he

SHERIDAN LE FANU
AND VICTORIAN IRELAND

Joseph Thomas Sheridan Le Fanu, *c.* 1843.
The portrait, together with a companion picture of Susanna Le Fanu,
was probably commissioned on the occasion of their marriage.

SHERIDAN LE FANU AND VICTORIAN IRELAND

W. J. McCORMACK

CLARENDON PRESS · OXFORD
1980

Oxford University Press, Walton Street, Oxford OX2 6DP

OXFORD LONDON GLASGOW
NEW YORK TORONTO MELBOURNE WELLINGTON
KUALA LUMPUR SINGAPORE JAKARTA HONG KONG TOKYO
DELHI BOMBAY CALCUTTA MADRAS KARACHI
NAIROBI DAR ES SALAAM CAPE TOWN

Published in the United States
by Oxford University Press, New York

© *W. J. McCormack* 1980

British Library Cataloguing in Publication Data

McCormack, W. J.
  Sheridan Le Fanu and Victorian Ireland
  1. Le Fanu, Sheridan – Biography
  2. Novelists, Irish – 19th century – Biography
  I. Title
  823'.8   PR4879.L7   79–40665

  ISBN 0–19–812629–8

Printed in Great Britain by
Billing & Sons Limited, Guildford, London and Worcester

for
Walter Allen

PREFACE

CERTAIN TECHNICAL difficulties confront the would-be biographer of Sheridan Le Fanu, which it may be useful to admit at the outset of this study. First, there is the problem of approaching a figure who, one hundred years after his death, has never attracted serious attention. The principal printed sources of information on his life are his brother's *Seventy Years of Irish Life* and his nephew's *Memoir of the Le Fanu Family*, in neither of which does the novelist receive any especial notice. Second, there is the absence of a reliable bibliography of Le Fanu's writings. Though I have attempted to remedy this deficiency in two appendices, the task of compiling a comprehensive listing of his periodical publications, and of collating the serial fiction and three-decker novels, remains for the future. Finally, surviving manuscript material is scarce and includes very little of literary—as distinct from biographical—interest. The surviving correspondence, which provides a mass of minor details of Le Fanu's life, unfortunately falls into clearly defined periods which leave much of his life unrecorded.

The absence of a Le Fanu bibliography has created a problem in choosing a text for quotation. From a cursory inspection of *Uncle Silas*, it is evident that the novelist tidied up his magazine text before passing it on to the publisher of the three-decker. Yet in many cases, Le Fanu's proof-reading of the books was less careful than of the serial, perhaps because he was also editor and proprietor of the magazine in which most of his fiction first appeared. For the general reader, copies of the three-decker and files of the *Dublin University Magazine* are equally inaccessible. In the following study the texts of the three-decker versions of the novels have been used, obvious misprints being corrected. For the stories in *The Purcell Papers*, the magazine texts is preferred, on the grounds that they were never collectively issued during Le Fanu's lifetime. Modern reissues of the better-known *In a Glass Darkly* have appeared frequently, but without any editorial apparatus. E. F. Bleiler's two anthologies, *Best Ghost Stories of J. S. Le Fanu* (New York, 1964) and *J. S. Le Fanu: Ghost Stories and Mysteries* (New York, 1975), include thirty stories with brief commentaries, and while these collections are warmly recommended to the general reader, Bleiler's eclectic choice of sources for his text renders them unsuitable for quotation.

For permission to quote from manuscripts and other copyright material in their care, I am grateful to the trustees, administrators, and officials of the British Library, Victoria and Albert Museum, National Library of Scotland, Bodleian Library, Swedenborg Society, National Library of Ireland, Trinity College, Dublin, University College, Dublin, Public Record Office (Dublin), Public Record Office of Northern Ireland, Representative Church Body, Royal Irish Academy, Registry of Deeds (Dublin), University of Illinois Library, New York Public Library, Houghton Library, and Pierpont Morgan Library. The staff of the Department of Older Printed Books and Special Collections at Trinity College, Dublin, and of the Leeds Library have provided services beyond the normal call of duty. Janet Woolley and Sally Croft typed my manuscript with efficiency and good humour.

Mrs Rachel Burrows, Dr Jean Laurie, and Mrs Susan Digby-Firth very kindly drew my attention to family records which included valuable sources of this study; each corresponded enthusiastically with me, shedding light on the obscurities of Victorian family history. I am happy to record my gratitude to them, and to add a special word of thanks to Mrs Digby-Firth for her advice on the Bennett Papers. But above all others, William Le Fanu and his wife Elizabeth have constantly encouraged me in writing this study, having placed their papers at my disposal and answered innumerable finicking questions. My debt to them must be expressed in terms of their great kindness and hospitality over the last six years. The portrait of Sheridan Le Fanu, as a novelist and as an individual soul, embodied in the following pages is exclusively my responsibility, but my task would have been impossible without the co-operation of the Le Fanu family. All manuscript material of Joseph Sheridan Le Fanu is quoted by kind permission of William Le Fanu.

School of English   W. J. McCORMACK
The University of Leeds

CONTENTS

LIST OF ILLUSTRATIONS

Joseph Thomas Sheridan Le Fanu, *c*.1843. (From an oil painting, artist unknown, in the possession of Mrs Susan Digby-Firth. Reproduced by kind permission.) *Frontispiece*

* Illustrations thus marked are reproduced from photographs commissioned for the present book.

ABBREVIATIONS

Diary   Diaries of William Richard Le Fanu (1816–94), preserved
             among the Le Fanu Papers at Chelmsford
D.U.M.   *Dublin University Magazine*
Illinois   Library of the University of Illinois, Urbana; the Bentley
             Papers
P.R.O.N.I.   Public Record Office of Northern Ireland, Belfast; the
             Dufferin and Ava Papers

When no source is stated for a manuscript, it may be assumed to be
preserved in the Le Fanu Papers.

INTRODUCTION: THE PAST

ACCORDING TO a note in his father's prayer-book, the future author of *Uncle Silas* was born 'at about half-past five o'clock AM' on 28 August 1814. Though no similar record establishes the place of birth, it is beyond doubt that Joseph Thomas Sheridan Le Fanu first saw the light of day at No. 45 Lower Dominick Street, Dublin. His father's family were Huguenots whose ancestor Charles de Cresserons had fought for William of Orange at the Boyne. Throughout the eighteenth century the Le Fanus had established themselves as comfortably bourgeois; as merchants and amateur bankers operating within the Protestant establishment, the novelist's forebears had acquired status and security. His paternal grandmother was a sister of Richard Brinsley Sheridan, and the alliance of Huguenot diligence and Irish brilliance produced its most enigmatic son in Sheridan Le Fanu.

'Sheridan' meant literary success and political nonconformity, an inheritance which proved embarrassing to the Victorian Le Fanus. Fortunately, in their splendour the Sheridans did not intrude on the daily lives of their humbler relatives. The comparatively closed ranks of the professional grades among the Anglo-Irish were perpetuated in intermarriage. The Le Fanus were related to the Sheridans by three alliances, to the Knowles by two, to the Dobbins by two, and to the Bennetts by two. Furthermore they retained surnames as Christian names, and perpetuated favourite names through four or more generations. Five generations of Le Fanus each baptized a child William, three of them adding Richard, and two Philip. The late county surveyor of Clare was properly addressed as Peter Le Fanu Knowles Dobbin; his grandfather and great aunt had both married Le Fanus who were first cousins, and his father had married his own second cousin. These alliances lend an air of hermetic completeness to an account of Le Fanu's life, for wherever one turns cousins nod in recognition. His fiction is laden with a sense of inescapable heredity; marriages and proposed marriages between blood relations proliferate. *Wylder's Hand* is the most striking case, where Dorcas Brandon rejects her cousin Mark Wylder to marry her cousin Stanley Lake, only to find that Stanley kills Mark, and is then himself killed. To add to the familiarity of the pattern behind the sensationalism, the narrator's name is Charles de Cresseron. Names recur in Le Fanu's fiction not from a lack of invention, but in keeping with a habit of the author's immediate clan. The heroes of *Uncle Silas* bear the surname Ruthyn—Le Fanu's Broughton relatives lived at Ruthyn in North Wales— the elder brother being Austin Aylmer Ruthyn Ruthyn, and the younger Silas Aylmer Ruthyn. The echoes are more than atmospheric: they are dangerous oscillations. For the moment we can partly explain them by pointing to the frequency of family names among Sheridan Le Fanu's nearest relatives.

A word or two about eighteenth-century Ireland from which the Victorian Le Fanus emerged. Lord Chancellor John Fitzgibbon acknowledged that:

the whole power and prosperity of the country has been conferred by successive monarchs upon an English colony, composed of three sets of English adventurers, who poured into this country at the termination of three successive rebellions. Confiscation is their common title, and from their first settlement they have been hemmed in on every side by the old inhabitants of the island, brooding over their discontents in sullen indignation.[1]

It was in this context that the Sheridans were so very odd— within a few decades Gaelic and Protestant, Jacobite and Radical. Indeed, oddness is a characteristic of Anglo-Ireland; Fitzgibbon, the hard-headed, boldly self-conscious Protestant supremacist, came of a humble Catholic family. The Le Fanus, arriving neither as conquerors nor sponsored colonists, made it their business to become assimilated into the privileged ascendancy, quickly shedding their French and Huguenot habits.

Le Fanus being in a sense too conventional, and Sheridans too renowned to require historical summary here, a moment can be spared for Sheridan Le Fanu's mother's family. Her father, Dr William Dobbin, was a Church of Ireland clergyman from Cork. During the stormy years from 1797 to 1809, he sat in

---

[1] John Fitzgibbon, Earl of Clare (1749–1802). Successively Attorney-General and Lord Chancellor in the pre-Union Irish administration, Fitzgibbon is traditionally regarded as the backbone of anti-Catholic feeling in the prelude to the Act of Union of 1800. Terence de Vere White provides a shrewd analysis of his character in *The Anglo-Irish* (London, 1972), pp. 94–110. For the extract from Fitzgibbon's speech, see ibid. 95–6.

St. Patrick's Cathedral stalls as prebendary of St. Michan's. During the rebellion of 1798 he was comforter and confessor to the brothers John and Henry Sheares in the days leading up to their execution as traitors and rebels. Dobbin's connection with them was more than professional, and there is a tradition that John Sheares was engaged to Sophia Dobbin to whom he sent a lock of hair on the evening before his execution. (A similar rumour about Fitzgibbon's love for a girl who preferred Henry Sheares intensifies the claustrophobia of Anglo-Ireland.) It seems that Dobbin shared some of these revolutionary sympathies, for his daughter Emma—Le Fanu's mother—preserved throughout her long life an admiration for the gallant Lord Edward Fitzgerald. Nor was 1798 the last moment of their involvement in revolutionary tragedy. In 1803 Dr Dobbin attended in his official capacity at the execution of Robert Emmet. According to Hamilton Maxwell, Emmet was 'a determined infidel', a radicalism in which Dobbin could not sympathize. No doubt conscious of his previous associations, the cleric strove with the condemned rebel and 'vainly endeavoured to eradicate the erroneous opinions he had imbibed upon the continent'.[1] The *mise-en-scène* would not be out of place in a novel by Le Fanu, Dobbin's grandson, for in his fiction unbelief and social disruption engage in uneasy dialogue.

In the north of Dublin, St. Mary's parish is one of the oldest ecclesiastical divisions of the city. In 1810 the rector was Dr Dobbin, who also held the vicarage of Finglas on the outskirts of the town. Among his curates was Thomas Philip Le Fanu, twenty-six years old, whose father was one of those Irish Protestants who had acquired a comfortable sinecure—he was 'Clerk of the Coast and Examiner of the Coast Accounts for the Outports'. Both the Dobbins and Le Fanus existed in the outer circle of the Anglo-Irish establishment, their hopes of advancement invested in the ranks of the clergy. Irish parochial clergy did not entirely live off the fat of the land; Dublin parishes were large and ill-organized, and the lower clergy spent much of their time in charitable work. Dobbin had virtually retired out to Finglas, but the curates were busy.

On 5 September 1804 some Dublin folk gathered at the Le Fanus', among them Emma Dobbin, one of the rector's daughters.

[1] W. H. Maxwell, *History of the Irish Rebellion in 1798* (London, 1854), pp. 432–3.

In 1810 an engagement between Tom Le Fanu and Emma was announced, and a rival suitor stepped forward at once. Theophilus Swift, a lawyer well stricken in years, informed the Dobbins that he regarded himself as Emma's acknowledged lover. The man, in fact, was a crackpot, and for that very reason—not to mention the social consequence of his name, his connection with Dean Swift's family—he was a dangerous nuisance. And a vocal nuisance; for once a rival was in the field, the old lawyer published his anguish in pamphlet form. Three editions of his self-justification were printed, each more impassioned, confused, and profuse with transcripts of missing correspondence than its predecessor. 'I would have burned . . . my two hands to the stumps, sooner than allow human eye to inspect a line of her letters, without her authority and permission.'[1] This was embarrassing nonsense, and Swift threatened to circumscribe the whole respectable world of the Dobbins and Le Fanus. Emma had to stay away from a ball at Glasnevin because of the buffoon's attendance. Tom received confidential letters from his rival only to find the texts reprinted in Swift's *Touchstone of Truth*, the ever-expanding dossier of his folly. To extinguish the sole ground for the man's crazy hope, Emma and Tom were married—furtively, according to Swift—on 31 July 1811. That effectively marked the end of Swift's interference in the Le Fanus' lives, but before he finally withdrew he delivered a warning to the curate: 'In the moral and political world, an Ill fate is often observed to follow states and families, and the same Ill fate to extend its shade over their remotest connections. The Dobbin family are an instance of it. Nothing but Misfortune attends their calamitous counsels.'[2] Whether Swift here alluded to Dobbin radicalism one cannot tell; the sense of the passage is no clearer than the rest of his utterance. But Tom's and Emma's later lives seem to substantiate Swift's prophecy; even their son was involved in the misfortunes of the Dobbins. Of Swift, thankfully, we hear nothing more.

The Le Fanus' first child, Catherine Frances, was born in Dominick Street in 1813, and there is no doubt that the future novelist was born here too. It has been claimed that the Royal Hibernian Military School was the birthplace, but this simply will not do. The child was born in August 1814, and his father was

---

[1] T. Swift, *The Touchstone of Truth* (n.p., 1811), p. 15.
[2] Ibid. 78.

not attached to the School until the following year. The child's Christian names honoured his grandfather, his father, and his grandmother's clan. A third child, William Richard, *was* born at the Military School in 1816; later in his *Seventy Years of Irish Life* William recorded the childhood adventures of the two brothers in the Phoenix Park. Joseph would have been less than two when the family moved from Dominick Street, and so it is certain that his earliest memories were of the Military School, the Phoenix Park, and the pageantry of the viceregal establishment. When in 1815 the Revd Thomas Le Fanu was appointed by the Lord Lieutenant to the chaplaincy of the School, the omens seemed to be reassuring. This was the kind of advancement a man of Le Fanu's station could expect, and the future seemed secure. The city was enjoying the prosperity of a wartime boom; local politics showed little sign of repeating the mistakes of the past. There could be no more insurrection; no more Robert Emmets. The Le Fanu children could sleep soundly, dreaming of their noble origins in France or of the security which the new country promised.

In search of the fully rounded character of a writer born to this inheritance, raised in a crisis of which he saw himself as a constituent, later composing fiction in which incident and emptiness virtually exclude the creation of character—in search of Sheridan Le Fanu—we may finally define him by circumscription, by comparing him with relatives whom he resembles in part, and with others from whom he differs. His biography might be seen as a tension between two poles—family identity and continuity, and personal isolation and self-questioning. Of course, he does no lack individuality; he is one of literature's eccentrics, and in Anglo-Ireland that does not rob him of representative interest. It is true that neither his friend Charles Lever nor his kinsman the Marquis of Dufferin and Ava drank green tea *and* read Swedenborg's *Heaven and Hell*—Le Fanu is no guide to average behaviour. Yet his life is significant and revealing in just the way a photographer uses a tinted filter, to bring out aspects of reality which normal vision ignores or excludes. We can see through Le Fanu's life and work a curiously neglected area—Victorian Ireland.

Victorian Ireland—the conjunction of terms is itself mildly surprising. Nineteenth-century Ireland has, for political and

literary historians alike, been exclusively the nursery of nationalism, of Charles Stewart Parnell and William Butler Yeats.
Victorianism, conversely, is still regarded as an essentially metropolitan culture, centralized, industrial, urban. Gustave Doré,
Charles Dickens, and the Tennyson of the Isle of Wight years are
its publicists. Yet Limerick and Dublin felt the effects of this
culture too, in their distinctive ways, and their experience tells us
much about the validity (or otherwise) of metropolitan assumptions. And by mid-century at least, Ireland had its middle classes,
confused though the Protestant element among them was by its
close association with the landed aristocracy. Beside the Protestant bourgeoisie of which William Le Fanu was an admirable
example, there was a similar body of Catholic professional men
and merchants. These were, however, still overawed by Protestant
control of the administrative heights, and tended to look back to
pre-emancipation cabins for their cultural identity. Despite Yeats
and Synge who came from the same church-infused background,
it is the Protestant middle classes who have been neglected. No
doubt they are partly responsible for this neglect themselves;
Yeats's unhistorical celebration of the eighteenth century as his
spiritual source is largely to blame. In praising Synge's contribution to a 'genuine' Irish literature, Professor Corkery and the
cultural nationalists ignored the degree to which Synge's mythology was a mask for tensions in his Protestant upbringing.[1]

Much of Le Fanu's later fiction is repetitive and, though this
feature may be obsessive rather than mechanical, a full study of
all his novels and stories cannot be justified. Fortunately Le Fanu
seems to have embodied the essence of his experience in *Uncle
Silas* with a formal economy missing in his other novels. The
success of that novel—and to a lesser extent the success of the
stories in *In a Glass Darkly*—is intimately connected with his
reading of Emanuel Swedenborg's theology. By a circuitous route,
this interest in Swedenborgian thought underlines the continuity
between Le Fanu and the generation of Yeats and Wilde. Having
read *Uncle Silas* and *In a Glass Darkly* with some attention to the
theological allusion, it is possible to see in the following remark of
Yeats's an unacknowledged debt to Le Fanu's fiction:

It was indeed Swedenborg who affirmed for the modern world, as

---

[1] See D. Corkery, *Synge and Anglo-Irish Literature; a Study* (Cork, 1931).

against the abstract reasoning of the learned, the doctrine and practice of the desolate places, of shepherds and midwives, and discovered a world of spirits where there was a scenery like that of earth, human forms, grotesque or beautiful, senses that knew pleasure and pain, marriage and war, all that could be painted on canvas, or put into stories to make one's hair stand up.[1]

The paintings to which Yeats refers may have been Blake's, but it is principally in Le Fanu's fiction that Swedenborgianism is incorporated into hair-raising plots. And the same theories of the soul and its remorse are put to dramatic effect in Yeats's play about Jonathan Swift, while in *Purgatory* the Le Fanuesque theme of a Great House destroyed by the depravity of its master is interwoven with a murder which must repeat itself according to the Swedenborgian formula. Seeing Le Fanu as a contemporary of Ainsworth's or Wilkie Collins's, we are inclined to forget that within his lifetime the giants of the Irish literary renaissance were born—W. B. Yeats, George Moore, J. M. Synge. As a child Oscar Wilde was occasionally a playmate of Le Fanu's children. The Victorians are closer to the generation of the modernist movement than the latter cared to admit.

As a child of the glebe-house, as editor of the *Dublin University Magazine*, as husband and widower, Le Fanu proclaimed his allegiance to the Victorian middle classes. His cousins and friends, even some of his bitterest foes, belonged to the same Protestant caste. He resembles them in many simple ways, the ways he pays his debts, writes his letters, takes his holidays. Common activities are significant because they constitute the shared life of an intricate if limited social group, less grand than they may have thought, but nevertheless powerful in business, in the professions, in education, in precisely those activities which defined Victorianism. Political historians have quite rightly concentrated on the Famine, the Land War, and Fenianism as the major events of Irish history before Parnell, but these themes necessarily limit our attention to the victims of time. Perhaps we can now look at some of the survivors who, though on nodding terms with hardship and some-

[1] W. B. Yeats, *Explorations* (London, 1962), p. 72. The passage comes from 'Swedenborg, Mediums, and the Desolate Places', first published in 1914. I have discussed the need to reconsider Yeats's idea of an Anglo-Irish tradition in the eighteenth and nineteenth centuries in 'Yeats and a New Tradition' (*Crane Bag*, vol. 3 no. 1, pp. 30–40, 1979). See pp. 36–7 for a particular discussion of Le Fanu in relation to Yeats's play *The Words Upon the Window-pane*.

times shaken by anxiety, spoke the language of Victorian success.

Two warnings are timely here. First of all, it would be wrong to say that Le Fanu was ever 'central to the lives' of the Dobbins, Barringtons, and Jelletts whom we shall meet in passing. Their lives circumscribe his in a way that is valuable simply because he was reticent and evasive. Secondly, the language of success was often a mask; Dobbins were sometimes poor, Barringtons in need of favours. Victorianism was a highly formal code of behaviour, and to understand it aright decoding is frequently necessary. The fact that his relatives were not irredeemably well-to-do, that his brother suffered (for a week or two) the agonies of the famous Victorian crisis of belief, makes it easier for us to see Le Fanu as a man of his time. He assumes importance and influence late in life when he found in sensational fiction a means to describe the extraordinary quality of his life, its urbanity and its closeness to violence. Essentially the common feature of his experience and of his fictional world is the idea of a society based on non-social assumptions, an experience outwardly social but really isolated and dangerously interior. Victorian Ireland is fascinating and relatively unknown, its daily routine a neglected part of the past which has moulded Yeats, Shaw, Parnell, and other distinctively modern figures. Its larger value as seen in Le Fanu's career can only be appreciated if we are prepared to make the connection between his failure to evolve a viable political stance in Ireland and his experiments in English sensationalism. Normal vision has its own censoring devices, and two sets of filters must be laid aside; one which excludes the middle-class Orangeman of 1840 as an historical irrelevance, and the other which dismisses sensational fiction as 'pulp'. With our vision adjusted we can watch the growth of a Victorian mind painfully engaged with the hidden Ireland of drawing-rooms and pole screens.

I

A CLERICAL WORLD

FOR ITS size Dublin is an extraordinarily renowned city, and has been made so by a succession of artists who, reluctantly in some cases, have been Dubliners. Jonathan Swift was sent into exile there; Goldsmith was nearly educated there, and, to skip a century, Yeats and Joyce were born there. Dublin is an old city; its continuity from Danish and Norman settlers is traceable below a more modern architecture. But it has never been essentially an Irish city; when Louis MacNeice called it the 'Augustan capital of a Gaelic nation' he was playing with paradox, a favourite weapon of Dublin's writers. To Swift it was both endearing and damnable; to Yeats it was an 'unmannerly town', a place of terrible beauty. Between Swift's death in 1745 and Yeats's birth one hundred and twenty years later, the city did not produce any comparable genius, but it did see the rise of the Georgian squares and terraces which still struggle to lend character to a modern capital. Partly because of Yeats's declarations, we are inclined to regard Dublin's Georgian architecture as quintessentially eighteenth century. In fact, some of the finest urban development in the city appeared at the turn of the centuries, and few of the best terraces were standing in Swift's time.

At the beginning of the nineteenth century Dublin suffered three traumas—insurrection in 1798, dissolution of the Irish Parliament in 1800, and Emmet's rebellion three years later. The city soon settled down to become for over a century a provincial town, known for eccentricity rather than genius. But the wars against Napoleon at least had given it importance as a recruiting ground; the Viceroy liked to cut a military dash, and for a few years Dublin Castle and the Phoenix Park kept up an appearance of vivacity. Charles Lever was not entirely joking when he exclaimed in *Jack Hinton:* 'Don't tell me of your insurrection acts, of your nightly outrages, your outbreaks, and your burnings, as a reason for keeping a large military force in Ireland—nothing of the kind. A very different object, indeed, is the reason—Ireland is garrisoned to please the ladies'.[1] To write a novel like *Jack Hinton* in 1843 was as good a way of forgetting the outrages of the period as Lever could think of; his literary analysis, and not his sense of period, is open to question.

Apart from the dashing officers and the dancing masters, Dublin society in 1810 was amply garrisoned by lawyers and Protestant clerics. Respectable society hardly recognized others grades of existence, and the gulf between high and low was complicated by religious differences. A tightly knit community revolved round the castle and the Viceregal Lodge; beyond it an outer circle of still respectable and largely Protestant middle-class professionals turned inwards in search of official patronage, and beyond them there was a general population—largely Catholic. 'Beyond' was the operative word in social distinctions, and beyond the city boundaries, 'beyond the pale' as the Irish phrase put it, the countryside extended these divisions into a landowning system of nearly barbaric character. Dublin was placed between the distant authority of Westminster and the mutinous estates of the upper classes, a dilemma which was not recognized, of course, in 1810. The Act of Union was intended in 1800 to heal the breach between England and Ireland, and had been accompanied by promises of emancipation for the Catholic majority.

The most lasting achievement of the campaign to repeal the Act of Union was the notion that Dublin had gone into a total decline after the dissolution of the Irish Parliament. Certainly, members of the Commons or the Lords no longer gathered in their town houses, dancing to a music of wit and prejudice. But their withdrawal left a vacuum which necessarily was filled. A satirical pamphlet of 1804, *An Intercepted Letter from J—— T——* (attributed now to John Wilson Croker), describes how the Parliament buildings were defaced by their new owners, the Bank of Ireland, whose taste, being arbitrary and bourgeois, was inferior. In a further passage Croker stressed the complacent supremacy of the new middle classes: 'They most wonderfully excell us in dignity; and it is not uncommon to see a shopkeeper sitting behind his counter in all the solemn state of a mandarine, and this indeed is but the *lex talionis*, for you can hardly imagine how many of the mandarines look like shopkeepers'.[2] The vulgar taste of

---

[1] C. Lever, *Jack Hinton the Guardsman* (London, 1897), p. 266.

[2] [J. W. Croker], *An Intercepted Letter from J—— T—— Esq., Writer at Canton to his Friend in Dublin, Ireland* (Dublin, 1804), p. 23.

merchants and bankers is an important element in Maria Edgeworth's *Absentee* (1812), and in describing post-Union Dublin
she drew on Croker's pamphlet.[1] But literature and politics were
not immune to the new forces at work in commerce, and two men
—both Catholics—soon emerged as the spokesmen of a new,
disgruntled, thoroughly bourgeois Ireland.

It has been said of Thomas Moore that he put Ireland back
on the cultural map of Europe, and his *Melodies* undoubtedly
achieved an enormous success. With more modesty, he can justly
claim to be the herald of Dublin's shopkeeper-merchants in
society. In politics he was a Whig with independent leanings; in
religion he was a luke-warm Catholic with a hotter aversion to the
Established Church. The faults of his verse are the inevitable
birthmarks of his age and class for he was that most discontented
of types, the recently liberated man who has just grasped how
thoroughly his past had been enslaved. No modern critic says
anything in favour of 'Blame not the Bard', and yet is it not a
complex apologia for the absence of political feeling in Moore's
work as a whole? As a liberal Irishman he recognized the greatness
of Richard Brinsley Sheridan, and when the champion died,
Moore determined to commemorate him. In search of material
he contacted the Le Fanus who reluctantly allowed him to copy
letters and memorabilia. In the matter of returning these, Moore
was a little careless. His *Travels of an Irish Gentleman in Search
of a Religion* (1833) gave great offence to churchmen like Thomas
Le Fanu, and it was fiercely reviewed in the *Dublin University
Magazine*. Despite these doctrinal antagonisms, there is no doubt
that Moore influenced the style of Victorian writing in Ireland.
By the time he died in 1852 even the *D.U.M.* had softened
considerably in its attitude to his limpid melodies.

The other *bête noire* of the Anglo-Irish ascendency was of
course Daniel O'Connell, in many ways the opposite of Moore—a
countryman, hard-headed and roughly spoken, scion of a tribe
who had thrived in the demanding conditions of Penal Ireland.
Although he was a landowner and a barrister, O'Connell was
regarded by his Protestant counterparts as an upstart and a
vulgarian. A recent historian declares him one of the most

---

[1] For an account of Maria Edgeworth's use of the pamphlet see W. J.
McCormack, '*The Absentee* and Maria Edgeworth's Notion of Didactic
Fiction', *Atlantis*, no. 5 (1973), 123–35.

successful liberal leaders of the early nineteenth century in Europe, but Anglo-Irish contemporaries were convinced that his aim was Catholic domination rather than liberal secularism.[1] Like Moore he was forced by circumstances to adopt a style which was likely to be misunderstood. The Catholic masses after 1800 were leaderless and demoralized; insurrection had brought the most terrible suffering, prefaced by unpalatably French principles. O'Connell had energy and organizing genius, and he worked for forty years to create an articulate public opinion in Ireland, representing the Catholic majority rather than the Protestant establishment. Arguably it was his challenge for the middle ground of Irish politics, the position between armed separatism and passive integration, which drove the Protestant gentry to adopt wholeheartedly the ascendency attitude. A resident gentry such as the Irish one, with its extensive involvement in the legal profession, might have seen that same middle ground as its proper sphere. In the face of O'Connellite provocation and the heightened sectarianism of the times, this resentment was transmuted into a charter for a new social pre-eminence; the Protestant gentleman of Ireland were the bastion of the Williamite constitution, of private property—of religion and civilization! Yet the Revd Thomas Le Fanu's grandfather had been a wine merchant like Moore's father—though a more prosperous one in keeping with the privileges of his church; and O'Connell and Sheridan Le Fanu were simultaneously members of the Irish Bar. In the Anglo-Irish scheme of things class could be discounted when it was inconvenient. The most effective answer to class insinuations was to create areas of exclusivism which were then presented to the world as the essence of Ireland. In this way the Church of Ireland became politicized; church and landed estate provided oases of security for the establishment in the years before Catholic emancipation. They were dangerously remote oases, remote from each other, from the new public opinion in Ireland, and from the realities of British politics. The church was particularly vulnerable, and 'the cause of religious reform got further [than land reform] because a minority Church could be deprived of privileges with less damage than any substantial shift toward Tenant Right . . . would have involved'.[2]

[1] K. B. Nowlan, *The Politics of Repeal* (London, 1965), p. 5.
[2] M. Hurst, *Maria Edgeworth and the Public Scene* (London, 1969), p. 22.

One further representative figure of Thomas Le Fanu's generation is worth a moment's notice, less prominent than Moore
or O'Connell but also more immediately relevant to the Church
of Ireland. The Revd Mortimer O'Sullivan summarized his view
of things for a House of Commons select committee in 1825:

The respectable class of the Roman Catholic laity are, generally, speaking, quite untinged with that political feeling which their religion might
infuse in them, and the very lowest classes would be led by the priest
of the parish, perhaps with as much effect as they would be led by the
Pope; but at present there is between the higher classes and those which
are very low, a class of persons becoming influential in the Roman
Catholic body who did not at all apply themselves to political concerns
before; and the middle class is that to which I look with most apprehension, for what is to be the future fate of Ireland.[1]

We know who O'Sullivan had in mind: the respectable Catholics
were men like Lord Trimbleston and Sir Edward Bellew, polite
petitioners for a concession; the 'very low' were of course anonymous, but could be found in party fights and the recesses of a
non-political landscape; the middle class were the lawyers and
agitators. But who was O'Sullivan? As his name might indicate, he
was born a Catholic; but educated as a Protestant, he had been
trained as the demagogue of Orangeism. The year after he en-
lightened the Commons he succeeded Thomas Le Fanu as
chaplain to the Military School, and throughout the 1830s and
the 1840s he was the chief ideologist of the *Dublin University
Magazine*, a role he shared with his brother Samuel, also a
convert and a cleric. His influence in the Church of Ireland was
very considerable not so much for the originality as the blatancy
of his views. The premiss lurking behind his evidence to the select
committee was that Protestantism and middle-class values were
eternal opposites, that the Established Church by its nature
precluded the possibility of a bourgeoisie in Ireland—unless this
dangerous innovation took root among the Papists. The notion
of an excluded middle class is familiar to readers of Yeats, and
its emergence in early nineteenth-century Ireland had important
consequences for the established clergy to whom it expressly
appealed.

North-west of Dublin the Phoenix Park stretches away from

[1] House of Commons, *Reports from Committees*, 1825, vol. 8, p. 461.

commerce and business to establish a green area in the suburbs, almost eighteen hundred acres bounded on the south by the river Liffey. In 1820 Chapelizod, Palmerstown, and Blanchardstown were still country villages visited perhaps by a carriage or two of holiday-makers from the city, but generally remote and self-contained. The park, which has its origins in the seventeenth century, had reached its present proportions and outline by Sheridan Le Fanu's birth, and while it was then as now a public park it also contained the principal residences of the British administrators. When the Le Fanus arrived from Dominick Street, Francis Johnstone was at work on the Viceregal Lodge, adding an Ionic portico to the south front. In the other notable houses of the park lived Robert Peel, the Chief Secretary, and William Gregory, his under-Secretary. In 1817 work began on the gigantic Wellington Monument, an obelisk of two hundred and five feet designed by Sir Robert Smirke. Duelling parties, building workers, and military tattoos were all elegantly contained in the vastness of the Phoenix Park, leaving the Hibernian Military School relatively undisturbed. The Revd Mr Le Fanu's duties as chaplain were not light, for the institution catered for about six hundred children. Most of the boys were destined to follow their fathers into the army, and at least one of the girls went into domestic service, staying with the Le Fanus for fifty-five years.

The park has not essentially changed. The trees are higher and denser in foliage. The long avenues which cross the centre of the green are covered in tar macadam rather than the dust of Le Fanu's day. Like a huge lens, it encapsulates a number of vital scenes in Irish social history; in 1842 a group of young men, sitting under a tree, hit upon the idea of a weekly newspaper in which to express their nationality—the *Nation* was conceived in the Phoenix Park; a few years earlier one of Europe's finest zoological gardens had opened, and a distinctive element of Dublin social life created; more sombrely in May 1882, the dust soaked up the blood of a Chief Secretary. The Phoenix Park recurs in Anglo-Irish literature from Le Fanu to James Joyce and Thomas Kinsella. Joyce drew on *The House by the Church-yard* as a source for the dirty deed in the park which lurks behind *Finnegans Wake*. The Phoenix Park's history brings together the warring elements of Irish society—the *Nation* and the viceroy, Le Fanu and the Invincibles, Victorian ladies watching polo, and James Joyce in pursuit of Haveth Childers Everywhere.

The Le Fanus stayed eleven years at the Military School, during which Joseph passed through an impressionable childhood. In *Seventy Years of Irish Life*, William provides examples of his brother's early genius, no more remarkable than any other claims for child prodigy. At about the age of six Joseph had a favourite amusement of drawing little pictures and writing some moral below them. In one, a balloon was floating high in the air, though two aeronauts had fallen from the basket and were tumbling towards the ground. The caption read: 'See the effects of trying to go to heaven.'[1] William's mind was less speculative, and his principal recollection was of trading his nanny for a red spaniel. The boys' life was regulated by their father's clerical duties, and by the military tone of a social world governed by the comings and goings of the highest dignitaries in the land. The nearest parish church was in Chapelizod, and the quaint little village between a weir and a bridge on the Liffey soberly impressed young Le Fanu with its antiquity.

An exception to the routine occurred in 1821. George IV had come to the throne in the previous year amid general celebrations, and he was anxious to consolidate his popularity with a tour of his Irish kingdom. Thomas and Emma were included among the guests at a levee and a drawing-room; as part of the Lord Lieutenant's retinue, the chaplain to the School was presented to His Majesty. The children watched the king's procession into Dublin from their grandfather's house in Eccles Street. The Phoenix Park with its official residences and vast open spaces was the ideal arena for military displays, and while the king presided Joseph and William Le Fanu watched a grand review of infantry regiments marching past in their white knee-breeches and long black gaiters. At seven Le Fanu had an eye for details of dress and appearance, and later he filled *The House by the Churchyard* with archaeological colour of this kind; amid the terrors of the plot he re-created imaginatively the ceremonial simplicity of his childhood. For to live at the centre of a constant, static spectacle—1821 being a heightened version of viceregal routine—was to acquire a distinctive mode of perception. Display, symbol, gesture dominated the military life of Dublin in the years between 1814 and

---

[1] W. R. Le Fanu, *Seventy Years of Irish Life* (London, 1893), p. 2. (Henceforth cited as *Seventy Years*.)

1826; the disturbed countryside was almost as remote as Waterloo. Of course, the Chief Secretary and his political staff were constantly in touch with developments across the country but that was a side to their activity hidden from a young boy. To him the officials were essentially ceremonial; their duties were public demonstrations of a political orthodoxy. The Phoenix Park, to an imaginative child, was an open-air cathedral, the liturgy political as well as religious, for the two can never be separated in nineteenth-century Ireland. Doubtless his father knew all about the implications of city life, the shopkeepers and their bills, relatives and their little problems. The boy only saw the splendid integrity of the Phoenix Park, its utter difference to the city and the countryside alike. It was an artificial landscape populated by symbolic figures.

Everyone recognizes Joyce's dark enquiries in *Finnegans Wake* as an exploration of the unconscious mind, and a public park may seem curious as a choice of imagery. But in his first novel, Le Fanu acknowledged that the park too had a past, a history less orderly than its modern playgrounds and promenades. The hero of *The Cock and Anchor*, wandering on the outskirts of Dublin sometime early in the eighteenth century, becomes ensnared in the park:

The close screen of the wild gnarled thorns which covered the upper level on which he now moved, still further deepened the darkness; and he became at length so entirely involved in the pitchy gloom, that he dismounted, and taking his horse by the head, led him forward through the tangled brake, and under the knotted branches of the old hoary thorns—stumbling among the briers and the crooked roots, and every moment encountering the sudden obstruction either of some stooping branch, or the trunk of one of the old trees; so that altogether his progress was as tedious and unpleasant as it well could be.[1]

Le Fanu convincingly translates the open playground of his childhood back into the ensnaring wildness of its past. Within the story this is appropriate and impressive in a novice writer. But the hero's entanglement is more profound than merely narrative. In fact, shortly after his immobilization by briar and root:

he saw, or thought he saw, a red light gleaming through the trees. It

[1] *The Cock and Anchor* (Dublin, 1845), ii. 303–4.

disappeared—it came again. He stopped, uncertain whether it was one of those fitful marshfires which but mock the perplexity of benighted travellers; but no—this light shone clearly, and with a steady beam through the branches; and toward it he directed his steps, losing it now, and again recovering it, till at length, after a longer probation than he had at first expected, he gained a clear space of ground.[1]

From here Edmond O'Connor sees that 'the light which had guided him streamed from the window of an old shattered house, partially surrounded by a dilapidated wall, having a few ruinous out-houses attached to it'. The anticipation is nicely rewarded: O'Connor finds not comfort but captivity. In the ruined house he falls into the hands of Jacobite conspirators who regard him as a spy. Now as narrative all this is ironic, for O'Connor is a Catholic himself, and only moves through Ireland at the risk of his liberty. But considered as a psychological symbol it is more illuminating. The hero, who is in love with a Protestant girl, is only luke warm in his Jacobitism; consciously he evades the agitator and the enthusiast, but in the dark wood he is drawn towards their violent conspiracy. The darkness reveals his deeper loyalties.

Further analysis of Le Fanu's novel would be out of place here, for we are primarily concerned with his childhood. But the setting of *The Cock and Anchor* is the scene of his earliest memories, and his transformation of the smooth lawns and dusty avenues into knotted thorns and dark sloughs is remarkable. The hero of the novel finds the park a secret place of conspiracy in favour of his despised religion and outlawed politics; it tells us what he inescapably is. It is difficult to avoid the parallel—that for Le Fanu his period in the Phoenix Park was a time of the closest identification with his very different politics and religion—his father a chaplain to a military establishment, surrounded by the pomp of the Williamite constitution which had proscribed O'Connor and his kind a hundred years earlier.

A working chaplain had to consider some of the outer world's pressures. The Church of Ireland might offer Thomas Le Fanu preferment in various forms. Curacy, which he had already experienced in St. Mary's under his father-in-law, was the lowest rung of the ladder. Down in the country, however, there were

[1] Ibid. 306.

parishes where scarcely a Protestant lived, areas in the southern and western counties where a rector literally had no congregation. In 1817 he was appointed rector of a parish in county Cork, Ardnageehy—'the windy heights.'[1] The tithe income was small, and as there was no glebe-house the rector was naturally an absentee. With few if any Protestants in the remote, mountainous, and Gaelic-speaking district, his absence was scarcely noticed. At the time, he saw his new office as an addition to his income rather than to his duties and, by the standards of the age, none could blame him. But the times were about to change.

In the light of political developments, his second opportunity to make contact with the greater Ireland 'beyond the pale' was crucial. Agitation for Catholic emancipation produced a moderate petition on the king's visit in 1821. That petition being rejected, the O'Connell juggernaut was launched in earnest, and soon civil war was feared. In 1823 Thomas Le Fanu was appointed rector of Abington, a parish on the borders of counties Limerick and Tipperary, on the edge of the Slieve Felim mountains. Limerick city was less than a dozen miles to the west, and a solid glebe-house had been built just a few years since. Perhaps the tithe income, even the joint income of two parishes, was not so great that he could throw up a chaplaincy in Dublin to bring a wife and three young children down to rural Limerick. He continued to be an absentee rector, now of Abington as well as of Ardnageehy. An incident in county Limerick in April 1823 may have influenced his decision. Lord Stradbroke repossessed part of his estate which had been let to a single tenant. Subdivision of the land, and sub-letting of plots, had resulted in forty or fifty families living off the original lease, and Stradbroke's action evicted four or five hundred people, 'prostrating' their cabins, and leaving them without support on the roadside. The incident raised fears of serious reprisals and outrage; Limerick had been placed under the Insurrection Act in February 1822, and now a new administra-

---

[1] Details of T. P. Le Fanu's ecclesiastical career are taken from printed sources listed in the bibliography below, and from manuscript material in the library of the Representative Church Body, Dublin. The most important of these documents are two tithe-applotment books for the united parish of Abington and Tuough for 1823–4 (MSS F/1–2) and a Vestry minute-book (MS E/7) commencing in 1811 and continuing throughout Le Fanu's career. A third tithe-applotment book, for Abington only, for 1826 is preserved in the Public Record Office, Dublin (TAB 17/61).

tor, Francis Blackburne, was appointed to uphold the law of eviction and seignorial rights. Abington, by all accounts, was a place to avoid in 1823.

His family also had a place in the rector's mind. Little of note had happened to them during their years at the Military School, and their toll of deaths and marriages was not greater than any similar family's. Perhaps the loss which the world noticed most—the death of R. B. Sheridan in 1816—was the least of their burdens. A greater blow of the same year was his sister Alicia's death, for it was she who symbolized the union of Sheridans and Le Fanus for her children and grandchildren. Other alliances became closer with the years, as when Dr Dobbin's son William married Alicia Hester Le Fanu in 1819.

Captain William Dobbin had been married once before, but after his wife's premature death, he had joined a regiment bound for the Peninsula. Dobbin saw some of the worst fighting of the campaign; he was wounded at Salamanca, in action at Vittoria, and desperately wounded in the head at Badajos. His marriage reinforced an alliance formed initially in the teeth of Theophilus Swift's defiance; Captain Dobbin was destined to fulfil the old bogey's dire prophecies. For as a result of his injuries he remained until his death something less than totally in command of himself. He was never mad; he was thoroughly sane by any medical definition. But what had originally been a romantic, in part affected, melancholy was magnified by his real sufferings into a constitutional inability to judge properly his fortune or misfortune. Like many other retired soldiers he became an officer in the Irish Constabulary, and was stationed at Borrisokeane, a market village roughly thirty miles from Limerick and Abington. Then in 1825 the 'Clerk of the Coast' died, bringing to a close the first generation of Le Fanus born on Irish soil.[1]

In 1826 the additional income of the deanery of Emly was given to Thomas and he brought his family out into the countryside. Leaving the Military School for Abington involved a total alteration in the scale of everything. Dublin was a capital, albeit a provincial one, with a history of centralized administration and the deference of other towns behind it. In contrast Abington was just a spot on the map, a remote village of no particular signi-

[1] Details concerning the Dobbin family are taken from a typescript family history, by kind permission of Mrs Rachel Burrows (née Dobbin).

ficance. True, Limerick was a seaport at the mouth of Ireland's longest river; but the Shannon, in dividing Connaught from the rest of the country, stood in much the same relation to Dublin as the Danube did to Rome in Ovid's day. Connaught was the wilderness, the Shannon its boundary, and Limerick an ambiguous bridgehead which could traffic in either direction. English travellers were often appalled by living conditions in the sister kingdom; Limerick produced unanimous indignation from radical and conservative alike. The level-headed Henry Inglis paid special attention to its degradation of humanity, and Thackeray thought its streets were 'black, ruinous, swarming, dark, hideous'. From the period of the Le Fanus' residence in county Limerick, William Cobbett's account of the city is perhaps the most moving:

In one street . . . I saw more misery than any man could have believed existed in the whole world. Men sleeping in the same wisp of dirty straw, or weeds, with their mothers, sisters and aunts; and compelled to do so, or perish; two or three families in one room, that is to say a miserable hole 10 feet by 8 or 9; and husbands, wives, sons, daughters, all huddled together, paying 6*d* or 8*d* or 10*d* a week for *the room;* and the rent paid to a *'nobleman'* in England . . . At a place in the country [near Limerick city] I went to the dwelling of a widower, who is nearly 60 years of age, and who had five children, *all very nearly stark naked.* The eldest girl, who is *fifteen years of age*, had a sort of apron to hide the middle part of her body before, and that was all she had. She hid herself, as well as she could, behind or at the end of, an old broken cupboard; and she held up her two arms and hands to hide her breasts. This man pays 30*s* rent for an acre of the poorest land.[1]

Even with its radical passion and italic emphasis, Cobbett's sketch of Limerick—town and county—is hardly exaggerated; others confirm his findings. We cannot say that Dean Le Fanu's family were unaware of these conditions, and yet *Seventy Years* devotes only a short passage to the local population:

They appeared to be devoted to us; if we had been away for a month or two, on our return they met us in numbers some way from our home, took the horses from the carriage and drew it to our house amid deafening cheers of welcome, and at night bonfires blazed on all the neighbouring hills. In all their troubles and difficulties the people came to

---

[1] W. Cobbett, *Rural Rides* (London, 1930), iii. 902–3. For other accounts of Limerick see H. Inglis, *Ireland in 1834*, and W. M. Thackeray, *Irish Sketch Book.*

my father for assistance. There was then no dispensary nor doctor
near us, and many sick folk or their friends came daily to my mother
for medicine and advice . . .[1]

This, of course, is not the whole story. William Le Fanu was
incapable of observing as Cobbett had done, because he did not
share the journalist's radical intentions; and Cobbett never manifested anything like the humour of *Seventy Years*, being obsessed
with change. That the people should need help daily (and from
the minister of a religion they rejected), while the Le Fanus might
be away for a month or more, is perhaps a more useful contrast
than any between political fact and nostalgic generality. Nor can
Cobbett's account of the district be accused of ignorance of
Abington, for he stayed less than a mile from the glebe-house in
the home of the Catholic priest. And the latter, Father Thomas
O'Brien Costello, recorded his own terse impressions of living
conditions in the parish: 'Mud walls, badly thatched; the bedding
consists of straw or rushes, not changed sometimes for years.
Some endeavour to procure bedsteads themselves; the bedding
is wretchedly bad . . . There may be about 100 instances of two
families residing in one cabin.'[2]

The priest's evidence is curtailed by the questionnaire he was
answering. A more syntactically rounded account of Abington
was smuggled into a short story by Sheridan Le Fanu a few years
later:

In the south of Ireland, and on the borders of the county of Limerick,
there lies a district of two or three miles in length, which is rendered
interesting by the fact that it is one of the very few spots throughout
this country, in which some fragments of aboriginal wood have found
a refuge . . . its vistas, in whose perspective the quiet cattle are peacefully browsing—its refreshing glades, where the grey rocks arise from
amid the nodding fern—the silvery shafts of the old birch trees—the
knotted trunks of the hoary oak—the grotesque but graceful branches,
which never shed their honours under the tyrant pruning hook . . .
This wood runs up, from below the base of the ridge of a long line of
irregular hills, having perhaps in primitive times, formed but the
skirting of some mighty forest which occupied the level below.[3]

---

[1] *Seventy Years*, p. 44.
[2] House of Commons, *Reports from Commissioners*, 1836, vol. 32 (supplement)
p. 218.
[3] *D.U.M.*, vol. 11 (Mar. 1838), 313.

Unlike the parish priest, the rector's son relies on picturesque conventions. He is writing fiction, of course, and no sustained comparison is advisable. Yet despite this special intention, Le Fanu's romantic landscape provides two crucial facts about the place which both Cobbett and his own brother had striven to describe. One is simply a visual topography, which was of no interest to the propagandist. The other is the sense of the place as a last resort, a surviving relic of those honours which have fallen to tyrants of every kind. Between the indignation of the journalist and the nostalgia of the autobiographer, the fictional evocation conveys different but fundamental facts, different but equally real emotions. Le Fanu was able to express this experience of Abington only after twelve intensely disturbing years.

Abington today is little more than the graveyard in which several Le Fanus are buried. Even in the 1820s the name scarcely denoted a recognizable village, merely commemorating a Cistercian monastery, the abbey of Owney (in Gaelic, *Uaithne Beag*). Nothing of the original abbey was visible in the Le Fanus' time, though legends lingered on in popular tradition. The Walshe family had acquired the monastery lands at the Dissolution, sparing the monks' lives; their successor in Caroline times, Joseph Stepney, ejected the recusants when he built a red-brick house and terraced garden where the community had gathered for five hundred years. Local people pointed to the road where the last monks had knelt to invoke judgement on their evictor. The consecrated land of the Protestant graveyard is the only survival of the monastic past in Abington, and even the place-name is gradually replaced by those of neighbouring townlands. During Dean Le Fanu's term in Abington glebe-house, a new settlement built by the Barrington family gradually superseded Abington, this new village being an extension of Murroe, hitherto little more than an inhabited roadside. Names gathered particular associations; the Catholic priest was based on Murroe and Boher and built his churches there, while the Anglican parish clung to the near obsolete place-name. The population of the parish was about 6,000 in 1822 when famine followed on a severe winter; natural disasters and emigration kept the figure reasonably steady during the Le Fanus' residence in the district.

When the Dean arrived in March 1826, he took particular notice of the neighbouring houses; not so much the cabins dotting the fields and hedgerows, but the sturdy, ugly, stone houses of the gentry. The glebe-house was one of the finest of these, built in a style of severe elegance. It stood (indeed still stands) back from the Green Road which led from the Catholic church of Murroe across the Dooglashla river. The river—it is about five feet wide—formed a natural boundary behind the house, giving it a sense of separateness (though not protection) from the countryside. The principal gentlemen of the parish lived farther west. In Madaboy House there was John Wickham, a Justice of the Peace and stalwart of the Anglican congregation. Clonshavoy belonged to another parishioner, Caleb Powell. The Evans family of Ashroe were Le Fanu's nearest neighbours, and though not educated folk, they had distinguished themselves during earlier disturbances. Captain Evans's father, a 'stirring magistrate', always began his reports with 'My dear Government'. But the most influencial family were the Barringtons who in 1826 lived in Clonkeen House. Matthew was Crown Solicitor for Munster, and his development of Murroe village was part of a programme to establish his heirs in almost feudal splendour. The building of Glenstal Castle, which became the family seat until the civil war of the 1920s, began about ten years after the Le Fanus' arrival and continued till 1849, providing jobs during the Great Famine of 1845–7. Apart from these, the Le Fanus' social life depended on their fellow clergy, who naturally lived at least as far away as the next parish. John Pennefather of Newport and George Madder of Ballybrood occasionally preached at Abington, and Madder (who was a bachelor) became a close friend. Few of these figures can take on much life for us now; they occur in correspondence or in *Seventy Years* but lack reality. Their significance is the smallness of their number. From a population of about six thousand maybe ten or a dozen families made up the circle of the Le Fanus' peers. The vast mass of the people lived for the most part below their consciousness, not as a result of callousness or snobbery, but because sectarian divisions and the poverty of the area isolated the glebe-house as effectively as the bend on the Dooglashla.

When the Le Fanus moved into the glebe-house, Catherine was thirteen, Joseph twelve, and William just turned eleven. Maria Walsh, who had been their nanny at the Military School, accompanied the family into their rural exile, and after the Dean's

death in 1845 she passed into William's service. A tutor, the
Revd John Stinson, was provided for the children. Apart from
French and English, which the Dean taught himself, the education of the boys was left in the hands of this aged cleric as they
prepared to go to Trinity College. For several hours each day he
sat with them in the school-room supposedly teaching classics
but in fact repairing his fishing gear. The brothers reacted in
different ways to this tuition of the Isaac Walton school; William
became an ardent fisherman, while Joseph educated himself in
his father's library. In *Seventy Years* William recorded a warm
tolerance of his tutor, but in a story written closer to the date
Joseph imagined a decidedly chilly and chilling cleric-tutor. Even
in his first years at Abington, he was a retiring, studious boy,
sometimes taking his book on the roof of the house when visitors
arrived, and pulling up the ladder to secure absolute seclusion.

The Dean was a collector of books, and though theological and
devotional literature crowded the shelves, there was plenty of
poetry, drama, and criticism also, editions of Shakespeare, Milton,
Smollett, Johnson, and Burke—the usual stock of a gentleman's
library. Irish dictionaries and Gaelic translations of the Bible
suggest that Le Fanu inexperience of native Ireland was not
wilful, and dozens of novels prove that Huguenot puritanism had
not extinguished the Sheridan love of literature. Several of the
books to which Sheridan Le Fanu refers in his own novels were
there on the shelves in Abington—Mrs Radcliffe's *Mysteries of
Udolpho* and de Quincey's *Confessions of an English Opium Eater*—
together with rarer shockers, *The History of the Devil* and *The
Mummy; a Tale of the Twenty-Second Century*. Though this was
the early diet of the future author of *The House by the Churchyard*
and 'Green Tea', the Dean's taste was more catholic; among his
prized volumes was a 1527 Boccaccio and a first edition of John
Donne's *Poems*. If the whole collection sounds dully conventional,
there were also books with intimate associations, Sheridan's
Pronouncing Dictionary and Moore's *Life* of R. B. Sheridan, which
proclaimed the permanence of the Cavan inheritance. On the Le
Fanu side there was less evidence; a copy of George Colman the
Elder's *Terence* recalled the dramatist's friendship with the
Dean's father, the 'Clerk of the Coast'. In 1830 a curious little
volume arrived, *Scripture Revelations concerning the Future State*,
with Swedenborg-like speculations on religion. The 1820s, how-

ever, were the high point of the Dean's book-buying, and later
falling-off underlines the difficult financial times which awaited
his family.[1] Joseph hardly needed a tutor in surroundings like
these, and eventually some serious misdemeanour led to Stinson's
dismissal. *Seventy Years* is silent as to the nature of the offence,
a silence which throws the malevolent tutor of Joseph's story,
'Spalatro', into an artificially dramatic light.[2] For years the family
hear no more of Stinson, only to discover him in the 1840s a
violent supporter of O'Connell's Repeal movement, playing party
tunes on the bagpipes and marching in processions.

A closer bond was usual between rector and landlord in nineteenth-century Ireland than that experienced by Dean Le Fanu.
Even when one or the other was an absentee, they had a common
interest in local society, one collecting rents and the other tithes.
The landlord was almost inevitably a Church of Ireland man, and
politically the rector was committed to the social *status quo*. In
Abington landlords counted for rather less than this; the Carbery
estate was burdened with entails and mortgages to a degree which
even the Rackrents would have found embarrassing, and the other
notable landowner, Lord Cloncurry, was typical of nothing in his
class. He had been imprisoned as a United Irishman in the Tower
of London, had subsequently met William Beckford (the author
of *Vathek*), and claimed an acquaintance with the Pope. Abington
Court, his Limerick home, was only a few hundred yards from Le
Fanu's church, but as he spent most of his time on his other Irish
estates, the second baron's influence on life in the glebe-house
was minimal. Given his radical politics and Catholic sympathies,
this was the way the Dean liked it.

Although an absentee for three years, Thomas Le Fanu had
not neglected his parish entirely. The rector of Newport had
acted as overseer at Abington, and a young clergyman with the
Trollopian name, John Bury Palliser, performed the usual
parochial functions throughout 1825. On 15 January 1826 he

---

[1] For a list of Dean Le Fanu's collection see *Catalogue of the Library of the
Very Rev. Thomas P. Le Fanu . . .*, a copy of which is preserved in the Royal
Irish Academy.

[2] See *Seventy Years*, pp. 7–9. There is no record of a Stinson in Church of
Ireland archives, though the Abington parish records indicate that he preached
on more than one occasion in place of Dean Le Fanu. If Stinson had not been
ordained (as his non-appearance in central archives would suggest) his dismissal
by the Dean would be understandable.

handed over officially to the newly appointed Dean of Emly, who arrived from Dublin in time for the Easter vestry meeting. These arrangements show that the Dean's eventual arrival in Abington was never in doubt. Indeed, he had preached in his own parish twice in late 1823, seven times the following year, and twice in 1825. Accusations of laxity would be ungenerous by the notions of his time and class.

Catholic emancipation was only three years away, when the general election of 1826 gave warning that the old anti-Catholic lobbies could not effectively defeat the mass organization of O'Connell's followers. His rhetoric and industry had welded together an unprecedented combination of priests, small business-men, and some liberal intellectuals. A weekly rent of £300 or more revealed the extent of O'Connell's support among the inarticulate peasantry, and the emancipation movement was the first popular 'machine' in British politics, a model for the later and unsuccessful Union Repeal agitation. The mood in Ireland from 1826 onwards was truly apocalyptic; prophecies circulated among the people of the final defeat of Protestantism; politicians weighed up their chances in a possible civil war. All this excitement was added to the normal turbulence of faction fights, the desperation of the hungry, the violence of highwaymen and stirring magistrates. The Phoenix Park, being a landscaped ideological garden, was the worst training ground for a country parson in the 1820s. With little or no experience of rural conditions, Dean Le Fanu had passed over an opportunity to adjust to the intensities of the countryside in 1817; even 1823 (seen in retrospect) might have been a better moment to move than 1826. The Catholic question now dominated every aspect of life, and relations between rector and priest were crucial in maintaining order in a deeply divided community.

Initially it seemed that he was remarkably lucky in his opposite number. Thomas O'Brien Costello had been on the best of terms with Le Fanu's predecessor, John Jebb. At a time when the majority of Catholic priests were living in rented rooms, in public houses, or in cabins no better than those of their parishioners, O'Brien Costello had built himself a solid residence in his native townland Farnane, and called it Castle Comfort. The social graces of the priest and the popularity of his own predecessor, would have helped Thomas Le Fanu to settle into his new responsibilities, had he arrived in 1823. Three years' absenteeism, however, had cost him much of this goodwill. In 1825 O'Brien Costello had given evidence to a select committee of the House of Commons, explaining the tensions in Irish society by pointing to a number of irritants. Catholics, he suggested, 'feel the degradation, which small as the number of persons of a different religion in the parish is, is excited by the supercilious conduct of some of those persons towards them in their transactions of life, shewing, that they feel a superiority by which others are degraded'.[1] In addition to this attempt to maintain a social distance between the minority and majority, the Protestant minister of a neighbouring parish was waging a missionary campaign, 'going through the streets of the village decrying the Roman Catholic religion . . . he tells the people they will be damned if they do not follow the Scriptures and go to church'. These vignettes of Anglican attitudes are valid in innumerable instances, but O'Brien Costello proceeded to refer specifically to his own parish and its absentee rector. He reported that Le Fanu had been in Abington but two or three times in two years, remaining once for a fortnight, and at other periods for a very short time. Absenteeism was not just a moral failing (in the eyes of the priest), but a palpable hardship imposed on the people who believed that a resident rector could give them employment or at least 'that his revenue would in some measure revert to them'.

The rector's income derived almost entirely from tithes paid by all landholders in the parish, Catholic and Protestant alike. In 1823 tithe for the united parish of Abington and Tuough was £1,179. 7s. 2d., the residents of Abington contributing just £839 of the total. As for the deanery of Emly, which Le Fanu acquired in 1826 and which was particularly attractive in that none of the usual duties of deans were required of him, it was valued at the time of his death at £650 per annum, and its worth in 1826 was probably similar. In all, the glebe-house had an income of about £1,800. In the first year of residence, however, Le Fanu's tithe income dropped to a total of £900, an unfortunate omen. When the priest and rector finally quarrelled at the beginning of the Tithe War, tithe income simply dried up, and the previous dependence of the people on the rector was transformed into a studied indifference to his existence.

[1] House of Commons, *Reports from Committees*, 1825, vol. 8, p. 423.

His parochial duties centred on Sunday service at twelve at the church on the monastic site. Services at Abington were sparsely attended. If the weather was particularly bad, no worshippers appeared, and the Dean simply went home. On 25 January 1829 there was a raging snow-storm, and the service was abandoned. On Palm Sunday, Charles Coote (rector of the neighbouring parish of Doon, and a cousin of Emma's) presided, but as the day was very wet and so few had turned up, no collection was taken. The weather had not improved by Good Friday when the Dean, who was back in Abington, preached no sermon and took up no collection. The major festivals brought out full attendances from the Abington faithful; on Christmas Day 1829 the Dean took up 17s. 4½d. and thirty-three people remained for Holy Communion after morning prayer. If we assume that thirty-three communicants were accompanied by as many unconfirmed children, then the congregation numbered about sixty. And, consequently, the Dean's flock amounted to approximately one per cent of the parish's total population; even if this proportion is doubled to allow for discrepancies between Catholic, Protestant, and civil parish boundaries, the Church of Ireland congregation in Abington was a tiny part of 'the people'.

Illness in the family sometimes affected the services, and shortly after his arrival in Abington, he was unable to preach 'one of the Rector's family being taken suddenly and dangerously ill'. This was almost certainly Catherine, just turned fourteen, whose subsequent disabilities made her a semi-invalid for the last ten years of her short life. She was the first of the Le Fanus to sense that the normality of their lives had an obverse reading, that the meagre appetite for the Word of God which her father's congregation displayed was of more than local significance. It warned of a general falling-off from the alliance of church and state which sustained the establishment; perhaps it even threatened a future invalidity of the revelations at the heart of the Christian mystery. A sensitive child, especially one whom illness had provided with ample time for reflection, could observe a basic irrelevance beneath the seemingly essential role of the Dean in local society. Another child might react differently, and the bonfires by the roadside, the ceremonial unyoking of the horses, assured her brother William of the family's real worth. Such exuberance and courtesy must be seen in the context of the faction fights which

perennially raged in Limerick, and the faction fights understood
as the necessary conjunct of a desperate dependence on the
'quality' for guidance, charity, and employment. If that cycle of
dependence and courtesy were once broken, if the people of the
cabins were once distracted from their excesses of ceremony and
riot, then the whole fabric of demonstrable relevance on which
William Le Fanu dotingly reflected might dissolve. Catherine Le
Fanu's illness persisted throughout the years at Abington like a
seed of doubt inside the glebe-house; to the mystically minded,
it might appear like an imperfect attunement between the house
and its ostensible status. Such disjunctions recur in her brother's
novels, where ailing or swooning daughters and unhappily ill
wives symbolize a malaise of the household and its inheritance.

In July 1828 Thomas and Emma received word that his sister
Elizabeth was dangerously ill in Bath, while his brother pressed
for money to meet their expenses. The money for a journey to
England Thomas proposed to raise on a short-term loan, but in
search of the medical expenses he was forced to turn to Captain
William Dobbin.[1] His letter suggests a less impressive degree of
security than the coldly elegant symmetry of the glebe-house or
the columns of calculating pittances in the tithe-applotment books:

I know it will grieve you and dear Lissy to hear that I have just received
the most dismal tidings from Bath. Poor Joseph, & Ormond the
surgeon, have both written to say that there is scarcely a hope for my
poor Sister. 'If you wish to see her,' says Ormond, 'you will make your
arrangements for leaving your home as soon as you can.' You may
imagine the wretched state of my unhappy brother, and to add to his
misery, the expenses of his & dear Betsy's illness have been in various
ways so enormous. Thus he writes me word that he is in immediate
want of one hundred pounds to meet the most pressing embarrassments.
Now I declare to heaven I have not 100 pence that I can lay my hand
on at the present moment . . . Will you, my dear William, under these
most painful circumstances lend me a hundred pounds on my note
with interest for one year? This will leave me time to make arrangements
for repaying you without interfering with other engagements that I
must fulfil in the interim. And I shall esteem it a real act of friendship.
I need not expostulate to you, who have a heart to feel for a friend,
upon the misery I at present experience. Poor Joseph just hardly able

[1] T. P. Le Fanu to W. Dobbin, 23 July 1828; quoted by kind permission of
Mrs Burrows.

to crawl—and my dear unhappy Sister fallen a victim to her devoted care of him.

Do dear William write me a line by return of post to say whether you can do this. If so the money can be sent after me to Bath in the form of a Bill. I will send my address from there and on receipt of it will enclose you my acceptance for the account on a year's note. As to our present account for the forty Pounds you were so kind as to lend me in London it stands thus

£40. 0s. 0d.

    Your first order of wines from O'Brien
    24 May £13. 14s. 6d.
    Yr Second Do 20 June £13. 12s. 6d.

                     27. 7s. 0d.
                         ————————
                     12. 13s. 0d.

The balance, on my return from Bath, I can settle either by wine, or cash as you please.

God bless you, my dear William. Emma joins in kindest love to Lissy & the children with your most unhappy
                        TPL

Two days later, on 25 July, Elizabeth Bonne Le Fanu died, and the Dean was away from Abington for August and September, settling up his sister's affairs. The make-shift financial arrangements, the payment of family debts through credit with the rector's wine merchant, the scraping of shillings together for a boat fare, may have been more common of nineteenth-century middle-class life than we can now imagine. Yet the significant point is the contrast between this understandable embarrassment and the scale of tithe income (*circa* £1,200), between the domestic anxiety and the public assurance.

Disturbances on the Stradbroke estate, which may have discouraged the Le Fanus from moving directly to Abington in 1823, sprang from the extremity of Irish social divisions. Individual acts of violence, assassination, and harassment occurred regularly and were regarded by the authorities and the Anglo-Irish upper classes as evidence of the irredeemable barbarism of the native, Catholic population. Apart from the justification which one may find in the conditions endured by the mass of the people, these murders and outrages were in fact special instances of an endemic violence. Faction fights were organized with a ritual attention to detail and protocol; the rival gangs bore grotesque titles and the plainest weapons, cudgels of blackthorn known as shillelaghs (after the village of Shillelagh in county Wicklow). Shanavests and Caravats (both named after Gaelic terms for items of clothing) and Coffeys and Reaskawallahs were the warring parties in Limerick and Tipperary. The Le Fanus' glebe-house was about midway between the Coffey stronghold at Newport and the Reaskawallah territory in the parish of Doon. 'Here is Coffey aboo against Reaskawallahs; here is Coffey aboo—who dar strike a Coffey?'—this taunt started a faction fight in Annagh bog which William Le Fanu witnessed. 'In an instant hundreds of sticks were up, hundreds of heads were broken. In vain the parish priest and his curate ride through the crowd, striking right and left with their whips; in vain a few policemen try to quell the riot; on it goes . . .'[1] In the end the Coffeys won, though a few were killed and many dangerously injured on both sides.

These fights were symptoms of the excessive energy and fertility of pre-Famine Ireland, and evidence also of the irrelevance of conventional codes of behaviour. 'A fair murder' was both a killing committed during a fair or market, and by the same token a reasonable, justified homicide. At the time of emancipation, many of the rival gangs combined to demonstrate their common support for Daniel O'Connell, whose influence channelled this over-abundant energy into more orthodox political forms. William Le Fanu took part in the reconciliation of the Coffeys and Reaskawallahs early in 1829. The latter faction, whose family name was Ryan, were marching from their headquarters through Cappamore towards Newport, their route lying alongside the glebe-land. They marched six deep in military formation, with music and banners, each man carrying a green bough of peace, the entire procession stretching back two miles along the dusty roads. William was easily persuaded to join in for a few hundred yards when he recognized 'a friendly peasant' among the marchers. At the end of the route there was an harmonious orgy of whiskey and rhetoric. To the Le Fanus, gazing over a deep hedge of ferns and foxgloves, it was at once a terrible exhibition of a power they lived beside and a promise of calmer days to come. *Seventy Years* makes no mention of Joseph Le Fanu's reaction to the march,

[1] *Seventy Years*, p. 34.

but if his younger brother participated it is hard to imagine him remaining behind. The tithe issue was still a year or two in the future as they listened to the Reaskawallah bands dropping into silence between the distant banks of the Green Road. The moment was an ironic crossroads in local history. The Ryans and Coffeys were putting away their ancient, internecine strife to become part of a regimented community paying dues to their politicians, making reasonable demands to parliaments they had scarcely heard of, and acknowledging the leadership of a middle-class caucus, attorneys, and committee men. They were taking the first unconscious steps towards a meaner, safer, modern Ireland; they were crossing, for the last time in their primitive formations, the Dooglashla bridge which rectors of Abington had kept in repair from time immemorial. But far from bringing agitation to an end, 1829 released frustrations and antagonisms which were less easily channelled into violent recreations. Reaskawallahs, denied their ritual, would be less tolerant of the benign but supercilious conduct of the glebe people.

Violence did not end in 1829, because it stemmed from the popular imagination and manifested itself in every aspect of life and death. The battles of the derrins, as they were called, took place whenever two funerals were due at the same graveyard on the same day. Intimidation and outright attack were employed to ensure initial occupation of the consecrated ground, in the popular belief that the last soul to reach Purgatory (i.e. the last corpse buried) had to carry water for all those who preceded him, his responsibility ending only with the arrival of another soul. Battles of this kind, in which blood was spilled, occurred at Abington graveyard while Joseph and William were boys, cries of victory or dismay drifting over the field which divided the glebe-house from the churchyard as rivals from Murroe and Barrington's Bridge fought on the banks of the river. The real interest of the superstition is the identification of the moment of burial with the entry of the soul into Purgatory, a survival into late Christian times of a material concept of religion. Like all folk myths which translate metaphysical concepts into physical incidents, it appeals to the literary imagination. Le Fanu used the idea of the purgatorial water-carrier in his first story, 'The Ghost and the Bone-setter', though his comic-gothic trappings scarcely allow any development of the implications.

The year of Catholic emancipation, 1829, was a disturbed one in Limerick and Tipperary. Between 11 April and 2 May four murders had been committed in county Limerick (excluding the city), according to the Limerick *Chronicle*, an average of one a week. On 3 August (a fair day) in Borrisokeane two factions arrived to fight by previous arrangement. Captain Dobbin, as the police officer in charge, tried to keep them apart; when one of his men had his skull fractured, he was obliged to read the Riot Act. He read the act three times in a futile attempt to disperse the rival mobs. Stones continued to pour down on his men, who returned fire and shot a man dead. The police were now under siege, and Dobbin read the act once more. The police fired; three men were killed, and a woman gathering stones was shot through the head. Finally, the military arrived with a piece of cannon to restore order in the town. There was nothing exceptional about the incident, apart from the pathos of Dobbin's oratory. There was an intentional element in Irish violence which directed it, as the century rolled on, increasingly towards the class of which the Le Fanus were representative. For the Tithe War (as the sporadic campaign against the Established Church was known) succeeded the faction fights; boycott and assassination took over from the casual head-cracking and outlawry of earlier decades. Sensitive children of the glebe-house, with few of their own caste within a dozen miles, were likely to absorb some profound reaction to this perpetual disturbance. In Le Fanu's later fiction, the isolation of the Great House was inexplicably disturbed by incidents of meaningless violence—brawling intruders in the parkland of *Uncle Silas*, the prostrate duellist in the Welsh wood of *Willing to Die*. To declare such acts meaningless, as the novelist virtually declares them, was to reserve some residual dignity and meaning to the Great House itself; nevertheless, the final fate of the House in each novel is desolation.

Wildness and death were not man's exclusive property; nature in the west contributed bountifully its own blatant theatricality to man's violence. In the hot summer of 1838, Joseph led a party of five out from his father's house to visit places of note in the neighbouring counties; the five were Joseph and William Le Fanu, John Walsh (afterwards Master of the Rolls), John Jellett (afterwards Provost of Trinity), and an Italian friend of the Le Fanus', Gaetano Egedi. Towards the end of their tour, the group

set out to walk the last fifteen miles across the Galtee Mountains
to Abington, having as guide a Gaelic-speaker from Tipperary.
The immensity of the mountains was emphasized by this imprecise
rapport between travellers and guide, and soon a romantic
appreciation overwhelmed the five:

It was a glorious sight as we looked back on the great plain below us,
with its green pastures and waving cornfields bathed in the light of
the setting sun. We could not rest long, and were soon on foot again,
and had nearly reached the crest of the range, when suddenly a fog
rolled down upon us, so thick that we could not see more than thirty
or forty yards . . . The guide tried to cheer us up by constantly saying
'Nabochlish' (never mind) [recte Ná bac leis] 'the houses is near, the
houses is near.' Once some fifteen or twenty yards from us, a horse
galloped past; as well as we could see he was of a chestnut colour.[1]

After further scrambling on the rocks, the party was encased in
absolute darkness when the moon went down and then, suddenly,
the fog lifted. Soon they encountered some late-returning
farmers, sat with them round a fire, joking and telling stories.
Joseph mentioned the horse which his group had seen in the fog:

All were silent, and looked one at another half-incredulous, half-
frightened. One of them, after a pause, said, 'There is no horse on the
mountain. What sort of horse was it that ye thought ye seen?' 'A chestnut horse,' said we. 'Oh begorra!' said our friend, 'they seen the yalla
horse.' Then turning to us, 'It's a wonder ye all cum down alive and
safe; it is few that sees the yalla horse that has luck after.'[2]

After this alarm the talk turned to the day's events. A land
steward had been shot near Bansha, and the younger men discussed the implications. William Le Fanu's account in *Seventy
Years* preserves a rough approximation to the dialect, but seems
unaware of the defensive manner of the conversation. One of the
farmer's boys said of the victim and his unknown assailants, 'Now,
why didn't they give him a good batin', and not to go kill him
entirely?' Another answered, 'They kem from a distance and
didn't like to go home without finishing the job.' At this time
Aherlow, which lay ahead of the Le Fanus, was one of the most
disturbed districts in the south; and clerical tithes being a
principal cause of agitation, the sons of an Anglican dean did not

---

[1] Ibid. 127–8.
[2] Ibid. 129–30.

hear the debate on murder without a shiver. As William half recognized, their friends for the night knew perfectly well who the murderers might be. An atmosphere of automatic, casual, and yet strangely intimate violence pervaded rural Ireland, and Joseph transposed the mood of his own youth back into history in his tales of the Jacobite and Penal times, written later in 1838 and in 1839. More specifically, his ballad 'Shamus O'Brien' is set here in Aherlow, a place which he visited only on this one occasion; and the remarkable aspect of the poem is that it celebrates a rebel of 1798 rather than a land steward or any other friend of his class and creed. Historical romance was to become a disguise for his feelings, and the murder near Bansha, the encounter on the mountain, and the rebel ballad are just the first elements of a deeply ironic and evasive treatment of society which he developed in his mature fiction.

The essence of society as Le Fanu grew to know it in his Abington years was the isolation of his people from 'the people'. A young Trinity undergraduate spending his time walking in the hills or lying on the glebe-house roof saw the landscape differently. To him it was populated by past solitaries as well as by the present throng. Nature itself provided him with the imagery to describe those early heroes; they were comparable to the aboriginal woods, the noble oak, the unspoiled leafage. Later in his career, when his historical romanticism had given way before a constitutional moroseness, he turned once more to the landscape of Abington. Now the picturesque is tempered with an autumnal gloom:

A deserted country. A wide, black bog, level as a lake, skirted with copse, spreads at the left, as you journey northward, and the long and irregular line of mountain rises at the right, clothed in heath, broken with lines of grey rock that resemble the bold and irregular outlines of fortifications, and riven with many a gully, expanding here and there into rocky wooded glens, which open as they approach the road . . . Lisnavoura, that lonely hill-haunt of the 'Good People'.[1]

As that last phrase reveals, this is a tale of the supernatural. Yet here after forty years, Le Fanu has described the landscape of places a few hundred yards from his father's glebe in terms which approximate to his own experience. Cobbett's overcrowded cabins

[1] *All the Year Round*, vol. 3 (new series), no. 62 (5 Feb. 1870), 228–9.

and half-naked peasants, the priest's statistical obsession with the present, even his own brother's easy and anecdotal sociability— none of these could express Sheridan Le Fanu's realization that his true home was a deserted country, a place of enveloping bewitchment. When the spiritual confidence of Anglo-Ireland was exposed and mocked, its religion bargained over, and its politics short-circuited, the O'Connellite present was abominable in the sight of the Le Fanus. To a potential novelist, landscape offered a surviving past, a palpable reality which had touched the victims of similar betrayals in history and had been touched by them. Landscape is full of irony in its multiple associations, bringing together the victors and vanquished of different ages in a slowly moving panorama which each generation had paused to observe. The society which Le Fanu evolved from the abnormality of county Limerick was one which bound together figures from the corners of time, rather than the immediately contemporary society which journalists analysed. It was a version of the Burkean democracy of the dead, and indeed Burke is the ideologist under whom the Protestant intellectuals of the *Dublin University Magazine* soon united.

2

A LOST COUNTRY

WILLIAM STEUART TRENCH, one of the few land agents to leave proof of their literacy, prefaced his reminiscences with the contented declaration: 'it has been my lot to live surrounded by a kind of poetic turbulence and almost romantic violence, which I believe could scarcely belong to real life in any other country in the world'. Referring more specifically to his early years in the southern midlands, he drew a sketch familiar to country Limerick households:

In disturbed times, when several murders had been committed in the neighbourhood, we habitually took our arms with us into the dining-room, and eat our meals with our loaded pistols on the table beside us, and our guns leaning against the chimney-piece. It is surprising, when one gets accustomed to it, how little this affects the appetite or weighs upon the mind.[1]

Though local dangers in southern Ireland were very real and special to the area, the general state of the kingdom in the early 1830s was not calm. Lord Melbourne's biographer recalls the nights of August 1830 when the Kentish countryside was lurid with blazing ricks. Bands of men roamed the lanes, breaking machines and beating up the landowners' agents. Soon there were pro-reform riots in the towns; Derby gaol was broken open, Nottingham castle destroyed, and the bishop's palace in Bristol fired. For more than a year the kingdom seemed on the edge of civil war, and in this state of panic the Reform Bill of 1832 was passed. Trench's choice of cutlery was not unique to his household or even to his province.

The causes of disturbance varied greatly from region to region, and in Ireland the passing of the Reform Bill had no effect on popular grievances. These principally revolved round tithes, which led back to questions of land usage and ownership. Tithes had been an irritant in Irish affairs since the eighteenth century,

---

[1] W. S. Trench, *Realities of Irish Life* (London, 1869), p. 42.

but in the 1820s and 1830s they became the focus for larger and weightier issues. Tithe opposition was an expression of Catholic indignation at the government's failure to honour the promises of emancipation made in 1800; it was a further indication of the growing political awareness of Irish Catholics and of the central role of the priesthood in political organization. The Tithe War also reflected in sectarian colours the deteriorating economic situation in Ireland after the Napoleonic wars, and the excessively high level of Irish rents. Finally, of course, it underlined the sectarian basis of society; the divisions, crudely stated, into a Catholic tenantry and a Protestant ascendency were indisputable in the area of tithe payment. Here Ireland differed from Kent or Derby. Even after 1829, when O'Connell's long campaign for emancipation was at last rewarded, sectarian feeling ran high, for emancipation had been primarily legal and parliamentary, whereas the tithe system remained a constant source of resentment among the poor masses. Tithe opposition had begun in 1830 in Kilkenny and Carlow, and the entire southern half of the country was caught up in the resistance by the following year. Tactics evolved as the campaign progressed, but essentially they were fabian—the organized driving of cattle away before the pursuing bailiffs. Traditional outrages, cattle maiming, house-burning, nocturnal ploughing of grasslands, intimidation, and, of course, murder, reinforced the passive campaign. Even before this explosion occurred, the Le Fanus had been given warnings of difficulties ahead. Arrears of tithes due to the Dean came to £8 in 1829, £45 in 1830, and £118 in 1831, an alarming progression which reached in 1832 £778. 11s. 11½d., virtually the entire tithe income for the year. In common with other similarly distressed clerics he applied for an advance from the authorities, receiving £310 in 1832.[1]

Limerick remained relatively calm during the early months of the war, but the spark came early in 1832. The Revd Charles Coote came to hear of some injudicious remarks on tithe made by his Catholic counterpart, Father Hickey. Coote, a vehement Brunswick Club man, immediately demanded tithe on the priest's holdings, in violation of custom. Hickey refused to pay and Coote distrained a cow and put it up for auction at the Pounding Field

---

[1] *Parliamentary Papers, 1833*, vol. 27, includes statistics of arrears of tithe and of advances in lieu of tithe, from which my calculations have been abstracted.

in Bilboa. These proceedings did not take place *in vacuo*, for Limerick was a populous county. Six thousand people crowded the village, with as many more watching from the surrounding hills. The government had sent in a troop of lancers, four companies of the 92nd Highlanders, and two pieces of artillery. Skirmishes broke out, and the number of casualties was contained only by the intervention of Hickey's curate who disciplined the angry mobs. Matthew Barrington, as Crown Solicitor for Munster, was instructed to investigate the incident, but no action was taken. Soon 'the people' were singing a new song:

> O Mr Coote, you have no right
> To cant the cow on Bilboa's height . . .

Much of this, though not the ballad, is recorded in William Le Fanu's *Seventy Years*, where the emphasis differs markedly from the popular account. To the Dean's son, Coote's cousin, the incident made 'weary work for the troops, as the day was very hot and bright'.[1] Coote became a marked man, and some of the resentment he inspired rubbed off on to the Le Fanus. None of the family went out alone, and they were at all times armed. When Catherine with some girl cousins, visitors to the glebe, ventured out unprotected, they were pelted with mud and stones, and any excursion by the family was greeted with shouts and cursing. On 20 April an attempt was made on Coote's life, and on another occasion he was, according to a local magistrate, 'stopped within three hundred yards of the Dean of Emly's gate by a ruffian mob who (but for his producing pistols . . .) would . . . have put him to death'. In the eyes of the people, the churchmen monopolized justice, for the magistrate was John Wickham, Le Fanu's churchwarden and assessor of tithes. Writing on 13 August, he gave an account of the Le Fanus' predicament:

A set of ruffians are in the daily habit in their passage to and from a bog in the neighbourhood of Dean Le Fanu's residence of using the most horrid threats and imprecations against that gentleman and his family threatening them with the fate of the Revd Messrs Going and Whitty who were murdered; and the daily and hourly insults to every member of the Dean of Emly's family are disgusting and terrific beyond measure.[2]

[1] *Seventy Years*, p. 61.
[2] Quoted by M. Tierney, *Murroe and Boher* (Dublin, 1966), p. 68.

The bog in question was the scene of the faction fight which William had watched in perfect safety a few years earlier; and the point of Coote's arrest by the mob was the junction of the Cappamore and Barrington's Bridge roads, where, in 1829, the family had happily watched the reconciliation of the factions. Within three years antagonism had focused on their solitary glebe-house, and behind the frail gates Joseph took his book—whether *The Mummy* or *The Scripture Revelations* we shall never know—on to the roof for seclusion. For him, the period became an area of experience to which he never referred explicitly either in journalism or fiction; it was repressed and channelled into other anxieties. William, on the other, was able to find in retrospect amusing details in the grim pattern. John Anster, translator of Goethe's *Faust*, came to spend a few days in Abington during the disturbances. As he drove from Limerick in the Le Fanus' car, the usual shouting followed him. Being slightly deaf, he heard the noise only and not the threatening abuse. Over dinner, and with a beaming face, he said to the Dean, 'I never knew I was so well known down here, but one's fame sometimes travels further than we think. I assure you, nearly the whole way as I drove from Limerick I was loudly cheered by the people.'[1]

The Tithe War threatened to shatter the holy alliance between church and state so revered by Irish Tories. The confidence of the ascendency depended largely on the integrity of this alliance, though in the 1830s landowners scarcely recognized the threat to their own position implicit in tithe resistance. Young though he was, Le Fanu recognized the wider implications; 'rents will be attacked, as tithes are now, with the same machinery, and with like success'.[2] Late in 1832 his father was appointed to a government commission inquiring into ecclesiastical incomes. As this necessitated a move to Dublin, the family were relieved by the temporary escape from Abington. Joseph was due to go up to Trinity in the autmn, and the official appointment simply allowed the others to accompany him. The Dean and Emma took a house in Williamstown Avenue in the southern suburbs, and the mobs of Doon and Murroe were left behind. But far behind also lay the comfortable tithe income. There were, of course, other sources of income, decanal fees, rents from patches of land inherited from

---

[1] *Seventy Years*, p. 63.
[2] Ibid. 70.

Sheridans and Le Fanus of the past. Yet this loss of tithes, if it persisted, was very severe. The following year Parliament passed the Church Temporalities Act, which reduced the establishment by two archbishoprics and eight bishoprics. At the parochial level it did nothing to ease the lot either of tithe payers or the rectors whose income dwindled for another year. The act, however, was seen by many churchmen as a sign of imminent doom. The Whigs were now in power, and Anglo-Irish Tories faced an alliance between O'Connell (their local and very personal foe) and their traditional opponents in Parliament.

In Trinity College radicalism had influencial supporters, and a group of young Tories launched the *Dublin University Magazine* to combat the new doctrines. The origins of this monthly journal, with which Le Fanu was later so intimately connected, are still obscure. The founders included Anster, whom the Le Fanus already knew, and Charles Stuart Stanford, editor for the first twelve months. The O'Sullivan brothers, Mortimer and Samuel, provided the ideological backbone. While the dual crisis in church and state was the impetus which launched the magazine, and polemic dominated the pages for several years, literature was large in the minds of the founders. Although everyone involved in the project was Trinity educated, there was no official connection with the College. In January 1833, when the first issue appeared, Le Fanu was a classics junior freshman, and as such he would have had little contact with the earnest young men of the editorial board. His brother came up in the autumn of 1833 as an engineering student. Down in Abington a curate, Benjamin Webb Bradshaw, lived in the glebe-house from April 1833 to December 1834 when he was 'obliged to give up the cure suddenly thro' indisposition', as the Dean expressed it; popular feeling in the district still ran high. He was followed by Austin Cooper, a curate *pro tempore* who remained at his post till the Le Fanus returned.

Captain Dobbin of Borrisokeane in 1833 made his own attempt to improve the family fortunes. In possession of deeds to property in Carrickfergus, he travelled north in the hope of recovering some ancestral holdings. Despite the documentation he had no success, and in his usual melancholy style he wrote to his children, 'if I were not in expectation of a letter from Mr Leonard Dobbin, I would set out immediately' for home. Leonard was one of the Armagh branch of the Dobbins, a prosperous banker. The contrast with his southern relative was marked indeed, for he had been elected as a radical MP for Armagh in 1832, smashing the Primate's long-established monopoly. For one reason or another the Captain found no consolation with the banker, and he gradually moved further into the decline which the absurd Swift had predicted in 1811.

The Dean, Emma, and Catherine had now to reconsider their position. With the commission's business completed, the ostensible reason for their presence in Dublin disappeared. In October 1834 the Dean wrote to the Prime Minister offering to resign his post, and hoping to elicit something better in return. Whether or not he was aware of the connection, he might have had a more personal introduction to Melbourne, for four years earlier Caroline Norton (a not-so-distant relative on the Sheridan side) had met the future Prime Minister and formed an intimate friendship with him. In the event Melbourne replied briefly that the Dean would be well advised to return to his post. And so in the early months of 1835 the Le Fanus prepared to quit Dublin once more and to return to the uncertainties of county Limerick. Catherine, twenty-one and in feeble health, naturally would continue to live with her parents. The two boys were established in their undergraduate courses and might be expected to stay in Dublin. But Trinity, unique among British universities, allowed a student to qualify for a degree by passing periodical examinations, without attendance at lectures or even residence in the city. This was known as the country-list system and, as R. B. McDowell has observed, the financial advantages of such an arrangement could not be overlooked 'in a country whose middle class was as poor as that of Ireland'. As a result the Le Fanu boys spent a large part of their university careers at Abington, being tutored by their father. In Joseph's case we know little of his doings beyond the casual details of *Seventy Years*, but the country list nearly cost William his life.

At the end of April 1835 the family reoccupied the glebe-house. Within a week a letter arrived from the Viceregal Lodge offering a chaplaincy. Here was an opportunity to escape permanently from the restrictions of rural Ireland, from the uncertainty, indeed the miserable inoperancy, of the tithe system, an opportunity to return to the scene of earlier happiness, the Phoenix Park. But the Dean did not hesitate in his reply, and the terms in which he wrote indicated clearly a stiffening of attitude even over his appeal of the previous autumn:

I request that you will present my respectful acknowledgement to the Lord Lieutn for his Excys good opinion of me, and for his intention of nominating me one of his Chaplains. At the same time I regret that I must decline the appointment; and lest my doing so should be interpreted as any personal disrespect of his Excelly, which would give me great concern, it is necessary that I should state my reason for declining this mark of his favour, which is simply this:—his Excy forms part of an administration pledged to the *appropriation clause*; a measure which I conscienciously [*sic*] believe tends to the destruction of the United Church of England and Ireland established in Ireland & such being the case I cannot as a dignitory [*sic*] of that establishment, connect myself officially with any member of a government so pledged.[1]

Behind the political terminology of the letter, there lies a simple truth: you cannot go back to the place that used to be; the place is changed, you are changed by what has intervened. This realization, merging with disapproval of the Whigs, is one Joseph would have approved. It is remarkable that, for all the atavism of his fiction, there are few instances of happy nostalgia.

Tithe income having never resumed, Abington continued to be a troublesome cure in mid-decade. Coote was still rector of Doon, at loggerheads with the local population; O'Brien Costello was still parish priest in Murroe. On his return to the parish, the Dean made no attempt to assert his position either through the local dispensary or through politics, and the year ended with a disquieting temporary closure of the church—ostensibly for redecoration. From 15 November till the last day of January 1836. ten weeks in all, services were held in the Petty Sessions House. This suspicious circumstance is made doubly curious by the use of the church on Christmas Day and the Sunday following, the implication being that the disruption of routine was caused by external pressures. The Anglican congregation existed in such tiny numbers that a momentary hint of intimidation, another indiscretion by Coote, could make closure of the church advisable. For the great festivals, however, a truce might be safely assumed to exist.

By 1836 Parliament had begun the task of legislating some

[1] T. P. Le Fanu to Lieut.-Col. Charles Yorke, Priv. Sec. to the Lord Lieutenant, 30 May 1835; from a copy among the Le Fanu Papers.

solution to the tithe question, and general disturbances—attacks on the mail coach, threats of death to anyone who paid, and sustained abuse of those who claimed tithes—had died down. More than four years had elapsed since the Le Fanus had enjoyed their proper income, four years of dwindling confidence during which they were forced to eat the seed-corn of their financial and spiritual inheritance. In the autumn the Dean directed his agent Edward Dartnell to publicize a 15 per cent reduction for all who were prepared to pay the year's dues. William, then aged twenty, and a cousin Robert Flemyng, undertook to distribute circulars explaining the terms of the abatement. On their first outing nothing remarkable happened beyond the usual hooting. 'Some of the houses were shut against us as the inmates saw us approach; at some few we were not uncivilly received, but were distinctly told that under no circumstances would one farthing of tithes ever be paid again.'[1] On the following day, 13 October, the two rode out towards Kishiquirk, a small village in the south of the parish. A threatening crowd shouted 'Down with the Orangemen! Down with the tithes!' Now the ambush was sprung; stones rained down from attackers behind the mound-fences, while the two riders pressed on without being stunned or unseated:

One man only was on the road, and, as we got near him, I saw him settling his spade in his hand as if to be ready to strike a blow. I presented my pistol at him. 'Don't shoot me,' he called out; 'I'm only working here.' But just as I passed him he made a tremendous blow at me; it missed me, but struck the horse just behind the saddle. The spade was broken by the violence of the blow. Down went the horse on his haunches, but was quickly up again, and on we went. Had he fallen, I should not have been alive many minutes; he brought me bravely home, but never recovered, and died soon afterwards.[2]

By a coincidence Caroline Norton wrote from London to her cousin on the day of this attack, regretting 'most earnestly and sincerely the effect upon [his] comfort of the present unsettled state of Irish tithes'.[3] The usual complaint was made to the authorities: Wickham, Justice of the Peace and churchwarden, wrote a report, and the Dean wrote directly to the new Under-Secretary, Thomas Drummond, explaining that he found it

---

[1] *Seventy Years*, p. 64.
[2] Ibid. 65.
[3] C. Norton to T. P. Le Fanu 13 Oct. (no year).

impossible to maintain his family without making an effort to recover at least some of his 'tithe property'. The years after the Le Fanus' return from Dublin spoke of deprivation and despair, less dramatically than the twelve months leading up to their hegira, but with an insidious authenticity. While pleading with his political opponents for financial support, while his heirs found the doors of cabins closed against them, the Dean and his family continued to live in the glebe-house, one of the largest occupied mansions in the district. Hidden forces sapped the vitality of the establishment; manifestations of hostility and death illuminated the general darkness of clerical life. Returning from church one Sunday shortly after the Kishiquirk incident, Charles Coote paused to let his horse drink from a stream. A thundering report and a cloud of smoke came from a little grove beside him. A blunderbuss had exploded prematurely: its shattered remains, a half-emptied whiskey bottle, and a quantity of blood were found under the trees.

The terrible horns of dilemma trapped men like Coote and the Dean. On the one hand they scorned offers of a sinecure in an administration they felt to be hostile to their ideals; on the other, they needed official protection in order to fulfil their pastoral duties. Their attitude to authority was necessarily ambiguous; the harmony of church and state had been fatally broken, and the consequences were not political or domestic merely. The strength of this divinely sanctioned world-view had suddenly waned; the all-pervading control of a Protestant, Tory God had failed, and chaos was imminent. Not simply the chaos of empty coffers and brawling in the lanes, but the spiritual chaos of a directionless world. Like St. Peter, they had been walking on water one moment, and now found themselves sinking. That Le Fanu's father was a dignitary of this threatened establishment, living in an exposed outpost while Tithe War raged, is important in the novelist's life. It is as well to emphasize the peculiarly Irish quality of this influence. Such a father related to his children not merely as progenitor, family chieftain, or tutor; he was the embodiment of a consciously maintained view of history, the ever present symbol of an anomaly—the established and rejected church. The history of this church reached back through con-fiscations, dispossessions, military impositions, to the remoteness of the Reformation—as the legends concerning Abington grave-

yard insisted. It is important to note how a status such as the
Dean's pervaded what, in a less contorted society, we might call
the privacy of his life. His income was a political salary in the
eyes of neighbours who spurned his guidance; his charity became
a tactic, his wife a spy in the dispensary. The spiritual dimension
of a rector's thought still took its bearings from the agony and
privilege of history; no corner of the soul, in extreme instances,
was free of these pressures. Le Fanu, reared in a glebe-house
during years of particular strain and impoverishment, is difficult
material for the 'pure' biographer. Pure biography assumes its
subject to be free from any overwhelming purpose, regards him
as a relatively self-governing figure, even when self-government
takes the form of impulsive surrender and abandonment of freedom. Dean Le Fanu, and after him Sheridan Le Fanu, saw themselves as both more and less than individuals. They were symbols
or embodiments of a particular view of reality, a once vital but
now collapsing historical coherence: their experience was typical
as well as personal. But they were also powerless victims of their
surroundings; their imminent fate was an existential nullity in
which society could proceed without the slightest reference to
their being. In Le Fanu's novels the lofty and embittered hermits
who appear as hero/villains have no identity, no reality beyond that
which they find, in desperation, in their guilt. At the beginning
of *Uncle Silas* the master of the Great House emerges out of the
blackness of the room, and in the conclusion another master
virtually lapses into suicide. The dissolution of the hero figure
parallels a spiritual disillusion, and in *A Lost Name* the close
association of belief with being is emphasized by the ill-starred
hero:

'I'd give something I could believe all that.'
He tapped with his finger the Bible that lay on the little table. . . .
'But believing, unluckily, isn't a matter of choice any more than
loving . . . just a sort of foreboding that makes me fancy I should like
to have something to go upon—I mean belief, idolatry, anything.'[1]

That moment from *A Lost Name* is not untypical of his fiction;
it is merely more precise in its use of religious terms than a dozen
similar scenes in *Uncle Silas*, *Guy Deverell*, *The Tenants of Malory*,
and *Willing to Die*. Several of his characters—Jane Lennox in
Guy Deverell and Francis Ware in *Willing to Die* for example—

[1] *A Lost Name* (London, 1868) ii. 118–19.

are quite definitely misled by their reading of Scripture; an open Bible is found by Ware's body when his suicide is discovered. The feature common to Le Fanu family experience in the 1830s and the later novels of Sheridan Le Fanu is a concurrence of social decline and religious questionings. More precisely, the doubting heroes of the fiction are the masters of disgraced houses, physically isolated and morally suspect. Obviously, there is not evidence sufficiently extensive to support a direct equation of this experience and the novelist's sources. But religious anxiety in his fiction cannot be dismissed as mere atmosphere. Reading *The Purcell Papers* (1838–40) and *Uncle Silas* (1864) we are inclined to think of Le Fanu as an Anglo-Irish story-teller and as a sensationalist in turn, as if these categories were mutually exclusive. Both books, though separated by twenty-five years, express a deep concern for religious certainties and doubts, the short stories symbolizing this in the persona of Father Purcell as narrator, and the novel by casting the principal characters as Swedenborgians. Details of Sheridan Le Fanu's upbringing in the violent context of Irish agrarian and sectarian strife may suggest that the improbabilities on which the sensational novel is said to depend were less improbable in county Limerick than in Derby or Kent. Beyond this, Le Fanu was growing into the Victorian frame of mind, being of the same generation, broadly speaking, as Alfred Tennyson and Matthew Arnold. When we come to look at the general pattern of his fiction we shall find that its conventions obliquely acknowledged both the pressures of local Irish experience and the wider implications of Victorian unease.

In 1832 Dublin possessed the only university in Ireland, an Elizabethan foundation with one college, Trinity. Like everything else in colonial Ireland, it had suffered from politics, and also from a geographical remoteness from other centres of learning. More insidiously it had been the victim of a sense of its own inferiority to the sisters at Oxford and Cambridge. It was said that the Fellows of Trinity made up in bad manners for what they lacked in scholarship. It had its traditions and legacies of personal oddness, like every other ancient foundation. Perhaps the liveliest legend was the recently deceased Vice-Provost, Jacky Barrett, a miserly recluse. He was known on just one occasion to have set

eyes on the sea—at Clontarf—which he described as 'a broad
flat superficies, like Euclid's definition of a line extending itself
into a surface, and blue, like Xenophon's plain covered with
wormwood'. Le Fanu's story 'The Watcher' gives an account of
Trinity in the days of Barrett's eminence.

In the 1830s the dignitaries were less colourful, though a recent
historian has described the Chancellor as 'a symbolic ogre of
reaction'.[1] Bartholemew Lloyd, the Provost, was a mathematician
of some distinction; he was succeeded in 1837 by Franc Sadleir,
a radical in politics and as such heartily disliked by the *Dublin
University Magazine*. There were seven Senior Fellows and
eighteen Junior, with about fourteen non-fellow professors and
lecturers. Mountifort Longfield, one of the more important of the
latter class, was professor of political economy from 1832 to 1834,
and he was succeeded not long afterwards by Isaac Butt. Both
men exercised considerable influence in the *D.U.M.*, Butt as
editor from 1834 to 1838, and Longfield as an occasional contributor and general adviser. There were also grinders in the college,
the lowest form of academic life, of whom Thomas Wallis
(graduated 1836) particularly interests us. Describing himself as
'professor of things in general and Patriotism in particular',
Wallis influenced many of his juniors in college, notably Thomas
Davis, the founder of Young Ireland. Le Fanu's relationship with
Wallis was one of uneasy respect rather than tutelage. Students
numbered about seventeen hundred when Joseph and William
joined their ranks, but as a result of the country lists, many of
these only appeared for examinations. If the boys' presence in
Abington from 1835 onwards is partly explained by the country-
list system, it also points to the relative stability of life in the
country after the initial violence of 1832. Kishiquirk was the
result of a dangerous miscalculation, but such incidents were rare.
For Le Fanu, life as an undergraduate at Abington was neither a
matter of intellectual discovery nor of sudden assault, but rather a
persistent undermining of status.

Stinson having been dismissed for whatever reason, the Dean
took charge of his sons' education. Joseph's progress with the
classics was unexceptional, and his name is absent from the lists
of place-winners. Yet he had enough talent to enter the scholar-

[1] R. B. McDowell and D. A. Webb, 'Trinity College in 1830', *Hermathena*,
no. 75 (1950), 2.

ship competitions in the summer of 1835, in which the examinations were confined by statute to the classics. The performance was negatively marked, the candidates with the lower scores succeeding. In mid-June he had the results, and transmitted them to his parents:

I am *not* in. 19 got it & my marks were 22. I got a 1 from the Provost. Wray from whom I expected a 1 or, at worst, a 2 gave me a 4. The answering was first rate. Ringwood got 1st on a tot of 9. The 3 next got in on a tot of 11 each. After which followed a tot of 12, & then one of 13, so that Lee who obtained 1st Scholarship last year, in our class would have been put down to the 7th. John Walsh is in, but did not get a high place.

This was a tolerable performance by a country-list man, and Joseph continued his letter with bits of college gossip:

The new fellow is Harte! 22 years of age! has not graduated 2 years and read so little & lived such a rakish life that a lad reading for scholarship in rooms underneath his, declared that he had not a quiet moment, owing to the laughing & uproar continually kept up in Hartes rooms . . . By the by, there is a very odd business about Stack the fellow—a *crim con*—with Lady Staples. If the matter is not ing[enious]ly patched up, he will be expelled. This matter will be a scandal to the Church & an injury to the conservative interest in college.[1]

Le Fanu's friends in Trinity were John Walsh and John Jellett, both members of the walking party who saw the 'yalla horse'; Jellett was studious and Walsh energetic. The wider circle of his companions were cousins—Flemyngs, Fergusons, and Homans. In time he found more acquaintances in the College Historical Society and the King's Inns, but he was never far from the company of relatives. These were for him the natural society which he as a countryman in town should seek, and the easiest friends which an introspective youth could mix with. Throughout his life he depended on his family for company, and in the last years only a few of his closest intimates, notably his brother, were welcome at his house.

Naturally there was an outer, perhaps defensive, shell to his personality. In December 1836 he declared his interest in debating and in student politics. 'I intend speaking on every occasion at the Historical Society, of course in a favourably conservative strain, and it is no small consolation to me to think that while I

[1] J. T. S. Le Fanu to T. P. Le Fanu, 16 June 1835.

am abusing the *Pisantry* in Dublin city, my brother may be shooting them in the country.'[1] A better attempt at humour concerned the son of the Newport rector:

Lysaght Pennefather has been making a 'Holy Show' of himself. He appeared, announced by name in the bills, upon the Abbey Street boards, & made a speech & also performed in a farce. I had the pleasure of seeing him. At the commencement of the piece for which he was announced, he came forward arrayed in Russia ducks (pleasant weather for the same), with a flaming silk waistcoat, and immense stack [hat], & his shirt collar up to his eyes. He had on an ill made green body coat & after three or four stiff bows he said with a rollicking piping air 'Ladies & Gents'—I shall not appear in the character for which the bills have announced me, but in one, which I am affraid [*sic*] (this with a sweetly conscious smile) you will consider much more appropriate, that of 'the Married Rake'.[2]

Le Fanu himself took up a more serious public stance. In the autumn of 1835, as a junior sophister, he qualified for membership of the Hist., as the successor to Edmund Burke's club of 1745 was known. The society had enjoyed varied fortunes since its formal inauguration in 1770; in 1815 it had been suppressed by the college authorities, and in 1820 revived as an extern society meeting in city hotels, Radley's in Dame Street or Morrison's at the corner of Dawson Street. The crisis of the 1830s provoked intense debates of Irish affairs; the emergence of Catholic power, the triumph of Whiggish reform, and the suppression of the Orange Order combined to frighten Irish Tories into a reconsideration of their place in the country. Early in his career as a speaker, Le Fanu reported proudly to his father that he had 'acquired the character of being posessed [*sic*] of the most imperturbable Brass'. In February 1836 Walsh was elected auditor (the premier office of the society) and Le Fanu treaurer. Indicating that even then the treasurer was regarded as virtual heir-apparent, he told his family, 'I suppose I may be auditor next session but as there is more trouble than honour or emolument connected with it I do not think I shall contend for it'.[3] High office required more ready cash than was available to him; on 5 June 1837 he complained to his mother:

---

[1] J. T. S. Le Fanu to Mrs E. Le Fanu, 22 Dec. 1836.
[2] J. T. S. Le Fanu to T. P. Le Fanu, 25 Apr. 1838.
[3] Ibid. 27 Feb. 1837.

but that I am treasurer of the H. Soc. I should be in abject want . . .
On the 19th of this month the College Historical Society will give a
great dinner at Morrisons rooms. I have been placed on the committee,
& to all who have that honour a ticket will cost 16s. Where is all this to
come from [?] I have not a *rap*. I am frightfully in debt to the Historical
Society.[1]

If his father does not come to his aid 'total ruin and public
disgrace' must be his fate—or so the letter ends. At the end of
the session, however, he was awarded the society's silver medal.

But disaster struck plans for the celebrations in Morrison's
Hotel:

The Grand Dinner of the Society has been blown up by the conduct
of the radicals, & in its stead we have gotten up a *conservative* dinner
with Butt in the Chair. (I am just beginning to become acquainted with
him, & like him greatly.) & in the way of lions we are to have Carlton
[i.e. William Carleton] & Mortimer O'Sullivan & to give us gravity &
respectability Samuel O'Sullivan, Mr Litton the barrister & professor
Longfield.[2]

For all this display of conventional Toryism, his political
horizons were broadened by the Hist. debates and dinners. He
spoke in favour of a tax on absentee landlords, a proposal supported
by some of the Anglo-Irish gentry who felt they were carrying a
burden which properly should be borne by a resident aristocracy.
It was at a meeting of the Hist. that Le Fanu gave an airing to his
'national ballad'; 'Shamus O'Brien', as we have already seen, had
been the outcome of unlikely circumstances—a midnight adventure
near Aherlow, a land-agent's murder, and the great underswell
of patriotic sentiment generated by Moore's melodies. For a
conservative, it was an odd recitation, its dialect as much as its
politics puzzling to the orthodox supporters of Wellington and
Peel:

> Just after the war, in the year ninety-eight,
> As soon as the boys were all scattered and bate,
> 'Twas the custom, whenever a peasant was caught
> To hang him by trial, barring such as was shot.
> There was trial by jury goin' on by daylight,
> And the martial law hanging the lavings by night.[3]

---

[1] J. T. S. Le Fanu to Mrs E. Le Fanu, 5 June 1837.
[2] J. T. S. Le Fanu to T. P. Le Fanu, 1 July 1837.
[3] Text of the version printed in *Seventy Years*, pp. 131–8; see p. 131.

As English poetry this cannot rate very high, but as Irish balladry it possesses two essential features—a speech from the dock, and a sentimental conclusion in which the hero escapes; the first points to the traditional ballad form, the second to Victorian drawing-room feeling. At the Hist. it produced a sensation; Wallis, the professor of patriotism, exclaimed 'Shake hands' and after a pause, 'Le Fanu say what you like. You must have something of the *real right feeling* in you, or you could never have written that.'[1] This was in April 1839, when he had become president of the society, a post akin to that of annual chairman. The auditor was Thomas Davis, Wallis's most renowned pupil, and subsequently the author of many national ballads.

A year earlier, an attempt was made to revive a debating society within the college walls as a rival to the extern Hist.; a despotic proposal, in Le Fanu's view, and he wished it no success. In the interminable constitutional crises of student societies, the Hist. was subsequently reconstituted. Charles Gavan Duffy, as Davis's biographer, meticulously recorded the inauguration:

At a meeting at Francis Kearney's chambers, 27 College, on the 29th of March, 1839, a new College Historical Society was founded. The original members consisted of ten Conservatives and ten Liberals; there was as yet no talk of Nationalists. The third name in the list was that of Thomas Davis, the preceding ones being John Thomas Ball, since Lord Chancellor of Ireland, and Joseph Le Fanu, afterwards distinguished as a popular novelist.[2]

Le Fanu's promotion, skipping the auditorship to become president, testified to his popularity with dedicated members of all opinions.

It is as well that the delicate arithmetic of the committee was expressed in conservative and liberal terms. By these he was clearly in the former camp, but had there been talk of nationalists, his place would be more difficult to define. Davis and Le Fanu had much in common, of course; both were intelligent middle-class Protestant lawyers in search of a means to express the predicament of their people. In time both voiced concern—Le Fanu near hysterically, and Davis unavailingly—that militant Catholicism would swamp all political initiative in Ireland.

---

[1] J. T. S. Le Fanu to Mrs E. Le Fanu, undated, postmarked Apr. 1839.
[2] C. Gavan Duffy, *Thomas Davis* (London, 1890), p. 14.

Davis's inaugural address to the Hist. is now famous in the liturgy of nationalism: 'Gentlemen, you have a country!' Though Le Fanu could never embrace the new creed so enthusiastically, both he and Davis were to varying degrees influenced by Thomas Wallis. Recent experience in the glebe-house did not encourage this flirtation with nationalism, and he was careful to spice his family correspondence with reassuring allusions to the conservative faction in the society. Even his ballad (which he did not publish for many years) offers only ambiguous evidence of radical thinking. Its politics are overtly nationalistic, but its form is deliberate pastiche and close to parody. The circumstances of its inspiration ensured as much. Yet as Davis's career amply demonstrates, nationalism (at least in the form of a vigorous scepticism of English ideas) had some appeal for the Protestant bourgeoisie. In extent and potential it was probably less significant than Davis and his followers imagined, though among intellectuals Young Ireland commanded respect. 'Shamus O'Brien' was in part a symbol of disenchantment with the alliance between an ascendency (or sections of it) in Ireland and a government in England. The rebel's pride and isolation are authentic. But Shamus is a peasant, one of the ruffian mob, and so his celebration is necessarily undercut by mimicry and sentimental evasion.

In the Hist. his closest friend was John Walsh, who like Le Fanu, was on the books of the King's Inns. With his brother William and his cousins, he was fond of practical joking and high spirits, but casual acquaintances saw less of this side of his personality. While preparing speeches for a debate in March 1837, Walsh and he dropped into the College Green coffee-house:

We were both very anxious about our speeches & looking I believe very funereal, when John in a solemn sepulchral tone, exclaimed to the listening waiter, bring us *coffin & muffies*. The man looked all aghast & I verily believe had not I over-heard & corrected John's *cacology*, he would have sent us to Bedlam, or at least committed us to the authorities to prevent a dreadful case of deliberate suicide. Of course we laughed a good deal. John was rather sheepish about it, & I had a great *crow* over him, but alas! how short lived is human triumph. I was deeply considering how I should reply to some argument of my opponent. I had just finished to myself a most eloquent period & was beginning another, when John who was employed I believe in a like manner requested me to hurry the waiter, & instantly in a loud voice of impatience I exclaimed *Mr Chairman*![1]

At this point the orators fled.

The active years in the Historical Society coincided with Le Fanu's legal training rather than his university course in classics, and his cronies were principally legal men. Apart from Walsh, the two friends of this period who retained his affection were John Ball and John Keogh. The Dublin Inns did not make excessive demands on their students' intellect but, by a survival of Tudor policy, candidates for the Irish Bar had to reside for a period at one of the English Inns. Even in this the regulations were dietary rather than academic, and the necessary dinners could be consumed in a few suitably timed excursions to the capital. Le Fanu and Walsh had arranged to share accommodation in London, but at the last moment the plan fell through. The delay was useful, for an allowance from the Dean had not arrived from Abington in time. Walsh had offered loans of money, and Keogh had arranged with London contacts to cover the bonds, which the Inns required, for his own and Le Fanu's security. At the beginning of May 1838 the two crossed over to London, and within a fortnight the Dean's bill followed them. Unfortunately it was not negotiable until the 28th, and Le Fanu complained that, as he had no fit clothes to dine in, his social life was very restricted. While still mourning the lack of a decent pair of shoes, he made contact with several relatives. Sheridan Knowles provided him with tickets for the Haymarket. Charles Sheridan threw him in complete confusion by introducing himself only as 'Paddy'. Other hosts were the Halls, Mr and Mrs Samuel Carter Hall, indefatigable editors and authors. 'Nothing could be more kind or hospitable,' he replied, 'I felt really quite at home (a strange sensation, you will say, for me).'[2] Within a few weeks of his arrival in London, his letters are by-passing all references to the law to concentrate instead on writing. He has met Butt, who invites him to write for a new paper in Dublin, the *Protestant Guardian*. He confesses to being engrossed in the second act of a tragedy. He announces another story, one of the horrible kind, which he will base on legends picked up at Kilkee. He is anxious that his parents should offer to put up the Halls at Abington during the summer. Each letter inevitably reveals his growing commitment to writing, at one level or another; and though he was probably unconscious of the discovery, by 1838 he had found a permanent way of life and a means of relating himself to the flux and ferocity of his country.

In 1834, when he was just twenty-one, Isaac Butt had become editor of the *Dublin University Magazine*. By the middle of 1837 Le Fanu was ambitious to write for the magazine, but the problem was an introduction to Butt. As far as the Hist. was concerned, the editor rarely attended. But the Grand Dinner, at first jeopardized by the liberal element in the society and then celebrated in full conservative exclusivism, brought Le Fanu into contact socially with the magazine's major contributors—the O'Sullivans, Carleton, and Butt himself. As Protestant supermacists they were an odd collection: the O'Sullivans who were ordained clerics were Catholic in origin; both Le Fanu and Butt who were sons of the glebe-house displayed erratic political tendencies, and Carleton's confused loyalties embraced nearly all of these positions and a few more besides.

His first story appeared in January of the following year, the first of twelve instalments of *The Purcell Papers* (a title posthumously bestowed by Alfred Graves). 'The Ghost and the Bonesetter' was not itself a remarkable production, but the subtitle promised more in the future: 'Extracts from the Ms. Papers of the late Rev. Francis Purcell, P.P. of Drumcoolagh'. It is of course paradoxical that a rector's son, writing at the end of a humiliating and costly Tithe War, should choose as a persona a fictional O'Brien Costello; that he should maintain the device for twelve instalments is a striking indication of his need for some disguise. Le Fanu used the parish priest, sometimes as narrator, sometimes as a moral and religious standard in the stories, in much the same way that Maria Edgeworth used Thady Quirk in *Castle Rackrent*. The priest, like the family retainer, was a privileged person with access to the secrets of a caste superior to his own. Any further uneasiness about a Papist narrator is largely dissolved by placing the stories in the remote early decades of the previous century. The priest is by now safely dead; his papers relate confessions and adventures dating from the first years of his ministry. Here lies an advance over 'Shamus O'Brien', for in choosing his historical milieu Le Fanu has moved back beyond the peasant-rebel to the heroic, defeated Jacobites whose lives were at risk in their own country. *The Purcell Papers*, as we shall see when we come to examine some of them in detail, achieve an impressive opacity and distance in their historical setting.

The magazine was informally organized. Butt, as editor, evidently had a team of assistants, but in the close society of Dublin intelligentsia little in the way of an office was required. A Scotsman, James McGlashan, who dealt with the magazine for its publishers (William Curry Jr. and Company), became the publisher himself in 1846. In the years of Le Fanu's first connection with the *D.U.M.* McGlashan had an important role in the production of the monthly issues and the payment of contributors. On at least one occasion Le Fanu gave him a story to cover a bill at Curry's bookshop. It is not clear whether Le Fanu belonged to the editorial 'team' when *The Purcell Papers* were appearing. He certainly contributed occasional articles on topical affairs, among them a paper on 'pawnbroking in Ireland' in December 1839. This was not the splendid Victorian public-spiritedness which it might appear, for his purpose was to publicize a recent pamphlet by Matthew Barrington. The two were neighbours in county Limerick; Barrington was a leading solicitor on the Irish rolls, and Le Fanu a newly called barrister. The anonymous flatterer admitted to his brother, 'I have puffed Barrington in the forthcoming No of the *D.U.M.* I wonder if the fellow has any gratitude.'[1]

Earlier in the year Barrington had himself sought tokens of gratitude from the authorities, in a manner indicative of the unsettled terms on which a professional man might advance in the dawn of Victorian Ireland. Thomas Drummond, a reforming and scrupulous Whig, had been glad of his support during an inquiry into crime in Ireland; Barrington had been rewarded by appointment as solicitor to the Shannon Commissioners. His ambition, however, was to sit in Parliament, but as Crown Solicitor he was disqualified. His proposal was that his son should be joined with him in his official capacity, that he would then temporarily resign to enter Parliament, while retaining his income

[1] J. T. S. Le Fanu to W. R. Le Fanu, 16 Nov. 1839.

through the son. Drummond's Scottish sense of propriety was not easily charmed; he was 'strongly impressed with the mischievous impolicy . . . of making such important public offices hereditary,'[1] and in the end Drummond's view prevailed. In his disappointment, the Crown Solicitor can be forgiven for ignoring his neighbour's flattery. It was this experience of uncertain and new rules of conduct which led, as a search for compensation and reassurance, to the ostentation of Victorian symbolism. By 1839 the great Barrington building programme in Murroe was well under way. The previous owners, the barons Carbery, had occupied a large tract to the north of Abington including the townlands of Cappercullen, Garranbane, and Glenstal. Cappercullen House had been their seat, but when the Barringtons finally acquired the Carbery interest, the house was in disrepair, the main floor having collapsed during a dance in 1820. A better site for a home was found in Garranbane, but the name did not appeal to the Barrington ear. With a judicious rightness of touch, Matthew built on the better site, and then annexed to his castle the name of a neighbouring townland, Glenstal. The *Limerick and Clare Examiner* praised Glenstal's 'Norman or baronial style'. The entrance to the billiard room was a facsimile of a door at Ely Cathedral. Another door displayed full size stone figures of Henry II and Eleanor of Aquitane, the latter carrying a stone sash with the words in Gaelic lettering '*céad míle fáilte*' (a hundred thousand welcomes). All the bedroom doorways were modelled on Irish Romanesque church architecture. (The Barringtons paid great attention to doors!) In time elaborately natural gardens and parks were laid out; lakes enlarged, and villages transported according to a controlling aesthetic. William Le Fanu, by then a prosperous railway engineer, designed a stone bridge in 1866 to connect the townlands of Cappercullen and Garranbane.

In his first term at the Bar, Joseph had not earned a 'stim'. Even during his excursions to London writing had threatened to overtake the law as an interest, and now fate was assisting with a vengeance. Yet in none of his fiction does he deal with the professional class in which he was reared. His imagination had been caught by the Carberys rather than the Barringtons, and the great houses of his fiction resemble more the ruins of Cappercullen than the bright splendours of Glenstal. His own family experience

---

[1] R. B. O'Brien, *Thomas Drummond* (London, 1889), p. 359.

was not so ruinous as the old eighteenth-century grandees who, had mortgaged townlands, estates, and the best part of counties nor of course so prosperous as the new lords of Glenstal. The Tithe War had finally petered out in 1838, when the government reorganized clerical finances to provide each rector with a fixed income. For Dean Le Fanu there were continuing minor difficulties: he had to mortgage lands, contest wills, and in general scrape and save in a manner unbecoming to a dignitary of the Established Church. In the Dobbin branch of the family, things were worse. Captain Dobbin's mission to Antrim having done nothing to revive his fortunes, he had left his post in Borrisokeane by 1836, probably as a result of the Whig reforms in the Irish constabulary. In August 1838 he found himself in a debtor's prison.

The circumstances are unclear. While attempts were made to buy him out, the Captain now languished in a very real despair for which his previous melancholy had been a fit preparation. Despite his friends' efforts he was still confined at the end of September when he sent an account to his daughters of the prison's causal violence:

27th. We have a delightful day this day, but unfortunately I can not enjoy it much. Mrs Edwards displeased the grand Governor of this Paradise the day before yesterday & was locked up in her room for that morning, & in the evening transferred to the Hospital where she has been confined ever since & of course I shall not have the key to the garden until she be let out. I did not see her put into confinement, but Captain Irwin says that he saw that brute Hugh Jones, the turnkey, drag her along the floor by the hair of her head. I hope that she will punish him when she is released—he & John Francis are two of the greatest brutes I ever saw.[1]

At the beginning of November, Joseph and William Le Fanu accompanied their uncle on the boat to North Wales 'on his liberation from his long and miserable confinement', perhaps suggesting that he was not entirely fit to travel alone. William returned directly to Dublin, while Joseph travelled on to London for a few more dinners at the Inns.

The fear of failure, particularly in business, controlled the lives

---

[1] W. Dobbin to A. and K. Dobbin, 26 Sept. 1838; quoted by kind permission of Mrs Burrows.

of a multitude of Dobbins. Pressures of conformism, of the need to preserve the appearance of prosperity when the reality had fled, reduced inner strength to a bundle of spasms. To sensitive and vulnerable individuals like Dean Le Fanu and his sons, the Captain's months in gaol were not without an ominous significance. Nor did the liberated debtor remain in decent exile in Wales; by the autumn of 1839 he was back in Dublin floundering in the shallow waters of debt. As this was the moment when Joseph was setting up in practice (hopefully) as a barrister, he was in no position to answer appeals, as he put it, on the text 'now a decree went forth from Captain Dobbin that all the world should be taxed'. As he told his brother, he was obdurate, and Dobbin 'ceased to importune'.[1]

Minor economic details are rarely valuable in themselves, but two circumstances make them especially significant for Le Fanu's biographer. Details of any kind concerning his life are scarce, and evidence of penny-pinching is more valuable when it relates to a family claiming allegiance to the ascendency, and residing in one of the premier houses of the district. Of the several mortgages which the Dean and his sons negotiated during the 1830s and 1840s, none is more revealing than that of 1841. Joseph and his father received an unspecified sum, and in return paid an annuity of £194. 4s. 10d. to someone called Alicia Tate for ninety-nine years or their lives. The real burden of the loan lay in the securities which the Le Fanus named: lands at Quilca and Drumratt (in Joseph's name, income £84 p.a.), and the income of his father's glebes, parishes, and deanery, assigned to a trustee to guarantee the annuity. To some this might look like simony and, whatever the exact position at law, it was a profoundly worrying contract for a conscientious priest of the church.[2] Le Fanu's sensational heroes—Silas Ruthyn, Mark Shadwell, and Francis Ware—emerge cloaked in debt; they struggle to maintain domestic stability in the face of hardship and temptation; they are clutched by the cold hand of doubt and despair; in the end each of them dies a suicide. In *Uncle Silas*, *A Lost Name*, and *Willing to Die*, written up to thirty years after the

[1] J. T. S. Le Fanu to W. R. Le Fanu, 16 Nov. 1839.
[2] For details of the mortgage see Memorial no. 1841/1/197 in the Registry of Deeds, Dublin; for Quilca and Drumratt rentals see MS 5634 in P.R.O., Dublin—the latter records Le Fanu's income of just £84 p.a. from 1846 to 1862 from these county Cavan properties.

'simonical' mortgage, there is a second justification for enquiries into family finances.

Apart from money-lenders and debtors' prisons, other institutions which haunted the Victorian mind (and threatened to monopolize the sensational novel when that literary subspecies emerged from the anxious imagination of suburbia) were asylums and private hospitals. As late as 1894, George Moore discovered public sensitivity on this issue, when he published *Esther Waters*. For earlier generations of Victorians, the problem was not one of propriety in writing fiction about mad-houses, lying-in hospitals, lunatics, and bastards—the cult of sensationalism revealed a positive desire to fictionalize these areas of life. In 'real life' the topic was becoming taboo; the family who had a child or relative in an asylum was never immune to the fear of discovery. Fundamental anxieties about religion, parental authority, and sexual drives lay at the root of at least some mental disorders, and these implications intensified the family guilt, forcing the secret into deeper areas of neurosis. If Victorian enlightenment knew enough to admit that the mad were not morally bad, there was still a residual fear that they might be *metaphysically* bad. Suicide, the ultimate blasphemy to the Christian, became closely identified with insane behaviour. The Le Fanus, in fact, had an afflicted cousin, Frances, and a crisis in her condition arose in July 1838. According to medical advice the woman's 'secret determination now was to put an end to herself'. And her sister, Alicia (Captain Dobbin's wife), had adopted a rigid indifference to Frances's plight, the indifference of terror. William Joseph Henry Le Fanu, in relating the medical report to his cousin, complained to the Dean that 'Lissy has given no manner of assistance on this trying occasion; she will not even allow Fanny's name to be mentioned in her presence; nor has she even read your letter lest you should have spoken of Fanny in it'—and much of this emphasized by underlining.[1] In the end the whole burden fell on Harriet (the victim's sister) and the Dean, who though deeply affected by his own calamities, strove to maintain a Christian charity in the face of his cousins' revulsion from the facts. Fanny survived the crisis by at least seventeen years.

The Captain's spell in the debtors' prison and his sister-in-

---

[1] W. J. H. Le Fanu to T. P. Le Fanu; text copied in T. P. Le Fanu to Harriet Le Fanu, 26 July 1838, and quoted by kind permission of Mrs Burrows.

law's insanity probably had their parallels in a million Victorian families; there is nothing intrinsically important about them. Yet coming as they did at the close of a long period of disappointment and hardship, they appeared to Le Fanu as part of a developing pattern, a downward swinging graph of insecurity, diminished confidence, and threatened faith. *The Purcell Papers*, written during these successive crises in the family, scrupulously avoid all personal references, but their general tone is of a shrunken capacity for life. Reversals of faith, death-bed exclamations of despair, ambiguous dual versions of supernatural themes, self-compelled if not self-inflicted deaths—these are the ingredients of tales which press back against an historical context, as if kept at arm's length by their author. Can it be an accident that these stories should conclude the decade of the Le Fanus' disillusion with their country, of their humiliation in a religious guerrilla war, of their domestic distress? As against coincidence, an answer can be found in the death of Catherine Le Fanu, for in that single incident there is a clearer body of evidence on which to consider the relation between Le Fanu's life and fiction, to consider whether the connections are merely chronological or more profoundly causal.

Catherine was the first of the Le Fanus to recognize the fallen world they had entered. Ailing for years, she had become the focus of her parents' home at Abington. Though this was her consolation in recurring illness, it exposed her to the chilly atmosphere of the locality to an extent which her more active brothers hardly experienced. At the age of twenty, in 1833, she drew up her will, a document revealing more spiritual unease than testamentary intention: 'being thank God, in as good health as I have enjoyed for the last three years . . . my earnest prayer to God is, that if once he sees me fit to die, he may mercifully take me, rather than let me fall back in Sin and Blindness.'[1] Perhaps we should see this compliance in death as hyperbole, for emotionalism in twenty-year-olds is a common result of evangelicalism. Yet Catherine's frailty was actual enough, and the conditions she lived in rough enough, to dampen hopes of longevity. She was not always an invalid, of course, and her brother William records in *Seventy Years* that in 1893 there were still old people in Abington who spoke of 'the good Miss Catherine' and of her good works.

[1] Le Fanu Papers.

One of her missions in the district was to teach English to Gaelic-speaking tenants, a mission made more difficult by the fact that the texts quoted in the instruction manual she used were taken in evangelical fashion from the New Testament.[1] This disguised proselytism cannot have lasted more than a year, for the hostility towards the Le Fanus provoked by Charles Coote curtailed casual excursions from the glebe-house. Catherine was herself attacked, probably in the spring of 1832, and, confined to the house thereafter, she became studious, publishing occasionally in the *Dublin University Magazine*. Her private diary is more interesting; after a temporary settlement of the tithe problem (possibly about the end of 1838), she recorded the family's difficult adjustment: 'Why should I ever desire more than that we should have a moderate fixed income, even though it were less than Papa had before the troubles.'[2] Side by side with this interior view of the household, there are her religious anxieties: 'It is not faith, but want of faith, that makes it necessary to fill our minds with any set of doctrines before we go to the Bible, as though that book would otherwise mislead us.' Fear of study was one of the unintended by-products of the evangelical method; self-examination might lead to scepticism instead of repentance, a paradox which puzzled her: 'What is the use of reading, if we only find doubts and difficulties increase by study . . . I find myself in an inextricable maze of doubt and uncertainty . . . Why is doubt so painful to me?' In March 1841 news reached her brothers in Dublin that Catherine was declining rapidly. Joseph and William hurried down to Limerick (a journey of about fourteen hours). According to William, 'great was her joy at seeing us and having us with her. She had feared that we would not arrive in time . . .'[3] On 25 March she died, and was buried in the cemetery beside her father's church. The Dean never recovered from the shock of Catherine's death, and his own death four years later was hastened by her loss. His sons hastened back to the city, Joseph to the newspaper world he had recently entered, and William to MacNeill, the engineer to whom he was apprenticed.

[1] W. R. Le Fanu of Chelmsford has in his possession Catherine's signed and dated (24 Dec. 1828) copy of *An Irish and English Spelling-Book being a Few Easy Steps to a Right Understanding of the English Language through the Medium of Irish* (Dublin, 1825, 2nd edn.).

[2] Le Fanu Papers.

[3] *Seventy Years*, p. 150.

It is worth looking back for a moment to the last of *The Purcell Papers*, the last piece of fiction which Le Fanu had published before Catherine's death. It is a slight piece of stage-Irishry, of which only the preface is noteworthy:

As I rode at a slow walk, one soft autumn evening, from the once noted and noticeable town of Emly, now a squalid village, towards the no less remarkable town of Tipperary, I fell into a meditative mood. My eye wandered over a glorious landscape: a broad sea of corn fields, that might have gladdened even a golden age, was waving before me . . . as I gazed on this scene whose richness was deepened by the melancholy glow of the setting sun, the tears rose to my eyes, and I said 'Alas my country! what a mournful beauty is thine; dressed in loveliness and laughter, there is mortal decay at thy heart . . .'[1]

This passage includes most of the assumptions underlining the Purcell stories—the associations of landscape, the contrast between the towns and the country, the declining fortune of Emly (the site of the Le Fanu sinecure). The passage is Le Fanu's farewell to Abington; henceforth newspaper proprietorship would necessarily keep him in Dublin. It also marks the redundance of the Purcell persona, as if to underline the importance of that device in Le Fanu's coming to terms with the disturbing landscape of his adolescence. The dialect tale which follows the narrator's apostrophe has nothing to do with the priestly persona or the eighteenth-century background of the series. 'The Quare Gander' is a comic squib marking the author's emergence from a prolonged and sombre meditation.

Until mid-July Le Fanu struggled on with his editorial chores, writing leaders, interviewing visitors, and finally retiring to his lodgings. William was frequently out of town, and he longed for some of his own people. 'I wish I could go down to Abington,' he wrote to his parents, 'I think I soon will.' Difficulties in the newspapers, election crises, a shortage of ready cash—a series of obstacles which never threatened to end—cancelled his often repeated intention to go home. Despite his intense loneliness in Dublin and his realization that he should visit his grieving parents, he was profoundly reluctant to renew contact with the mortal decay of the rural landscape. Catherine's death had fallen like a boom across the hopes implicit in the final Purcell tale. It had

[1] *D.U.M.*, vol. 16 (Oct. 1840), 390.

been his first encounter with death; he had stood by the deathbed of an adored sister, just one year his senior. Death, which had been a theme in his stories, had now followed him home. Increasingly, journalism in Dublin and politics in the wider world began to irritate or bore him; his letters hint at a state of unusually reduced vitality:

It is very melancholy to me being all alone here, having no one of my immediate family near me, & being constantly fagged & harassed. I have no one to talk to & I never get any letters unless I write first, which from utter want of spirits & depression I can only do with dullness & effort, although constantly thinking of you & my father & William. Every minute this day my eyes were filling with tears.[1]

In May Mortimer O'Sullivan suggested a distraction—writing a novel—but Joseph felt that he could not start until he had extricated himself from current newspaper problems. On 11 July he gave his mother a further account of the proposed trip home: 'I am going to write a story for McGlashan in a great hurry as I owe him a large bill. I will do it this week in my leisure time, so that when I get down to Abington I shall not have anything to bother me.[2] But the trip was once again postponed, and the story—whether written promptly or not—did not appear in the *Dublin University Magazine* for close on eighteen months. Reasons for the delay are obvious in the story itself.

'Spalatro' was the longest tale which Le Fanu had written to date; it represented such a departure from *The Purcell Papers* and displays so tortured an imagination that it requires closer examination here if we are to place it in the context of his family life. Spalatro was an Italian bandit, and the story proceeds in the form of a memorandum written by his confessor just before the bandit's execution. (In this it maintains some continuity with the Purcell persona.) Spalatro had no time for Christian consolations, primarily because his early tutor, a monk, had taken 'a strange pleasure in unsettling all the most established convictions of my mind, and in thus plunging me into an abyss of fearful uncertainty and scepticism from which I have never quite escaped. This kind of metaphysical conversation he not infrequently seasoned with

---

[1] J. T. S. Le Fanu to Mrs E. Le Fanu, 26 June 1841.
[2] Ibid. 11 July 1841.

indirect and artful ridicule of religion . . .'[1] But this satirical monk had fled from his post as tutor, when he was discovered by Spalatro assaulting the latter's sister. A year later, when Spalatro himself left his home to journey to Rome, he fell into the hands of banditti, and the first part of the tale reaches its climax in a disgusting murder which Spalatro is forced to witness. His horror is intensified by the knowledge that he was the intended victim. The second part of the tale, published the following month, provides initial relief from this fascinated horror. The hero/villain reaches the city, and mixes with Carnival revellers. After some aimless wandering he is finally led into a ruinous building by a virtuous-looking old man. Under magical conditions, a girl of 'preternatural loveliness in limb and feature, but pale and bloodless as the dead', emerges from 'a light semi-transparent vapour, which rolled and eddied in cloudy volumes'.[2] The woman drinks a crimson liquid which Spalatro had earlier suspected to be other than wine, and 'the glow of life spread itself gently over the face and limbs of the girl'.[3] When he is finally liberated from this scene, he finds himself suddenly in a crowded church, where his abrupt appearance causes a disturbance. The future bandit becomes fascinated by the woman he has thus seen, attempts to locate her strange house once more, chances to see the old man and the girl in a church, and follows them despite admonishing gestures from the girl. Ultimately he is caught up in a Bacchanalian festival in the house. Revulsion and indulgence contend in his mind, and he comes to consciousness lying in the now ruined and empty aisle of a church. From this moment he believes himself damned by these follies; he turns to crime without any further fear of the consequences.

The two parts of the tale are linked by the crimson blood so freely spilled in the first and so libidinously consumed in the second. The degree of dislocation behind these grotesque images can be gauged in a curiously disintegrated incident in the opening scene of Part Two. A tantalizing harlequin leads Spalatro away from the revellers, and then instantly is transformed into the sardonic monk of his childhood, the assailant of his sister:

[1] *D.U.M.*, vol. 21 (Mar. 1843), 340–1. In the editor's (Charles Lever's) diary the two parts of 'Spalatro' in March and April 1843 are attributed to 'Lefanu'; the original diaries are preserved in the Pierpont Morgan Library, New York.

[2] Ibid. (Apr. 1843), 452.

[3] Ibid. 453.

Suddenly he [the spectral monk] stopped before me, and by an unearthly sympathy I was constrained to do the same: he sate down upon
the earth; by an irresistible impulse I did so likewise. We were opposite
to one another—face to face, and scarcely a yard assunder. He tossed
his arms wildly in the air—I could not choose but do the same . . .
and the dreadful passions themselves possessed me in succession,
while all the time, independently of these malignant inspirations, there
remained within me, as it were looking on, a terrified self-conscious-
ness.[1]

Even those who are cautious of fashionable cult words, and who
are suspicious of psychiatry, cannot entirely prohibit the term
schizoid here. In more precise and restrictive terms, Le Fanu
has created in fiction a *praecox* feeling, similar, if less impressive
because less controlled, to those in Hogg's *Confessions of a Justified
Sinner* and Poe's 'William Wilson'.

'Spalatro' alerts us to a pattern which recurs in many of Le
Fanu's tales and novels—the pattern of the hero's elimination by
suicide—for the taunting spectre monk finally drives the young
man to draw his knife: 'He placed his hand within his bosom—
my hand copied the gesture, and rested upon my stiletto: he drew
a dagger from his breast—I drew my poignard from mine. At
the next instant his weapon was at his throat, and mine at mine.
Another moment and HELL would have had its victim . . .'[2] At
the crucial moment, Christian interpretations reassert themselves
—Hell would have been a suicide's fate. Having previously
destroyed his faith, the old tutor (officially a Christian priest) has
now tempted Spalatro with the ultimate and unforgivable sin.
Walter Houghton quotes a grim remark of Thomas Carlyle's
which is appropriate here, 'From Suicide a certain aftershine . . .
of Christianity withheld me.'[3] But by the end of the tale, Spalatro
has lost even this aftershine; he believes himself as damned as
any suicide. The tale certainly emphasizes religious contexts: the
first tempter is a hypocritical priest, and the second manifests
herself in a church which is initially crowded and finally ruined
and deserted. The narrator is a Christian priest but, like Purcell,
of a denomination to which Le Fanu was hostile on political
grounds. Does this not mask a greater alienation from Christianity,

[1] Ibid. 448.
[2] Ibid. 448.
[3] W. E. Houghton, *The Victorian Frame of Mind* (New Haven, 1957),
pp. 73–4.

the full implications of which he disguises in conventional anti-Catholicism? At his remote post as pseudo-translator of the priest's recital of the bandit's confession, he concludes with a few significant words addressed to his editor: 'All around us is darkness and uncertainty. To what thing shall we say I understand thee? All is doubt—all is mystery . . . in short, in the words of our poetic countrymen "It's all botheration from bottom to top." '[1] Are these last words those of an incipient schizophrenic author or of a devious and near-imperceptible narrator? Whatever one's answer the concern of the tale is primarily religious. But when the date of composition is recalled, it is impossible to ignore domestic influences. 'Spalatro' is the only story Le Fanu is known to have written between the death of his beloved sister in March 1841 and his marriage in 1843. He had never been a particularly pious child; his brother records several practical jokes which the Dean found near-irreverent. But surrounding this levity of his, the entire fabric of the household—its daily routine, its income, its politics, in the largest and most active sense, its *culture*—was religious. Throughout a prolonged assault on this outpost of orthodoxy, it was Catherine who perceived the more than local implications, who suggested that a deeper spiritual deprivation also threatened their identity. The crisis apparently past in 1841, Catherine herself was finally 'taken'. The shock for her brother was profound. Had his levity infected her; had the partly conventional, partly instinctive debate on supernaturalism in *The Purcell Papers* corrupted her soul? Did she on her dying day possess whatever attitude to religion that would assure her of bliss, rest, oblivion—or whatever was at stake?

But if the religious anxiety of 'Spalatro' can be related to Catherine's death, what are we to make of the libidinous elements in the tale? Two features only might be said ostensibly to point to possible biographical sources:—the presence of a beloved sister and of an (exaggeratedly) wicked tutor. Superficially these are not connected to the murder in Part One or the blood-drinking in Part Two. But 'Spalatro' is really a complex piece of ventriloquism; the multiplicity of figures and voices does not establish a variety of attitude or experience. The harlequin/monk in leading Spalatro aside operates in suggestive parallel to the pious old man who leads him to the blood-drinking beauty. Similarly, Spalatro's

[1] *D.U.M.*, vol. 21 (Apr. 1843), 458.

home and the scene of the murder are connected by a serving girl who had worked in the former and who later warns Spalatro of the plot to kill him. And again, Spalatro's assailants are banditti and he later becomes a bandit. The crucial question would seem to be this—if the monk with dagger is Spalatro's double, is Spalatro not implicated in the assault on his sister, superficially attributed to the monk? The structure of Part Two seems to confirm this; the dead girl is linked to the earlier narrative by the guide who brings Spalatro to her; the blood she consumes mirrors the blood spilled in Part One. That these associations cannot be made explicit is implied in the warning of mortal danger which the blood-consuming beauty mutely gives to Spalatro in response to his infatuation. It may be preferable to see her, not as a vampire (as the surface narrative suggests), but as a surrogate figure in the disguised pattern. She accepts the blood spilled in his stead; she rejects his offer to follow her; she too is part of the ventriloquism.

This last point is important because it absolves Spalatro from the logic of a simple-minded reading of the tale as guilt in incest. It must, however, also serve to confirm him in a more comprehensive sense of guilt. The surrogate figure stands for him and instead of him; but a surrogate at another level is the same figure also. In this nexus of identification and separation we can recognize a schizoid tendency. Spalatro ignores the dead woman's admonishment, but he is nevertheless separated from her. He avoids the impulse to suicide, but still feels that he is damned. Psychological biography, like 'military intelligence', is often a contradiction in terms, but there is one observation of a psychological nature which 'Spalatro' permits: Le Fanu assumes in the patterning of his ventriloquist techniques that the sexes are not mutually exclusive classes, but rather complementary energies which depend on each other for definition. Though crudely dramatized here, it is a strikingly modern assumption about human sexuality. The hero's passionate search for a dead woman (who also stands for his survival) is the first instance of powerful sexual feeling in Le Fanu's fiction, a feeling which he will rarely describe. Instead he will translate his assumptions about sexuality into formal aspects of the fiction, into a recurrence of female narrators for example. Death and love appear as themes in harness, and the ultimate formalism of the later fiction is annihilation dramatized as suicide.

This lengthy analysis of 'Spalatro' may be excused on several grounds: it is the first time the tale has been recognized as Le Fanu's work and examined as such; it dates from a period when he was not known to be writing, and in its extremity of symbol it exemplifies his cast of mind in a startling manner. But at the biographical level it also helps to explain an otherwise innocuous and baffling letter which he wrote to his father in December 1842, and the letter in turn supports our view of the story as concerned with religious anxiety:

I know that William is very anxious to go into the Church & that he does not wish to speak to you about it. I have been thinking the matter over very much & without telling him the result of it, I am persuaded that for many reasons his doing so would be *better* than his continuing at the engineering. And first of all I ought to say that he is not the least unreasonable about the matter, but wishes to leave it intirely [*sic*] to your determination & is resolved whatever that may be to abide by it cheerfully.

My chief reason for thinking his wishes prudent, is that I have been led to think, from all I can learn from the best authorities in my reach, that the engineering profession is declining rather than advancing & that any posision [*sic*] in it must be both slowly reached & precarious, and it is more than probable that for many years he would have to draw his full allowance from you. Now he *has* a wish to go into the Church, not from any unworthy motive & I think that both for his & yours & my mother's happiness, & for *his immediate & ultimate interest* it would be advisable to let him take orders.[1]

The baffling feature of the entire business is William's silence. Though it is not extraordinary that Joseph, the elder son, should raise the matter of his brother's career, it is strange that at no point do we find William expressing any wish to take orders. None of his surviving letters (admittedly few in number), nor the private diary which he kept from the mid-1840s until his death at the close of the century, nor his autobiography, refers to a vocation. This is not to say that Joseph invented the whole idea; presumably William had mentioned the possibility in vague terms at some point. But if he had really wanted to go into the church, it would hardly have been necessary to *persuade* the Dean. And Joseph's letter of persuasion presents arguments which are not

[1] J. T. S. Le Fanu to T. P. Le Fanu, 8 Dec. 1842; the manuscript of this letter is incomplete.

only unconvincing ('the engineering profession is declining') but also unconvinced in themselves. What then lies behind Joseph's encouragement of another's passing interest in the church as a career? There is a discrepancy between the letter and the performance, which locates eagerness on Joseph's side of the balance. William, it need hardly be repeated, remained an engineer; but if Joseph had been effective in directing him into the church, he would have made a positive contribution to an orthodoxy which he found personally indigestible; he would have made a vicarious reconciliation with the church. In seeing Le Fanu as a doubter at this period, we have little or no first hand contemporary evidence to go upon; his natural reticence did not allow him to express religious or philosophical opinions directly. There is, on the other hand, the nervous iteration of supernatural themes in *The Purcell Papers*, and, later, more explicitly religious anxieties in a fragmentary diary and in the sensational novels. The reading of the letter accords with one further feature of Sheridan Le Fanu's fiction—its indirection. Here he may be attempting to resolve his own uncertain commitment by urging the commitment of his brother to orthodox Christianity; in the mature novels he frequently solves narrative difficulties or moral problems by stylistic or structural means.

We can now recognize in Le Fanu strongly Calvinist traits, an anxiety about the efficacy of faith, about the nature of passion, and the influence of a determinist fate. William James's phrase for such personalities was that they must be 'twice-born in order to be happy', or that they must die to an unreal life before rebirth into the second and real world. For Le Fanu this cast of mind was synchronized to a drastic objective change in his social environment. The world of a child is naturally simplistic and monistic: Joseph's childhood had advanced into consciousness amid the pageantry and formal landscape of the Phoenix Park. Authority, orthodoxy, and esteem were neighbours; kings walked by, and the school chapel had no rival. When he was twelve, the family went out to claim its portion of the redeemable world, to represent this harmony of church and state before the people of Abington. Suddenly it seemed that this moment had been chosen for the triumph of rival claims. Departure from Dublin now seemed in retrospect to have been an expulsion rather than a hopeful exodus. The glebe-house grew into itself, shrank behind its doubtful privileges. Le Fanu drew up his ladder for seclusion, while commotion at the gates announced the aroused antagonism of those to whom the Dean officially ministered. Arrears of tithe mounted in the ledgers; appeals to government funds brought in a little help and with it the seed of further despondency. It was perhaps disillusion with this landscape, so dissimilar to the parkland of the Military School, which drove Le Fanu to depict it as a categorically different world, one of mortal decay in which the buoyancy of a harmonized faith was lacking. The years of the Tithe War could only be stoically tolerated, and then solely in the hope that some rebirth might renew the world. But the conclusion of social strife brought the infinitely more difficult crisis of Catherine's death; and whereas *The Purcell Papers* have their roots in the disturbed soil of Irish history, 'Spalatro' speaks— indeed screams—of an intolerably private loss, an inarticulable disruption in which all values are lost.

The macabre story of the Italian bandit is an isolated exotic in Le Fanu's work, coming in the middle of the otherwise vacant years between *The Purcell Papers* and *The Cock and Anchor* (1845) —vacant in terms of literature, that is. It marks a realization that the second birth of the soul is a tissue of false hope; damnation is never so irreversible, never so inexplicable and absolute, as in 'Spalatro'. Such spiritual despair might be conquered by a brave engagement with the outer world. Vacillating between two interpretations of this sense of loss—the product of some external social disaster, or the consequence of a failure of vision and moral development—he was still sufficiently committed to the business of writing to resume his enquiries. His parallel involvement in politics and fiction between 1838 and 1848 will provide an opportunity to explore his uncertainty. In both political action and fictional analysis he sought to regain a lost country, all the more painfully desirable in its continuity with the idyllic landscape of his youth.

3

FICTION AND POLITICS

THE TWO decades following the great Reform Act produced a new
wave of historical novelists. Sir Walter Scott had died in 1832,
but William Harrison Ainsworth, Lytton Bulwer, and G. P. R.
James continued to meet the demand for historical romance, and
in 1841 Dickens published *Barnaby Rudge*. Though Scott
remained the formative influence, many models were available to
Le Fanu in commencing his career as historical novelist. As an
Irishman he was affected by native practitioners also, though they
in turn owed as much to Scott as did James or Ainsworth. John
Banim, Gerald Griffin, and William Carleton had consolidated a
sub-tradition of Anglo-Irish fiction in the wake of Maria Edgeworth's *Castle Rackrent*, *The Absentee*, and *Ormond*. Irish writers
favoured the shorter tale to the multi-volume novel, and Banim's
Tales by the O'Hara Family, Griffin's *Tales of the Munster
Festivals*, and Carleton's *Traits and Stories of the Irish Peasantry*
were earlier landmarks on a map to which Le Fanu made his own
contribution with *The Purcell Papers*. Class and denomination
placed all three of his predecessors in closer intimacy with the
general population than the reclusive son of an Established Church
dignitary. His work emerged between the distant models provided
by Ainsworth and Lytton-Bulwer, and the colourful, shapeless,
but informed anecdotes of Griffin and Carelton.

The costumery of *The Cock and Anchor* and *The House by the
Churchyard* owes something to Ainsworth, but for Le Fanu's
earlier tales local comparisons are more useful. In 'The Aylmers
of Ballyaylmer', Griffin described the arrival of an Irish magistrate
at his demesne; the coach is ceremonially unyoked, bursts of
wild laughter and the music of 'villainous instruments' accompany
the returning magnate along a road lined by crowds of ragged
tenants and cheering urchins. One of the latter 'had clambered
up a gate pier and sitting cross-legged on the back of a stone
monkey, secured himself by passing his arm around the neck of
the dilapidated pug; while with the other he twirled his little

hareskin cap above his head, and added his share of noisy triumph to the general voice'.[1] Griffin, the Limerick hedge-scholar, had here invented a fictionalized scene which Le Fanu, the Limerick gentleman, had actually experienced. Yet nowhere in *The Purcell Papers* is there immediate and vivid incident such as Griffin's. Neither in the grim tales of death, nor in the comic interludes, nor the exercises in folk tale, is there any confrontation between diverse figures such as the magistrate and the urchin. Instead Le Fanu provides the confessions of eighteenth-century squires or the antics of anonymous peasants, never letting confession and antic coexist within a single story. There is no neatly unifying image of a peasant on a gate-pier, emblematic of a future revolution. Griffin, of course, had been writing in London in 1826, the year the Le Fanus had gone down to county Limerick, and between 1826 and 1838 the crowds at the glebe-gate had grown hostile.

Though not all of *The Purcell Papers* are of equal merit or interest, there is behind the least of them a consistent historical background. In a preface, Le Fanu anonymously addressed his readers:

In looking over the papers of my late valued and respected friend, Francis Purcell, who for nearly fifty years discharged the arduous duties of a parish priest in the south of Ireland, I met with the following document . . . To such as may think the composing of such productions as these inconsistent with the character of a country priest, it is necessary to observe, that there did exist a race of priests—those of the old school, a race now nearly extinct—whose habits were from many causes more refined, and whose tastes more literary than those of the alumni of Maynooth.[2]

With this last aside at the O'Brien Costellos of southern Ireland, Le Fanu introduces his eighteenth-century priest. The first tale is an exercise in pseudo-Gothic comedy, and need not detain us. In the second, 'The Fortunes of Sir Robert Ardagh', the basic ingredients of Le Fanu's fiction are already present—the doomed master of the Great House, supernatural intrusions or at least intimations of such, and a concern for formal properties in the narrative.

[1] G. Griffin *Holland-tide* (London, 1842), pp. 63–4; quoted by T. Flanagan, *The Irish Novelists* (New York, 1959), p. 215.
[2] *D.U.M.*, vol. 11 (Jan. 1838), 50.

Ardagh's story is directly told in Father Purcell's words, with a few 'editorial' notes to add verisimilitude. But there is more to it than the sum of the events related. The tale begins with a brief sketch of the popular, traditional account of Ardagh's fate, involving a pact with the Devil who turns up (complete with sooty hair) to drag his victim over a precipice. Purcell purports to dismiss all this as the unfortunate accretion of exaggerated superstition, and offers an historical account based on Lady Ardagh's evidence, this revision forming the second part of the tale. When we are told that Lady Ardagh had married Sir Robert after his return from the Continent in 1760, the reference to Europe mutely identifies the family as Catholic and Jacobite; in a later version Le Fanu gave them the name Sarsfield, a name as closely linked to Irish Jacobitism as Cromwell to English Protestantism. The second part of the tale tends to corroborate the crude 'synopsis of the first, though the narrator insists that 'the two narratives are irreconcilable'.[1] There are minor divergences, but on a crucial point the two concur: Robert Ardagh dies on a day fixed and anticipated. Instead of the wild despair and melodramatic struggle of the traditional version, Lady Ardagh's evidence reveals that her husband had announced the date of his death quite calmly and had assembled some relatives to console her when the inevitable occurred. On their arrival, he locked himself in his room and died peacefully before midnight. If Le Fanu's intention was to demonstrate the diverging tendencies of oral tradition and written history the result is indeed satisfactory, but in no sense has the supernatural element been eliminated. All the marks of a Faustian pact are retained—the arrogant servant, the unexplained wealth, and the anticipated death. The traditional version is ludicrous even within its own conventions, and the second is to follow in contrast; contrast, however, in the form of a higher corroboration. In the dual structure of the tale, Le Fanu is perhaps rewriting the terms on which supernatural belief might be dealt with or questioned in fiction.

The next tale in the series, 'The Last Heir of Castle Connor', undermines this assured tone, for whereas 'Ardagh' had moved from despair at death to stoical resignation, the new story reverses the order. The young heir returns after three years on the Continent, and in the company of Purcell (also young in these

---

[1] Ibid. (Mar. 1838), 317.

distant days) he goes to a ball. A mysterious and sullen stranger, who stands aloof from the night's amusements, is greeted only by O'Connor; this stranger is subsequently named as Fitzgerald, a notorious duellist.[1] Despite Purcell's efforts a quarrel arises between O'Connor and his dangerous acquaintance. At this point the hero, a dashing and energetic fellow, suddenly becomes fatalistic and inert; he insists that his death is inevitable; he prepares his will, and even tells Purcell that he will fire wide of Fitzgerald to avoid having blood on his conscience. After many delays and uncertainties which Le Fanu handles with skill, the duel takes place. O'Connor fires first and fires wide; he is then mortally wounded by Fitzgerald, who flees from the spectators with extraordinary swiftness and ease. Once again the story takes a curious turn: though severely wounded, O'Connor begins to believe that he will survive. Confident of this he tackles the surgeon who announces that death is imminent:

As the surgeon uttered these terrible words, the hands which O'Connor had stretched towards him while awaiting his reply fell powerless by his side: his head sank forward; it seemed as if horror and despair had unstrung every nerve and sinew; he appeared to collapse and shrink together as a plant might, under the influence of a withering spell.[2]

Clearly Ardagh and O'Connor are explorations of the same predicament, that of men in life facing death's inevitability. Their despair knows nothing of Christian consolations, which appear solely in the device of the narrator's vocation. In 'Ardagh' a metaphysical dimension is preserved, but it is the devilish, negative dimension; in 'Castle Connor' cruel fate replaces Providence.

'Strange Event in the Life of Schalken the Painter', published a year later in May 1839, takes this concern with the reality of the supernatural a stage further. In many ways it is the most successful of *The Purcell Papers*, being less crudely death-focused than its

---

[1] The duellist's name is perhaps significant in identifying the real villain of *The Purcell Papers*. George Robert 'Fighting' Fitzgerald (?1748–1786), notorious duellist and murderer, had been born into the Anglo-Irish ascendency, and became a vigorous supporter of the Volunteer reform movement and of the earl-bishop of Derry. As such he might be seen as a precursor of the radical conservative groups with which Le Fanu was associated in the early 1840s—and simultaneously—a symbol of Le Fanu's unease at his own deviation from orthodox Toryism and Unionism. His friend, John Walsh, published a three-part sketch of Fighting Fitzgerald in *D.U.M.* between July and September 1840.

[2] *D.U.M.*, vol. 11 (June 1838), 727.

companions. Schalken is in love with the ward of his master, Gerard Douw, but has not told him about their attachment. A mysterious suitor asks for Rose's hand in marriage, with displays of wealth which Douw feels in no way obliged to refuse. When the agreement has been ratified, the suitor reveals himself as a Demon Lover, a figure of terrible appearance and power, who plucks Rose away from the safety of her protector and lover. Even here the energy of the tale is concentrated on the principal characters' willingness to discount a supernatural explanation of the stranger's behaviour; he does not reveal his true nature until they have committed themselves to his normality. Le Fanu appears to bring the tale to a climax in a tomb, but at the last moment this scene is announced as existing in Schalken's dreams. When the conclusion is finally reached, there is still uncertainty about the reality of what Schalken has seen; the emphasis is explicitly on Schalken's conviction to the neglect of any assurance or direction for the reader: 'To his dying day Schalken was satisfied of the reality of the vision [of Rose beckoning to him in a crypt] which he had witnessed, and he has left behind him a curious evidence of the impression which it wrought upon his fancy, in a painting executed shortly after the event . . .'[1] Significantly the painting depicts a girl with an arch smile beckoning someone forward, and not the demonic figure of the dream's climax. The girl's white veil and dress 'is not strictly that of any religious order', a phrase which raises (by imperfect denial) a religious association in the temptress's represenation.[2] If the Dutch setting seems out of place in *The Purcell Papers*, Le Fanu provides a provenance for the Schalken painting, which involves a supporter of the House of Orange, a settler in Ireland; the emergence of the Demon himself is entirely fitting in a continental context, when Ardagh and O'Connor have been destroyed apparently through merely visiting Europe.

In these stories the Irish gentry are revealed to be Catholic primarily by their continental associations, just as surely as Ardagh's wealth and O'Connor's fatal acquaintance have continental origins. Links with France and Spain had been the political life-blood of eighteenth-century Irish Jacobites, and in dramatizing the fate of Ardagh and O'Connor Le Fanu seems to say that Catholicism is acceptable so long as it avoids political (i.e. continental) associations. The decade before publication of the *Papers* had seen the greatest resurgence of Catholicism in British political life since the reign of the Stuarts; at least to Protestant Tories, it seemed that the Williamite constitution which had been secured only by the overthrow of the Stuarts was now virtually in jeopardy. *The Purcell Papers* advance in a kind of code a portrait of Le Fanu's own caste under pressure from a new regime; if we read nineteenth-century terms into the tales, their significance is evident. His account of the Ardaghs and O'Connors springs from the anxiety of Protestant landowners, magistrates, and clergy, and in the face of humiliation celebrations of lost causes and heroic defeat in the manner of Walter Scott are in order. A continental source of evil is doubly useful in this code; not only does it point to the merely formal Catholicism of the characters, it also hints at the revolutionary French doctrines which had threatened Great Britain since 1789. Emmet, Hamilton-Rowan, and O'Connell, to name just three, had spent time in France, and though they each drew different conclusions from their European spell, none of them had the good of the Williamite constitution at heart. French principles had first propagated subversive Jacobitism and Catholicism, and now revolutionary Jacobinism and irreligion. The Continent was a portmanteau image for all that a high-Tory family dreaded.

Repeatedly Le Fanu announces that his narrator-priest had ministered in the southern counties of Ireland and when specific names are required, he mentions Limerick and Tipperary, on the borders of which he had himself lived since 1826. Such Gothicism on the doorstep was unusual, for the cult generally favoured foreign settings. Le Fanu's intention was to acknowledge —perhaps more to himself than to the reader—that the adventures of eighteenth-century Jacobites had a more immediate signi-ficance than the historical. His landscape is not merely geographic; indeed the landscape assumes an importance in the tales which includes some duties normally allotted to casual imagery, to character or incident. A district is 'rendered interesting by the fact that it is one of the very few spots throughout the country, in which some fragments of aboriginal wood have found a refuge'. These humanizing terms—aboriginal, refuge—are expanded into a social landscape relating past to present:

But now, alas, whither have we drifted?—whither has the tide of civilisation borne us?—it has passed over a land unprepared for it—it has left nakedness behind it. We have lost our forests, but our marauders remain—we have destroyed all that is picturesque, while we have retained everything that is revolting in barbarism.[1]

After this opening, the narrative of 'Ardagh' reverts to its proper context of eighty years earlier. 'Castle Connor' begins with some trite emotion stimulated by the 'ruins of time' and becomes gradually more precise:

There do, indeed, still exist some fragments of the ancient Catholic families of Ireland; but alas! what *very* fragments. They linger like the remnants of her aboriginal forests, reft indeed of their strength and greatness, but proud in decay. Every winter thins their ranks, and stews the ground with the wreck of their loftiest branches[2]

This overture prepares us for the image of O'Connor's death—'he appeared to collapse and shrink together as a plant might, under the influence of a withering spell'—and indicates the hero's representative role. Landscape substitutes itself for a kind of characterization, and in absorbing O'Connor the symbolic woodland softens the issues of personal victimization, political and denominational alienation which otherwise might make him unmanageable. Such difficulties in writing fiction had been admitted by the founder of the Anglo-Irish tradition, for in 1834 Maria Edgeworth confessed that 'It is impossible to draw Ireland as she now is in a book of fiction—realities are too strong, party passions too violent . . .'[3] No doubt the historical setting and non-individual characterization of 'Castle Connor' saved Le Fanu from the controversies implied in a tale primarily concerned with politics and religion, and when the tale was also written in a personal code the need for such techniques was all the greater.

Certainly, he was less successful in controlling his material in those few of the *Papers* where he attempts to deal explicitly with the Protestant past. 'Passage in the Secret History of an Irish Countess' reads more like a blue-print for a tale than the thing itself, and 'Chapter in the History of a Tyrone Family' concludes its tale of bigamy with a too convenient madness and suicide. In

---

[1] Ibid., vol. II (Mar. 1838), 313.

[2] Ibid. (June 1838), 713.

[3] A. J. C. Hare (ed.), *The Life and Letters of Maria Edgeworth* (London, 1894) ii. 202.

'The Bridal of Carrighavarrah' Le Fanu visibly toys with and abandons the explosive theme of intermarriage between the sects, allowing the opposing families to merge into his generalized eighteenth-century and implicitly Catholic background. There is some evidence that his sister Catherine may have influenced his decision to attempt these 'Protestant' tales, which are also marked by their lack of interest in the supernatural. The important development in this otherwise unhappy experiment is the substitution of the Great House for the aboriginal forests; where previously sylvan imagery and a nervous interest in the supernatural had framed the tales' crises, the 'Protestant' tales opt decisively for domestic interiors and explicitly criminal offences. The fatal agents (arrogant servants and invincible duellists) are replaced by thoroughly human villains, whose crimes (murder and bigamy) are violations of civil law. The synchronization is remarkable: the introduction of Protestant contexts and criminal villains. Conscious guilt, of course, takes on larger proportions in the novels which Le Fanu subsequently built on the plots of 'The Irish Countess' and 'The Tyrone Family':—*Uncle Silas* and *The Wyvern Mystery*. There was a limit to the *Papers*' potential; even the priestly persona could not sustain an endless series of anecdotes. Purcell himself, however, embodies one of the recurring issues of Le Fanu's fiction, despite his seeming invisibility as mere narrator. His loneliness as a solitary figure in a withered landscape, the custodian of painful memories and confessions, provides another context for the Gothic deaths and damnations. The narrator is a Christian believer but, even in those tales where he is involved in the melodrama, his belief cannot reach others. He is condemned to be a looker-on, sometimes racked by guilty feelings of his inadequacy, and always bringing his sacred office to bear on the same grim experience—the death of those who have left behind his consoling creed. Solitude is the destiny which the central figures face, and in some cases the result is self-destruction, suicide, the absolute but purely formal escape from solitude. Naturally these acts of self-destruction may be seen as the forerunners to the suicides of *Uncle Silas*, *A Lost Name*, and *Willing to Die;* sensational fiction would appear to be their proper home. But in the context of *The Purcell Papers*, a context political both at the historical and immediate level, suicide may have a ponderous symbolism also.

Many literary discussions of suicide are of the kind which gives bad taste a bad name, but as a symbol *in* literature it need have no biographical reference either prophetic or autobiographical. *Werther* and *Obermann* had established the symbol of suicide in modern literature more permanently than the rash of alleged suicides which followed the publication of Goethe's novel. Within a fictional or poetic structure there is a range of related symbols, the static and stifling images which convey a paralysed or horrified consciousness. Suicide is, paradoxically, the epitome of self-possession and the negation of self; it may symbolize an experience available to men who share a common history as well as to a solitary victim. Its paradoxical logic, employed as symbol, can refer to broader matters than self-killing, to spiritual or ideological contradictions, even to unconscious collective urges which never acquire the name of action. The last heir of Castle Connor was finally a representative figure absorbed into a dying landscape; his 'suicide' was not even depicted as a single act of violence on his own body, but rather an attitude towards his fate which lead him to expect death in such a way as to make death inevitable. The diffused self-destruction of this figure is not the literary reflection of a 'biographical' suicide; it is a condensed symbol of a movement in history which Le Fanu saw as parallel to his own caste. Throughout the period when he was publishing *The Purcell Papers*, he was active in Dublin political circles, and to correlate his political expressions with his fictional creations is to penetrate to a further layer of significance in his life.

The Anglo-Irish ascendancy, and particularly the resident gentry on whom the burden of carrying the ascendancy's responsibilities in the countryside had fallen, existed in a state of dislocation in 1838–40. At loggerheads with its sectarian foes at home, it was also deeply suspicious of its traditional ally, the imperial government at Westminster. Caught between the new and aggressive power of Irish Catholics and the distant authority of English politicians who openly repudiated their identity of interest, it was forced to examine its alternatives. For many the safest course was an absolute trust in the British Tories; surely Wellington and Peel were incapable of the selfish ingratitude of a Melbourne or Russell! The Whig government would sooner or later be replaced, and the temporary alliance of O'Connell and Westminster dismantled. But as the decade came to a close, and the humiliated Irish conservatives watched helplessly the dissolution of the Orange lodges, the abolition of bishoprics, and the first moves towards municipal reform, some at least wondered if more drastic resistance might not be needed. Any such initiative must drive the Anglo-Irish on to their own resources, cutting them off from sympathizers in Britain and leaving them face to face with the resurgent Catholic population. Unilateral action, if taken to the extreme, must lead to isolation and perhaps the discovery of a loss of nerve or an inadequacy of determination. The ascendency's cultural training since 1800 had emphasized the Union as the guarantee of Tory interests in Ireland, and the upsurge of Catholic activism in the intervening years confirmed the Anglo-Irish belief in the united parliament. The temporary supremacy of a reforming government was hardly a pretext for overturning this arrangement—unless, of course, its reforms went so far as to destroy the privileges of ascendency. And once destroyed by a Whig government, it would be politically impossible for a Tory administration (no matter how determined) to recreate the old hegemony.

Among the many groups formed after the suppression of the Orange Order, the Irish Metropolitan Conservative Society determined to maintain a brave public face at its weekly meetings. Conservative House was 19 Dawson Street, between St. Anne's church and the Lord Mayor's residence—the headquarters today of the Royal Irish Academy. In 1837 the officials included Isaac Butt and John Francis Waller (a founder of the *Dublin University Magazine*) and a similarity between the Society's policy and the magazine's editorials was particularly marked during Butt's editorship. The membership generally was drawn from the obscurer branches of the Irish aristocracy, the county magnates, and the captains of militia. The vice-presidents included Chidley Coote, a kinsman of Emma Le Fanu; A. S. Hart, the Trinity Fellow whose rakish life had been the subject of comment in Le Fanu's undergraduate letters; and Colonel Henry Bruen, MP for Carlow since 1812. The President was Hodgkinson, Vice-Provost of Trinity, and the secretaries included both Butt and Mountifort Longfield; in these key positions the academics were able to infuse some intellectual rigour into the I.M.C.S.'s deliberations. Butt and Le Fanu were the two members who subsequently achieved permanent distinction—neither of them as conservative politicians. Le Fanu's involvement with this Tory ginger group had its effect on his literary career; his friend Percy Fitzgerald recalled how he had early thrown himself into local politics, 'which had rather a prejudicial effect on his nature, his gloomy imagination giving them larger proportions than they deserved'.[1] In fact, it was not so much his single-minded commitment to the Tories which moulded his sombre imagination, as the paradoxical combination of several activities carried on simultaneously.

For all his fondness for seclusion, he possessed a vigorous public style, the sensitive mind thus seeing to its own defence. In November 1838 he made his début as a conservative public speaker. He had already published 'Robert Ardagh' and 'The Last Heir of Castle Connor', the most eloquently Jacobite of *The Purcell Papers*, and in the previous summer he had experienced the unnerving encounter with agrarian violence on the Galtee Mountains. As if to counterbalance this curious prelude to Williamite rhetoric, the same month (November) saw the publication of 'Passage in the Secret History of an Irish Countess', the first of the *Papers* in which confiscator Williamites are portrayed. Such a counterbalance is solely an ironical one, for instead of a monopoly of Jacobite heroics his fiction now introduced Williamite guilt. In the circumstances the speech, though overblown, is revealing:

Worshipful Sir and Brethren, although in other earlier times Protestantism in Ireland had been exposed to dangers which have rendered a strict and defensive confederation among its members absolutely necessary to its existence, yet at no time have its professors been so unequivocally called upon, as at the present, by extreme urgency and danger, to band themselves together in its defence. At other times the warfare to which we were exposed, though sanguinary and exterminating, had in it nevertheless something of an open and a manly character —the men who sought our property and our lives, had the courage in the attempt to peril their own; open rebellion was preferred to secret assassination and in the broad day-light, and in the field of battle was shed that blood which now flows in the secrecy of murder and of night.[2]

---

[1] P. H. Fitzgerald, *The Lives of the Sheridans* (London, 1886) ii. 469. It appears that Fitzgerald included his brief reference to Sheridan Le Fanu at the prompting of the novelist's brother. In an undated letter Fitzgerald admitted to William that 'there is not much to be got'.

[2] *The Warder*, vol. 17, no. 895 (17 Nov. 1838), 3.

In this unconcealed admiration for earlier generations of resisting Catholics Le Fanu reveals the logic of his *Purcell Papers;* Sarsfields or Ardaghs had a nobility of which O'Connells are incapable. But he concerned himself as a writer with the defeated heirs to the wars of William and James rather than with the wars themselves. His attention was always drawn to the displaced and exposed figure who, like young O'Connor, becomes a representative of his class and sect. Similarly, in his public oratory, Le Fanu emphasized the abandoned position of his own people in language as bitter as his condemnation of agrarian outrage:

in all our former struggles . . . whenever Protestantism in Ireland was persecuted, assailed and imperilled, the government of England sympathised and supported; and it was reserved for Lord Melbourne's whig administration, by abandoning and seeking to destroy the interests of Protestant Ireland, to compromise the character and the honour of Protestant England, for never until the accession of that noble lord to office, had England failed in the hour of danger, to redeem her pledge of protection, and left the Protestants of Ireland wholly unsustained and unencouraged, to abide the assaults of their malignant inveterate enemies; and never before had a British government been found so sordid and so mean as, at the price of the patronage and the emolument of place, to sell their independence and their honour to a Popish leader, and enlisting themselves among the foes of Protestantism, to break down her bulwarks, waste her strength, betray her safety, mock her prayers . . .[1]

The Popish leader was, of course, Daniel O'Connell. Irish Protestants bore him so violent an animosity that their balance of judgement was often upset solely by his influence. Earlier in 1838, Le Fanu had written to his father telling of various public meetings of the Liberator's which he was attending, among them an anti-slavery rally. 'I heard him at the Corn Exchange on yesterday. He is greatly knocked up & seems very much subdued. He looks quite old & wrinkled, which he did *not* about a year ago.'[2] This was written while the first of *The Purcell Papers* were appearing. But two years later his attitude to O'Connell had changed dramatically.

In October 1840 the last of the *Papers* appeared, 'The Quare

[1] Ibid.
[2] J. T. S. Le Fanu to T. P. Le Fanu, dated 'Friday 1838', to which a later hand (?T. P. Le Fanu's) has added 'about the 21st. April'.

Gander' in which Father Purcell took his mournful leave of the mortally decaying landscape. At Conservative House on 19 October, the anonymous author's public rhetoric was flecked with personal antagonism:

Mr O'Connell has been, throughout his whole political career, the sworn exterminator of Protestantism—he is one whose political existence, from youth to decrepitude, has been one of sordid hypocrisy, and of utter and savage selfishness—who has achieved his own political elevation at a sacrifice of human life, greater than any mortal pestilence has caused, and at an expense of human crime which must be slowly paid for [by] ages of national degradation—and one who, having seen the victims of his hatred laid in the graves of martyrdom, and those of his perfidy and cajolery exposed upon the gibbets of their country, now approaches the verge of his iniquitous existence, unaffected by the visitings of remorse, with a soul in which every passion, but that of unquenchable malignity had perished, and a heart which so far from being touched by the awful approaches of death and judgment, seems not to anticipate the coldness and corruption of the grave.[1]

The change of opinion between the letter of April 1838 and the speech of October 1840, from O'Connell's wrinkles to jeers at his decrepitude, may spring from an attack of galloping rhetoric. (The I.M.C.S. was not always the brightest company, despite the several dons.) Yet the occasion of Le Fanu's outburst against O'Connell was important in the Society's history, and his contribution was symptomatic of a fundamental uncertainty.

Rumours had been gathering earlier in 1840 that the I.M.C.S. favoured more radical forms of Toryism than those of the orthodox politicians at Westminster. A motion had been presented calling on the Society openly to declare its total loyalty to the party. Butt, however, realizing the tactical error of adding fuel to the controversy, tried on 19 October to channel the discussion into a procedural wrangle. In such a compromising situation, Le Fanu felt obliged to express his own detestation of O'Connell publicly, lest any rumour-monger accuse him of apostasy. He was, nevertheless, compromised by an earlier private debate at Conservative House, and the venom of his denunciations perhaps measures the degree of his embarrassment. Rumours of discontent in the I.M.C.S. could not have been fully and honestly denied: a desire for radical alternatives had already been expressed

---

[1] *Dublin Evening Mail*, 21 Oct. 1840.

at an August meeting, and the extraordinary form which this
desire took is captured in Joseph Le Fanu's dutiful letter to his
mother:

I went down to the Conservative Society & took an active part in a very
hot debate which for good reasons was not reported: it arose most
unexpectedly & I think you will be surprised to hear that the subject
was the repeal of the Union—the question being what advice the
Society should give in their address to the protestants of this country
upon the movement. Some spoke most vehemently in favour of an
open declaration for repeal & none spoke directly against it. The fact
is that the Whig policy, or rather the policy of the conservative opposition who claim to give up Ireland, has completely unsettled the
protestants and every thing seems to promise a speedy & tremendous
revolutionary explosion.[1]

Here was the atavistic dream of a Protestant-dominated Irish
parliament of the kind extinguished in 1800, a parliament elected
on a severely restricted franchise. Such longings for an eighteenth-
century solution to a nineteenth-century crisis clearly startled
the dreamers of the Irish Metropolitan Conservative Society.
Le Fanu's active part in the hot debate puts him among those
who, at the least, gave Repeal some positive consideration. But
Anglo-Ireland was haunted by its past corruptions, its roots in
conquest, and its ignominy in vote-selling, and none of those
present in Conservative House that August evening had the nerve
of a John Fitzgibbon. Though his diatribes denounced the
'Robespierres of the Ribbon faction' and warned of the
'ascendency of Popish superstition', Le Fanu also feared the
consequences of Protestant isolation. There was no solid base for
the dream of a restored and exclusive Dublin parliament:

The Roman Catholics are an important political power, & as full as
ever of treason. The lower classes of all religions have acquired a
smattering of information & have consequently acquired a kind of
expansive ambition which will soon make itself felt against the higher
orders. The Roman Catholic gentry of the professions are generally
infidel and revolutionary & the protestants from first to last *unsteady*.[2]

'Infidel and revolutionary'—these are the twin evils which France
stands for, and in *The Purcell Papers* religious despair and social

---

[1] J. T. S. Le Fanu to Mrs E. Le Fanu, undated, postmarked 21 Aug. 1840.
[2] Ibid.

collapse result from continental sojourn. The 'unsteady' Protestants of the tales are unique in their own criminal inheritance.
The interaction of fiction and politics in Le Fanu's thought is
plain in his treatment of O'Connell who, as he 'now approaches
the verge of his iniquitous existence, unaffected by the visitings
of remorse', more closely resembles a fictional creation than a
political foe. If there was one definable ground on which Protestant Repeal was totally unacceptable it was the appearance
of a link with O'Connell: 'I would cast to the winds all considerations of political convenience and aggrandisement, rather
than suffer it to be believed by my silence, or by any other
implication, that I was willing to submit to the contamination of
such a leadership as Mr. O'Connell's . . .'[1] That was in October
1840, the month in which Father Purcell bid farewell to the
landscape's mortal decay, and the implication surely is that Le
Fanu's detestation of O'Connell ultimately penetrated the 'code'
of his historical fiction to make the identification of his own caste
and the earlier Jacobites intolerable. The rejection was unfortunate, for the *Papers* had allowed Le Fanu to explore areas
of his experience other than the political, notably his uneasy
concern with supernatural belief. When the crisis of Catherine's
death arose, the fictional response ('Spalatro') lacked the control
which *The Purcell Papers'* persona had previously provided. And
behind the fear of O'Connell and the refusal to countenance
unilateral political action lay fears about the spiritual quality of
his inheritance, fears ultimately involving larger issues of identity
which merged with the religious unease.

Virtually five years elapsed between the last of *The Purcell Papers*
and the publication of *The Cock and Anchor* with which Le Fanu
resumed his commitment to Irish historical fiction. In the interim
political and personal developments affected him in a manner
which gradually encouraged a return to writing. He had, of
course, already entered the lesser world of journalism in an effort
to supplement his income as a barrister. By September 1840 he
had an interest in two Dublin newspapers, the *Statesman* and
The Warder. Apart from his instinct to write, journalism was the
best means of creating a public opinion sympathetic to a conservative with reservations about official party policy. In buying

[1] *Dublin Evening Mail*, 21 Oct. 1840.

his way into the papers, he was forced to accept a mortgage on the property which still left the previous owners (notably a troublesome Huguenot cleric, Charles Marlay Fleury) with some control over editorial policy. In the case of the *Statesman*, his lack of freedom was particularly irksome in that the paper's tone had offended many in the Tory camp whom he needed to impress. Its 'low' tone brought down fatherly disapproval which he was anxious to show was unearned. In a letter which has, regrettably, survived only in part, he stressed the utter impotence of his position:

My vote is overruled by the other two [proprietors] both of whom are agreed in the propriety of continuing the present editor . . . *I* proposed converting the paper into a merely political one, but was overruled. *I* proposed changing it into a staunch Church paper but was *overruled*. I have no power over the Statesman and wash my hands of all responsibility for its tone alike in point of style & of feeling.[1]

It was perhaps then fortunate that the paper died in October 1846, though Le Fanu had ceased to write leaders for it twelve months earlier. Apart from *The Warder*, a robust champion of Irish Toryism in which he retained his interest until 1870, his involvement in Dublin newspapers in the 1840s proved to be a troublesome and costly business.

Defending the conservative interest in print had quickly turned into a tiresome drudgery, and Catherine's death added a deeper tone to his disillusion. Even the 1841 election could not rouse his former vehemence, though the eventual victory of the Tories suggested that the wrongs of a Whiggish decade might now be reversed. His father's right to a bishopric, he feared, might be overlooked or lost through the Dean's unbending rectitude. But down in Abington, the election brought no alteration to the popular mood. Caleb Powell of Clonshavoy had been elected a Whig MP as if to bring the taint of reform politics into the congregation. When O'Connell launched his 'monster' meetings in favour of Repeal, Powell welcomed him to Murroe. The Dean's tiny congregation became a metaphor for meek compliance in Powell's opening address: 'This meeting today—the countless thousands who surround me . . . will disperse as orderly as our congregation down in Abington church, consisting of six or

---

[1] J. T. S. Le Fanu to T. P. Le Fanu, undated; manuscript of this letter is incomplete, and survives only from the second leaf.

twenty, does on Sunday.'[1] *The Nation*'s report added a heckler's cry: 'You have exaggerated, there are only 24.'

At the same time, Joseph in Dublin was consolidating his position in the legal world with a useful sinecure in the courts. In 1842 Chief Justice John Doherty arranged the post of Tipstaff to the Court of Common Pleas for him. He was anxious to distinguish this nominal office from 'the worthies who call silence & convey penny-post communications from one side of the court to the other', but in the absence of any income at the Bar the regular salary was welcome.[2] A connection with the courts probably had other attractions, for shortly after his appointment he was hopeful suitor of a QC's daughter. A new phase of his life, with Abington left far behind, was dawning.

The Dean's life was now almost spent, and the circumstances of Joseph's promotion as head of the family were not auspicious. Making his will in 1844, his father found his property hedged in by embarrassments and apologies. Lands left to his widow would be burdened by mortgages, and William's inheritance would amount to two books (Walton's *Angler* and a New Testament) and a ring with a Persian inscription. To Joseph he bequeathed a cornelian ring, a silver tankard with the family arms, and a set of Swift's works edited by Thomas Sheridan. In order that even this reduced heritage might be preserved, the Dean directed that his library be sold and the proceeds used to liquidate his debts. A shrunken worldy estate symbolized spiritual anxieties: 'I desire that my body may be kept until unequivocal signs of death shall have taken place; and that with the least possible expense (consistent with propriety) it be buried in my burial place in the churchyard of Abington, and laid beside the remains of my only, my beloved & ever-lamented daughter, Catherine.'[3] The fear of premature burial was not uncommon: among victims of the phobia was Daniel O'Connell. Its psychological causes are obscure but often included a rationalized uncertainty about the existence of a future life, for the obsession flourished at times and in places where orthodox belief was coming under pressure. Less pretentiously, it can be seen as a projected hypersensitivity

---

[1] *The Nation*, 17 June 1843, 593.

[2] J. T. S. Le Fanu to T. P. Le Fanu, dated 'Monday'; the Dublin Directory lists Le Fanu as Tip-staff from 1842 to 1852.

[3] Probate of the will is recorded in the P.R.O. Dublin.

to the horrors of a paralysed consciousness, a theme which recurs in Sheridan Le Fanu's tales from *The Purcell Papers* to *In a Glass Darkly*.

Between Catherine's death in March 1841 and the Dean's in June 1845, Joseph and his mother nurtured an intimacy which was intensified, if anything, by their separation. Lonely in Dublin, he valued the food-baskets and occasional delicacies which she sent to him as more than culinary relief. The Dean, though a sophisticated man and a player of the harp, had not inherited the creative talents of the Sheridans; on balance Joseph found it easier to discuss his writing with Emma. While midway through *The Purcell Papers* he had ambitions on a larger scale. First, there was the play confessed to in a letter from London, but within weeks it had fallen a victim to plot complications; it lacked incident and variety, qualities which the *Papers* rarely required. Though he returned to the task intermittently during his life, play-writing never suited Le Fanu's abilities. In April 1839, with 'Schalken' in the press, book publication had already occurred to him. Seven *Papers* were now printed, with perhaps one or two more in preparation. Through the Dobbins, he was confident of an introduction to Richard Bentley, one of London's most energetic publishers with whom Dickens was associated. April 1839 was a high-point of Dobbin–Le Fanu co-operation, for Le Fanu had published in the *Dublin University Magazine* several anonymous letters which had been in the Dobbin family for generations.[1] The letters—they were in fact unsigned copies made at the time of composition—were addressed to King James II, informing him of conditions in Ireland before the crisis of 1688. He had previously published two Swift letters, heirlooms in his own family, in the previous September's *D.U.M.*, and in editing

---

[1] 'Original Letters, No 2—Political', *D.U.M.*, vol. 13 (Apr. 1839), 431-8 (misnumbered 348). The texts of these two letters, together with those of six others in the same hand and of the same character, were published in *Notes and Queries* in 1882 (6th series, vols. 5-6, Apr.–July 1882) by the Dublin antiquarian, William Frazer. In a prefatory note Frazer writes: 'I purchased [the letters] some time since, with other papers belonging to the late Mr. Lefanu, the novelist and writer, which were sold in Dublin after his death . . . At the end of the book there is a short paragraph, written in lead-pencil by Mr. Lefanu, in which he states, 'I finished these curious letters 12 July, 1839 . . . The MS. belonged to Dr. Dobbyn.' (Vol. 5, 321-2.) I am grateful to the late Dr J. G. Simms, sometime Fellow Emeritus, Trinity College, Dublin, for discussing the historical context of these letters with me.

the Jacobite spy reports he stumbled on a further historical retreat from the Penal years of Father Purcell's career. 'An Adventure of Hardress Fitzgerald, a Royalist Captain' (published in February 1840) was his first experiment in full-blooded and bloody military romance, a tale of the wars of William and James later incorporated into *The Fortunes of Colonel Torlogh O'Brien*. Family hardship, even on the Dobbin side, had its casual effect on Le Fanu's development. To counterbalance this influence, his courtship of Susanna Bennett ran parallel to his early struggles with the novel form. In May 1841, a month of lasting influence, Mortimer O'Sullivan had advised him to attempt a longer tale than those allowed by the Purcell formula; and on 20 May, the Bennetts entertained both Joseph and William to dinner in 18 Merrion Square South, the house in which the sensational novelist later spent the final twenty years of his life. George Bennett was the leading barrister on the Munster circuit, a thin, Tory-principled man.

In July 1842 Le Fanu was disappointed to hear that Folds, the Dublin printer, was rumoured to be going out of business. Though he had no complete manuscript at hand, he was taking stock of publishing possibilities. In January 1843 he reported to his mother: 'I am getting on my best with my story. I think I am doing it at least as well as any I have done. I hope you will like it.'[1] Though this sounds like another short tale rather than a novel, it also sounds unlike the ghastliness of 'Spalatro', the first tale to appear after this date. During a ritual appearance at the Four Courts in January 1843 he determined to write to the Spottiswoode publishing family in London, with whom the Le Fanus had some personal contacts. He still had no manuscript to offer, but had great hopes of starting the third volume by mid-February. These plans involved the insertion of 'Jim Sulivan's Adventure in the Great Snow', a dialect tale from *The Purcell Papers*, in the final chapters of the novel. 'Jim Sulivan', however, does not appear in any of Le Fanu's novels, and the manuscript in progress may have been ultimately rejected or abandoned.

But by June a novel had been dispatched to London, where its fate was closely observed by Sheridan Knowles—hardly a rock of sense in business matters. Delay was dispiriting, and with the Bennetts out of town for the summer, Le Fanu was again the

[1] J. T. S. Le Fanu to Mrs E. Le Fanu, undated, postmarked 24 Jan. 1843.

victim of brooding loneliness. In these moods he found relief in his mother's letters, treasuring her gossip, and requesting from her occasional country recipes. By October the Bennetts had returned to Dublin and, with his marriage only three months away his spirits soared. A basket of provisions from the glebe-house brought 'capital' turkey and 'beautiful' bacon. But the pattern of his feelings in the months leading up to the publication of his first novel is far from simple. *The Cock and Anchor* is amongst other things the story of a thwarted courtship, written during or just after the author's successful courtship of Miss Bennett; it is also an eloquent celebration of Jacobite defeat and Catholic suffering in 1710, written during a period of Le Fanu's most vehemently anti-Papist oratory, much of which—for example a speech delivered at the Rotunda in June 1843—was far more widely publicized than the weekly cabals in Conservative House. There is in fact reason to believe that *The Cock and Anchor* was not the first novel which he had written, though it must retain its premier position in any account of his Irish fiction. Visibly implicated in the respectable Tory circles of the Bennetts as well as the somewhat zanier orthodoxy of the Irish Metropolitan Conservative Society, anonymity for the novelist was *de rigueur*.

The first few months of married life were agitated to some extent by Joseph's nervousness about his novel's fate. A letter of 5 March 1844 reported a variety of domestic successes, but no news of the manuscript:

My own darling mother

We are nearly settled in our new house, & were most agreeably surprised by poor Willie's popping in this morning. He is I think in very good spirits & as far as I can judge in the highest honour & confidence with MacNeill. All your presents my darling Mother arrived safely & Sue is absolutely delighted with them. The china was exactly the thing she wanted & most liked. We are as happy together as possible & I think never will have any more disputes. She is a most kind hearted goodhumoured little mortal. She is in first delight with the servants Catherine & Kitty [;] & Mrs Bennet, her aunt is also most highly pleased with them, & told Sue she was most fortunate in getting them. We are uncommonly snug & happy together. Sue had a letter from Mr. Bennett the other day in which he spoke in the most affectionate terms of *both* of us.[1]

[1] J. T. S. Le Fanu to Mrs E. Le Fanu, 5 Mar. 1844. See below pp. 111–114 for a fuller account of the domestic context of Le Fanu's marriage.

The house to which the couple had returned, 15 Warrington Place, was well placed in the southern Dublin suburbs, overlooking the languid waters of a tree-lined canal. By the end of March, Le Fanu's mood in writing to his mother was less unruffled:

I have been longing for a letter from you. Your dear letters are the greatest delight to me, & indeed I never saw any extacies more extravagant than poor little Sue's whenever the post brings her a letter in your welcome hand ... Not having since heard from Miss Spottiswoode who used to be so very punctual in acknowledging my letters . . . I would therefore be greatly obliged to you if you would write to her mentioning the fact of my having written at great length and also stating the purport of my communication, namely to ask whether she could make any interest for me through Mr. Andrew Spottiswoode with any publisher & mentioning that I look to *publication* as my fixed object & to remuneration only as a secondary one . . . I would write myself at once were I sure that my letter had not reached her, but it would not do to to [sic] treat her twice to the same story from the *same person*, so I think it better to wait until I see what effect yours may have. I enclose for my father also poor Wm Dobbin's letter. Poor Catherine Brady has been suffering very much from her side for the last three days. Poor William visits me & I think looking very well . . . As to my poor novel I begin to fear that like water and other good things, it is doomed to lie at the bottom of a well, being too good for vulgar eyes. However, as I have pretty well lost all ambition except that of living free from fighting and absolute hunger & nakedness this reflection does not trouble me so much as a few years since it would have done.[1]

This fussy repetitiveness stands in contrast to the colourful rhetoric of Le Fanu's speeches and the suavity of his fictional villains. The indiscriminate labelling of all and sundry as 'poor'— including his robust and successful brother—is a further mark of innate insecurity. In the light of these casual revelations, the nakedness and hunger may not have been entirely fanciful. Behind the curtains of Warrington Place lives of quiet desperation flickered in the uncertain Victorian dawn. Money was not plentiful; politics was embarrassing, the inner life a conflict of obligations. None of these inhibitions appears in *The Cock and Anchor*, where the lovers are oblivious of debts and ideologies; it is their relatives who squander blood and guineas.

But *The Cock and Anchor*, or at least its publication, lay some

[1] Ibid., 25 Mar. 1844.

distance away in the future, and the context in which it was written included both public as well as private concerns. In Le Fanu's case each of these areas was precariously founded on recent upheavals. His parents had passed from the prestige of local magnates with spiritual functions to the dependency of a 'moderate fixed income'—a transformation which seemed to question the reality of their spiritual values. Le Fanu was never entirely at home with the ultra-blue Toryism of the Cootes, for the simple reason that he acknowledged the existence, albeit the frequently distasteful existence, of Ireland round about him. And his family experience also included some radical memories— Dr Dobbin befriending the Sheares brothers, Emma Le Fanu venerating Lord Edward Fitzgerald. The moment which Emma chose to record her theft of Lord Edward's relic, April 1847, is a significant one, drawing together the private and public domains, a moment poised between her son's most explicit fictional Jacobitism and the insurrection of 1848. It was the time of Young Ireland, of a resurgent and romantic nationalism in which Protestant and Catholic (in theory at least) sought to be reconciled. For, just as the family tradition of Toryism contained a sub-plot of occasional radicalism, so Le Fanu's generation at Trinity produced Thomas Davis as well as Isaac Butt. To the Young Irelanders under Davis, Repeal of the Union was not an atavistic temptation indulged behind closed doors, but a policy of sound integrity. As a result of nationalist success in the twentieth century, Davis and his fellows have been long regarded as proto-revolutionaries, whereas their primary instinct was anti-Whig. Where their conservative counterparts in the *Dublin University Magazine* and The Irish Metropolitan Conservative Society were defensive, introspective, and hostile to change, the Young Irelanders welcomed new ideas, encouraged experiment, and looked to the past as the obedient midwife of the future. Their methods were the classical Victorian bourgeois ones: an energetic newspaper (*The Nation*), libraries, reading-rooms, and all the trappings of educational propaganda. Articulate to a fault, Young Ireland seemed at the time to be the dominant intellectual movement in politics and in general cultural discussion. But it was perhaps no firmer rooted in Irish life than were the cherished traditions of momentary radicalism in the instinctively cautious Le Fanus.

As *The Nation* made a conscious effort to cultivate good relations with the *Dublin University Magazine*, inevitably relations of some kind developed. James Clarence Mangan and William Carleton contributed frequently to both, though in Carleton's case there was more recrimination than co-operation in the exchange. John Walsh, Le Fanu's friend from Hist. days, and M. J. Barry, subsequently a close friend of William's, also published in the rival magazines. The apex of this mutual understanding came in 1845 (the year of *The Cock and Anchor*) with Davis's death, Samuel Ferguson publishing his moving lament in the *Dublin University Magazine*. It was Charles Gavan Duffy in particular who stressed the common interest of the magazines. As a professional journalist, he had been involved in May 1838 in launching a press association in Dublin, into which he welcomed the staff of literary journals. Le Fanu possibly met Gavan Duffy as early as May 1838 but—whatever the date of their first encounter —the journalist always spoke sympathetically of the novelist, even after relations between the two magazines had deteriorated. In 1845, some years after John Banim's death, it was thought necessary to petition the government on his widow's behalf, and the committee which Gavan Duffy dragooned into united action testified to his temporary success in bridging ideological gulfs: it included Daniel O'Connell, John Anster, William Smith-O'Brien, Isaac Butt, Charles Lever, Thomas Davis, Samuel Ferguson, William Carleton, James McGlashan, M. J. Barry, Sheridan Le Fanu—and Gavan Duffy himself. (Respect for Banim was probably the sole cause in which the committee could have been united.) If one compares Banim's *Boyne Water* and Le Fanu's *Cock and Anchor* and *The Fortunes of Colonel Torlogh O'Brien*, it is not difficult to see the debt which the younger writer was repaying by his service on the committee, but Le Fanu's participation is remarkable especially as the O'Sullivan brothers held aloof. He was separating himself from the clerical influences of the previous years; *The Cock and Anchor* has neither the nervous supernaturalism nor the sly anti-Papist footnotes of *The Purcell Papers*. Young Ireland may have encouraged this emergence from earlier obsessions, but it was only possible as a result of the Irish Tories' disillusionment with Peel's new government. In recording his memories of Young Ireland, Gavan Duffy acknowledged that Le Fanu's real sphere was the Tory one:

Joseph Le Fanu was the literary leader of the young Conservatives, and Isaac Butt was their political leader; both were at this time engaged, privately and unknown to each other, in writing historical romances which would present the hereditary feuds of Catholics and Protestants in a juster light to their posterity. Their books were published anonymously and not for some years after they were begun, but I can state on their authority respectively, that they had constantly in view in pursuing their task to gratify the new sentiment which the *Nation* had awakened.[1]

Now Butt had been Le Fanu's witness at his wedding in December 1843, and so the secrecy with which each regarded his novel-writing was indeed near absolute. Butt's novel was *The Gap of Barnesmore*, published in 1848, and Gavan Duffy names *Torlogh O'Brien* as Le Fanu's. With *The Cock and Anchor* appearing in 1845 and the first instalment of *Torlogh O'Brien* in April 1846 it would not seem that the latter was a long time in the writing, unless it was in fact written before *The Cock and Anchor*. 'Jim Sulivan's Adventures', which was intended for inclusion in the third volume of a manuscript nearing completion in February 1843, never appears in any Le Fanu novel, but a similar piece of dialect and folklore does appear at the end of *Torlogh O'Brien*— this suggesting that it was the first manuscript on which Le Fanu worked. And although *Torlogh O'Brien* was published after *The Cock and Anchor*, the second novel has more apprentice awkwardness, being both shorter and cruder in construction. On balance then, it seems that the publication of Le Fanu's first two novels reversed the order of their original composition. Gavan Duffy's evidence actually goes further than this, for in June 1846 he was approached by James McGlashan in connection with the serialization of *Torlogh O'Brien*. The anonymous author was uneasy about his treatment of Patrick Sarsfield, the military leader of the Irish Jacobites, and through his publisher he asked Gavan Duffy's opinion of a forthcoming instalment. In due course the journalist made various suggestions which, it seems certain, Le Fanu accepted, for his characterization of Sarsfield and the Duke of Tyrconnell—even of King James himself—is relatively free from bias. In a useful assessment of this disappointing novel, Nelson Browne has surely but unwittingly placed his finger on Duffy's contribution to *Torlogh O'Brien* and the author's assimilation of it:

[1] C. Gavan Duffy, *Young Ireland* (London, 1880), pp. 501–2.

Le Fanu allows himself to be dazzled by the haughty Viceroy, by his almost Satanic magnificence, and by the immense power he wielded. Yet there is one moment when after an interview with the villainous intriguer, Miles Garrett, the Viceroy pauses to survey the night sky through a window of Dublin Castle and in that moment the inner nature of the Duke is revealed to us. Behind the outward show of pompous vanity, there lay a mind unconvinced by the passing enthusiasms of the hour, a heart not untouched by misgivings for the future, and a soul yearning for something more permanent than the baseless fabric of the almost visionary Court, with its futile, faithless courtiers and its unlucky, misguided king.[1]

The Viceroy's power is Gavan Duffy's contribution, surely, and the disillusion and reserve Le Fanu's. Though *Torlogh O'Brien* is less well written than *The Cock and Anchor*, its peculiar condition of having been constructed before *The Cock and Anchor* and amended afterwards help us to see the significance of certain large images in the better novel.

Le Fanu's reliance on Gavan Duffy's advice is particularly striking when we remember the secrecy with which he hid his project from Butt, his personal friend and political associate. Though he could be vicious about O'Connell, he was obviously affected by the Young Ireland programme. Nevertheless, the tone he adopted in reviewing the *Nation*'s anthology in his own paper, *The Warder*, remained cautious:

The *Nation* is written with a masculine vigour, and with an impetuous singleness of purpose which makes every number tell home. It represents the opinions and feelings of some millions of men, reflected with vivid precision in its successive pages, and, taken for all in all, it is a genuine and gigantic representative of its vast party.[2]

In the circumstances of Le Fanu's background and his recent

[1] N. Browne, *Sheridan Le Fanu* (London, 1951), p. 35. Gavan Duffy transcribes the relevant pages from his diary, adding explanatory comments in square brackets: '19th (June)—To call on McGlashan *in re* "Torlogh O'Brien" and his anonymous project. [Mr. Le Fanu, who was writing his national story of "Torlogh O'Brien", asked me to look at the proofs, and consider whether he had done justice to Sarsfield (the popular hero of that era), and Mr. McGlashan, his publisher, wrote me a note on that subject, which possesses a historic interest from the use he made of the correspondence a couple of years later:— "My dear sir,—Many thanks for your note and your valuable suggestions. I have sent it to Le Fanu . . .]"' C. Gavan Duffy, *Four Years of Irish History 1844–1849* (London, 1883), p. 77.

[2] Quoted by C. Gavan Duffy, *Thomas Davis*, p. 141; and *Young Ireland*, p. 284.

political associations, this no-praise of *The Nation* was praise indeed. *The Cock and Anchor* (which the Young Irelanders' paper obligingly and enthusiastically reviewed) is far less restrained, and there the seeds of Davis's gospel of historical reinterpretation, meeting the disguised self-analysis of *The Purcell Papers*, flourished almost without reservation.

The story is set in the last days of Wharton's viceroyalty. Edmond O'Connor, a Catholic secretly returned from exile, is in love with Mary, sister of Sir Henry Ashwoode, Protestant, Whig, and scoundrel. The two dominant conflicts in the baronet's life are his resistance to his sister's love-match and his own falling into the hands of Nicholas Blarden through gambling, forgery, and blackmail. Rarely do the central figures converge on a single house or place, for class separates Ashwoode from the vulgar ruffianism of Blarden, and religion separates him from O'Connor and his associates. Indeed Le Fanu makes no attempt to show how Edmond and Mary contrived to meet each other in the first instance. Ashwoode's vice is an extension of political intolerance and rapacity, while O'Connor in contrast is not greatly concerned in ideological matters. The returned exile, however, meets eloquent enthusiasts for the old regime, and their exhortations are the most vivid of the novel: 'over-ridden, and despised, and scattered as we are, mercenaries and beggars abroad, and landless at home—still something whispers in my ear that there will come at last a retribution, and such a one as will make this perjured, corrupt, and robbing ascendancy a warning and a wonder to all after times.'[1] The terms in which Le Fanu describes the Williamites of 1710 are as violent as any he had used of Daniel O'Connell; repeatedly the novel condemns 'the usurpers, the perjurers, and the plunderers who now possess the wealth and dignities of this spoiled and oppressed country'.[2] These indictments of the Whig regime are never answered either by O'Connor (to whom they are addressed) or the Ashwoodes (whom they implicitly condemn). While he is indifferent to such exhortations and denunciations, O'Connor is not unaffected by political passion, though his involvement is presented as an accidental one. When he loses his way in the tangled wood near Finiskea House, ensnaring vegetation draws him towards the heart of a Jacobite con-

---

[1] *The Cock and Anchor*, i. 20.
[2] Ibid. iii. 15.

spiracy. To emphasize his real identification beneath the surface 'accident', O'Connor here meets and is rescued by his father's dearest friend who, though a rescuer, is also a conspirator. The danger which O'Connor faces is that he shall be refused recognition as his father's son. There is a deeply ironical logic to Le Fanu's presentation of the unwilling politico, for the site of this ensnarement is the latter-day Phoenix Park, the site of the Le Fanus' closest identification with the Williamite establishment.

The connection between this plot and the author's own political ideas is complex. He had been led, perhaps without adequate consideration, into the counsels of the Irish Metropolitan Conservative Society, an extreme if slightly ludicrous conservative forum. His motives were those of family honour and caste loyalty, but experience quickly taught him that politics brought more torment, dirty work, and paradox than he had imagined. As he told his mother, he simply wished to live free from fighting. In *The Cock and Anchor* O'Connor is similarly placed, surrounded by zealots whose beliefs he shares but whose fanaticism he deprecates; he too wishes simply to settle down quietly with his beloved Mary. Although at this level the novel is anti-political, Le Fanu makes it clear that O'Connor is opposed by an ideology (Whiggery) which he too detested. The Whiggery of 1710 was Protestant, but that of 1845 had powerful Catholic connotations. Whiggery throughout the ages was the betrayer of traditional powers and properties. 'What is Whiggery?' Yeats asked in 'The Seven Sages'. His definition would have pleased the author of *The Cock and Anchor:* 'a levelling, rancorous, rational sort of mind'.

If this sounds like critical ventriloquism—attributing to an eighteenth-century Catholic the anxieties of a nineteenth-century Protestant—then Le Fanu himself sanctioned the tactic. O'Connor, walking through Dublin, pays a very un-Catholic attention to St. Patrick's Cathedral, and the tavern he stays in has a most inappropriate antiquity in which 'the saintly Cromwell might have smoked and boozed'.[1] The Cromwellian metaphor dogs O'Connor to a degree inexcusable if he were simply a Jacobite hero; his kindly guardian, we are told, looked very like a 'Cromwell guiltless of his country's blood'.[2] The evidence of

---

[1] Ibid. i. 73.
[2] Ibid. i. 167.

O'Connor's real significance is not restricted merely to these anomalous images, for the novel introduces a third political standard—the Protestantism of Jonathan Swift. In the seventeenth chapter Le Fanu allows Swift and Joseph Addison to stand in momentary contrast to the flippant corruption of their master, Wharton. As characters they are weightless, but as emblems of right government and true Christianity they make a point economically. They also rescue, perhaps insufficiently, *The Cock and Anchor* from the rigid pattern of team confronting team by introducing the possibility of a political attitude drawing the best (for Le Fanu, the most conservative) qualities from each party. Furthermore, for Le Fanu, Swift had a personal relevance as the fountain-head of a family tradition stretching back through the Sheridans to the years of the Huguenots' arrival in Ireland. The close of the novel echoes other personal associations; the two lovers are separately making their way towards Ardgillagh, a 'wild wooded domain' in a southern county. This, of course, is really Abington, and the protector to whom Mary Ashwoode appeals is her uncle Oliver French, a sound Protestant Tory of the Swift variety. Yet he is also a negating figure, for his protection is helpless in the face of corrupt Whartons and violent conspirators; he is an invalid and a hermit; his mansion is already in the first stages of collapse. Nor does Ardgillagh see any reunion of the lovers, as the heroine dies before Edmond reaches her. As a bonus, however, Mary's death may be seen as Le Fanu's successful purging of the trauma of his sister's death.

The merits of *The Cock and Anchor* are commonplace. It is a gripping story, richer in incident than character. Though it is more fluent than *Torlogh O'Brien*, the two share a central image of great significance. Like Charles Lever's *Jack Hinton* or Butt's *Gap of Barnesmore*, Le Fanu's Irish novels adopt the plot of 'racial marriage'. The romantic narrative, of hero and heroine from different camps falling in love, enacts in fiction the Young Ireland programme, the reconciliation of Catholic and Protestant, Celt and Saxon, in the common name of Irishman. But where the more conventional saw Victorian female vulnerability in the aboriginal, the female in Le Fanu's fiction is associated with corruption and confiscation—though innocent herself—and the male is dispossessed and relatively helpless. While this may take on psychological importance in the light of his subsequent treatment of the sexes, politically the implication is of his pessimistic toleration of *The Nation's* policy. He accepted the outer shape of this historical fiction but rewrote its inner logic to accord with his own defensive view of history. Compared to *The Purcell Papers*, however, this new view of history was more dynamic; the obsessive claustrophobic imagery of 'Robert Ardagh' and 'The Last Heir of Castle Connor' had been exchanged for an extended metaphor which at least posited a union between opposites. Willing to explore this 'racial marriage' in two novels, Le Fanu's treatment of the theme varies between *The Cock and Anchor* and *Torlogh O'Brien*. In the first he felt compelled to make two crucial reservations: the enterprising hero or heroine is willy-nilly manipulated by the excesses of his or her party to a degree which virtually excludes individual initiative and freedom, and—equally important at least—the locus of their frustrated union is the semi-ruined landscape of Ardgillagh/Abington, its personification a bed-ridden old bachelor. Here political pessimism, or the caution which led to rejection of the dream of Repeal at the I.M.C.S., finally conquers the exploratory myth.

In *Torlogh O'Brien* Protestant Grace Willoughby and Catholic Torlogh O'Brien are married, and the location is specifically called Muroe, that is, the Catholic parish coterminous with the Dean's Abington. Thus the dying imagery which draws *The Cock and Anchor* to a close—ruined Ardgillagh, bedridden Oliver French, the expiring heroine, and the exiled soon-to-be-slain hero—is replaced by a marriage (two marriages in fact), solemnized in the same place. If Gavan Duffy adjusted the portrayal of Sarsfield and Tyrconnell in April 1846, it seems reasonable to attribute this optimistic conclusion to the influence of the Young Ireland movement. Yet *The Cock and Anchor* is recognizably Le Fanu's true assessment of the potential of Irish politics and the significance of Irish history, for in retrospect we can see that it accords with the tenor of his subsequent fiction as well as that of *The Purcell Papers*. *Torlogh O'Brien* is the odd man out.

In 1845 when Le Fanu's first published novel reached the public, a sense of political fluidity affected both conservative unionists and liberal nationalists. The latter were more anxious to proselytize than their opponents, whose embarrassment was compounded by the contempt which they felt Peel held them in.

Gavan Duffy, who had been successful with a press association
in 1838 and now with the Banim committee, soon had graver
reasons for seeking the conservatives' aid. Famine and epidemic
spread throughout Ireland, and with Davis dying in September
1845, the leadership of Young Ireland fell to Gavan Duffy. To
combat the government's complacency, a general assembly of
Irish opinion was proposed. The organizers were careful to limit
the expressed aims of the notion to effective action against famine,
but it was nevertheless clear that such a gathering would bring
Tories and Radicals together on a more substantially political
programme than any previously attempted. William Smith-
O'Brien, fellow Repeal MP with Caleb Powell for county Limerick, secured the support of a few country gentlemen, and there
were fanciful rumours that Protestants as a body might swing
towards nationalism in the extremity of the country's plight.
Among the intellectuals, Samuel Ferguson, Isaac Butt, Dr Henry
Maunsell, and Le Fanu promised their assistance. Maunsell, the
least known of the four, later became Le Fanu's partner in the
Dublin Evening Mail, and his recruitment to this joint action-
committee gave some promise that the middle-class Protestants
of Dublin were not entirely beyond redemption. Samuel Ferguson,
whom Gavan Duffy recruited personally, was less ordinary;
scholarly, sensitive, but hardly original, he had none the less
publicly identified himself with the idea of a Protestant movement
for Repeal. Throughout his long life his combination of literary
nationalism and social conformism made him an archetypical
Victorian. The more difficult recruits, Butt and Le Fanu, were
the responsibility of John Mitchel and John Francis Meagher.
Gavan Duffy must have had every confidence of Le Fanu's
support when he chose these intermediaries, who were decidedly
more aggressive Repealers than Gavan Duffy himself. Thomas
Wallis, the professor of patriotism in Le Fanu's Trinity days,
had warned the Young Ireland leader: 'Beware of scaring the
timid or wavering among them by any untimely trumpeting of
the ultimate consequences of their accession . . . We shall see
now what Butt and Le Fanu, and the other minds of the young
Conservative party, have to say for themselves.'[1]

If tact was required in handling a Tory of Le Fanu's nervous
disposition, then Meagher was an unwise choice of negotiator

[1] Reported by C. Gavan Duffy, *Four Years of Irish History,* p. 405.

who did not earn his nickname (Meagher of the Sword) for tact. It still remains incontestable that in the spring of 1847 Le Fanu promised his support to Mitchel and Meagher for the Irish Council. In 1846 he had made a sardonic assessment of the dangers to Young Ireland arising from within its own camp:

It remains to be seen, however, whether, the Repeal party is worthy of an organ of sterling genius and integrity. If the *Nation* is crushed, it is clear there exists not a particle of independence in Popish Ireland . . . With all their errors and mischief to answer for, the Young Ireland party carry with them the sympathies even of those who hate Repeal . . .[1]

Perhaps the same forensic interest in seeing how they would stand up to Popery and Whiggery prompted him to join Mitchel and Meagher the following year. April 1847, of course, was an exceptional moment in Irish history. Engineering at Burnfort near Mallow, William Le Fanu rescued a number of corpses from the dogs, a service he could have repeated through a year's tour of the island. Extraordinary measures were given desperate consideration in the face of what Irishmen of all creeds recognized as a disastrous imperial policy.

Despite this widespread realization of the country's peril, the *Dublin University Magazine* said comparatively little about the Famine in the years between 1845 and 1847. Carleton's historical but tragically topical *Black Prophet* was serialized from May to December 1846, and in April 1847 Butt returned to the columns with a forty-page analysis of the national disaster and the remedies it called for. The invitation from Mitchel and Meagher coincided with this initiative by his colleague and friend, and as his own *Torlogh O'Brien* had completed its final instalment, Le Fanu was carried over by its concluding imagery of reconciliation into agreement with the Young Irelanders. Nothing came of the Irish Council, and perhaps its very ineffectiveness allowed Le Fanu to extend tentatively his new contacts. *The Nation* had risen in his estimate, perhaps because its Tory counterpart was in the doldrums. Conservatism in Ireland had little to offer either intellectually or practically, and the haters of Repeal—among them some who flirted with the idea in 1840—were essentially haters of O'Connell. Gavan Duffy recorded that *The Nation* gained new contributors in 'Black '47', including one who 'bore

[1] Quoted ibid. 268.

an historic name, familiar not only in Ireland but throughout Europe'. Might this not be Sheridan Le Fanu, whose combination of names included just this blend of fame and exoticism, of local and foreign elements? The meagre details known of this anonymous contributor would confirm rather than refute the speculation, for he had said to Gavan Duffy: 'Though I do not agree with you in politics, I admire and value your definite truthfulness and consistent advocacy, and would gladly do anything in my power to assist, either in prose or verse, the literary department of your journal.'[1] Le Fanu must be a candidate here as Gavan Duffy's unknown supporter. 'Shamus O'Brien' had been written eight years earlier, and remained unpublished; *Torlogh O'Brien* (Le Fanu's repetitive use of names is already evident), in which Gavan Duffy had had a hand, was now being issued in a single volume; there was no shortage of ostensibly 'national' material in his file. A Tory, who had gone so far as to welcome a delegation including Mitchel and Meagher, might well proceed to write verse for Gavan Duffy. Yet the fact remains that nothing definite is known of any contribution of Le Fanu's in *The Nation*.

The events of the next twelve months destroyed this *rapprochement* between liberals and conservatives. First, Daniel O'Connell's death was exploited by his followers to whip up pious emotion of so decidedly Catholic a kind as to scare off any nervous Protestant recruits to the Repeal cause. Then the general election of 1847 resulted in a landslide for those Repealers whose instinct was O'Connellite rather than Davisite; worse still the old alliance between Irish political Catholicism and English Whiggery seemed sure of revival. But most decisively for those whose tolerance of *The Nation* sprang from the futility of any other Protestant initiative, an insurrectionist faction suddenly emerged among the Repealers. Prominent among these were Mitchel and Meagher, Le Fanu's contacts of the previous April, and with them William Smith-O'Brien, MP for 'Ardgillagh'. In an instant, or so it seemed, Le Fanu's active political acquaintances revealed themselves as secret revolutionaries. Whereas in 1840 he had toyed with Repeal because otherwise 'every thing seems to promise a speedy & tremendous revolutionary explosion', in 1848 he found that his cautious acceptance of the Irish Council had put him in league with insurrectionists and socialists. The

[1] Ibid. 461n.

reservations which held *The Cock and Anchor* from a conclusive endorsement of *rapprochement* had been more than justified; the trouble was that Le Fanu's impulsive mind did not find these reservations an adequate consolation. Had he not committed himself unreservedly in *Torlogh O'Brien*, making a fatal admission, nurturing a mortal contamination? This son of the glebe-house had betrayed his heritage, had joined counsel with the ungodly, tainted his soul with treason. Only such a feeling of guilt and of revulsion against the self could have produced 'Some Account of the Latter Days of the Honorable Richard Marston of Dunoran', the tale with which Le Fanu greeted the 1848 Insurrection, an act of rebellion incited by men whom he had encouraged and led by men of his own class and locality.

Though 'Richard Marston' had begun to appear as early as April, and insurrection did not break out till July, the tale was written in the heady context of revolutionary alarm. It was a year of revolt in Europe, and in Ireland Mitchel's *United Irishman* inflamed the imagination of Smith-O'Brien, Meagher, and a few others. On 21 July Dublin was proclaimed, and by the end of the month the entire episode was virtually closed. William Le Fanu, now living in county Cork, recorded without anxiety on 3 August that Smith-O'Brien was rumoured to be marching on Cork with two hundred thousand men; by the following Sunday news of his arrest filtered through to Rathpeacon House. Yet William's calm was not quite undisturbed: on 2 August several of his friends had been arrested in Cork city on a charge of treason. One of them, Michael Joseph Barry, was a contributor to the *Dublin University Magazine* and *The Nation*, and the others, Denny Lane and Isaac Varian, were Protestants and members of Smith-O'Brien's inner council. The closeness of treason did not shock William as it did Joseph; he visited his friends in gaol and recorded his opinions in his diary. Months later, Caroline Norton, whose liberal but realistic social views William shared, wrote inquiring about the rebel trials, and speculated 'if these tedious uncertain ceremonies increase the respect for the law or *fester* in the people's minds'.[1] She reported that 'Smith-O'Brien's sister is gone to Madeira with her sick husband without hearing the verdict. I suppose there can be but one verdict, but the difficulty will be what punishment.' Given the authorities' adroitness in

[1] Caroline Norton to W. R. Le Fanu, 11 Oct. 1848.

choosing juries, the verdict was guilty, the sentence death. But the government had no wish to hang, draw, or quarter a baron's son, and so, after much delay engendered by the traitor himself, Smith-O'Brien was transported in July, Mitchel having already reached the Australian settlements.

Le Fanu's retreat from contamination began with Mitchel's prosecution for sedition in March 1848, and 'Richard Marston' follows on that trial rather than the July skirmishes. Le Fanu was worried by the trials, and used the *Dublin University Magazine* for diatribe as well as fiction; in June (just as the tale was concluding) he wrote of Mitchel:

It is impossible to read his speeches and writings, and not to be impressed with the striking evidences everywhere apparent, of that impetuous abandonment of self, which characterises the genuine fanatic . . . Mitchel wrote and spoke irrespectively of display; he gave us no pompous metaphors, no affected quaintness, no vapid parodies upon the style of 'Sartor Resartus'. He seems to have been equally destitute of vanity, and of fear. Ireland republicanised and communised was his engrossing idea . . .[1]

This is the vehemence of a man denouncing sins which he had all but committed himself, and until we reach Mitchel's republicanism the assessment is not without sympathy. It continues in ambiguous discussion of fanaticism, in the course of which the less impetuous epigoni are lacerated with scorn. Towards the end discordant notes are heard; apparently oblivious of Mitchel's and Smith-O'Brien's Protestant background, Le Fanu declares that 'the supremacy of British law in this country is actually maintained by and depends upon, the loyalty of Irish PROTESTANTS'. And then his anti-Catholicism leads him openly to sympathize with the prisoner:

To the cowardly deference to Roman Catholic disaffection, which has so uniformly characterised the Whigs, is attributable that policy of procrastination which has ended in making Mitchel a felon, his wife bereaved, and his children fatherless—all rather than enforce *at once* the milder law of sedition, to which four months since the now ruined convict was amenable—and this is mercy![2]

The moral was clear: an earlier warning would have saved Le

---

[1] *D.U.M.*, vol. 31 (June 1848), 785–786.
[2] Ibid. 788.

Fanu himself from taint by these rebels; just as Mitchel was now irrevocably a felon, so he was irredeemably contaminated. The error lay in placating Catholic opinion, in seeking the marriage of the sects and the tribes which *Torlogh O'Brien* had sanctioned.

Two familiar images, now urgently distorted, dominate 'Richard Marston'. Symbolic misalliance of the hero/villain blends with a continental source of corruption in the person of Mlle Eugenie de Barras, governess to Marston's daughter. Eugenie transcends the traditional role of arrogant servant by acting also as fair seducer, and the whole tale of murder, bigamy, adultery, and suicide is overlaid with a supernatural gloss pointed up by the motto which opens all three instalments: 'When Lust hath conceived, it bringeth forth Sin: and Sin, when it is finished, bringeth forth Death.'[1] The plot is quickly told: Marston murders his house-guest and cousin, Sir Wynston Berkley, and allows suspicion to fall on a servant, Merton. Eugenie blackmails her master, replaces her mistress, marries Marston when he is widowed, and, to add incest to injury, brings her 'brother' into the household only to have him finally exposed as her rightful husband. Marston commits suicide, convinced that his victim retains 'spurious life'.

It is, however, the manner and not the matter of the story which is important. From the outset there are apparent anomalies. Long before she is implicated in evil, Eugenie fears that she must be an 'ominous thing' in her mistress's eyes. When Marston discovers a liaison between Sir Wynston and Eugenie, it is he Marston who throws 'a guilty and furious glance' at the offenders. These details appear in the first instalment, and the second goes some way towards externalizing them—Marston's guilty look becomes an affair and an elopement, and Eugenie achieves a near-Satanic hold over the master. When Marston (the real murderer) discovers Merton skulking in the demesne, he shouts 'murderer' and fires his pistol which fails to go off. In fact Marston and Merton have been advancing in parallel through the story. At the outset, Marston had recalled a gipsy's prophecy that he would kill his cousin, while Merton simultaneously begs permission to leave Dunoran to avert some unknown calamity. On the night of the murder Merton is seen near the baronet's room,

[1] Jas. 1:15.

with blood on his hands, and his disappearance the next morning is taken as a mute confession. As narrative 'Richard Marston' raises the moral chestnut about intention and commission. Le Fanu isolates two extremes in Marston (who actually but perhaps unknowingly kills) and Merton (who knowingly intends to kill but discovers his crime already committed). These may appear to be figures in contrast but in fact they should be seen as twin images of one central personality shown in montage. Nor is Merton the only secondary figure into which the title-character's actions are drawn. Berkley is a memento of Marston's past, and the urge to kill stems from revulsion against the past and its folly. At the second climax, Marston's suicide repeats Berkley's death in that both die in the same manner and by the same hand, a point which Le Fanu emphasizes. In this melodramatic plot we can see a single obsession—the futile attempt to obliterate the past, to cancel Fate.

The past is identified by Eugenie, the continental. It is her liaison with Berkley which spurs Marston to kill, but Marston is soon himself ensnared in an illicit sexual alliance with her. When he is tormented by visions of his victim dogging him in squalor and contempt, it is clear that this Berkley is a self-projection of Marston's impoverished and ostracized condition. Ultimately only suicide wipes the slate clean. If the governess stands for the French principles of *The Purcell Papers*—and she is both an usurper in the Great House and a seeming demon—her role has been prefigured in Marston's relationship with his legal wife. Pious and neglected, Mrs Marston is weightless in the plot. Her husband has already lost the religious convictions which sustain her; his scepticism is both the cause and the expression of their estrangement. Consequently, as the tale opens we find Marston already half-way towards a total reorientation of his existence. The Frenchwoman not only replaces Mrs Marston as wife but also as the temporary focus of Marston's entire vision of life. This focus can never be permanently established, because she is in league with his victim; in fictional terms a dangerously narrow cycle of alliances tightens round the hero/villain; in ideological terms Marston is subversively attaching himself to values which he also needs to annihilate. Marriage between opposing forces is the grand motif of the two novels which preceded 'Richard Marston', and the contradiction of this theme is now dramatized in the

volatile alliance of Great House and French principles. Le
Fanu's flirtation with Gavan Duffy, Mitchel, and Meagher, his
response to Young Ireland and *The Nation*, is the energy behind
this study in inescapable guilt. Unlike *The Purcell Papers*,
'Richard Marston' flamboyantly eschews all allusions to a political
dimension; in its setting and locale it is only sufficiently precise
to deny any identification with 'Ardgillagh'. This silence is itself
a political volte-face.

To a high Tory of Le Fanu's kind, and especially one who
had experienced the violence of the Tithe War, French principles
involved more than political morality. Shaken by his self-betrayal
in *The Cock and Anchor* and *Torlogh O'Brien*, he reintroduced into
'Richard Marston' the religious unease which had been dormant
since the beginning of the decade. The Protestant rector,
Dr Danvers, plays a part superficially analogous to that of Father
Purcell, but profoundly more significant. He emphasizes the
importance of belief in the proper maintenance of the Great
House. Marston's discussions with him begin in indifference but
soon reach the high pitch of a desperate search for understanding.
The only fixity which he can achieve is despair; to his spiritual
comforter he says wearily, 'We have squabbled over religion long
enough, and each holds his own faith still. Continue to sun
yourself in your happy delusions, and leave me untroubled to
tread the way of my own dark and cheerless destiny.'[1] It is not
Danvers, however, who must be shaken off but Marston himself:

The human mind, I take it, must have either comfort in the past, or
hope in the future . . . otherwise it is *in danger*; to me the past is
intolerably repulsive—one boundless barren, and hideous golgotha of
dead hopes and murdered opportunities—the future still blacker and
more furious, peopled with dreadful features of horror and menace.
Sir, I do not exaggerate—between such as past, and such a future, I
stand upon this miserable present . . .[2]

Here is the rejection of longing which will characterize Le Fanu's
mature fiction and which already had been noted in his father's
clerical career. A correlation of Le Fanu's fiction and politics is
not achieved simply by an attempted autobiographical reading of
'Richard Marston', for the named figures—Marston, Merton,

---

[1] *D.U.M.*, vol. 31 (June 1848), 731.
[2] Ibid. 741.

Berkley, Eugenie—merge into a contorted continuum which prevents any identification with them. Instead, parallels to the political world are found in the concealed symbolic actions of the fiction—the anticipated guilt, the postponed and projected suicide. How far had Le Fanu compromised himself by allowing Gavan Duffy to colour his portrait of Sarsfield? What was the real enormity of his dealings with Mitchel and Meagher? These self-lacerating questions spurred his attack on Whiggery and rebellion in the June and July articles in the *Dublin University Magazine*: 'Richard Marston' dramatizes similar enquiries. Did guilt require the commission of an offence, or simply the intention? Did death punish equally the actual and intending killers? If Marston had abandoned his traditional love, pious and socially recognizable Gertrude Marston, and allied himself with the foreign, subversive, and ultimately demonic mademoiselle, Le Fanu himself had drifted from the Tory *Dublin University Magazine* towards the crypto-revolutionary *Nation*. Nor was it possible simply to walk back into the straight and narrow path, for the automatic assumption of religious belief which true Toryism required was no longer available to him. Whether doubter or outright sceptic, his self-conscious anxiety about belief barred the way back to his father's harmony of church and state. Politically he had separated himself from the orthodox party-men, and imaginatively he could not return. Le Fanu's heroes from Marston onwards will be moulded by that betrayal; they will lose belief in God but still fear the Devil; they will live in the discrepancy between faith and salvation, for scepticism cannot simply be abandoned. And whereas the heroes of *The Purcell Papers* were enlarged to the point of being representative of their despised class and creed, the future heroes will be mavericks, shunned by their peers and suspected in their own communities.

The 1840s were traumatic years for Sheridan Le Fanu. They established an actual area of offence in which he discovered his own conflicting interests, his own momentary but affecting self-betrayal. In psychological terms, he treated the decade as a hysterical personality reacts to trauma, circling round and round in painful fascination. Even more potent was the discovery that the outer world offered little or no opportunity to him to alter the conditions of his existence; there was no escape from the dark country of his anxieties, for class kept him from the adventurism of *The Nation* and doubt held him aside from full-blooded reaction. A brave engagement with the world had resulted only in a dangerous isolation, an exploration of reconciled antagonisms had produced a paradoxical self-division.

4

LOVE AND DEATH

IN MAY 1841, when Joseph and William Le Fanu first visited the house on Merrion Square which subsequently became the novelist's home, George Bennett presided over a large family. Jane, his eldest surviving daughter, had married Delves Broughton in 1835, and in time she became the mother of Rhoda Broughton whose fiction first appeared in the *Dublin University Magazine* under Le Fanu's editorship. There remained four sons and four daughters: George who married Henrietta Kinehan in 1845 and died in 1853; John who became head of the family on his father's death and lived at Grange in King's County; Elizabeth Pigot who was born on 17 June 1815 and remained unmarried; Eleanor; Edmund; Mary and William (who was just fourteen in 1841). Susanna was the third youngest of the family, being eighteen at the time of her meeting with Le Fanu. Among the guests at Bennett's was G. W. Hemans, son of the poetess and an engineering colleague of William's.

Within two and a half years Le Fanu had married Susanna Bennett, but the course of their courtship remains obscure. The imagery of frustrated courtship in *The Cock and Anchor* may be nothing more than a conventional feature of the Scott-ish models which he had chosen, but within the Bennett circle there were further complications. Among the girls, the liveliest was Elizabeth, 'Bessie', closer in age to both Joseph and William than Susanna. By mid-1842 Joseph was in correspondence with Bessie, employing a half-bantering, half-defensive code to describe his relationship with the Bennett girls. 'Miss Smith' was the code-name of the girl to whom he might declare his intentions, but in the few letters which survive it is not clear whether Bessie or Susanna is referred to; at times the ambiguity appears to be deliberate. He writes to Bessie for 'Miss Smith's' address (suggesting that Bessie is not the object of his immediate interest) but proceeds to declare that he has been in 'agonies of suspense', 'expecting the required information relative to the great case of E. Bennett v.

E. Smith, and I have now once for all to inform you . . . that unless I am treated with the utmost candour & the utmost confidence I can not professionally take any further part in "Bennett v. Smith".'[1] In a subsequent letter the same jaunty style is maintained though the incidental imagery becomes significant if we recall that Le Fanu was shortly to write 'Spalatro':

My dear Miss Bennett

You can not be more afraid of me than I am of you. To your terrified letter I sit down in a panic to write a reply. This comes of mutual detection. I am acquainted with your malice & you are cognisant of my malignity. Mutual acquaintance has produced reciprocal trepidation and I am convinced that nothing but a scheme of such a diabolical nature as that which your note develops could have established a communication between us.

I have sketched in my mind the kind of epistle for Miss Smith—a sort of passionate, romantic, semi-religious effusion such as a sentimental Puseyite might be supposed to indite, but I do not know where to send it. Where does Miss Elizabeth Smith make her layer [i.e. lair]? . . . A dreadful thought strikes me. Just suppose me to have penned, as you suggest, my anonymous tale of love, and suppose by the malice of the Devil (whom I take to be an especial friend of Miss Smith) some accidental break down in the machinery of the affair to convict me plainly of the authorship of the passionate document, and suppose—Oh thunder & turf—suppose my receiving an answer duly addressed to Joseph Le Fanu Esq 2 Nelson St. accepting (for a desperate wretch like that will do anything) I say *accepting* my offer & (Merciful heaven!) calling on me to fix the happy day, and suppose old Smith naturally anxious, upon any terms, to get rid of his youngest darling & justly believing that no impulse short of demoniac possession could make any man take her off his hands . . . Suppose me I say to yield—the thought is too tremendous for human endurance. My brain reels.

I can readily imagine your villainous enjoyment as you behold me in funeral procession return to breakfast after having suffered hymeneal execution. I can conceive your visiting my bride and imagine your wishing me joy—you *joy*!—Add thumbscrews & crucifixion, any torture but that.[2]

---

[1] Bennett Papers; J. T. S. Le Fanu to Elizabeth Bennett, dated Sunday 31 July. All subsequent references in this chapter to 'Bennett Papers' refer to letters from Le Fanu to Elizabeth Bennett, with identifying date (where possible) added.

[2] Bennett Papers; undated letter concluding 'Sunday (!!!) 2 Nelson St.'

Difficult though it be to recapture the precise tone in which these letters were written—and read—a nervous discrepancy between what is stated and what is implied is obvious. Le Fanu's lack of sympathy with 'Miss Smith's' religious views (or at least those of her family) is emphasized by the manner in which he dates his letter—'Sunday!!!'—thus confessing himself a letter-writer on the Sabbath. In an undated letter, probably of August 1842, he is careful to establish a formal mode of address to his future sister-in-law, though the substance of the letter is, if anything, even more suspect than the imagery of daemoniac connivance in love-pacts:

My dear *Sister*
... I am happy to hear that you were fitting yourself for the fulfilment of my production when you return to Dublin. I am happy I repeat that you are acquainting yourself with the duties of married life & imbibing principles of conjugal obedience & fidelity from that, shall I call it, *inspired*, volume which I sent by post to her in whose obedience I am most interested. My other reasons for purchasing the book are to be found in the resemblance (which I proudly admit) between my *character* & that of Bluebeard, & between Susy's style of beauty & that of *Mrs.* Bluebeard. Perhaps the latter weighed most with me. I must now conclude. So believe me ever my dear old adviser your affectionate *brother*.

J. T. S. Le Fanu.[1]

The first acknowledgement of Joseph's status as suitor to Susanna which survives is this curious letter in which Bessie's participation in amateur dramatics, her practical education in married life (the family were staying with Mrs Jane Broughton at the time), and Joseph's recommendation of *Bluebeard*, are all framed in a letter which stresses the brother/sister relationship which should exist between him and Bessie. Susanna indeed appears only in the mechanical phrase—'her in whose obedience I am most interested'—and in the allusion to Bluebeard's victim.

Between this flirtatious correspondence with Bessie and his eventual marriage to Susanna, Le Fanu published 'Spalatro', a story in which daemoniac possession, religious hypocrisy, and sexual fantasy mingle strangely. Catherine Le Fanu's death in March 1841 undoubtedly contributed much to the psychological

[1] Bennett Papers; undated letter: the envelope in which it is preserved suggests that it was posted in August 1842.

disturbance which the story reveals, but the intervening correspendence with Bessie Bennett provides further evidence of Le Fanu's nervous concern with the themes which flourish exotically in the short story. But despite certain Bennett reservations (understandable in the light of Joseph's relationship with Bessie) he was married to Susanna on 18 December 1843 in St. Peter's Church, by consistorial licence. The Revd George Bennett, the bride's eldest brother, conducted the service, and the official witnesses were Isaac Butt and Edmund Bennett.[1] The couple travelled to Abington Glebe in time for Christmas, though not before the wedding breakfast which Joseph had teasingly prophesied to Bessie eighteen months earlier. On St. Stephen's Day he wrote from his parents' home to his old adviser:

My dear little Bessie
I sit down to write with real pleasure to you, my good, old, sincere friend. Dear Sue is looking very well, but [?scraggy] She & Miss Knowles are becoming bosom friends, sing duets together, etc. I think I never saw my father & mother take such a fancy to any creature as they have done to my dear little wife. They are *delighted* with her. She sings & plays for them & chats away I think a great deal more than I ever heard her do at home. She is as merry as a lark, & for my part I am ten thousand times more in love with her than ever. This day she is looking better & even prettier than she has done for the last week. I write this note exclusively upon the subject of little Sue & the impression she has produced here, as I thought you would wish to hear of it. I remain my dear little old Sister,
Ever I am affectionately
J. T. S. Le Fanu
Write me a note you grand old cronie.[2]

An unusual honeymoon letter to somebody whom he might have felt it more delicate to leave in peace. Bessie, however, continued to attract attentions from risky sources, and within a few years she had disgraced herself in the family by secretly encouraging the affection of Charles Marlay Fleury, an elderly and married Huguenot clergyman who, by an ironic coincidence, had been a troublesome partner of Le Fanu's in *The Warder*. The years from 1838 to 1841 had been largely given over to the Irish Metropolitan Conservative Society, in which Le Fanu had hesistantly

[1] Details taken from the marriage register of St. Peter's Church, Aungier Street, Dublin, by kind permission of the Revd Canon Richard Dowse.
[2] Bennett Papers; letter headed 'Abington Glebe Tuesday 26 Decr. 1843'.

but persistently considered a radical adjustment of his political
loyalites. In the succeeding two years, courtship at Merrion
Square and by correspondence had carried this pattern of conflicting interests into his emotional life. It is not therefore surprising that, after December 1843, he turns to fiction to investigate in historical symbolism the tensions to which he had been
increasingly subject over the previous decade. *The Cock and
Anchor* adopts the conventional image of marriages between
warring factions, but in Le Fanu's case it is impossible to identify
either politics or marriage as the symbolism through which the
other is investigated. If 1848 had not, by its suddeness, destroyed
this intimate bond between theme and symbol, Sheridan Le
Fanu's historical fiction might have grown into something more
complex and fine than the two novels he had completed before
the rumours of violence and revolution disturbed the balance of
his imagination.

Though the writer in Le Fanu suffered a temporary eclipse
in 1848, ordinary reality persisted with a consoling richness.
Joseph and Susanna's first child, Eleanor Frances, was born on
10 February 1845, and fifteen months later a second girl was born
on 21 May 1846 and christened Emma Lucretia, after her paternal
grandmother. A son, Thomas Philip, arrived on 3 September
1847. At the age of thirty-three Le Fanu was the head of a growing household and, with the death of his father in June 1845, the
head of a larger family community also. As far as his income was
concerned, family inheritance did not provide adequate resources,
and he and his wife depended on his commercial rather than
professional earnings. The Bar had more or less failed him, and
partly by choice he came to rely on his interests in journalism for
his livelihood.

Given the desperate rhetoric of Protestant ascendency
journalism, the newspaper business inevitably brought problems
as well as profits, and on at least three occasions in the early years
of his marriage Le Fanu was involved in libel actions connected
with his papers. In 1845 a jury awarded £500 to Messrs Malcomson of Waterford (with costs against the defendants) resulting
from a letter in *The Warder* complaining generally of the evils of
the factory system. Le Fanu unwisely tried to take the case to a
higher court, with the result that on 9 August he was forced to
publish a bitter admission:

When the last publication of the Warder issued to our subscribers, the type, the printing machine, steam engine, and every article in the office of this journal, were under seizure by the officers of the Sheriff of the city of Dublin, under an execution at the suit of Messrs. Malcomson, for the damages recovered in their action. The execution was issued at a time when both propriators [*sic*] were absent from town.[1]

But the victims appeared to have bowed before the Court's decision and paid up in this instance. In connection with a controversy surrounding the dismissal of two prominent Orange magistrates, *The Warder* rashly accused the Lord Lieutenant of treachery to the cause it assumed him to support. The dispute raged between the editorial columns of *The Warder* and the *Dublin Evening Post* in the autumn of 1849. On 17 November Le Fanu's paper issued a warning to its rival, a warning which contained hidden evidence of insecurity:

We are authorised to state that one of the propriators [*sic*] of this journal, who has been attacked by name in a series of articles in the *Dublin Evening Post* is about to institute proceedings . . . We have to state that the gentleman so assailed is not the editor of this journal, and that the office of Tipstaff is not now worth ten pounds a year; although in the time of the gentleman's predecessors, it was of great emolument. It is unnecessary to inform any one at all acquainted with our courts of law that the office of Tipstaff has always been filled by gentlemen of high respectability.[2]

This action appears to have been settled out of court, though not before Le Fanu had been exposed to considerable abuse and ridicule.

He had reserves of good humour which helped him to cancel (or at least postpone) the effect of these tribulations. In March 1846 the two Le Fanu brothers with some engineering cronies of William's took a trip to London. The Adelphi Theatre could hardly supply amusement enough for the party, who travelled to Woolwich where they had 'one grand deal of fun'. According to William's meticulous diary, 'we put all our hats in a row in a field, and pelted them with stones, which afforded us great sport, but did our hats no good . . .'[3] The following year William's im-

---

[1] *The Warder*, 9 Aug. 1845, 4.
[2] Ibid. 17 Nov. 1849, 4.
[3] Diary, 29 Mar. 1846.

promptu suggestion of more fun got him into trouble with Susanna who had, admittedly, just given birth to a son three weeks earlier. (She would not allow Joe to go to Cork on the train with William.) The diary reports that Joe is a 'Wictim of Connubiality' and that Susanna gave her brother-in-law 'a grand rating', telling him that she hated him and that he was 'the most malicious person she ever knew'.[1] Relations between the two brothers survived of course, and in January 1848—just before the events reflected in 'Richard Marston' got under way—Joe read William an act and a half from a comedy in progress. Though William thought it very amusing, the play seems to have been a victim of those reversals of loyalty and ambition which 1848 came to stand for in Le Fanu's career.[2]

Throughout their lives William was a steadfast friend to his less stable brother, though as early as 1846 one of the recurring features of their relationship had been established. Practically the first entry in William's dairy records that Joe owed him £300 which, by the end of 1847, had become £367. As a railway engineer William was on the iron road to success, a fact which cost him £70 in a defaulted agreement involving Isaac Butt in 1848. The elder brother made hesitant, extreme, and ambiguous commitments to a radical realignment of Irish loyalties in his anonymous writings; William's more urbane manner allowed him to invite Morgan John O'Connell (the Liberator's son) to breakfast, to visit friends in prison when they were under suspicion of treason. The contrast is of diametrically opposed psychological types, brothers who nevertheless maintained a friendship of which William (who constantly bore the brunt of his brother's difficulties) never once made an adverse criticism in the privacy of his diary.

In 1850 Le Fanu was gathering together some of his tales for publication as a Christmas collection of *Ghost Stories and Tales of Mystery*, but publication was delayed until the New Year. 'Richard Marston', the story originally written during the gestation period of Irish rebellion, was included, but in an amended form which transferred the setting to England, altering the title to 'The Evil Guest'. This change of title emphasizes the continuity between Le Fanu's Irish historical fiction and the first tale of his reformed imagination, 'The Mysterious Lodger', which

---

[1] Diary, 20 Sept. 1847.
[2] Ibid. 7 Jan. 1848.

had been published anonymously in the *Dublin University Magazine* in January and February 1850. Apart from the similar titles, the two stories share an English setting, with the influence of a guest whose identity is at times nearly confused with that of the master of the house. But, whereas Richard Marston had been the luckless heir to landed estate, the nameless narrator of 'The Mysterious Lodger' is a meek, modern, city dweller worried by a debt of just £200.[1] It is not a good story, nor even an interesting one, unless we are prepared to consider the light it may shed on the author himself. Some details which the narrator provides are clearly inapplicable to Sheridan Le Fanu, though we are also told that the narrator's father had been 'a good, plain, country clergyman'. Religion, in fact, is the theme of this curious parable of a daemonic lodger who wears the modern garb of devilish concealment—goggles and respirator. The narrator is a student of 'Voltaire, Tom Paine, Hume, Shelley, and the whole school of infidels, poetical as well as prose'.[2] And the tenant whom he chooses in preference to a 'clergyman in ill health' describes himself as 'a Voltaire, without his luxuries—a Robinson Crusoe, without his Bible—an anchorite, without a superstition'.[3] The attempts which the narrator had previously made to undermine his wife's faith are successful in the lodger's more artful arguments, and the poor lady soon finds herself unable to pray; almost echoing Richard Marston she declares that there is something in her that resists prayer. Despite his earlier scepticism, the narrator is so repelled by his lodger's manner that he is willing, though unable, to help his wife find her old beliefs: 'inconsistent in me as the task would have been, I would gladly have explained away her difficulties, and restored to her mind its wonted confidence and serenity, had I possessed sufficient knowledge for the purpose.'[4] Before any restoration can be effected, the two children of the household die, apparently through the agency of the mysterious lodger. Dreams, omens, and the suffocation of a little girl in her coffin add conventional horror to the tale of lost faith. As in 'Spalatro' and in the curious relationship between Berkley and Marston in 'Richard Marston', the identity

[1] *D.U.M.*, vol. 35 (Jan. 1850), 54.
[2] Ibid. 54–5.
[3] Ibid. 59–60.
[4] Ibid. 63.

of two figures is suggested: the nameless narrator says of Mr Smith, his tenant:

all that he had said had floated through my own mind before, without order, indeed, or shew of logic. From my own rebellious heart the same evil thoughts had risen, like pale apparitions hovering and lost in the fumes of a necromancer's cauldron. His was like the summing up of all this—a reflection of my own feelings and fancies—but reduced to an awful order and definiteness, and clothed with a sophistical form of argument.[1]

Even when the lodger is not explicitly presented as the articulator of the narrator's own scepticism, a scepticism he had directed at his wife's faith, the relations between man and wife are contorted and ambiguous. One night she had risen from bed, feeling that for once she might be able to pray but 'somebody . . . clutched her arm violently near the wrist, and she heard, at the same instant, some blasphemous menace'. Screaming, she wakes her husband and catches his wrist 'in her icy grasp' and climbs 'trembling violently, into bed'.[2] Here, the narrator makes no attempt to suggest the real existence of their tenant; it is a scene of unconscious conflict, a scene repeated with variations later in the tale:

The room was perfectly dark, as usual, for we burned no night-light; but from the side of the bed next her proceeded a voice as of one sitting there with his head within a foot of the curtains—and merciful heavens! it was the voice of our lodger.

He was discoursing of the death of our baby, and inveighing, in the old mocking tone of hate and suppressed fury, against the justice, mercy, and goodness of God. He did this with a terrible plausibility of sophistry, and with a resolute emphasis and precision, which seemed to imply, 'I have got something to tell you, and, whether you like it or like it not, I *will* say out my say.'[3]

The persecution ends only after the death of both children, and the narrator finds consolation in the advice of another mysterious stranger. This figure about whom 'there was a grace, a purity, a compassion, and a grandeur of intellect in his countenance, in his language, in his mien, that was beautiful and kinglike' has appeared in the wife's dreams, and now speaks in biblical terms.

[1] Ibid. (Feb. 1850), 226.
[2] Ibid. (Jan. 1850), 64.
[3] Ibid. (Feb. 1850), 225.

He expounds a gospel of salvation through suffering, and in the last paragraphs of the tale he blesses the narrator and his household. But this angel of consolation never enters the house in which the lodger has been triumphant, and when the narrator's wife finally recognizes him through the window as a figure from her dreams 'there was a seraphic smile on her face—pale, pure, and beautiful as death'.[1] Little in the story itself can link its narrative to Sheridan Le Fanu's life, though the distancing techniques of *The Purcell Papers*—the historical dimension and the presentation of character as political type—have disappeared. Instead of the traditional treatment of the supernatural (the demon lover, the arrogant servant), 'The Mysterious Lodger' balances the influence of belief and scepticism by depicting the narrator as placed between two strangers; the advocate of belief, however, is even further removed from the narrative than was Father Purcell, and death informs the metaphor with which the tale closes.

In January 1851 Le Fanu published three 'Ghost Stories of Chapelizod' in the *Dublin University Magazine*, utilizing traditions recalled from his childhood in the Phoenix Park. These are the earliest signs of his mature fiction, being trial pieces for *The House by the Churchyard*, the first of the twelve novels written between 1861 and his death in 1873. Here his relation with the narrative is virtually that of an editor simply presenting the facts of legend, and none of the problems connected with a possible identification of narrator and author arise. Indeed his direct treatment of local material led to some good-humoured complaints, as he reported to his mother:

I was very much flattered by your appreciation of my Chapelizod Ghost Stories & was yesterday rather shocked by McGlashan [now the publisher of the *D.U.M.*] shewing me a letter from Sam O'Sullivan asking 'why has Le Fanu killed poor Bob Martin, who is now alive & well & filling his vocation as Sexton [?]' The possibility of this had struck me when I introduced him but I scouted it, for I remember him when I was a child, an old man. There can be no doubt that the story is a horrid libel on him & I live in daily expectation of a message.

The letter continues with further literary and familial gossip:

I yesterday met [William] Carleton [;] he had met Dick Knowles in London who was enquiring how I was & is writing away in a *ladies'*

<hr />

[1] Ibid. 235.

Newspaper but Carleton says 'the most bigoted papist he ever met in the course of his life', a bold assertion from a man familiar with the Irish priests. So that the Jesuits have made a mouthful of poor little Dick. Poor Sue is thank God, better, but still unable to walk up or down stairs . . .[1]

The two Le Fanu brothers were very attached to their mother, who shared a house with William until he married in 1857. She remained Joseph's only confidante until her death in 1861, a disaster which somehow released him from a compact of silence and permitted him to resume novel-writing. In the early 1850s their relationship included all the mutual assistance which characterized the Victorian family. William was retained by the directors of the Great Southern and Western Railway Company to investigate alternative Irish ports for development as a trans-Atlantic packet station, and Joseph's journalistic connections were naturally exploited to support William's findings. James McGlashan favoured the port of Galway, while William was reporting in favour of Cork. Joseph, however, was no economist and had to complain to his mother that the 'rascal Willy' had given him no material for an article on the packet station 'as at present I do not know a single good reason except the cheapness of coal why it should be in Ireland at all'.[2]

In 1852 Sheridan Le Fanu took steps to revive his political fortunes, after the embarrassment of 1848, by seeking the Tory nomination for Carlow county. If he were to have any hope of success, he needed the support of one of the sitting members, Colonel Henry Bruen, who had held the constituency virtually without interruption since 1812. The Colonel had been a vice-president of the Irish Metropolitan Conservative Society in the 1830s and might be expected to recall Le Fanu's more orthodox political past rather than his fictional deviations. In April William came to his brother's assistance in the pre-election manœuvres, but despite their canvassing the Colonel decided to stand once more. At the general election he was returned with John Ball (a contemporary of Le Fanu's at the Bar), but before the year was over the old man had died. Disregarding this second opportunity, Le Fanu made no further attempts to get a nomination, and the

---

[1] J. T. S. Le Fanu to Mrs E. Le Fanu 15 Jan. 1851.
[2] Ibid.

seat passed to Bruen's son. The commitment to action in the outer world had lasted less than six months.

Despite his mother's influence and his brother's constant assistance in money matters, Sheridan Le Fanu inevitably became closely involved in his wife's family. George Bennett, the father of the Munster Circuit, had been born in 1777 and in July 1850 he and his wife moved with their unmarried daughters to Sodylt Hall, Shropshire. Though George Bennett lived into his seventy-ninth year, there was a high mortality rate in his family, three of his thirteen children died under the age of one year, and his fifth son, Jonathan Lovett Bennett died of pleurisy in 1840 at the age of twenty. These deaths, though unexceptional in Victorian statistics, began to accumulate as a family burden, a burden Sheridan Le Fanu was peculiarly ill-fitted to acquire as dowry. In 1849 Cecilia Georgina, a daughter of Edmund Bennett, a witness with Isaac Butt at Joseph and Susanna's wedding, died aged eleven months. Among those who testified to her identity at the burial was Sheridan Le Fanu, and the inexplicable horror of a child's death finds morbid expression in 'The Mysterious Lodger' published early the following year: 'why has not civilisation abolished these repulsive and shocking formalities? What has the poor corpse to do with frills, and pillows, and napkins . . .'[1] Ill-health dogged both Joseph and Susanna—scarletina, rheumatism, gout in his case, and a recurring ailment probably of psychosomatic origins in Susanna's.

In the spring of 1851, she fell seriously ill. Her sister, Bessie, was living outside Ireland, partly as a result of her flirtation with the Revd Mr Fleury. Once again, she and Joseph began to correspond, and he maintained something of the ambiguity of his letters of 1842–3. The tone of his comments on his wife's health, on Bessie's admirer, on politics and newspapers, suggests that he instinctively absorbed attitudes and mannerisms from the individual with whom he was in immediate contact. Thus, with Bessie Bennett, he was casual, witty, and even *risqué*; with his mother pious and responsible; there is even a letter written in baby-talk to his younger son while the boy was at Rugby. This negative sympathy is another aspect of the novelist's ability to reach imaginatively inside characters of contrasting styles, but it is also a manifestation of his personality's central fluidity. The

---

[1] *D.U.M.*, vol. 35 (Feb. 1850), 232.

principal characters of Le Fanu's novels are absorbed with the problem of their own identity, which they often find is definable only in terms of guilt. In this light we should see Le Fanu's letters to his sister-in-law as being the product of her imagination as well as of his; the *double entendre* is a matter of mimicry rather than moral ambiguity. The earliest of these letters describes the unfortunate Fleury and then passes on to mention Susanna Le Fanu's apparent recovery:

I saw your old man yesterday. His 'fit has left him weak'. His face is withered above & puffy below, & of the colour of a floured chicken in a poulterer's shop. His clothes are fit for nothing but to make mops of & he had a large hole in the front of his shirt through which his parchment bosom was visible . . . I did not shew your letter to Sue, as Mrs. Bennett thought she might be jealous at getting none herself. So I have kept it a secret & should you write to her do not allude to *it* or to Mary's or I should get into a scrape.[1]

Two weeks later, on 20 May 1851, Le Fanu describes his wife's recovery more fully but allows his humour to satirize his father-in-law:

Poor little Sue is now thank God doing well. I carried her down to the drawingroom today where she lies on the sofa. She is not of course permitted to stand, nor indeed can she sit, yet. The dear little mother quite well. The father had an indifferent night, hot & coughing, attributable to having dined *hotly* with Alderman Kinahan & left the house *without* his respirator. Fleury is almost quite well but did no duty on Sunday.[2]

Injunctions against telling Susanna about correspondence between the Bennetts and her husband were repeated on several occasions. Not only Bessie but her sister Mary and her mother were in the conspiracy. When Susanna developed scarlet fever, the risk of infection being transmitted complicated the motives of the conspirators, and Joseph requested that Bessie should write to him at the University Club—a pointless precaution, as far as medicine is concerned, as the risk lay in transmitting infection on letters *from* Joseph. But before this graver crisis, the Le Fanus made a trip to the Bennetts' new home in Shropshire where Joseph helped to establish the garden. Writing to Bessie

[1] Bennett Papers, 7 May 1851.
[2] Ibid. 20 May 1851.

in exile, he reported that 'the plants I put down in the garden at Sodylt are doing best of all, & so I please myself with the thought of having left a memorial of my visit at that sweet place, which I fear I shall not see for a long time again.'[1] By June 1852 his correspondence with his sister-in-law was flourishing. Either he shared Bessie's attitude to religion or was drawn into a dangerous mimicry of her scepticism; and, with the Fleury flirtation as an additional source of banter, the correspondence took on a more intimate tone, revealed a more personal need for companionship on his part:

I do not myself fear infection except from *patients*, but I know that some people do & that even a letter however welcome on some accounts, is to them at best what the ocean in a breeze was to Lord Byron 'a pleasing terror'. I am however delighted to hear that neither you nor dear Mary are afraid & that I may soon hope for some news of your diving & paddling in the sea of Barmouth & of all your other doings, sayings & plans. With respect to *Antipathiser* he is not the nameless individual whom you obviously suspect, but a philosophical accoucheur & pie-house Christian called Peebles, who lives in Dorset Street & gives good dinners to the apostles & a good delivery to their wives. If you have any message to send to this Evangelical accoucheur you can communicate through some one of you clerical correspondents as I do not know him. As to your impertinence about my *scrap* containing as much infection as a *long letter*, *that* I pardon for its imbecility. The degree of infection is proportioned to the surface, & a square inch is to a square foot as 1 is to 144! I sent therefore in my scrap about 144 times less infection than I send in this present writing. If however you take the complaint (which notwithstanding your 'sauce' I don't desire.) & become a 'scarlet lady' in that sense, you are not to blame me for it.[2]

Such joking, even if it be ascribed to Le Fanu's tendency to assume the attitudes of his correspondents, could hardly have pleased his wife. His relations with Bessie had been curious from the outset, and Susanna had become increasingly nervous with the passing years. It is unlikely that she knew of this correspondence and certainly was ignorant of its contents. Nevertheless, as Joseph's later diary reveals, she had sensed a fundamental insecurity in their marriage. In 'An Authentic Narrative of a

---

[1] Ibid. 6 Sept. 1851.
[2] Ibid. 19 June 1852. The 'pie-house Christian called Peebles' was no frivolous invention; John Peebles, M.D., F.R.C.S.I., lived at 26 Upper Dorset Street and was surgeon-accoucheur to the House of Industry hospitals.

Haunted House' which Le Fanu published in 1862, he describes
a summer resort to which the narrator and his wife have retired
as invalids. He dates the story to about eight years earlier, that is,
to 1853 or 1854. Illness and convalescence are recurring images
of isolation and relationship in his fiction.

During the first ten years of their marriage, the Le Fanus had
spent various prolonged periods at Bray, Malahide, and Kings-
town—any one of which would fit the description in 'An Authentic
Narrative'. It is difficult to follow their movements during this
period. They lived in Warrington Place till 1850, and sometime
shortly afterwards moved into Merrion Square with the Bennetts.
George Bennett was in the process of retiring to Shropshire, and
may in fact have vacated his Dublin house in order to provide
Susanna and her husband with a home sufficiently large for their
growing family. In February 1853 her brother George (who lived
in Belfast) died of a fever and was brought to Dublin for burial.
He was only forty, and he was quickly followed to the grave by
two of his brother Edmund's children in 1853 and 1854. Bennett
mortality is important because of Susanna's reaction to it, its
effect on her religious attitudes, and Sheridan Le Fanu's concern
in writing of such themes. But after 'An Account of some Strange
Disturbances in Aungier Street', published in December 1853,
he did not attempt fiction for nine years, being caught up in the
increasing tension of his own domestic life, a tension probably
noticed by none outside the house on Merrion Square.

On 1 August 1854 the Le Fanus' fourth child was born, some
seven years after his elder brother. George Brinsley Le Fanu was
christened in honour of his maternal grandfather and his father's
illustrious ancestor. Family life seemed to have resumed its
normal outer forms; the Le Fanu brothers took walks to the
Grand Canal to watch the skaters; Susanna accompanied them
to the theatre and to promenades at the Viceregal Lodge. Joseph's
social life flowered in 1856; with his wife and his brother he
dined at Croker Barrington's, where his distant cousin Lord
Dufferin was a guest of honour; on 5 April the two brothers were
entertained at dinner in Dublin Castle by Lord Carlisle, the
newly appointed Lord Lieutenant. Under the surface, however,
pressure was building up within the Le Fanu family circle.

On Sunday 1 July 1855 William Le Fanu had gone to
St. Stephen's Church in Dublin, where the curate, the Revd

Henry Galbraith, preached on the text 'This man receiveth sinners'. William was struck by the sermon and immediately resolved to change his way of life, to repent, and to turn to God. When he reached home, he entered these resolutions in his diary, and put 1s. 11d. in the poor-box. The following Sunday he sought some devotional reading among his books and papers, read some of Butler's *Analogy of Religion* and 'Poor dear Catherine's writings'.[1] His church attendance, reading, and text-transcribing persisted to the end of the year, and as Joseph and Susanna's Merrion Square house was within sight of St. Stephen's Church, William's Sunday duties brought him into further intimacy with them. On 18 November he and Susanna stayed for Holy Communion after the regular service, though there is no reference in the diary to Joseph's devotions. During the early part of 1856, William and his sister-in-law established a habit of either taking lunch together or walking on Sunday afternoon through the suburban streets to Donnybrook. On 1 January they called to a reception at the Viceregal Lodge and left their names. On 23 January Joseph and William attended a levee together. Throughout this period, normal social duties were performed, but William in his recent religious fervour increasingly sought Susanna's company or, alternatively, she found his company as a believer helpful and pleasant. Joseph participated in the dinners, lunches, and sometimes even the walks, but apparently neglected his church attendance. There was nothing remarkable about William's religious experience; it was briefly intense but constantly circumscribed by Victorian rectitude. It never led him to the extremes of evangelicalism, with its rejection of the theatre and games— recreations which William enjoyed throughout his long life. It is not surprising to find that his period of fervour (which lasted between a year and eighteen months) came to an end with his engagement and marriage; it was in fact a very ordinary expression of low-key Victorian anxiety.

For Susanna, however, the tensions were more fearful. Her health constantly gave cause for unease, and her temper was at times irascible. Her parents had retired to Shropshire, and her relatives in Ireland were scattered from Belfast to King's County. She was living once more in the house on Merrion Square in which she had grown up, now in the company of her husband

[1] Diary, 15 July 1855.

and four children. Money was still a problem, and whether she knew it or not, her husband's debt to William was mounting; at the end of 1855 it had reached £500. To a nervous young woman, the roll-call of family deaths in these years was deeply disturbing, and the crisis of her father's death on 26 May 1856 brought about a major disruption of her emotional and spiritual life.

According to her husband's very brief diary, written two years later, Susanna had experienced trials of faith even before George Bennett's death:

A little before the death of her beloved father . . . my darling's mind was harrassed [sic] with incessant doubts about the truth of revealed religion. She was acute in detecting apparent weakness, & quick in suggesting difficulties, and I was much distressed, for she was too volatile & rapid to bear a protracted & minute argument, & although I thought I had the answer to her objection, yet her attention generally failed & passed off to some other difficulty before I had completed my reply. It grieved me to see my darling's faith unsettled & obscured . . .[1]

In such circumstances it is easy to see how valuable a companion William had been to his tormented sister-in-law, whose husband had not experienced the quickening of faith which she desperately sought and yet fought against. The language of Sheridan Le Fanu's memorandum is similar to that of 'The Mysterious Lodger' where the narrator's wife cannot pray, where the narrator is willing but unable to explain away her difficulties and restore her mind to serenity. In the melodrama of the fiction, two children die, their deaths being virtually assumed as inevitable by their mother: in the diary Sheridan Le Fanu records that Susanna reacted in a similar fashion: 'If she took leave of anyone who was dear to her she was always overpowered with an agonizing frustration that she should never see them again. If anyone she loved was ill, though not dangerously, she despaired of their recovery.'[2] Her volatility did find public expression on occasions. William had married Henrietta Victorine Barrington on 15 January 1857, and their first child was born on 30 December. Susanna was asked to be god-mother at the christening in

---

[1] This fragmentary diary has been transcribed and published by Jean Lozes, 'Fragment d'un journal intime de J. S. Le Fanu . . . 18 mai 1858', *Caliban* (new series), vol. 10, no. 1 (1974), 153–64. Though the extracts published in this study are based on an independent examination of the manuscript, references are provided to Lozes's transcription, 160.

[2] Lozes, 161.

February 1858, but refused in what William called 'a fit of Grumps'. Clearly, religious uncertainty could have prompted this refusal, though at the time Ellen (the Le Fanus' eldest child) was seriously ill with pleurisy. In either instance (or in both) the situation bore a striking resemblance to the domestic and spiritual crux in 'The Mysterious Lodger'. The contrast with William and Banky (as Henrietta was affectionately known) could not be more pronounced; the day after their marriage he had regaled her with a reading of 'The Last Heir of Castle Connor', one of Joseph's sombre early stories.

On 26 April 1858, two months after the fit of grumps, Susanna was taken dangerously ill with an hysterical attack. William spent all of the following day in Merrion Square supporting his brother in what soon proved to be Susanna's final struggle with death. At ten in the morning of 28 April she died. Within an hour, Joseph was writing to his mother:

My darling little mother,
   The greatest misfortune of my life has overtaken me. My darling wife is gone. The most affectionate the truest I think.
   Banky will write to you today. I do not well know what I am writing. I cannot believe it. Oh you cannot imagine the poor little letter to you which she was writing at the moment her attack seized her. My head is confused & I cannot say more. Pray to God to help me. My light is gone. For God's sake, write to me all you can ever remember of her. I thank my God for all his undeserved mercies. I have prayed in agony to be delivered from this most frightful calamity. But into his wise & merciful hands I put all things. I pleased myself with the thought that she would have outlived me for many years. She was wiser than I & better & would have been to the children what no father could be. I prayed to God for Christ's sake to accept her. She had true religion in her heart, & was always yearning after God & Christ, but so lowly in her thoughts of her spiritual state, that she was always asking me— unworthy—to pray for her. Oh my darling mother, you have lost much in her, but to me she was the light of my life & light in every day. I am trembling, but I beg of you to write to me. I had my farewell word—Oh look through her letters to you & copy any words in which she said I loved her & was kind to her. I adored her.
                                        I am your affectionate son
                                                J: S: Le Fanu[1]

[1] J. T. S. Le Fanu to Mrs E. Le Fanu, 28 Apr. 1858.

William took charge of the funeral arrangements, paying the fees at Mount Jerome cemetery. No immediate member of the Le Fanu family had died since they had left Abington in 1845, and so it was inevitable that Susanna should be buried in the Bennett vault—as indeed she had stipulated. Friday 30 April was bitterly cold in Dublin. Snow lay on the ground as the funeral moved out of the city towards the southern suburbs. At eight o'clock Susanna, who was not quite thirty-five years old, was laid beside her father and her two brothers. William remained with his brother for the remainder of the day. In the afternoon they travelled out to the Phoenix Park to take a walk under the trees. The weather continued foully for days, with thunder, lightning, and hailstones, but William escorted his brother and the four children on repeated visits to the park. Later in the year the elder boy, Philly, came to stay with his uncle in Bray.

Bereavement naturally disoriented Joseph, but a particularly disturbing feature of his wife's tribulations was its apparent conformity to a pattern already described in his fiction. Whether or not 'The Mysterious Lodger' describes the psychological state of the author's household, Susanna's behaviour subsequently had followed the suggestions implicit in the fiction—irrational anxiety for the life of those around her and a despairing concern for her own soul had now culminated in sudden and anguished death, just as the last image of the tale had shown the narrator's wife bathed in the sweet smile of the dead. In his letter to his mother, Le Fanu was naturally distraught but there is as much insecurity of self as grief for the deceased in the final sentence— 'copy any words in which she said I loved her & was kind to her'. On 18 May he began to write an account of his wife's death into a notebook, and in this privacy these insecurities and anxieties flourished. The diary opens with a long invocation of God the creator of life and controller of death. The general tenor is one of resignation, if not compliance, in the face of bereavement. When he turns to consider medical aspects of Susanna's sufferings, fear shines through: 'I will not trouble myself with the faithless thought that the errors of art or the misapprehensions of the beloved patient hastened her death. In these events there is no such thing as chance, and, over all seeming accidents preside [*sic*] the eternal dominion of our Heavenly Father, a controul

[*sic*] the most minute and power immeasurable.'[1] Immediately
after this nervous declaration there follows an account of Christ's
trial and crucifixion which concludes that every detail of his
death was prearranged and approved by God, and that by
extension God has sanctioned her death also: 'God be praised.
I can rest upon this as upon a rock. I must trouble my self no
more about Doctors, or their measures, or what might have been.
It was the will of my heavenly Father that she should die exactly
when & as she died & in that certainty ends all speculation.'[2] Much
of this orthodox consolation reached him through his mother, to
whom he wrote again on 22 May:

I cannot tell you what gratitude I owe to my adored Redeemer for the
comfort which through you he had vouchsafed to me. The sting of
death & the victory of the grave are gone & I would not bring my
darling back to danger & pain. My tears are happy now. I would not
wish my grief less for it brings me nearer to my Saviour, of whose
marvelous [*sic*] love I have had so many proofs, not only during my
happier days, but specially throughout this past sorrow. You, my dear
little mother, must consult somebody upon the symptoms which you
mention. If you will not, at least apply a wet towel to your head . . .
but you ought to see a homoeopathist.[3]

Le Fanu's anxieties about the treatment of his wife, and her
misapprehensions, stem from the rival claims of conventional
medicine and homoeopathic practice. It is not entirely clear who
favoured homoeopathy—which was more fashionable in mid-
Victorian times than it is now—but the nervous self-interrogation
about doctors and their measures is entirely understandable if
Joseph and Susanna held diverging views on medicine. Religious
consolation was, however, two-edged and Le Fanu resumed his
diary meditations with an account of his wife's spiritual state, now
showing her as neither sceptical nor content, but, if anything, in
greater straits:

Never did I see or imagine a creature having no deliberate or pre-
sumptive sin to affright his conscience so humble before God, in
Christ, so abject, so self-accusing, so prostrate in spirit, so wrung with
anguish of grief and penitence which in her prayers broke forth in
tears & groans, as my darling Sue. She was always asking prayers of

[1] Lozes, 157.
[2] Ibid. 160.
[3] J. T. S. Le Fanu to Mrs E. Le Fanu, 22 May 1858.

others, & though she constantly prayed in agony of spirit & such sorrow, she thought herself unworthy even to offer prayer to God . . .[1]

The notebook continues with extensive allusions to Martin Luther's *Table-Talk*, which the widower was evidently using as devotional literature. Luther's notion of humility especially appeals to him:

I am sure that this vale of humility, need and tribulation was that best adapted to the character of my beloved wife for the purpose of keeping her mind constantly engaged upon religion, her interest incessantly awake and active in searching the Scriptures, & her spirit in the anguish & humility of prayer. Had she been confident she might have relaxed; & relief might have ended in carelessness. But though she had constant glimms of hope there was always anxiety sufficient to maintain the tension of her mind & to disrupt that repose which had it been established might have been dangerous.[2]

This is a drastic theology of doubt, and its reliance on tension and disruption points to the diarist's need for reassurance. The emphasis shifts towards Le Fanu's own religious concern and his relationship with Susanna, already suggested in the account of her successful evasion of his counter-arguments during her sceptical period:

One night soon after her death I was tortured with the thought that if she had secured the love of her saviour she would have had an assurance of it & a confidence that it was so. I felt as if my heart would break & in my agony I prayed to God my Redeemer for comfort upon this point, & in the paroxysms of my misery I repeated the prayer again & again. When I became exhausted & began to reflect, I said to myself 'Is this not an unreasonable petition. I cannot look for a miracle, & yet without any, how can I be satisfied?' & so I turned over the leaves of my Bible to find my place and as I did a thing was presented to my mind, not as if reasoned all by myself for I had turned my attention to recover my place in the Bible, but suddenly as if spoken by another 'Did not you love her, & yet was she ever quite confident of your love?' Oh how well I knew it. I loved her almost to idolatry. She was always doubting & sometimes actually disbelieved my love, though I was then both declaring & showing it day & night. It was a beautiful & convincing answer, the force of which was to me delightful & irresistible, and with all the strength of my heart I blessed & thanked my gracious God for it.[3]

[1] Lozes, 161.
[2] Ibid.
[3] Ibid. 161–2.

This confession, at once illogical and painfully vivid, substantiates the suspicion present in the letter, which Joseph had written to his mother an hour after his wife's death, that marital difficulties had been complicated by religious differences, and these in the last days intensified by conflicting views of medicine. In the diary he thirsts for accusation—the accusation that his wife's unhappiness is explicable in terms of his suspect love—in order to reassure himself of her spiritual welfare. He describes her spiritual state, first in terms of scepticism and recovered faith, and then of her fear of damnation and exclusion from bliss. In his fiction we find several instances of this attenuated faith, with only the negative and terrifying aspect of revelation retaining its potency. But the diary concludes with a final summary in which renunciation replaces both scepticism and despair, a bleak afflatus:

All her scepticism had vanished & her faith was never for a moment clouded, the idea of death was constantly present to her mind, and its gloom & horror most beautifully softened, while its chastening influence was always present. Her conversation & her correspondence were full of this great subject & of her hopes & longings for eternity, and all this had been brought about gradually within little more than a year & most remarkably & in the greater part during the last winter.[1]

Such intrusion into the recesses of a novelist's marriage may seem unwarranted. However, previous commentators have entirely misrepresented relations between Joseph and Susanna, proceeding to link their view of the marriage to their interpretation of the fiction. For example, William Le Fanu in *Seventy Years of Irish Life* provides a skeletal account of his brother's life, observing that 'his wife, to whom he was devotedly attached, died in 1858, and from this time he entirely forsook general society, and was seldom seen except by his near relations and a few familiar friends'.[2] Naturally, the intimate details provide a less clear-cut image of the marriage. A later commentator, who was under no obligation to the strict code of Victorian decorum, speaks of the marriage as 'an exceptionally happy one'.[3] The intimacy of Sheridan Le Fanu's fragmentary diary is valuable because it warns that the religious questioning of the novels is not merely incidental, that it springs from a continuing and real

---

[1] Ibid. 164.
[2] *Seventy Years*, p. 151.
[3] Nelson Browne, *Sheridan Le Fanu*, p. 23.

experience of doubt and a search for assurance. It is worth noting that the misgivings eventually adhere to the bereaved husband as much as to the dead wife; questions as to whether the right doctor had been chosen, whether Susanna had been confident of Joseph's love, whether the argument against scepticism had been pressed home—all these refer immediately to Sheridan Le Fanu's responsibility. And when he suddenly finds comfort it is in the form of self-accusation.

The diary of May 1858 only revealed part of the truth about the psychological state of the Merrion Square household in the months leading up to Susanna's death. To his mother Joseph wrote a lengthy account of her dreams:

she one night thought she saw the curtain of her bed at the side next the door drawn, & the darling old man [i.e. George Bennett, her father], dressed in his usual morning suit, holding it aside, stood close to her looking ten or (I think) twelve years younger than when he died, & with his delightful smile of fondness & affection beaming upon her, I think she also said that his hand rested on the bed clothes as he used to place it. The words were as you say 'There is room in the vault for you, my little Sue', & with the same tender happy delightful smile he moved gently away as if he were going softly out of the door letting the curtain fall back. She lighted a candle & got up in the hope, if I recollect rightly, of seeing him again, & little Ellen who slept on the sofa & is easily awoken, was so, & asked her if she wanted anything; she answered 'no my darling' & bid her go to sleep. She told the 'vision', for she said that she was positively awake when she saw it, to little Ellen in the morning. I have examined her [i.e. Ellen] since I wrote the above as to her recollection & she says that the words were, when he placed his hand on the bed, 'Ah, little Sue, you are very poorly', & she replied 'Oh! no, I am pretty well' & then he said ['][there is room in the vault & will you win the race & get there first.' Little Ellen is confident that these are the very words she told her in the morning, & I recollect now that she mentions it, a portion of them which had escaped me. Little Ellen too is quite clear that she told her that her attention was first attracted by a sound as of the door opening & that this had startled her as she knew it was locked. She told little Ellen that she was certain it was *not* a dream. 'I think', she said, 'it was a sort of vision that God sent me, to prepare me.' In the morning having told it to me she said 'it is my warning'. She cried a great deal but not in agitation or grief, but with a sort of yearning, as it seemed to me, after the darling old man, & she dwelt with delight upon the beaming smile of love with which he had looked on her all the time. She told me &

little Ellen also that she was not in the slightest degree frightened at seeing him, but she was startled by the sound of the door opening & feeling nervous lighted the candle.

This dream is delightful to me, & although, when the poor darling when suffering, used to speak of the dream, & to say 'well, I'll win the race' & to speak in floods of tears, as it were to the old man with a longing to be lying beside him, it used to pain me. Yet, having seen that wish fulfilled exactly, for she lies by his side, the rememberance of it is a comfort, & I can think of her without horror or desolation.[1]

A rambling letter, perhaps, but of special interest for a post-script which Le Fanu added to the concluding paragraphs of domestic gossip: 'Will you keep this statement of the dream as I shall want to refer to it, intending to write down all the particulars I can recollect of her of every kind & this is carefully written, & some incident without a reference to it simply is forgotten[?]'

The appearance of George Bennett in his daughter's dreams complicates the already complex emotional base of her religious anxieties. Moving into her father's house, she was returning to the site of her childhood, which recalled her life before her marriage to Sheridan Le Fanu. If we are to take the evidence of letters and diaries seriously, we can hardly avoid the conclusion that the domestic distress depicted in 'Richard Marston' and 'The Mysterious Lodger' has a bearing (however oblique) on life in the author's home. If this be the case, Susanna's emotional and religious attitudes would seem to have been attuned to anxiety even before she and her husband came to live on Merrion Square. With the death of her father in 1856, the avenue back to an imaginatively stable past disappeared, and in its place her mind evolved images of the absolute retreat, incorporating the figure of her father as sanctioning her rejection of life. Freudians would doubtless see this preference for the father instead of the husband as sexually motivated; and Sheridan Le Fanu's own revelations in his dairy make it clear that marital difficulties combined with religious anxiety to produce a painful nexus of negative reactions. On the Bennett side of the family, it was accepted that all had not been well in the marriage; for, recording her daughter's death in the family prayer-book, Mrs Bennett had pointedly written: 'My darling Susy died at No 18 Merrion Square Wednesday 28 April 1858 suddenly. She was laid with her

beloved father and two brothers in the vault at Mount Jerome
near Dublin beloved and bitterly lamented by those who *knew*
her loving and attractive nature.'[1] The underlining is a dramatic,
if implied, condemnation of Le Fanu. Years later, when he
rewrote 'Richard Marston' as *A Lost Name*, he unconsciously
justified and answered the condemnation with the hero's weary
recognition that 'believing, unluckily, isn't a matter of choice any
more than loving'.[2]

Whatever the precise mechanism of Susanna's vision, her
experience in Merrion Square permanently marked her husband's
view of the house. In his earlier fiction, the Great House featured
only to a limited extent, but when he resumed writing in the
1860s the house became the centre of a series of novels. The
device may be a standard one in late-Gothic and sensational
fiction, but in Sheridan Le Fanu's case the Great House is
presented with an intensity of feeling which stems from psychological experience, not to say shock. To add to the tension in this
bond between house and master, Le Fanu was never the owner
of 18 Merrion Square. After his wife's death he held it on a lease
from John Bennett at a yearly rent of £22. 10s. However, by
1868 he owed his brother-in-law close on £900, and was consequently obliged to mortgage his leasehold interest back to
Bennett, with the result that when he died in 1873 his children
had to vacate their home immediately. Le Fanu's tenure in
Merrion Square was always fraught with uncertainty; the im-
posing architecture disguised the realities within.[3]

Sheridan Le Fanu's financial position contrasts obviously with
his brother's, for in 1858 William calculated that his income for
the next two years would be in the region of £9,000. He already
held shares in various railway companies, and as an engineer-
administrator aged forty-two he had hardly reached the zenith
of his earning power. It would be wrong, however, to conclude
that Joseph was the exception in his financial instability. Elsewhere in the family circle, insecurity and hardship were familiar

[1] Transcript kindly supplied by Dr Jean Laurie, in whose possession the
Bennett prayer–book remains.
[2] *A Lost Name*, ii. 118–19.
[3] Registry of Deeds, Dublin, Memorial 1868/4/57. The deed, dated 13 Jan.
1868, recites that Le Fanu owed John Bennett of Grange, King's County,
£942.10s. worth of 3 per cent Consols equivalent at the price of the day to
£876.10s.6d.

guests. Captain William Dobbin's son, the Revd William Peter Hume Dobbin, had been appointed chaplain to Dr Steeven's Hospital. Dobbin with his wife and a large family were obliged to live on the premises in very confined quarters, and the unpleasant conditions were further complicated by Dobbin's need to take in a private pupil to supplement his meagre salary. Given the chaplain's parentage, he may have been eccentric as well as impoverished, but there is something pathetic in the Hospital Committee's directing him in January 1866 'to prevent in future the disfigurement of the gallery by having the top of the windows stuffed with old clothes'.[1] William Le Fanu was in the habit of calling on the Dobbins after a Sunday visit to the Phoenix Park.

The household at Merrion Square attempted to maintain its ordinary routine, though Le Fanu's mother expressed anxiety about the children's welfare from time to time. A French governess was employed to look after them, and to encourage their fluency a rule was introduced that all conversation at meal times should be conducted through French. The girls were allowed to keep their mother's guitar, and took tuition in music. But it was principally on the question of religious instruction that old Mrs Le Fanu expressed her anxiety; her son assured her that he read about thirty verses from the Bible to the children each day, though he added that he thought it 'very necessary never to make religion irksome to children, but interesting which is quite easy if people will only be at the pains to try'.[2] In March 1861 Mrs Le Fanu died. Some time before her death, he had been considering a renewed contact with the outer world, and in January 1861 he had persuaded William to lend him £2,000 to buy the Dublin *Daily Express*, a project which was never completed.

Le Fanu's letter to his brother is a curious document, not least because it is addressed to 'My dear Richard', that being William's second Christian name and as such very rarely used:

My dear Richard,
    I have completed an arrangement for the purchase of the 'Daily Express' as also a most desirable one with Knox for the final termination of the competion [sic] between the two papers & for a transference to me of the entire body of his evening subscribers amounting to more than

---

[1] T. P. C. Kirkpatrick, *The History of Doctor Steevens' Hospital* (Dublin, 1924), p. 79.
[2] J. T. S. Le Fanu to Mrs E. Le Fanu, dated 'Thursday'.

one thousand (nearer to fourteen hundred) & have made all calculations as to working expenses in every department & detail, & find that the result will be to place me in possession of a well-protected property of great value. Your loan of £2,000 will enable me to carry it out forthwith. I can give you my bond with power of Atty. to confess judgment, but you would not enter it without special reason for so doing, as there is now a publication called the 'black list' in which they print the names of all who have judgments against them, & there is publicity & annoyance in appearing in it. Croker will tell you however how effectual a security a bond is, as on entering judgment you can convert it into a mortgage upon any property belonging to me. I shall pay the interest punctually.

Believe me Richard,
Your affectionate brother
Joe

Private Do not let a word get out as its being known prematurely would probably cause much trouble.[1]

By 1861 Le Fanu had acquired an interest in the *Dublin Evening Mail* in partnership with Dr Henry Maunsell, and the purpose of the agreement with Knox clearly was to consolidate his position in the newspaper world. Yet the very terms on which he sought to improve his position reveal his extreme vulnerability. He could rely on his brother's support, but any rumour of such a need for support endangered him. Doubtless, such contradictions abound in the archives of Victorian business, but there is a particular point to Sheridan Le Fanu's dilemma: as co-editor of the *Dublin Evening Mail* he articulated the ambitions and demands of the city's middle class, especially the Protestant and Unionist élite. Nor was he capable of the devil-may-care contempt for money worries and respectability which enabled his sometime friend Isaac Butt to survive crisis after crisis. Propriety was important to Le Fanu, who now found himself perilously isolated from the sources of self-congratulation and complacency on which so many Victorian virtues depended. His political past was ambiguous and compromising, and made progressively more embarrassing by Butt's gradual abandoning of Orangeism and conversion to nationalism; his business interests were hemmed in by debts and mortgages, and made progressively more embarrassing by

---

[1] J. T. S. Le Fanu to W. R. Le Fanu, 16 Jan. 1861. W. R. Loughheed has explained the curious mode of address by suggesting that Le Fanu was writing to his brother-*in-law*; however, Susanna had no brother named Richard.

his brother's effortless success. And his emotional life had been
shattered by the death of his wife, a disaster which generated
painful self-scrutiny and self-accusation. These were not pro-
pitious circumstances in which to resume a career in writing;
nevertheless they were the personal energies which shaped
Sheridan Le Fanu's later fiction. His mother's death probably
silenced the only voice which could have identified his experience
had he expressed it in fiction; apart from her he had no intimate
friends and no confessors. The children were too young to
recognize their father in Austin Ruthyn, the narrator's father in
Uncle Silas, or to realize that the Persian ring which plays so
sinister a part in *Wylder's Hand* is similar to that which Le Fanu
had inherited from his father in 1845. William could be trusted to
read any new fiction in the same way in which he had read 'The
Last Heir of Castle Connor'—as something fundamentally unreal,
an entertainment. In July 1861 Sheridan Le Fanu bought the
Dublin University Magazine, thus providing himself with the
means to publish his own fiction without any intervening agent
or editor having an opportunity to alter a jot or tittle. As a further
protection of his privacy, Le Fanu chose to publish his first novel
of the 1860s under a pseudonym; he chose Charles de Cresseron,
a name which underlines the importance of the past, especially
the family's past, in his fiction. After *The House by the Churchyard*, he did not resort directly to pseudonymity in publishing
his novels, though Charles de Cresseron is retained as the
narrator of *Wylder's Hand*.

Images of exile and a concern for the past dominate all of Le
Fanu's sensational fiction, from *The House by the Churchyard*
(1861–3) to the posthumously published *Willing to Die* (1873).
The House by the Churchyard, set in the village of Chapelizod in
the year 1767, utilizes childhood memories of the Phoenix Park
and the Hibernian Military School. Two dominant features of
the book are the Royal Irish Artillery, barracked nearby, and the
refined kindliness of the rector, Dr Walsingham. The story is not
thematically strong; the central narrative is often submerged in
the festivities of social life, the minor crises of romantic sub-plots,
and the emergence of a strangely disjointed and yet palpable
manifestation of the supernatural. The book remains one of Le
Fanu's most enjoyable if shapeless novels, an inimitable mixture
of grave and gay things and a plot so complicated that one forgets

that a plot exists only to have the delicious rediscovery of terror surprise one again and again. Though Le Fanu plunges quickly into the dark adventures of mid-eighteenth century Chapelizod, a fervent note of nostalgia is sounded at length in the opening chapter:

As for the barrack of the Royal Irish Artillery, the great gate leading into the parade ground, by the river side, and all that, I believe the earth, or rather that grim giant factory, which is now the grand feature and centre of Chapelizod, throbbing all over with steam, and whizzing with wheels, and vomiting pitchy smoke, has swallowed them all up.[1]

The novel then presents a narrative of the past explicitly as a retreat from the grimy present; the warm and gossipy snug of the public house in *The House by the Churchyard* contrasts directly with the less generous account of Chapelizod in *The Cock and Anchor*, a novel which, despite its limitations, struggled to make a comprehensive statement concerning Irish realities. Chapelizod is a retreat in geographical terms also, a thoroughly unimportant place far enough removed from Dublin (in 1767) to avoid the turmoil of city life, and rescued from rural obscurity by the presence of the regiment. The village community is in no sense a typical one: neither commerce nor agriculture plays much part in its economy. Throughout the novel there is a subdued carnival mood; and food, drink, song, and scandal are prominent in the daily lives of the residents. Only the rector and the doctor—and of course the publican—seem preoccupied by professional responsibilities. The abnormality of Chapelizod is given point by the presence of the military who ensure the political orthodoxy of the community—a haven of historical loyalism created by Le Fanu amid the increasingly determined national resurgence of nineteenth-century Ireland—and who also guarantee an artificial Protestant majority in the village, for 'the R.I.A. were Protestant by constitution'.[2] Harmony is further advanced, however, by the presence of the Catholic priest, a man intemperate only in his drinking. Father Roach's attendance at the regimental dinner indicates a tolerance which is paralleled by Le Fanu's silence on all questions of ideological dispute. Nevertheless, there are hints

[1] *The House by the Churchyard* (London, 1863), i. 4.
[2] Ibid. 172. It may be timely to repeat Elizabeth Bowen's warning (in her introduction to the 1968 edition of the novel) that the R.I.A. should not be confused with I.R.A!

that this harmony is fragile and, like the Jacobite O'Connor in *The Cock and Anchor*, metaphor constantly embarrasses the priest. A disrespectful song about Lenten fasting, strictly a Catholic tradition in Ireland, is followed by a more pointed and personal recipe—for roast roach! Although the priest is accommodated into the general account of Chapelizod society, remarks at a metaphorical level indicate the abnormality of his position. This is characteristic of *The House by the Churchyard*, that the implications of its setting are not consistently maintained in the detail of the novel. There is a contrast between the decorum of village life and the unexplained mysteries which intrude. Society and landscape, seen as the framework of incident and character, do not extend the range of the plot but stand in contrast to it. But only some of these intrusive mysteries are directly connected with the plot of murder and confession: others remain unexplained by anything on the page.

Le Fanu serialized *The House by the Churchyard* between October 1861 and February 1863. Despite his acquisition of the *Dublin University Magazine*, publication opportunities were limited in Dublin, for James McGlashan had died and with him the principal outlet for book publication for a writer of Le Fanu's political loyalties. Consequently, he undertook to finance the printing of his first serial novel in three-decker form. He spent £78 on printing a thousand copies, £21 on binding them, and £62 on paper. Distribution, however, proved difficult for a self-help publisher, and Le Fanu was lucky to sell five hundred copies to the London publisher, Tinsley, who issued *The House by the Churchyard* in a new binding in 1863.[1] London publication brought him to the attention of Tinsley's rivals, and he negotiated a contract for a successor to *The House* with Richard Bentley. But Bentley insisted on 'the story of an English subject and in modern times'.[2] And Le Fanu obediently wrote *Wylder's Hand* in conformity to these requirements. Superficially, all his subsequent novels—with the exception of *Morley Court*, a new title but in fact virtually a reissue of *The Cock and Anchor*—conform to the Bentley formula, a formula generally applicable to the sensa-

---

[1] For an account of the publication history of *The House by the Churchyard* see Michael Sadleir *XIX Century Fiction* (London, 1951), i. 200–3.

[2] British Library, Add. MS. 46642, R. Bentley to J. T. S. Le Fanu (copy), 26 Feb. 1863.

tionalist school. Nevertheless, Sheridan Le Fanu insinuates into his modern English settings many of the characteristics of the Irish past. Elizabeth Bowen, herself an Anglo-Irish novelist of exile and contained despair, wrote that *Uncle Silas* always struck her as 'an Irish story transposed to an English setting'. This is of course literally true, for Le Fanu had adapted and expanded the plot of his Purcell story, 'Passage in the Secret History of an Irish Countess'. Miss Bowen's analysis goes much further than literal truth, of course:

The hermetic solitude and the autocracy of the great country house [in *Uncle Silas*], the demonic power of the family myth, fatalism, feudalism and the 'ascendency' outlook are accepted facts of life for the race of hybrids from which Le Fanu sprang. For the psychological background of *Uncle Silas* it was necessary for him to *invent* nothing. Rather, he was at once exploiting in art and exploring for its more terrible implications what would have been the norm of his own heredity. Having, for reasons which are inscrutable, pitched on England as the setting for *Uncle Silas*, he wisely chose the North, the wildness of Derbyshire. Up there, in the vast estates of the landed old stock, there appeared, in the years when Le Fanu wrote (and still more in the years *of* which he wrote: the early 1840s) a time lag—just such a time lag as, in a more marked form, separates Ireland from England more effectually than any sea.[1]

For reasons which are already evident, Le Fanu's experience indeed justifies Elizabeth Bowen's guesses and intuitions. In writing critical introductions to both *The House by the Churchyard* and *Uncle Silas*, she reveals herself to be a discerning reader of a kind of fiction generally disregarded by professional critics. One final observation of her's on *Uncle Silas* confirms her innate understanding of Le Fanu's psyche (it is important to remember that she knew nothing of his diaries and letters):

Uncle Silas is, as a novel, Irish in two other ways: it is sexless, and it shows a sublimated infantilism. It may, for all I know, bristle with symbolism; but I speak of the *story*, not of its implications—in the story, no force from any one of the main characters runs into the channel of sexual feeling. The reactions of Maud, the narrator-heroine, throughout are those of a highly intelligent, still more highly sensitive, child of twelve. This may, to a degree, be accounted for by seclusion and a repressive father—but not, I think, entirely: I should doubt

[1] Introduction to *Uncle Silas* (London, 1947), p. 8.

whether Le Fanu himself realised Maud's abnormality as a heroine . . .
We must in fact note how Maud's sensuousness (which is un-English)
disperses, expends itself throughout the story in so much small change.
She shows, at every turn, the carelessness, or acquiescence, of the
predestined person: Maud is, by nature, a bride of Death.[1]

The exile locations of Le Fanu's fiction are not merely geographically remote, but are expressions of a deeper dislocation
of the individual from society, a dislocation of certain modes of
feeling from their usual emotional context. In *The House by the
Churchyard*, Chapelizod is explicitly an anomaly: landscape stands
aside from narrative. Though this is true of the plot generally, it
is most strikingly evident in an episode which inevitably recalls
Le Fanu's experiences between 1848 and 1858. The chapter in
question is called 'An Authentic Narrative of the Ghost of a
Hand', and in it Le Fanu describes how a 'white and plump'
hand taps at windows and doors as if to gain admission, and
subsequently leaves its print in the dust of a parlour table. The
hand is then seen on several occasions inside the house; it is quite
literally disembodied, appearing to resemble a toad in its horrid
completeness and integrity. At a climax of this persecution, the
tenant of the house, Mr Prosser

drew the curtain at the side of the bed, and saw Mrs Prosser lying, as
for a few seconds, he mortally feared, dead, her face being motionless,
white, and covered with a cold dew; and on the pillow, close beside
her head, and just within the curtains, was, as he first thought, a toad—
but really the same white, fattish hand, the wrist resting on the pillow,
and the fingers extended towards her temple.[2]

The career of this plump, slightly moist hand is one of the
sensational passages for which Sheridan Le Fanu is celebrated.
But within *The House by the Churchyard*, the incident is quite
pointless; the Prossers are not characters referred to in any other
connection; the period of their tenancy has long passed before
the novel opens, and the hand never manifests itself to anyone
else. Within Le Fanu's experience, however, the plump white
hand recalls a detail stressed in the account of Susanna Le Fanu's
dream: that her visitant (her dead father, Le Fanu's father-in-
law) rested his hand in the dream 'on the [bed]clothes as he used
to place it' when he was alive. And there is an oblique confirma-

[1] Ibid. 9.
[2] *The House by the Churchyard*, i. 128.

tion of George Bennett's posthumous activity within *The House by the Churchyard* in an incongruous detail of Prosser's appearance at the moment when the ghostly hand is discovered by his wife's head: 'a heavy ledger, connected with his father-in-law's business being under his arm'.[1]

It might be wholly unremarkable that a novelist should include incidents from his own experience in his fiction were it not for the fact that, as a sensationalist, Le Fanu is generally regarded as a merchant in the wildly improbable. Yet here in the most macabre incident of *The House by the Churchyard* one finds the recreation of a profoundly intimate and disturbing personal experience. *Uncle Silas* has been cited previously as presenting in the figure of Austin Ruthyn a thumb-nail self-portrait of the author. In *A Memoir of the Le Fanu Family*, his nephew isolates a few obvious details and then expands on them:

There are touches in his description of Austin Ruthyn of Knowl in *Uncle Silas* which vividly recall him in his later days and his favourite room at the back of his house in Merrion Square to the writer of this Memoir: 'Many old portraits, some grim and pale and others pretty and some very graceful and charming, hanging from the walls. Few pictures except portraits, long and short were there . . . His beautiful young wife died . . . This bereavement I have been told changed him, made him more odd and taciturn than ever . . . He was now walking up and down this spacious old room . . . It was his wont to walk up and down thus . . . He wore a loose black velvet coat and waistcoat. It was the figure of an elderly rather than an old man, but firm and with no sign of weakness.' The room in Merrion Square contained like that at Knowl the portrait of a handsome young man with a buff waistcoat and chocolate-coloured coat and the hair long and brushed back. The picture which thus suggested the description of Uncle Silas in his youth, is believed to be a likeness of George Colman the younger, whose father [was] a friend of the novelist's grandfather.[2]

If Le Fanu's self-portraiture were nothing more than a matter of costume and furniture, it would indeed be unremarkable. But in *Uncle Silas*, as in *The House by the Churchyard*, he creates a scene reminiscent of his late wife's visionary torments. The narrator, Maud (whom Elizabeth Bowen found both sexless and sensuous), retires to bed one night very shortly after her father's death:

[1] Ibid.
[2] T. P. Le Fanu, *A Memoir of the Le Fanu Family* (Manchester, [1924]), p. 59.

Everybody at all nervously excitable has suffered some time or another by the appearance of ghastly features presenting themselves in every variety of contortion, one after another, the moment the eyes are closed. This night my dear father's face troubled me—sometimes white and sharp as ivory, sometimes strangely transparent like glass, sometimes all hanging in cadaverous folds, always with the same unnatural expression of diabolical fury.

From this dreadful vision I could only escape by sitting up and staring at the light. At length, worn out, I dropped asleep, and in a dream I distinctly heard papa's voice say sharply outside the bed-curtain: 'Maud, we shall be late at Bartram-Haugh.'[1]

This invitation, virtual command, of a dead father to his daughter becomes even more reminiscent of George Bennett's 'There is room in the vault for you, my little Sue' when we examine the imagery of death which surrounds the house at Bartram-Haugh, the home of Maud's uncle Silas.

Indeed, Le Fanu's best fiction—*Uncle Silas* and *In a Glass Darkly*—is amenable to formal and stylistic criticism to a degree surprising in sensationalism. The characteristic Le Fanu plot conforms roughly to the rules of the Wilkie Collins school: there is murder, suicide, attempted bigamy, a little detection, a great deal of sentiment, sleep-walking, lunatic asylums, shipwrecks, and debtors' prisons. A synopsis of any of these tales is strangely pointless, for the real significance of the fiction lies elsewhere, in recurrent imagery, in symmetrical patterns, in the use of female narrators. As far as the sensational narratives are concerned, the most important feature is perhaps the suggestion which Le Fanu generally creates that his hero or heroine stands at one extremity of a process which began in the past. In *The House by the Churchyard* mystery surrounds melancholy Mr Mervyn, really Lord Dunoran, whose father died in disgrace in prison. In *Wylder's Hand*, which makes a robust attempt to be contemporary, the principal character is dead throughout most of the narrative though this fact only emerges in the last few pages. In *Uncle Silas* the brothers Austin and Silas Ruthyn live in their separate stately hermitages, both blighted by an offence committed in their youth. In *Guy Deverell* the wicked baronet is appalled to meet a youth identical to a man whom he had killed in an unsporting duel many years since. These narratives do not

---

[1] *Uncle Silas*, ii. 52–3.

simply expose past crimes and guilty consciences; they show us the historical past acted out in the present, sometimes in ironical mimicry, sometimes with a metaphysical *frisson*.

The view that the work of an artist is a distinct area of experience separated in every important aspect from his life is deeply rooted in the romantic tradition. It is ultimately a theory of the artistic personality which distinguishes between an ordinary universe and a special, sanctified world of the imagination. Yeats had encapsulated this view in the poem, 'The Choice', where he declares that

> The intellect of man is forced to choose
> Perfection of the life or of the work,
> And if it take the second must refuse
> A heavenly mansion, raging in the dark.[1]

But the choice is never so impossibly absolute, the alternatives never so perfect. 'The life' is as much an abstraction—considered in isolation thus—as 'the work', for the life of any individual is not merely the sum of incidents and feelings which he has experienced; it is also a structure, an order, which relates one individual to another, to a community of individuals, and to the individual's view of himself. Life cannot be directly contrasted with art, for each contains and extends the other.

Nevertheless, the critic who insists on the autonomy of art highlights a problem which his opponents often ignore: by what means, according to what criteria, may two different modes of experience (the one active, the other verbal or at least symbolic) be related? The Socialist Realist, who insists that literature must emulate life and yet provide a model for life, finally denies the common-sense distinction between a tractor and a tract. In the case of Sheridan Le Fanu's life and work, there is at least one discernible characteristic of his experience which provides a link between 'the life' and 'the work'. In the terms of narrative plot, it is the recurring revelation of the past in the present, the implicit declaration that what is happening in the immediate context of a scene has already happened. At one level, we may speak of this as a kind of predetermined action—only that which has occurred can occur now. But at a more fundamental level,

[1] *Collected Poems* (London, 1963), p. 278.

this characteristic of Le Fanu's plot denies the concept of action; it is stasis which dominates his fiction, and not action. This paradox is closely related to the suicidal patterns of *The Purcell Papers*, where suicide (in various formal guises) epitomized both the negation of will and its assertion. Thus we find that in *Uncle Silas* a figure emerges in the opening chapter from the utter blackness of wainscoting in a darkened room, and in the closing chapter another figure virtually lapses into non-existence through a suicide which Le Fanu effectively implies but does not specify. There is a narrative connection between these two figures (they are the brothers Ruthyn about whom various tales are told), but the *formal* relationship between the two is infinitely more suggestive in its symmetry, its nihilistic patterning. To turn to Le Fanu's life, it could be argued that similar patterns exist in his political behaviour, his emergence from a darkened Tory background into an ambiguous action which must be cancelled and concealed in order to preserve the original links with reality. To argue thus emphasizes the difficulty of establishing criteria by which two differing modes of experience may be compared—one is constantly betrayed into sleight of hand by analogy or metaphor. Nevertheless, *The Cock and Anchor* and 'Richard Marston' can only be understood as fiction if the political context of their composition is admitted as relevant; the autonomy-critic may observe patterns and forms, but he cannot appreciate their significance. To take a simple example from *The Cock and Anchor*, we may find a critic who notices that Edmund O'Connor is on at least two occasions associated by metaphor with Oliver Cromwell, but the significance of this is more than a neat parallelism of allusion, more even than a conventional irony.

The static plot which occurs in much of Le Fanu's fiction is closely connected with more extreme forms of stasis, and it is these which illustrate the relationship between the life and the work. Hyperstasis is a condition in which an object is held in excessive isolation from those motions or circumstances by necessity attendant on it. In psychological terms, one would speak of a morbid attention to a particular object to the neglect of the context and hence to change its significance. But hyperstasis is not solely a psychological condition. It may be a legitimate method of presenting an object when certain intense effects are required; everyone is familiar with those night-time photographs of busy streets in which a multitude of golden lines are present, where in a less hyperstatic depiction one would see individual motorcar headlights separated in time and space. Both in its psychological and artistic senses, hyperstasis is concerned essentially with perception. In *The House by the Churchyard* the anachronistic incident of the hand haunting Mr and Mrs Prosser brings together both psychologically powerful impulses and symbolic intentions; indeed the principal fault of the incident is that the relation between the father-in-law's ledger and the novel as a whole is entirely arbitrary and private. But in method, the hand is presented hyperstatically; nothing else is admitted into the depiction, for the hand is infused with some unknown intensity which blacks out, as it were, all other circumstances. The hyperstatic quality of the scene is quite pervasive; the bed is reduced to pillow and curtain, while Mrs Prosser is referred to solely as face, head, and temple. In Le Fanu's letter reporting his wife's visionary disturbances, there are similarly concentrated images—the dead George Bennett's sweet smile and his hand resting on the bedclothes are repeated on several occasions. Susanna's vision, being an unconscious manifestation of a single central image, exemplifies the hyperstasis of psychological obsession. Her husband's fiction, potentially at least, may come to exploit the hyperstasis of artistic method. In *The House by the Churchyard* it appears that unconscious impulses are at work, but *Uncle Silas* provides clearer evidence of Le Fanu's powers of symbolic organization and the limitations within which his imagination operated.

5

UNCLE SILAS:
A HABITATION OF SYMBOLS

IN *Chronicles of Golden Friars* Le Fanu tried to create a fictional context in which nature and society, surrounding a Great House, take on more active roles than those we have observed in *The House by the Churchyard*. In the three tales collected under this title, and in one or two more using the same setting, he introduced the village of Golden Friars which, as even the name suggests, carried idyllic or paradisal associations; in the longest of the chronicles, 'The Haunted Baronet', it is seen

standing by the margin of the lake, hemmed round by an amphitheatre of purple mountain, rich in tint and furrowed by ravines, high in air, when the tall gables and narrow windows of its ancient graystone houses, and the tower of the old church, from which every evening the curfew still rings, show like silver in the moonbeams, and the black elms that stand round throw moveless shadows upon the short level grass . . . There it rises, as from the stroke of the enchanter's wand, looking so light and filmy, that you could scarcely believe it more than a picture reflected on the thin mist of night.[1]

Despite this initial vapidity of the landscape, 'The Haunted Baronet' develops considerable momentum in the manner in which it treats natural imagery. Sir Bale Mardykes is persuaded to cross a lake to haunted Cloostedd forest, where he encounters a strange environment:

As he walked under the shadow of these noble trees, suddenly his eye was struck by a strange little flower, nodding quite alone by the knotted root of one of those huge oaks.

He stopped and picked it up, and as he plucked it, with a harsh scream just over his head, a large bird with heavy beating wings broke away from the midst of the branches. He could not see it, but he fancied the scream was like that of the huge macaw whose ill-poised

---

[1] *Chronicles of Golden Friars* (London, 1871), i. 281–2.

flight he had watched. This conjecture was but founded in the odd cry he had heard.

The flower was a curious one—a stem fine as a hair supported a little bell, that looked like a drop of blood, and never ceased trembling. He walked on, holding this in his fingers; and soon he saw another of the same odd type, then another at a shorter distance . . .[1]

After some time, the baronet comes upon a human figure

seated upon the grass, a strange figure, corpulent, with a great hanging nose, the whole face glowing like copper. He was dressed in a bottle-green cut-velvet coat, of the style of Queen Anne's reign, with a dusky crimson waistcoat, both overlaid with broad and tarnished gold lace, and his silk stockings on thick swollen legs, with great buckled shoes, straddling on the grass, were rolled up over his knees to his short breeches.[2]

Sir Bale is gradually able to make the connections necessary to understand something of this strange region:

Looking at the unwieldly old man, with his heavy nose, powdered head, and all the bottle-green, crimson, and gold about him, and the long slim serving man, with sharp beak, and white from head to heel, standing by him, Sir Bale was forcibly reminded of the great old macaw and the long and slender kite, whose colours they, after their fashion, reproduced, with something, also indescribable, of the air and character of the birds.[3]

The natural world and humanity here act as a metaphor for each other; no absolute distinction between them exists in Cloostedd, for it is a symbolical world in which Sir Bale discovers reality. Through the chance finding of a portrait in Mardykes Hall, he recognizes the gaudy figure in Cloostedd as his own ancestor, his guilty ancestral past. The scenery is not merely decoration; it is the landscape of the past and—simultaneously—of Sir Bale's troubled conscience. The symbolical implications in the birds and flowers are achieved by two complementary techniques: first Golden Friars is presented in 'moveless shadows', and Cloostedd reposes 'in the stirless air'—this is the excessive isolation from the motions inherent in nature, which creates the altered significance of the focal features. Then the tension involved in this

---

[1] Ibid. ii. 209–10.
[2] Ibid. ii. 211.
[3] Ibid. ii. 213.

creative distortion is revealed in the awkwardness of the birds'
ill-posed flight and the perpetual trembling of the flowers.

In Le Fanu's fiction generally, it is possible to distinguish
between the explicit treatment of the supernatural in short stories
and tales, and the neglect or disguise of that dimension in the
longer novels. 'The Haunted Baronet' successfully accommodates
its curious landscape into a narrative of supernatural events,
which still conforms to an over-all definition of Le Fanu's concern with the past. *Uncle Silas*, the most complex of the novels,
also takes particular care of the way in which landscape is introduced and exploited. But here, unlike 'The Haunted Baronet',
the fiction presents two faces, one narrative, the other less
directly evident. In narrative terms, it becomes obvious that the
landscape does not respond to man in the conspiratorial manner
of the shorter tale, though when Maud ventures out from her
uncle's house on a blackberrying expedition her experience even
of the landscape is constricting:

People can't go on eating blackberries always; so after a while we
resumed our walk along this pretty dell, which gradually expanded
into a wooded valley—level beneath and enclosed by irregular uplands,
receding, as it were, in mimic bays and harbours at some points, and
running out at others into broken promontories, ending in clumps of
forest trees.

Just where the glen which we had been traversing expanded into
this broad, but wooded valley, it was traversed by a high and close
paling, which although it looked decayed, was still very strong.[1]

We are still within the conventions of the sensational novel,
here, with imprisoning palings and anticlimactic picnics. But the
natural imagery—of mimic bays and broken promontories—
establishes a deeper level of enclosure than the stout wooden
fence. Though the landscape is typical of the cultivated parkland
surrounding an English country house, artificially planned and
naturally maintained, the effect is to create a further level at which
Bartram-Haugh is marked off from a world outside. In describing
the gardens round the house, Le Fanu emphasizes form and style
at the expense of vivacity; they are compared to a carpet, and thus
the natural takes second place within the metaphor to the arti-

---

[1] *Uncle Silas* (London, 1864), ii. 119–20.

ficial. Similarly, human figures are repeatedly described as being like a portrait, 'Rembrandt-like' or '*á la* Wouvermans'. The effect is to reduce the spontaneity which we expect in fictional characters, to frame them in emblematic poses rather than in situations or activities. The world of *Uncle Silas* is slowly built up against the resistance of rigid barriers and static images. Significantly the first landscape which Maud introduces is one seen from within her father's house, through a window:

I was the only occupant of the room; and the lights near the fire, at its further end, hardly reached to the window at which I sat.

The shorn grass sloped gently downward from the windows till it met the broad level on which stood, in clumps, or solitarily scattered, some of the noblest timber in England. Hoar in the moonbeams stood those graceful trees casting their moveless shadows upon the grass, and in the background crowning the undulations of the distance, in masses, were piled those woods among which lay the solitary tomb where the remains of my beloved mother rested.[1]

This motionless scene is framed in the window, a picture of landscape which leads Maud directly to reflections on her father's recent intimations about an 'approaching visitor'. Austin Ruthyn, Maud has already told us, has become a Swedenborgian having abandoned the Church of England; and relating the coming visitor to her father's 'unearthly and spectral' religion, she recalls an earlier visitor who had taken her for a walk many years earlier when her mother had died:

He led me into the garden—the Dutch garden, we used to call it— with a balustrade, and statues at the farther front, laid out in a carpet-pattern of brilliantly coloured flowers. We came down the broad flight of Caen stone steps into this, and we walked in silence to the balustrade. The base was too high at the spot where we reached it for me to see over; but holding my hand, he said, 'Look through that, my child. Well, you can't; but *I* can see beyond it—shall I tell you what? I see ever so much. I see a cottage with a steep roof, that looks like gold in the sunlight; there are tall trees throwing soft shadows round it, and flowering shrubs, I can't say what, only the colours are beautiful, growing by the walls and windows, and two little children are playing among the stems of the trees, and we are on our way there, and in a few minutes shall be under those trees ourselves, and talking to those

[1] Ibid. i. 25–6.

little children. Yet now to me it is but a picture in my brain, and to you but a story told by me, which you believe.'[1]

The child Maud and her Swedenborgian visitor advance in the direction he has suggested,

along the grass lane between tall trim walls of evergreens. The way was in deep shadow, for the sun was near the horizon; but suddenly we turned to the left, and there we stood in rich sunlight, among the many objects he had described.

'Is this your house, my little men?' he asked of the children—pretty little rosy boys—who assented; and he leaned with his open hand against the stem of one of the trees, and with a grave smile he nodded down to me, saying—

'You see now, and hear, and *feel* for yourself that both the vision and the story were quite true . . .'[2]

The first landscape, which Maud sees from the window, is, as she expresses it, a picture of a landscape; it is distant, static. Nevertheless the passage pictures a natural landscape with the possibilities of movement and temperature and growth. The second landscape is encountered indirectly also: on this occasion the distance is not merely a physical one caused by intervening glass and masonry, but is categorically distinct. We see the place first through the 'vision' of the Swedenborgian; like Maud, to see it we must believe it. In a manner resembling the garden in the opening section of T. S. Eliot's 'Burnt Norton', this is an ideal landscape; the objects have 'the look of flowers that are looked at'. In stylistic terms, we can examine the use of moderately inappropriate word-collocations to intensify the reader's apprenhension of the scene: the trees have stems and not trunks; 'trim' attaches itself closely to 'walls'; the approach is by a 'grass lane'. By these gentle disturbances of the predictable word-order, and by the tone of anticipation, the mere reality of the scene is questioned. There is now a *perfect* climate; it is not temperate or mild, but absolute and unchanging. Maud rightly suspects a spiritual meaning in the Swedenborgian's stories.

Thus *Uncle Silas* begins with the interior of the focal house and then commences a retreat from the normal representation of landscape and setting. We have so far noted two stages in this

[1] Ibid. i. 27–8.
[2] Ibid. i. 28–9.

retreat—if that is what it is—the static pictured landscape framed in the drawing-room window and the visionary scenes of the visiting minister. The process is quickly taken a stage further when Maud relates how her childhood companion led her towards the tomb in which her mother had been recently buried. As they look at the tomb the Swedenborgian asks her what she sees; she replies that it is the place where 'poor mamma' is buried; in the Swedenborgian's words, it is 'too high for either you or me to see over'. 'But Swedenborg sees beyond it, over, and *through* it, and has told me all that concerns us to know. He says your mamma is not there.'[1] Naturally the child is panic-stricken by this announcement, fearing that her mother's body has been stolen in some way. She continues:

I was uttering unconsciously very nearly the question with which Mary, in the grey of that wondrous morning on which she stood by the empty sepulchre, accosted the figure standing near.

'Your mamma is alive, but too far away to see or hear us; but Swedenborg, standing here, can see and hear her, and tells me all he sees, just as I told you in the garden about the little boys and the cottage, and the trees and flowers which you could not see, but believed in when *I* told you. So I can tell you now as I did then; and as we are both, I hope, walking on to the same place, just as we did to the trees and cottage, you will surely see with your own eyes how true is the description which I give you.'

I was very much frightened, for I feared that when he had done his narrative we were to walk on through the wood into that place of wonders and of shadows where the dead were visible.

He leaned his elbow on his knee, and his forehead on his hand, which shaded his downcast eyes, and in that attitude described to me a beautiful landscape, radiant with a wondrous light, in which, rejoicing, my mother moved along an airy path, ascending among mountains of fantastic height, and peaks, melting in celestial colouring into the air, and peopled with human beings translated into the same image, beauty, and splendour.[2]

This third, specifically celestial, landscape draws the retreat further away from a matter-of-fact, 'things-are-as-they-seem' environment. Or, to alter the perspective, this third stage of the process widens the implication of natural imagery throughout

Uncle Silas. Maud is assured that one can only enter this heavenly scene through the 'gates of death'. Nevertheless the effect of the imagery dilutes the absoluteness of death; complete and utter separation from the world of the living is dissolved by the use of a relative standard (distance) as the distinguishing characteristic of the place of the dead. Accepting for the moment the authenticity of the children and their cottage, we may also accept that the Swedenborgian convinces Maud of his visionary power simply by describing what he can see and what she will in a moment see when she walks further on. By the close parallel between this device and the account of the celestial landscape the two are equally plausible to the reader. Consequently, those 'mimic bays and harbours' are not merely the casual metaphor of an adolescent narrator; nor can we accept simply as euphemism Austin's constant references to the excursion or unknown journey which he must shortly make. Anticipating his death Austin refers to his 'excursion'; describing the mother's death the Swedenborgian says she is 'alive but too far away to see or hear us'. The difference between the dead and the living, as far as the author describes it, always refers to a topographical dimension. Of course, it will take more than assertion of this concept to integrate it into a satisfying fiction.

The incident where Maud looks through the drawing-room window and sees the landscape as a picture has a parallel in the second part of the novel, after her removal to Bartram-Haugh. In a narrative largely exploiting the set theme of a damsel imprisoned in an old house or castle, it is to be expected that much of Maud's experience is gained by peeping through windows or across boundary walls. The subjectivity of these glimpses is well conveyed in an incident where, after an interview with her uncle Silas, Maud is unable to sleep:

it was past two o'clock when I fancied I heard the sound of horses and carriage-wheels on the avenue.

Mary Quince [a servant] was close by, and therefore, I was not afraid to get up and peep from the window. My heart beat fast as I saw a post-chaise approach the court-yard . . . I was obliged to keep my cheek against the window-pane to command a view of the point of debarkation, and my breath upon the glass, which dimmed it again almost as fast as I wiped it away, helped to obscure my vision.[1]

[1] Ibid. ii. 170-1.

It is not necessary to deny that this is a naturalistic detail in order to suggest that it is also something more than that. Maud's apparent passivity in the face of danger is perhaps partly explained by her discovery that the very act of seeing, of attempting to comprehened, leads essentially to a blurring of the object, just as her breath dims the window-pane. The incident presents in the conventions of sensational fiction the consequences of a hyperstatic mode of perception; the object effectively changes by becoming a subject. Many of her glimpses beyond the barriers reflect back inwards to the heart of her isolation; thus the exploration of the windmill only serves to incorporate its inhabitants in the scheme of ensnarement being woven around her.

Maud is only safe when she has overcome this subjective instinct to assimilate objects and so to be hypnotized before them. We see in the final paragraphs of *Uncle Silas* a sense of relief, an indication of vision cleared and adjusted to the external world: 'I have penned it. I sit for a moment breathless. My hands are cold and damp. I rise with a great sigh, and look out on the sweet green landscape and pastoral hills, and see the flowers and birds, and the waving boughs of glorious trees . . .'[1] The whole movement of the novel is to reverse slowly the priority in its dominant metaphors, where life is merely a reflection or expression of some static order or pattern, to release the human face from the formal order of portraiture. It is principally through the introduction of landscape that Le Fanu reveals the power of this abstract dimension. Characters fail to travel, not simply because the senatational novel rejoices in isolated settings and lonely horizons, but perhaps also because of the associations which physical distance acquires in those discussions of the place of the dead. The whole symmetrical structure of the book revolves, as we shall see, around the journey which Maud makes from her father's house at Knowl to her uncle's at Bartram-Haugh.

Given Sheridan Le Fanu's unusual cast of mind, this treatment of landscape might appear to be simply the unthinking product of an undirected imagination. Fortunately there is a point of comparison which effectively disposes of the problem. *Wylder's Hand* (written immediately prior to *Uncle Silas*) treats its setting in an entirely different way. The novel opens with a broad panorama of English countryside gradually focusing on the Brandon

[1] Ibid. iii. 322.

family home. The vision is initially harmonious; landscape and society are constantly interchanging, and much of the detail in nature is man-made—farmstead and parkland. Society is seen to emerge from nature and to resemble it in orderliness and discretion. The landscape, in turn, responds to the presence of humanity with deference. All this stands in direct contrast to *Uncle Silas* where the landscape—as in the blackberrying incident—signally fails to respond. And in *Wylder's Hand* the exposure of the villain is presented in two interrelated images in which society and nature rebel against his fraudulent aspirations: discrepancies in his alibi (the inability of society to conceal his guilt) are paralleled by the erosions of an earth bank in which he has buried his victim (the revelation of guilt by nature). Throughout *Wylder's Hand* characters move easily from the town to the Great House, from the dark undergrowth which surrounds the house to the ballroom and the election riot. Characters in *Uncle Silas* experience the greatest difficulty in achieving any freedom of movement, and are constantly restrained by the nature of their fictional world. In fact, Le Fanu's deliberate rejection of the 'things-are-as-they-seem' world of *Wylder's Hand* in writing *Uncle Silas* undoubtedly stems from his dissatisfaction with that view of reality. In *Uncle Silas*, instead, we find that man includes the landscape as it were, which is seen as basically subjective, interior or metaphorical. This is, partly, the result of contrasting roles played by the narrator in each novel. Charles de Cresseron, the narrator of *Wylder's Hand*, is a minor character who can take what is virtually an objective view of events; being neutral in relation to the principal antagonists, he does not invalidate their subjective worlds but instead provides a perspective on them for the reader. Landscape through de Cresseron's eyes may accommodate not only the village but also the narrative and the *dramatis personae*, and ultimately the imposter is obliged to comply with the narrator's sense of verisimilitude. In *Uncle Silas*, however, Maud Ruthyn is both narrator and principal character. In addition to the incidental consequences of her 'imprisonment'—the glimpses of the world through window-frames and other artificial contours—there is the fact that her view of the world as narrator is identical presumably, to that of the intended victim of the sensational plot. In describing the world of the novel she describes herself, her predicament. Silas Ruthyn's house at

Bartram-Haugh is designed to enclose a courtyard from which escape is impossible; the landscape of the fiction is modelled on the same pattern, implying enclosure, constantly referring inwards.

Both *Wylder's Hand* and *Uncle Silas*, despite the obvious differences, impose similar burdens on their characters. In *Uncle Silas* character is restricted in articulation by the absence of any explicit relation between character and context; much of the characterization of the book is negative. In *Wylder's Hand* the other extreme may be observed; context (society and nature) is active and benign to an extent which drains character of initiative and function; so much of the characterization here is formal, depending on the logic of context rather than the freedom of personality of individual characters. Elizabeth Bowen has described this habit of Le Fanu's as an 'oblique and more than semi-mistrustful view of character'.[1] Restricted in the degree to which his characters can exert their freedom and articulation, he is obliged to adopt other methods of conveying human relationship. Formal organization and metaphorical implication lead us further into *Uncle Silas* than narrative or psychological characterization. (For these reasons the English setting of the work seems less important than it would in a novel of the realist tradition.) Nevertheless, a story depends on the people it is told about, and we appreciate *Uncle Silas* initially by learning what happens to those characters who, on closer examination, turn out to be agents of another and different expression.

How do the characters of *Uncle Silas* fare if Le Fanu's notion of character is so attenuated? With most of them there is little difficulty, for the majority of named individuals operate more as stage hands who move boxes or bodies at the direction of the principals. Apart from servants at Knowl and Bartram-Haugh, the only characters of importance outside the Ruthyn family are Dr Bryerly the Swedenborgian, and Mme de la Rougierre, Maud's governess. As a character the Frenchwoman is revealed from the outside; instead of a psychological study, or even a tolerably factual explanation of how she gets mixed up with Silas, we encounter her wet grin, her cadaverous jaws, and her shrill, disturbingly broken speech. Bryerly too is introduced by way of description of his physical appearance—lean and sallow—and

[1] Introduction to *The House by the Churchyard* (London 1968), vii.

his dress, that of a Glasgow artisan in his Sunday best. Maud quickly reveals herself as imaginative, impulsive, naïve, haughty towards servants, compliant before her father.

It is primarily with her uncle Silas that Maud is involved in intricate relationship, yet the early part of the novel, when she is living at Knowl with her father, provides an exemplary account of how character is used in *Uncle Silas*. Superficially, Austin Ruthyn's aloof nature aids the peculiar treatment of character, by throwing responsibility on to the narrator. Maud initially can only ask us to believe in the intimacy between father and daughter, because his personality resists the demonstrative. But this relationship of assumed affection becomes active and explicit when Austin decides to instruct Maud as to what she must do when he goes—as he soon must—upon a journey. He learns that Maud is willing to risk sacrifice in order to clear the family name, that she feels able to resist the influence of outsiders who cannot understand the importance of this mission. There then follows a crucial passage in the novel, bringing together, either by participation or by allusion, all the principal characters, and explicitly relating them to each other: Austin addresses Maud:

'Your Uncle Silas', he said, speaking suddenly in loud and fierce tones that sounded from so old a man almost terrible, 'lies under an intolerable slander. I don't correspond with him—I don't sympathise with him—I never quite did. He has grown religious, and that's well; but there are things in which even religion should not bring a man to acquiesce, and from what I can learn, he, the person primarily affected —the cause, though the innocent cause, of this great calamity—bears it with an easy apathy which is mistaken,—and such as no Ruthyn under the circumstances ought to exhibit. I told him what he ought to do, and offered to open my purse for the purpose; but he would not, or *did* not; indeed he *never* took my advice, he followed his own, and a foul and dismal shoal he has drifted on. It is not for his sake—why should I?—that I have longed and laboured to remove the disgraceful slur under which his ill-fortune has thrown us. He troubles himself little about it, I believe—he's meek, meeker than I. He cares less about his children than I about you, Maud; he is selfishly sunk in futurity— a feeble visionary. I am not so. I believe it to be a duty to take care of others beside myself. The character and influence of an ancient family is a peculiar heritage—sacred but destructible; and woe to him who either destroys or suffers it to perish!'[1]

<hr>

[1] *Uncle Silas*, i. 230–1.

We see here the establishment of a particular relationship, hitherto inarticulate, between Austin Ruthyn and his daughter. In the words of the American critic Richard Chase (discussing the varieties of fiction generally), Austin and Maud come to share *idealized emotion*: their relationship is formalized into a Trust, after which obligations are accepted by Maud and confidences spoken by Austin.[1] The Trust is abstract in that it refers to obligations overriding personal priorities, and is exclusive in that the influence of others is antagonistic to the understanding which the trustees articulate. The heart of the matter is the acceptance of a risk of sacrifice in order to clear the family name; such emotion is symbolic, its feeling directed away from personalities and towards an abstract objective. Significantly this consolidation of the emotionally symbolic relationship is the longest speech which Maud recalls ever hearing from her father. It is only with this development that we see Maud moving into a central area of the narrative, but there is no corresponding development of parental or filial emotion, but simply a recurring allegiance to the Trust. In Austin's will it is given explicit terms which carry Maud from Knowl to Bartram-Haugh.

The concentration of Austin's character in this symbolic emotion focused on Maud seems to extend to his dealings with minor figures also. His treatment of Mme de la Rougierre, when she is accused of rifling his desk, is stiff and resolute, lacking indignation or passion. He so thoroughly embodies certain attitudes that he is, for the reader, drained of all other emotions. We meet him stepping from a hidden corner of a room; his smile is compared to a Rembrandt expression. Yet when he emerges from these frames, he is free only to adopt equally rigid attitudes. The result, however, is far from being a paradigmatic personality; there are inconsistencies and self-allusions. He is religious, but his daughter seems uneducated in his beliefs. Having castigated his brother's conduct and referred to his own sense of a duty to others, Austin admits a curious comparison which unconsciously hints at possible culpability: 'He cares less about his children than I about you, Maud.'

When she takes up residence at Bartram, in accordance with her father's will Maud moves through two adjustments in her

---

[1] See Richard Chase, *The American Novel and its Tradition* (London, 1958), esp. the opening chapter.

attitude to her uncle. First, she unstitches the elaborate fantasy she had created as a child standing before Silas's portrait in Knowl, long before she had ever thought of living as his ward. This fantasy is itself an abstract relationship based on the creation of a heroic, martyred figure appropriate to her admiration. The picture, and her fantasy, had been crucial in acting as visible evidence of the substance behind her father's Trust. Gradually, at Bartram, Maud replaces this view of Silas with a rigid embodiment of herself as the endangered heiress, which inevitably casts Silas as the wicked uncle. Maud's reaction to him is not merely one of curiosity rewarded by fear; she constructs a victim in her imagination with whom she identifies herself. Narrative details such as the caged bird or the peasant girl who is beaten with a cudgel act as external emblems of her own self-portrayal. Maud's sensitivity increases her apprehension; shortly after her arrival at Bartram she thinks of Silas that 'the living face did not expound the past, any more than the portrait portended the future'.[1]

Although Silas is not frequently in visible evidence at Bartram— he is never seen outside the building, and keeps almost exclusively to his own room—Maud's casting of herself establishes him as the dominant if dormant partner in their rigid emotional bond. There is some recognition of this fascination on her part:

When I looked at him, his eyes were upon the book before him; and when he spoke, a person not heeding what he uttered would have fancied that he was reading aloud from it.

There was nothing tangible but this shrinking from the encounter of our eyes. I said he was kind as usual. He was even more so. But there was this new sign of our silently repellant natures. Dislike it could not be. He knew I longed to serve him. Was it shame? Was there not a shade of horror in it.[2]

It may seem that Silas displays less rigidity in his responses than Austin. He welcomes Maud, he tries to cajole her, he conspires, and he assaults. If his welcome is insincere then at least we can add hypocrisy to the list of his resources. But the emotional bond, the fascinated horror, with which they regard each other must predominate in any account of his relationship with Maud. Despite the fact that we meet him through her highly coloured account, and despite his relatively few appearances, Silas is

---

[1] *Uncle Silas*, ii. 111.
[2] Ibid. iii. 127.

described in a multitude of visual details. If Austin's rigidity had
dominated the early part of the novel, then it is Silas's appearance
which plays a similar role in the second. He is the only figure of
whom we are given a detailed physical description, apart from the
thumb-nail introductions of servants, menials, and minor characters. Maud, the heroine, is not emphasized as a delicately
beautiful girl nor as a handsomely sturdy one. Her father is seen
mainly in shadows of darkness and light. Thus Silas's appearance,
decidedly odd as it is in its many descriptions, is not only distinctive in itself, but marks him off from the other characters who
lack any comparable detail. The effect is to suggest virtually an
added dimension to his existence.

The predominant aspect of Silas's appearance is his white hair
and his phosphorous eyes; references to these are so numerous
that it is unnecessary to draw attention to them specifically.
Indeed, Silas scarcely makes an entrance into either the action
or Maud's speculations without an escorting commentary on his
extraordinary appearance. He is not, however, simply an ema-
ciated Count Fosco, for the significance of these accounts is
deeper than the disturbing effect of his gaze. We should in fact
take care to distinguish between the effect which his eyes, hair,
and so on have upon Maud within the narrative and the effect
which her narration should have upon the attentive reader; far
from adhering to the deranged naturalism of the sensational
school, *Uncle Silas* is a self-conscious artefact, a verbal order.
At first we can distinguish between the ostensibly naturalist
details (whiteness of hair, leanness of body) and metaphorical
extensions of these details (such terms as 'phosphorous', 'necromantic', and other more complex images). But, given Maud's
tendency to perceive hyperstatically, it is difficult to maintain an
absolute distinction between what seems to be her unadorned
description of her uncle and her metaphorical elaborations on the
description; as a narrator her mode of perception generates
metaphor automatically. Her initial encounter with Silas produces
this vignette:

A face like marble, with a fearful monumental look, and, for an old
man, singularly vivid strange eyes, the singularity of which rather
grew upon me as I looked; for his eyebrows were still black, though

his hair descended from his temples in long locks of the purest silver and fine as silk, nearly to his shoulders.[1]

Here Maud's perceptions operate by inversions of conventional mechanisms—she is startled by the *vividness* of the man's eyes, and the more extended her observation the less familiar he appears. From this point onwards a consistent imagery is used to describe Silas, and one becomes aware of the importance of the manner of saying rather than the matter. Virtually on each occasion when Silas appears he is described in terms drawn from the vocabulary of death. In Maud's first impression of him, this imagery is still implicit, though we notice the face 'like *marble*, with a fearful *monumental* look', two terms which relate to each other by reference to monumental sculpture (i.e. tombstones). And so we can analyse what Maud found startling in Silas's initial appearance—it was those aspects which did not conform to the imagery of death—the bright eyes and the black eyebrows. She multiplies her terminology rapidly; soon Silas is an 'appari- tion, drawn as it seemed in black and white, venerable, blood- less . . .'[2] Here the effect is achieved by eliminating diversity of colour which in turn produces the perception of Silas as something drawn, that is, static. When she reviews the events of the day she utilizes four terms intimately associated with death to describe her uncle:

Uncle Silas was always before me; the voice so silvery for an old man— so *preternaturally* soft; the manners so sweet, so gentle; the aspect, smiling, suffering, *spectral*. It was no longer a shadow; I had now seen him in the flesh. But after all, was he more than a shadow to me? When I closed my eyes I saw him before me still, in *necromantic* black, ashy with a pallor on which I looked with fear and pain, a face so dazzlingly pale, and those hollow, fiery, awful eyes! It sometimes seemed as if the curtain opened, and I had seen a *ghost*.[3]

Maud reports to us that other residents in Bartram-Haugh saw Silas, if not in the same light, at least in the same imagery. His own daughter Milly says of his indisposition, 'Well, I don't know what it is, but he does grow very queer sometimes—you'd think he was dead a'most, maybe two or three days and nights

---

[1] Ibid. ii. 100–1.
[2] Ibid.
[3] Ibid. ii. 110–11. Emphasis added.

together.'[1] Some time after the occasion of this remark, Maud visits Silas in his room, and now explicitly draws on the same imagery as her cousin: 'In a white wrapper, he lay coiled in a great easy chair. I should have thought him dead, had I not been accompanied by old L'Amour [a servant], who knew every gradation and symptom of these strange affections.'[2] There is of course a natural explanation for Silas's behaviour; he takes excessive doses of laudanum. But there are reasons for ignoring this explanation. Firstly, the plot in *Uncle Silas* is largely a matter of conventional gestures—wicked uncles, lonely houses, defenceless maidens, and loyal servants—into which laudanum fits inobtrusively. Then there is the recurrent imagery used to describe Silas's condition, an imagery which has nothing to do with biological excess. In a fiction where metaphor tends towards symbol rather than simile—as in the introduction of landscape—this consistent application of death-imagery cannot be ignored. And finally, the pattern of *Uncle Silas*, the relationship between characters, locations, and events, substantiates, as we shall see, the implications of the recurring imagery.

Le Fanu, in varying the manner in which he applies his death-imagery to the figure of Silas, displays some subtelty, for the villain is rarely allowed to appear simply as sensational; references surround him in one form or another. Apart from the naturalistic details, and the metaphors of death which Maud progressively ascribes to him, a series of literary allusions continue the preoccupation with death, and extend its reference beyond Silas himself. His servant is described as a struldbrugg, that is, one of the creatures from Swift's *Gulliver's Travels* whose existence, having no end, effectively converts life into death. Another Irish allusion conveys an even more transcendental implication, when Maud mentally quotes a poem of Thomas Moore's in response to a glimpse of Silas:

> Oh, ye dead! oh, ye dead! whom we know by the light
> you give
> From your cold gleaming eyes, though you move like
> men who live.[3]

This transitional state between death and life features also in a

---

[1] Ibid. ii. 158.
[2] Ibid. ii. 167.
[3] Ibid. ii. 252.

passage from Scott's *Lay of the Last Minstrel* which Lady Monica Knollys draws on to describe her hermit cousin:

I mean Silas . . . my dear. Honestly, is he not very like Michael Scott? . . . Well, no matter. Michael Scott, my dear, was a dead wizard, with ever so much silvery hair, lying in his grave for ever so many years, with just life enough to scowl when they took his book.[1]

It is not surprising that Silas himself contributes to the growing implication of his death-association through what would be, in any novel of the classical realist tradition, a purely hyperbolic passage; Silas repents of a vindictive thought, dismissing it as 'the galvanic spasm of a corpse. Never was breast more dead than mine to the passions and ambitions of the world.'[2] This is a fine example of the non-referring nature of metaphor in *Uncle Silas*, where any consideration of galvanic electricity would be laughable, and yet where the constant implication of metaphor leads inwardly to the substance of the metaphor itself. Metaphor does not describe something; it is not secondary to a more real world which it enhances; it is that something, is the real world of the novel.

Maud gradually comes to reflect consciously upon the problem of Silas's condition. While sitting up with one of the servants by his bedside 'a new and dreadful suspicion' began to haunt her for he 'lay still and motionless as if he were actually dead'.[3] When Silas rises from this prone position, his movements are described by verbs of motion which are limbless:

The figure of Uncle Silas rose up, and dressed in a long white morning gown, *slid* over the end of the bed, and with two or three swift noiseless steps, stood behind me, with a *death-like* scowl and a simper. *Preternaturally* tall and thin, he stood for a moment almost touching me, with the white bandage pinned across his forehead, his bandaged arm stiffly by his side, and diving over my shoulder, with his long thin hand he snatched the Bible, and whispered over my head, 'The serpent beguiled her and she did eat'; and after a momentary pause, he *glided* to the farthest window, and appeared to look out upon the midnight prospect.
It was cold, but he did not seem to feel it.[4]

[1] Ibid. ii. 259.
[2] Ibid. ii. 215.
[3] Ibid. ii. 301.
[4] Ibid. ii. 305–6. Emphasis added.

All this Maud sees, significantly, framed and reflected in a mirror; there is no reciprocity between the two persons in the room. Maud is by now driven to distinguish Silas's nature from the normal and representative as she finds it in others:

His nature was incomprehensible by me. He was without the nobleness, without the freshness, without the softness, without the frivolities of such human nature as I had experienced, either within myself or in other persons. I instinctively felt that appeals to sympathies or feelings could no more affect him than a marble monument. He seemed to accommodate his conversation to the moral structure of others, *just as spirits are said to assume the shape of mortals.*[1]

Having made this categorical distinction, Maud tries to evaluate Silas: 'it seemed somehow to me, that his unknown nature was a systematic blasphemy'.[2]

Not surprisingly Maud then alludes to *Faust,* and indeed we are as close to the poetic world of Goethe or Blake as to the novelistic tradition of the Victorians. As Le Fanu shared an interest with both poets in Swedenborgian religion, it is clear that some clarification may be sought from this source. But Silas, already verbally clothed in symbolic description, appears even more central to the novel when we look at the pattern in which he moves in relation to the other figures.

In seeking the underlying pattern of *Uncle Silas,* we have to pay particular attention to some features of the early part of the book which are too easily ignored because they are assimilable into a crudely sensational reading. According to such a reading Austin Ruthyn is the righteous father whose faith in family honour is betrayed. Certainly Maud's account at face value is of a man morally and religiously upright. What we see of Austin himself indicates that this is close to his own opinion. Yet the most striking feature of his household is the lack of interest he takes in his daughter's religious training; if he is deeply convinced of the benefits of religion, then he has failed to extend these to others; his wisdom or insight is personal and exclusive. His cousin Lady Monica Knollys, taking the common-sense approach, has noticed something of this; she describes Austin, after his death, as having

---

[1] Ibid. iii. 120–1. Emphasis added.
[2] Ibid. iii. 121.

been 'a man who had forgotten the world and learned to exaggerate himself in his long seclusion'.[1] Austin ironically substantiated
such criticism in his outburst about Silas's wrongs, by admitting
that his brother is *more careless* than he is of the children's welfare.
The implied neglect is not acknowledged in modesty, for the
surrounding utterances are complacent if not self-righteous.

At Knowl there is a portrait of Silas—it is our first introduction
to him—in front of which Maud dedicates herself to his restitution.
Thus, as Austin establishes his Trust with his daughter, there is
always present the shadow portrait of the suspect. (Austin at the
same time is repeatedly described as having a Rembrandt-smile,
Rembrandt-expression, and so forth.) The duality of portrait/
subject is invoked throughout the novel, and a portrait represents
a rigid projection of idealized personality, formal and remote.
When we read the pages where Austin confides in Maud, we are
aware of this formality, a mannerism which disposes the figures
as in a painted scene. Maud sees nature as a still-life framed in
the window. At Bartram-Haugh, it seems at first that the dilapidation and carelessness of style of the place symbolizes a
fluidity of implication, but this assumption by the reader is
simply a consequence of the narrator's mistaken first impressions.
Soon an even greater inflexibility of attitude, a hypnotic emotion
emerges, externalized in Maud's discovery of the stout paling
which, like the Ruthyn family spirit, is decayed though strong.
In the scene where her uncle snatches the Bible from her, Maud
perceives everything in the obverse imagery of a mirror which
formalizes Silas into 'the figure of uncle Silas' and ensures that he
speaks 'over' Maud's head and only appears to look out on to the
night, apparently unfeeling of the cold.

Continuity between the first and second part of *Uncle Silas*
is guaranteed by Maud's removal from Knowl to Bartram. But
other continuities are nearly as precise. Bartram, though evidently
more neglected, is an isolated country house similar in its situation
and its occupants to Knowl; it is even suggested that Caen stone
steps are found at both—though this is hardly an unusual feature,
the parallel references are noteworthy.[2] There is then a symmetry
of location, revolving round Maud's journey from her father's
house to her uncle's. Both houses share certain visitors who are,

---

[1] Ibid. ii. 40.
[2] Ibid. i. 28, ii. 85.

so to speak, stable—Mme de la Rougierre, Lady Monica Knollys, Dr Bryerly. Incidents which occur early in the book are echoed or repeated at Bartram: two unacceptable suitors approach Maud at Knowl, Monica's protégé, Captain Oakley, and the insolent stranger in Church Scarsdale churchyard whom she subsequently identifies as Silas's boorish son, Dudley. Both of these reappear at Bartram-Haugh, Dudley with the inflated insolence which familiarity with the terrain provides, and Oakley whose unexplained and pointless second emergence only serves to underline the symmetry of his action. Scenes of violence at Bartram, as when Hawkes beats his daughter or when the rival suitors fight, recall the ruffians brawling in the Knowl parkland. The distinguishing feature in this symmetrical pattern is the presence of Austin in the first part and Silas in the second. We have already seen that Silas, while personally absent from Knowl, has been present through an early portrait emphasizing his gallantry and beauty and thus inspiring Maud's worship of him. However, he only takes on active life, as far as we can see, after Austin's death. When Maud gets her first imperious letter from him, she feels as if she 'had received a box on the ear'.[1] The point of succession is as precise as the inheritance of a title: immediately after Austin and Maud enter into their abstract Trust concerning Silas, Austin dies and Silas emerges. Until Austin's death he had been inert, a personality postponed. Now having seen the vocabulary of death which surrounds Silas, we can hardly find the moment of his emergence insignificant. Silas is called into being by Austin's death.

What further evidence does the book provide for so unusual a disposition of characters? First, there are certain symmetrical patterns deepening the unity of the entire structure and encouraging the perception of a continuity between Austin and Silas. Second, there are references, from Maud's subjective imagination, dissolving still further the tenuous autonomy of Austin and Silas. And finally there is the crucial document of the last will and testament, the expression of the Trust and the instigator of sacrifice, which can only be reasonably interpreted by abandoning belief in the separate existence of the Ruthyn brothers.

The plot of *Uncle Silas* as a whole can be summarized as a symmetrical pattern. At Knowl it revolves round the growth of a

[1] Ibid i. 322.

relationship between an old man and a young girl; this reaches
its climax with the establishment of 'ideal relation' and 'abstract
emotion' between them; the man then dies and the girl departs.
At Bartram the pattern is repeated; the crisis of undertaking is
the attempt on Maud's life (which precipitates Silas's death),
prefigured at Knowl by Maud's submission to the risk of sacrifice.
A symmetry of essential action is added to the symmetries of
location, minor incident, and characterization. Maud's narration
contributes enormously, but subversively, to the pattern identifying Austin and Silas. Immediately after her father's death she
dreams of him; he has an 'unnatural expression of diabolical fury',
and speaks to her warning that they will be late at Bartram-Haugh.
In other words, Austin, visualized in terms which shall soon be
applied in more detail to Silas, insists that *both* he and Maud shall
go to the house in which the imagery of death abounds. This
incident finds its own echo, in deference to the all-controlling
symmetry of the novel, at the crisis of the second part. Maud,
having attempted to escape from Bartram, is confronted by a
furious uncle; she swoons: 'When I came to myself I was drenched
with water, my hair, face, neck, and dress. I did not in the least
know where I was. I thought my father was ill, and spoke to him.
Uncle Silas was standing near the window looking unspeakably
grim.[1] Recollecting the incident the next morning, Maud repeats
her impression of the meeting: 'My recollection of what had
passed in Uncle Silas' room was utterly confused, and it seemed
to me as if my poor father had been there and taken a share—I
could not remember how—in the conference.'[2] Austin's appearance in Maud's dream, insisting that he (though dead) will go
with her to Bartram, is repeated here where she declares on two
occasions that her father somehow participated in the scenes at
Bartram.

When we bear in mind the explicitly transcendent implications
of landscape introduced at the time of Maud's first meeting with
the Swedenborgians, and their interpretation of her mother's
death in topographical terms, we can hardly avoid the conclusion
that the world of Bartram is the post-mortem recreation of Knowl,
and that Silas in some way is the dead soul of Austin. Austin
himself has maintained the equation of death and travel by his

[1] Ibid. iii. 209–10.
[2] Ibid. iii. 211.

references to his coming death as a journey which he must make. Maud's journey in the coach from Knowl to Bartram is the only detailed account of travel in the entire book; other exits and entrances are as abrupt as a cuckoo-clock. Silas, the master of Bartram, does not move beyond the house at all. When Maud finally sets out on what is meant to be a trip to France, physical distance turns in on itself and she ends up in a more remote corner of Bartram. After the central journey of the novel, there is no possibility of further movement.

All this evidence pointing towards Silas as the post-mortem continuation of Austin's career depends on formal examination, the essentially symmetrical pattern of action and character, the non-referring nature of metaphor, the preference for manner rather than matter. Nothing so concrete as an identifiable 'imita-tion' of outer reality can be found—at least as far as the secular notion of reality is concerned. There is, however, an opportunity to test the logic of *Uncle Silas* against a reading which accepts Austin and Silas as separate persons. The will is understood by all to embody Austin's belief in Silas's innocence, and Lady Monica Knollys regards the prospect of life at desolate Bartram as the fulfilment of Austin's forecast of sacrifice for Maud. How-ever, he had specifically told her that the risk of sacrifice was slight, virtually non-existent. Consequently, when he spoke of sacrifice he referred to something other than residence with Silas and the isolation that would entail. There is of course an illogicality in Austin's will, for there is no essential connection between establishing one man's innocence and demonstrating another's belief in that innocence. Austin disguises his attitude to Silas, indeed minimizes the reality of that other person, by advancing a fundamentally 'Austin-centred' proposal—by entrust-ing his daughter he shall demonstrate his own belief. It is this attitude which Lady Knollys criticizes sharply when she tells Maud 'Your poor father's idea of carrying it by a demonstration was simply the dream of a man who had forgotten the world and learned to exaggerate himself by his long seclusion.'[1] The sentence is full of accusations; the will reveals not proof but demonstration, it is a dream, created by an isolated figure who no longer sees himself as he merely is. The will, the fulcrum on which the symmetry depends in that it authorizes the central journey of the

[1] Ibid. ii. 40.

novel, reveals its own internality, its neglect of the logic of the external world. Only by dissolving the distinction between Austin and Silas can any sense be made of the document. Then it is a projection of fear, a need for assurance, and an admission that this reassurance cannot be found in the Austin/Silas psyche. The demonstration falls on Maud.

Silas replaces Austin in all the relationships and actions which had been built up at Knowl, and these are mirrored in the more hectic light of Bartram. The nature of this replacement is in several respects curious. Firstly, the political and denominational attitudes attached to Austin and Silas are similar; each is apolitical, a heretic in religion, a student of Swedenborg. The residual emotional attitudes still attaching to Austin after the Trust has been established with Maud—sternness, introspection, a preference for seclusion—are paralleled in Silas when he emerges actively in the latter half of the novel. Both men suffer from some unspecified disruption of normal health, and their deaths are immediately linked with the crux of an abstract relation with Maud. There is also a more cogent connection between the two figures; we have already noted the lack of contact between them— no correspondence, no sympathy—while secondary presences are maintained (Silas's portrait at Knowl, Austin's spectral participation in Maud's recovery of consciousness at Bartram). Austin's account of Silas fits Austin himself: 'he has grown religious, and that's well'.[1] But Austin's account of himself (his sense of duty towards others and so on) is entirely unsubstantiated. He combines pride with self-ignorance. He refuses to know himself, and the knowledge he suppresses is projected first as rumour on to remote Silas, and then as certainty when that figure is more closely tested. Ignorance of himself, ignorance of the world; those features of Austin's culminate in the negative character which is explored in the shadow existence of 'Silas'.

Is this a feature unique to *Uncle Silas;* does an explanation lie solely within the book itself? Certainly the remaining novels reveal no equally sustained pattern, though there are crude parallels to the central feature of *Uncle Silas* (its replacement of one figure by another who is in some sense not distinct from the first). In keeping with the realist sympathies of the novel form, these are usually disguised as sensationalist revelation or coin-

[1] Ibid. i. 230.

cidence: thus in *Checkmate* Walter Longcluse turns out to be
Yelland Mace of old, long thought dead but in fact merely transformed by plastic surgery; in *The Tenants of Malory* Mr Dingwell
finally reveals himself to be the long-lost black sheep whose death
he has announced earlier to a relieved family; more schematically
in *Willing to Die*, Mr Carmel and Mr Marston alternate in our
view like the heraldic devices of rival moralities. What is lacking
in these later novels is any deeper logic than that of melodrama.
Uncle Silas, because of its pervasive symmetry and metaphor,
asks the question as to why this pattern should persist in clearer
terms. An answer might be sought in the ideological consistency
which the romance—to make a tactical distinction from the novel
form—cultivates; in the case of *Uncle Silas* Swedenborgianism is
important in this regard. And if the remainder of Le Fanu's
novels offer only a mute and imprecise conformity to a pattern
seemingly peculiar to *Uncle Silas*, then we can turn once more to
an area which has already proved fruitful—the comparison of a
short tale. 'The Haunted Baronet' provides a complementary
account of character to that implicit in *Uncle Silas*, for what Le
Fanu must pass over silently in the longer fiction—the actual
continuity across death—is detailed in the shorter tale, and
accompanied by a concise explanation.

The central point of 'The Haunted Baronet' is the drowning of
pathetic Philip Feltram, and it is important to notice how Le
Fanu stresses that there is no doubt about his death, no question
of cataleptic trance or medical oversight. The ghoulish attendants
have laid out the corpse, when they are disturbed in their tea-
drinking. 'Each lady looked aghast, and saw Feltram sitting
straight up in the bed, with the white bandage in his hand, and
as it seemed, for one foot was below the coverlet, near the floor,
about to glide forth.'[1] This description is close to that of Silas
Ruthyn's movements just when Maud had begun to suspect that
he was actually dead. Though the resurrection of Philip Feltram
terrifies the household of Mardykes Hall, it had been foretold in
the cryptic words of a vagrant 'sir' or preacher. Just when the
ladies by the side of the corpse witness Feltram's resurrection,
Sir Bale Mardykes is having a troubled dream:

It seemed to him that he got up, took a candle in his hand, and went

---

[1] *Chronicles of Golden Friars* ii. 123.

through the passages to the old still-room where Philip Feltram lay . . .
He found the body of poor Philip Feltram just as he had left it . . . with
traces of suffering fixed in its outlines . . . 'Gone in weakness!' said
Sir Bale, repeating the words of the 'daft sir', Hugh Cresswell; as he
did so, a voice whispered near him, with a great sigh, 'Come in power!'[1]

The dream coincides with Feltram's resurrection, for the scream
which wakes Sir Bale is that of the body-washers. And the new
Feltram is indeed come in power, much as Sir Bale's return to
Golden Friars had been feared among the villagers. The reversal
of roles is accompanied by Feltram's oracular account of himself:
'myself, and not myself . . . as like as voice and echo, man and
shadow'.[2] Feltram's subsequent influence over his master makes
Sir Bale's tyranny seem a mere shadow; and Sir Bale's death, the
circumstances of which he had known in advance, produces an
exclamation directly echoing the earlier drowning of Feltram:
'Where is Sir Bale Mardykes now, whose roof-tree and whose
place at board and bed will know him no more? Here lies a chap-,
fallen fish-eyed image, chilling already into clay, and stiffening
in every joint.'[3] The power of Bale over Philip is exactly reversed
and intensified; the death of one echoes the intermediary death
of the other. Instead of identity, fixity, and responsibility, the
attributes of character are image, shadow, echo. 'The Haunted
Baronet' indeed would make a suitable text for Jungian analysis,
with its alternations of 'feminine' and 'masculine' attitudes in
Bale and Philip.

For the logic of the tale is of the weak Philip learning the secrets
of Sir Bale by following earlier victims (of Bale's ancestors, rather
than of himself) into the lake, and then returning to channel an
appropriate vengeance on the present lord of Mardykes Hall: the
victim triumphs; guilt *is* punishment. With its explicitly supernatural imagery, the tale incorporates a resurrected figure, whom
we can bear in mind in turning again to *Uncle Silas*'s similar
pattern of life becoming death, ignorance becoming knowledge.
We have come to a point in the density of the novel where we
must either seek some all-illumining light, or be content to see
every reliable feature of the classic novel dissolve before our eyes.
In other words we have to find some substitute for the realistic

[1] Ibid. ii. 109–10.
[2] Ibid. ii. 155.
[3] Ibid. ii. 325.

plausibility which some aspects of the book have travestied—a transcendent landscape, attenuated or bifurcated character, neglect of the logic of time.

The theories of Emanuel Swedenborg (1688–1772) were at one and the same time a product of the Enlightenment and a radical reaction against the basic direction of eighteenth-century thought. As a physical scientist and a mystic, Swedenborg brought together in his own personality the warring claims of reason and inspiration, and attempted to reconcile the categories of matter and spirit. When he came to systematize his religious beliefs he resorted to a methodology apparently scientific though his experiences were highly internalized and personal. The Swedenborgian Doctrines expounded a revelation additional to that of the Christian Church, disclosing the essential unity of matter and spirit, appearance and reality. While being a precursor of the Romantics, Swedenborg also represented a vulgarization of some Platonic concepts preserved in England through the Cambridge school. Blake, at first absorbed by the Doctrines, ultimately came to despise them. Nevertheless, their influence has been far from negligible—Blake, Goethe, Emerson, Tennyson, and Yeats all responded to aspects of Swedenborgianism.

The average reader, asked to estimate the prominence of the Doctrines in *Uncle Silas*, might compare their intrusion to the role of the Plymouth Brethren in George Moore's *Esther Waters*. The comparison is useful in so far as religious belief does not condition the behaviour of the Ruthyns, just as Esther's formal allegiance is cast aside by more powerful influences in her life. It would be a mistake to dismiss the question of Swedenborgianism in *Uncle Silas* solely on the grounds that the characters do not themselves take it very seriously. We have already learned that the named individuals in the book do not resemble in important ways characters from a realistic novel. Maud Ruthyn introduces her father's religious beliefs without embarrassment:

There was not even that mild religious bustle which sometimes besets the wealthy and moral recluse. My father had left the Church of England for some odd sect, I forget its name, and ultimately became, I was told, a Swedenborgian. But he did not care to trouble me upon the subject. So the old carriage brought my governess, when I had one, the old housekeeper, Mrs. Rusk, and myself to the parish church every

Sunday. And my father, in the view of the honest Rector who shook his head over him—'a cloud without water, carried about of the winds, and a wandering star to whom is reserved the blackness of darkness'—corresponded with the 'minister' of his church, and was provokingly contented with his own fertility and illumination; and Mrs. Rusk, who was a sound and bitter churchwoman, said he fancied he saw visions and talked with angels like the rest of that 'rubbitch'.[1]

Throughout the first half of the book Austin is the magnet to which Swedenborgian traces adhere. After the initial announcement of his theological position, references to religion are made with greater economy and subtlety. Maud's encounter with the Swedenborgian minister had already been discussed in connection with his anticipation of a 'visionary landscape' from which he leads on to an account of the Swedenborgian notion of death. But although Austin is the focus of this preoccupation he does not monopolize it; as a Swedenborgian he might have been isolated in the parish, but among the characters of *Uncle Silas* he appears, on closer examination, to be typical rather than exceptional. Apart from Lady Knollys and Cousin Milly—who are natural counterparts to their spiritually preoccupied relatives and, as such, have little influence in the narrative—all the characters are linked to the ideas of the New Jerusalem Church. In the case of minor characters, the links are sketched very lightly; on the other hand, Dr Bryerly's allegiance is specific and professional for he is the point of Swedenborgian orthodoxy in *Uncle Silas*. The importance of this role is expanded by his also becoming Austin's medical adviser and the administrator of his estate. Le Fanu even goes to some trouble to include the French governess in this spreading Swedenborgian presence.[2]

While the explicit emphasis relates to Austin, two processes gain momentum to implicate other figures in the philosophy of Swedenborg. First, our belief in Maud's comparative ignorance of the Doctrines is dissolved, and secondly, references to Silas Ruthyn's religion become more specific and recognizably Swedenborgian. The common characteristic of these disciples is the isolation which they impose on themselves—not merely a physical isolation—for each despises the beliefs of his co-religionists. Austin condemns Silas's selfishness, and his sinking into 'futurity'.

[1] *Uncle Silas*, i. 5–6.
[2] Ibid. i. 48.

Silas jeers at Bryerly's combination of visionary religion and fiscal ability, while Bryerly himself attempts to keep Maud away from Silas's home. Maud's introduction to her uncle's piety is provided by the curate: 'I don't say that there may not be some little matters in a few points of doctrine which we could, perhaps, wish otherwise. But these you know are speculative, and in all essentials he is Church . . .'[1] The curate is 'not very wise'. And when Maud reads some letters of Silas's she discovers that his vagaries in 'a few points of doctrine' are more considerable than the curate realized:

If here and there occurred passages that were querulous and even abject, there were also long passages of manly and altogether noble sentiment, and the strangest rodomontade and maunderings about religion. Here and there a letter would gradually transform itself into a prayer, and end with a doxology and no signature; and some of them expressed such wild and disordered views respecting religion, as I imagine he can never have disclosed to good Mr. Fairfield, and which approached more nearly to the Swedenborg visions than to anything in the Church of England.[2]

At this point Maud seems to uphold a solidly 'Church' attitude, but to display also a deeper knowledge of Swedenborgian intricacies than she had earlier admitted. Lady Knollys's attitude is brisker: she thinks Swedenborgians are 'a sort of pagans' and 'all likely to be damned'.[3] Bryerly, at the time of Austin's death, fills in some details of Silas's religious history, and it is subsequently made clear that Silas possesses some of Swedenborg's writings, among them *Heaven and Hell*, which Maud had tried to read as a child. This little volume from Silas's library serves to bring together three of the students of the Doctrines. On one of his irregular visits to Bartram-Haugh, Bryerly waits in semi-hiding to speak with Maud. As she approaches he closes on his finger the copy of *Heaven and Hell* which Maud had borrowed from Silas's library to read—again. He is anxious to know that she is being well treated and, to illustrate his fears about the other inhabitants of the house, he cites *Heaven and Hell* to the girl:

It was in that awful portion of the book which assumes to describe the condition of the condemned; and it said, that independently of the

[1] Ibid. i. 237.
[2] Ibid. i. 258.
[3] Ibid. i. 94.

physical causes in that state operating to enforce community of habitation, and an isolation from superior spirits, there exist sympathies, aptitudes, and necessities which would, of themselves, induce that depraved gregariousness, and isolation too.[1]

We find here the same unanimity of attitude, though at drastically separate levels, between Lady Knollys and Bryerly which is evident also at the reading of Austin's will. Lady Knollys, the voice of common sense and so merely rhetorical in the context of *Uncle Silas*, speaks of the Swedenborgians' being damned. Bryerly, to emphasize a point about Silas and his house, cites Swedenborg's account of hell. Crucial to this view of hell is the isolation which has been initially condemned in Austin and perpetuated in Silas.

Maud finally terminates her narrative with several apostrophes which reveal that she has not been indifferent to the spiritual enquiries of the Scandinavian mystic. Immediately before the attempt on her life, she describes the skylines seen from a small window in Bartram-Haugh:

A thin glimmering crescent hung in the frosty sky, and all heaven was strewn with stars. Over the steep roof at the other side spread on the dark azure of the night this glorious blazonry of the unfathomable Creator. To me a dreadful scroll—inexorable eyes. The cloud of cruel witness looking down in freezing brightness on my prayers and agonies.[2]

Here is a further example of the static qualities of Maud's imagination; confined in a house, she sees the vastness of the sky solely as a further dimension of stasis, focused cruelly on her. In more specifically Swedenborgian terms she attempts to interpret her experience:

This world is a parable—the habitation of symbols—the phantoms of spiritual things immortal shown in material shape. May the blessed second-sight be mine—to recognise under these beautiful forms of earth the ANGELS who wear them; for I am sure we may walk with them if we will, and hear them speak.[3]

In this final paragraph, Maud entirely contradicts the opinion of visionary claims implicit in her initial account of her father's religion.

[1] Ibid. ii. 196–7.
[2] Ibid. iii. 294.
[3] Ibid. iii. 323–4.

Throughout *Uncle Silas*, the only Swedenborgian text which is named is *Heaven and Hell*, originally published in 1758 as *De coelo et ejus mirabilibus et de inferno, ex auditis et visis*, and intended by Swedenborg as an introduction to his vast theological system. Though its style is unbending, *Heaven and Hell* is admirably concise, a feature which aids our application of its doctrines to several puzzling incidents in Le Fanu's novel. Swedenborg taught that the universe is a symmetrical system with hell at the lowest and heaven at the highest level. The mortal world of man, considered on one axis, may be seen to occupy a middle place. Although he is able to use physical terms, such as the points of the compass, to describe the future life, he insists that his heaven and hell are spiritual worlds. Their structures, however, are exactly similar to this mortal world of man. In *Heaven and Hell*, he tells us that the forms of man, of heaven, and of hell are similar:

Since the whole heaven resembles one man and is a Divine spiritual man in the greatest form in its very likeness, so heaven, like a man, is arranged into members and parts which are similarly named. Moreover, angels know in what member this or that society is. This society, they say, is in the head or a certain province of the head, another in the breast or a certain province of the breast, that, in the loins or a certain province of the loins, and so forth.[1]

The nature of man is directly relatable to the alternative future worlds, one of which becomes each soul's destination. The topographical detail in which the future worlds may be described, involving the suns and equinoxes of heaven and hell, is revealed through *correspondences*, a vast series of correlations between every feature of the mortal or natural world and of the future worlds. Swedenborg elaborated thousand of instances of these correspondences, providing an internal sense of the Word, in his *Arcana Coelestia*, but the synopsis in *Heaven and Hell* is quite adequate for our purposes: 'The whole natural world corresponds to the spiritual world, not only the natural world in general but also in every particular. Therefore, whatever in the natural world comes into existence from the spiritual world is said to be in

---

[1] *Heaven and Hell* (London, 1958, trans. J. C. Ager), paragraph 65. All quotations from Swedenborg in this chapter are taken from this edition, henceforth cited as *Heaven and Hell*, with paragraph numbers.

correspondence with it.'[1] Much of his demonstration of this doctrine is based on a deciphering of the Book of the Revelations of St. John the Divine, and the whole apparatus derives from the Platonic concept of Ideas underlying manifestations.

The relationship between man (in the mortal world) and angels (in the spiritual worlds) is strikingly different from the mythology of, say, Milton's *Paradise Lost*, for the angels whom Swedenborg describes were all originally men of 'this world': 'They wish for this reason that I should declare from their lips that in the entire heaven there is not a single angel who was created such in the beginning, nor in hell any devil who was created an angel of light and cast down, but that all, both in heaven and hell, are from the human race.'[2] Thus, although we are led into a world which is far from ordinary, at all times the beings which we meet—the angels as Swedenborg calls them—all originate in familiar mortal life. This involves the acts of mortal life as crucial in deciding whether a spirit is related to heaven or to hell. Crucial to an understanding of the Doctrines is Swedenborg's stress on the importance of the 'world of spirits'. Just as the mortal life of man takes a middle place between heaven and hell, considered on one axis, so the world of spirits is intermediary between the mortal life and the final resting place of the soul. It is a kind of inverted Purgatory for, instead of working off in punishment or purification the consequences of sin prior to final salvation, souls in the world of spirits are gradually attuned either to heaven or hell by a process of self-revelation:

The world of spirits is not heaven, nor is it hell, but it is the intermediary place or state between the two. For to that place man comes at first after death, and then, after a certain time, he is either raised up into heaven or cast down into hell, in accord with his life in the world.[3]

There is a perpetual equilibrium between heaven and hell. From hell continually breathes forth and ascends an effort to do evil, and from heaven there continually breathes forth and descends an effort to do good. In this equilibrium is the world of spirits . . . in equilibrium because every man after death enters first the world of spirits, and is kept there in a state like that in which he was while in the world, and this would be impossible if there were not a perfect equilibrium there;

[1] Ibid. 89.
[2] Ibid. 311.
[3] Ibid. 421.

for by means of this the characters of everyone is explored, since there they are left in the same freedom as they had been in the world.[1]

The resemblance between the world of spirits and the previous life is part of the pervading symmetry of Swedenborg's system—and indeed of his literary style. If the heart of religious speculation is the problem of salvation, the originality of Swedenborgianism lies here. For Swedenborg taught that Judgement is indirectly by deeds committed in the mortal world; but it is only in the world of spirits that the real character of these deeds is revealed as one is drawn gradually towards either hell or heaven.

There are therefore four fundamental tenets of Swedenborgianism relevant to the ideology of *Uncle Silas*: the symmetrical cosmology, the doctrine of correspondence, the world of spirits as the place of judgement, and the possibility of appearance and speech between men and angels. This final point is directly connected to Swedenborg's own life and may be dealt with before we pass on to study correspondence and judgement in the text of *Uncle Silas*. Swedenborg believed that he himself had seen and spoken to many angels, some of whom were in heaven, others in hell, and a few who were in the world of spirits so recently that their funerals had scarcely been arranged![2] This accessibility of spiritual beings depends on a man's interior sight and on the doctrine of correspondence, but the result in *Heaven and Hell* is fully documented:

Because angels are men, and live together as men do on earth, they have garments, dwellings and other such things with the difference, however, that as they are in a more perfect state, all the things they have are in greater perfection.[3]

It is better, however, to bring forward the evidence of experience. Whenever I have spoken with angels face to face, I have been with them in their dwellings. Their dwellings are precisely like the dwellings on earth which are called houses, but more beautiful. In them are chambers, inner rooms and bed-rooms in great number. There are also courts and around them gardens, flower-beds and lawns. When they live in societies, their houses are near one another, one alongside another, arranged in the form of a city, with streets, roads and public squares exactly like the cities on our earth. I have been permitted to

[1] Ibid. 590.
[2] Ibid.
[3] Ibid. 177.

wander through them, looking about on every side and occasionally entering the houses. This occurred when I was fully awake, and my inner sight was opened.[1]

Thus, before we look for any consistent application of Swedenborgian doctrines in *Uncle Silas*, we can at least be assured that they admitted the possible description of spiritual beings and states in visual terms.

In search of a starting-point from which to trace the influence of Swedenborgianism in *Uncle Silas* we can do no better than recall Maud's initial encounter with the visiting minister at the time of her mother's death. He had said to her: 'I see a cottage with a steep roof, that looks like gold in the sunlight; there are tall trees throwing soft shadows round it, and flowering shrubs, I can't say what, only the colours are beautiful, growing by the walls and windows, and two little children are playing among the stems of the trees . . .'[2] Though even to a secularist paradisal tones are audible here, Swedenborg can confirm explicitly the correspondence of gardens: 'In general, a garden corresponds to heaven as intelligence and wisdom, so that heaven is called the garden of God and paradise, and by man the heavenly paradise.'[3] If this does not take us very much further than the first chapters of Genesis, we find a more detailed account of gardens and those—like Maud—who learn to see them:

By those who are intelligent, gardens and paradises full of trees and flowers of every kind are seen. The trees there are planted in most beautiful order, entwined in cross-beam formation with arched entrances and encircling walks. All is of such beauty as to beggar description. There, walk those who are in intelligence, gathering flowers and weaving garlands with which they adorn little children.[4]

At the outset of her experience of the Swedenborgians, Maud was invited to walk on further with the minister to 'that place of wonders and of shadows where the dead were visible'; the implications of travel are extended when we observe that the journey between Knowl and the metaphorically intense world of Bartram lends substance to this equation with a spiritually altered state. *Heaven and Hell* expounds this doctrinally: 'in the spiritual world,

---

[1] Ibid. 184.
[2] *Uncle Silas*, i. 28.
[3] *Heaven and Hell*, 111.
[4] Ibid. 176.

distances have no other origin than from differences in the state of interiors'.[1] We can be reasonably certain, then, that Le Fanu was not merely attributing Swedenborgianism to his characters, as Moore makes the Waters family Plymouth Brethren, to establish a particular social or moral dimension; he has utilized concepts from the Doctrines which can be traced to the only Swedenborgian text mentioned in the novel. The world of *Uncle Silas* is, as the narrator finally recognizes, a 'habitation of symbols'.

Considering the essential action revolving round the narrator's idealized emotional bond or trust, the symmetry of locations and minor figures and incidents, and the direct continuity of Austin/Silas, we find that in *Uncle Silas* something happens twice. The plausibility of this repetition cannot be found on a purely terrestial level; it implicates all the metaphysical aspects of the symbolic landscape so deliberately introduced in the early chapters. Now Swedenborg held that, in the world of spirits, the recent dead carry their memories and appetites which are so to speak 'run through' again, in order to explore the real character of the soul. In his account in *Heaven and Hell* he allowed for all the incidental detail which Bartram (in the metaphorical garb of death) provides in Le Fanu's novel; the recently deceased

sees as before, he hears and speaks as before, smells and tastes, and when touched, he feels the touch as before; he also strives, desires, longs for, thinks, reflects, is affected, loves, wills, as before; and one who is delighted with studies, reads and writes as before. In a word, when a man passes from one life into the other, or from one world into the other, it is like passing from one place unto another, carrying with him all things that he possesses in himself as a man; so that it cannot be said that after death, which is only the death of the earthly body, the man will have lost anything of his own. Furthermore, he carries with him his natural memory, retaining everything whatever that he had heard, seen, read, learned of, or thought in the world from earliest infancy even to the end of life . . .[2]

Not only does the soul newly arrived in the world of spirits feel it to be similar to mortal life but 'he then does not know but that he is still in the world unless he gives attention to what he encounters'.[3] And Swedenborg elsewhere even abandons this

---

[1] Ibid. 42, and see also 192.
[2] Ibid. 461.
[3] Ibid. 493.

tenuous means of distinguishing between life and death, for he declares that 'when a man has become a spirit he does not know otherwise than that he is in his own body in which he had been in the world and thus does not know that he has died'.[1] If we are right in thinking Swedenborgianism structurally important in *Uncle Silas*, such passages from *Heaven and Hell* as these effectively eliminate all logical objections to the formal analysis that Silas is a continuity of Austin, the metaphorical implication that Silas is the post-mortem existence of Austin, a pattern underlined by so many other parallels of incident and setting. Even the recurrence of minor figures from the Knowl section fits into this pattern and finds justification in one of the more vulgarized and vulgar doctrines of *Heaven and Hell*: 'So all, as soon as they come into the other life, are recognised by their friends, their relatives, and those in any way known to them; and they talk with one another, and afterwards associate in accordance with their friendships in the world.'[2]

But the condition of the dead in the world of spirits is not static. They are, after all, being explored and their real character discovered so that they may be drawn towards either hell or heaven. The account which Swedenborg gives of the initial withdrawal from the body is consistent with Le Fanu's description of Silas's trances and apparent stupor.[3] Similarly the gradual revelation of the soul's real moral condition is paralleled in *Uncle Silas* by Maud's gradual awareness of her danger, of her uncle's intentions. The description of Silas's outburst of rage, significantly stimulating Maud to believe that her father is present, resembles *Heaven and Hell*:

When such in the other life come into the state of their interiors, and are heard speaking and seen acting, they appear foolish; for from their evil lusts they burst forth into all sorts of abominations, into contempt of others, ridicule, and blasphemy, hatred and revenge; they plot intrigues, some with a cunning and malice that can scarcely be believed to be possible in any man. For they are then in a state of freedom to act in harmony with the thoughts of their will, since they are separated from the exteriors that restrained and checked them in the world.[4]

---

[1] Ibid. 461.
[2] Ibid. 494.
[3] Ibid. 440.
[4] Ibid. 505.

In this revelation and active memory of their real moral condition in the world, the dead continue to accept the immediate and exclusive reality of their mental processes, seeing them as no reflection of the past. Judgement too does not refer, as far as they experience it, back to any mortal offence but relates inward to the revelation of their interiors: 'no one in the other world suffers punishment on account of the evils he has done in this world, but only on account of the evils that he then does'.[1] This sophisticated notion of remorse is exploited by Yeats in *The Words upon the Windowpane* where, through a medium, we hear the agonies of Jonathan Swift 'reliving' the crises of his life in search of a final resting place. Le Fanu's narrative is consistent with this metaphysic, for Silas is first of all rumoured to have killed a house guest, and ultimately demonstrates the methods he employed by assaulting Maud; he is exposed not for the offence of which he was originally believed guilty, but for a later correspondence or representation of it. The so-called original murder (of Charke, the house guest) has taken place prior to the Knowl/Bartram journey, whereas the assault on Maud occurs after the death of Austin and in the place reached after the novel's sole journey.

If Silas accommodates himself to this interpretation by the unshakable evidence of metaphor—the associations of death used in his description—what are we to make of Austin? Is it merely the Bartram-Haugh section of the novel which drops, as it were, through a trap-door into the metaphysical depths? There are attractions in this view, for it would satisfy the minimum demands of a Swedenborgian plausibility, while still retaining for the story a solid grip on mundane reality. But the result must leave more questions unanswered—what is the nature of the Austin/Silas continuum, or more specifically, what is the original cause of the diabolical revelation which Silas displays? For, although the two sections of *Uncle Silas* are true to the general symmetry of Swedenborgianism, the novel is more than a diagram, a geometrical paradigm. We have already noticed that some hint of Austin's altered value is provided even before the journey to Bartram, when he appears in Maud's dream with 'an expression of diabolical fury'. In *Heaven and Hell*, the immediately dead are described curiously: 'When, however, the internal of man has not been opened above, but only beneath, it is still, after it has

[1] Ibid. 509.

been loosed from the body, in a human form, but a horrible and diabolical form, for it is not able to look upwards towards heaven but only downwards towards hell.'[1] Though this may explain the immediate appearance of the previously untarnished Austin, there is still the larger problem of the exploration of the Ruthyn soul— using 'Ruthyn' here to refer to the unity across the continuum of Austin and Silas. What fault, appropriate in magnitude to justify the 'ridicule, and blasphemy, hatred and revenge' of Silas, can we identify in Austin's conduct?

There are many indirect though sustained accounts of Austin Ruthyn's isolation: 'an immense distance separated him from all his neighbours'. No parochial community involves Knowl; no visitors stay overnight; even relatives like Lady Knolly are discouraged. Every possibility of broader horizons has been excluded —politics abandoned, travel and remarriage rejected. The motive or consequence of this isolation is always a pride of which Austin himself is unaware. His loyalty is to family honour rather than to any individual member of his family. His will—to continue the analysis of surface references—reveals further self-centred interests in its desire to demonstrate his own belief rather than to establish a real innocence. Much of this is explicable in Swedenborg's account of pious recluses:

I have spoken with some after death who, while they lived in the world, renounced the world and gave themselves up to an almost solitary life, in order that by an abstraction of the thoughts from worldly things they might have opportunity for pious meditations, believing that thus they might enter the way of heaven. But these in the other life are of a sad disposition; they despise others who are not like themselves; they are indignant that they do not have a happier lot than others, believing that they have merited it; they have no interests in others, and turn away from the duties of charity by which there is conjunction with heaven. They desire heaven more than others; but when they are taken up among the angels they induce anxieties that disturb the happiness of the angels, and in consequence they are sent away; and when sent away they betake themselves to desert places, where they lead a life like that which they lived in the world.[2]

Even the visions which Austin seeks may not be genuine, may indeed indicate the basic self-love of his personality:

[1] Ibid. 314.
[2] Ibid. 360.

Those who meditate much on religious subjects, and are so intent upon them as to see them as it were inwardly within themselves, begin also to hear spirits speaking with them; for religious subjects, whatever they are, when man dwells upon them by himself and does not modify them with various things that are of use in the world, penetrate to the interiors and dwell there, and occupy the whole spirit of the man, and even enter the spiritual world and act upon the spirits there. . . . I have sometimes talked with them, and the wicked things they infused into their worshippers were then disclosed. They dwell together towards the left, in a desert place.[1]

Spiritual pride and enthusiasm might be rewarded by the dilapidation of Bartram, a desert place lacking all the correspondences of wisdom and community—gardens and streets. But Le Fanu has hardly justified the extraordinary revelations of the Bartram section with indications of previous guilt of this magnitude. Perhaps his intention is precisely this: to show that so innocuous an isolation as Knowl's leads in the end to the mania of Bartram. The principal difficulty in interpreting the contribution of Swedenborgianism to *Uncle Silas* lies in the sparcity of other references to the Doctrines in Le Fanu's work; only *In a Glass Darkly* specifically repeats his Swedenborgian allusions, and then in a less symbolically integrated manner than *Uncle Silas*.

It is clear that the symmetrical structure of the Swedenborgian metaphysic could be schizophrenic in origin. The psychopathological element in the Doctrines resembles schizophrenia not only in its hallucinatory visions and voices and irresistible commands, but also in its elaboration of the 'split mind' into a mystical system. Everything happens twice; there is a correspondence for every particular thing, a dual existence for each perception. But the schizoid personality is moved by the conviction that immediate things are inadequately *real*, and so he creates a further illusory world in which he can believe. Swedenborg stresses an element of neo-Platonism which comes close to this position; in *Heaven and Hell* he approves of those who know that nature is dead.[2] Just as the schizophrenic drives himself from what is unacceptable to what is unsubstantiated, so the Swedenborgian system leads

[1] Ibid. 249.
[2] Ibid. 489.

towards solipsism and implosion. If herbs and grasses signify scientific truths, what do scientific truths signify? If heaven appears like the earth, how can we tell the difference? If angels can appear to men, can talk and dress and eat like men, how can we distinguish between them to call them separately angels and men? The distinction between the dead and the living, seemingly absolute, is in fact elusive: Swedenborg may speak of them as separate and distinguishable, but his criteria can never ultimately define a difference—the dead (spirits) may appear normally to us without our being aware of the fact. Even more catastrophically, the dead do not know that they are not alive. If neither the living nor the dead can tell the difference, how can one speak of a difference? These contradictions could be multiplied by a closer scrutiny of *Heaven and Hell* where inversions of the present world are advanced as accounts of a future world. The system of correspondence is so hermetically and completely sealed that no external criterion remains by which it can be tested or proved; the result is a metaphysical oscillation of values feeding themselves on their 'inner sense'. In morals, symmetry takes the form of ambiguity, if not outright self-contradiction: *Heaven and Hell* recommends that in this life a man should participate in the delights of the world, but also teaches that in the future life he shall be punished if his 'reigning affection' has been for this world. It is a manual of religious instruction which condemns religious enthusiasm; it is written by one who saw visions to warn against people who make such claims. In the future life, even punishment and reward are indistinguishable, for each soul is drawn towards its own delights. The dissociation inherent in this central feature of Swedenborgianism can be observed in its most radical form when the Doctrines, with all their schizoid features, specifically condemn the dominant aspect of all schizophrenic experience— isolation. Those who turn from the world and from human society to cultivate the visionary world see 'falsities as truths'. *Heaven and Hell* is more diagnosis than cure, a call for treatment rather than a declaration of health.

Accounts of both Swedenborgianism and schizophrenia must take second place in an analysis of Sheridan Le Fanu's fiction. The fundamental mechanism of psychotic behaviour is the projection on to another figure, real or imagined, of feelings which the personality cannot admit as its own. These feelings need not

be justified in any external sense; they are part of the creation of
an alternative and more real world, being the stimulus towards
that act of imagination. The impulses behind such a mechanism
may vary, but a sense of guilt related to a diminished personal
identity is a powerful motivation. Austin's account of his condemned brother resembles such a projection, and it is reinforced
by the metaphors of portrait and mirror which surround both
figures in the surface narrative; significantly the reader never sees
Austin and Silas together. Neither of these male figures is absolutely real; each is a dim reflection of an original personality
obscured from our view by the power of its own illusion. Nor is
Austin/Silas the only example of such a bifurcated presentation of
personality in Le Fanu's fiction, though it the most thorough and
the most symbolically suggestive. In *Wylder's Hand* Stanley Lake
the villain is mistaken for Mark Wylder his victim on at least one
occasion, and Lake's handwriting becomes totally accepted as
Wylder's. Just as Silas Ruthyn appears only after Austin dies, so
Lake must logically disappear with the discovery of Wylder's body
in Redman's Dell. In *Wylder's Hand* 'villain' and 'victim' are not
mutually exclusive and distinct, for the characterization of the
novel disguises a greater unity which, however, may not be
publicly presented. Again, in *Willing to Die* there is a scene where
the sinister Marston occupies a seat in so perfect a resemblance
to the habit of saintly Mr Carmel that they appear as the negative
and positive forms of the one photograph.[1] Such narrative cameos
of duality take on a further significance in the context of Le Fanu's
recurring plot, where the would-be murderer finds that his sin
has already been committed. Indeed, the dilemma of Carmel
Sherlock in *A Lost Name* is precisely that of the schizoid personality, whose position becomes one of increasing passivity.
Even one's offences become projected on to another figure, who
robs one of the reality of guilt-in-fact, thus driving the psychosis
deeper inwards. Yet, if we abandon psychology to concentrate on
artistic organization—arguing perhaps that a story told twice has
become a form—we still find that the form is self-destructive,
implosive. What Le Fanu omits from his story—an adequate
preparation in 'Austin' for the atrocities of 'Silas'—is precisely
the sense of reality even in guilt. The story is not told against any
background of transcendent reality nor of social coherence, but

---

[1] *Willing to Die* (London, 1873), i. 144.

against itself. There is no external reference to substantiate the motivations of its figures, for they are the creators and victims of a solipsistic universe; formal perfections there may be, but they are the paradoxical absolutes of a suicidal control of will and consciousness. It is inevitable therefore that Le Fanu should introduce, albeit conversationally, discussion of a religious belief in which some absolute criterion might be found. But it is only the residual belief which we discovered in *The Purcell Papers*, the Gothic legacy which perpetuates the Devil while denying the reality of God.

In the prologue to *In a Glass Darkly* he attempted to establish a distinction between inner and outer meanings. These five tales purport to be based on the papers of a physician, Martin Hesselius, who like Bryerly before him combines medical skill with a spiritual diagnosis. In the scanty details provided by the narrator, we can see similarities between Hesselius's methods and those of Swedenborg—Hesselius is said to have written *Essays on Metaphysical Medicine* and his patient in 'Green Tea' is a reader of the *Arcana Coelestia*:

His treatment of some of these cases is curious. He writes in two distinct characters. He describes what he saw and heard as an intelligent layman might, and when in this style of narrative he had seen the patient either through his own hall-door, to the light of day, or through the gates of darkness to the caverns of the dead, he returns upon the narrative, and in the terms of his art, and with all the force and originality of genius, proceeds to the work of analysis, diagnosis and illustration.[1]

It is in this way that *Uncle Silas* should be read, first as the intelligent layman's tale of terror and mystery, and then as a symbolic pattern in which metaphor transforms landscape and characterization into a symmetrical order. Perhaps the two sections of the novel, centred on Knowl and Bartram, should not be considered as having a chronological relation to each other, but rather they are, so to speak, simultaneous.

None of Sheridan Le Fanu's other novels provide a comparable problem for the literary critic; they are for the most part repetitive and awkwardly constructed. Only 'The Haunted Baronet' and the tales of *In a Glass Darkly* possess the same concern for

[1] *In a Glass Darkly* (London, 1872), i. 5.

complex organization and symbolic consistency. The five tales culled from Dr Hesselius's papers offer variety and unity in their treatment of Le Fanu's obsessive narrative of suicide, for whereas the novels often exploit the act of self-destruction as a spasm virtually unconnected to the over-all movement of the plot, the tales present a series of variations on a theme for which suicide is a convenient short-hand description. In 'The Room in *The Dragon Volant*' a young Englishman adrift in France immediately after Napoleon's final defeat is caught up in a conspiracy of which he is the intended victim and an unconscious partner; when he finally realizes that his colleagues intended to bury him alive he reflects despairingly:

I now understood their frightful plan. This coffin had been prepared for *me*; the funeral of St. Amand was a sham to mislead inquiry; I had myself given the order at Pere la Chaise, signed it, and paid the fees for the interment of the fictitious Pierre de St. Amand, whose place I was to take, to lie in his coffin, with his name on the plate above my breast, and with a ton of clay packed down upon me; to waken from this catalepsy, after I had been for hours in the grave, there to perish by a death the most horrible that imagination can conceive.[1]

Beckett's consciousness at this moment is significant; he has perceived the element of self-destruction in his death though it exists purely on a formal level. Like Lady Jane Lennox in *Guy Deverell* religious thoughts only torment him: 'I tried to pray to God in my unearthly panic, but only thoughts of terror, judgment, and eternal anguish crossed the distraction of my immediate doom.'[2] In the novels, Le Fanu presented in isolation a particular victim of self-destruction: in *Uncle Silas* it is the speculative dreamer, Ruthyn; in *Guy Deverell* (where the suicide is diffused and confused) it is Jekyl Marlowe, the sensual epicurean; in *A Lost Name* Mark Shadwell declares himself a self-sufficient rationalist. Apart from *Uncle Silas*, the novels are less than impressive, failing to convince the reader of their structural integrity—incidents often intrude upon the narrative as a whole, and obscure digressions sometimes embarrass the fiction. But in *In a Glass Darkly* he assembled tales dealing in turn with each of these types, epicurean, rationalist, and dreamer. Beckett in 'The Room in *The Dragon Volant*' is thoughtless and dangerously

---

[1] Ibid. iii. 23–4.
[2] Ibid. iii. 24–5.

innocent, but Captain Barton in 'The Familiar' is a committed whig and sceptic. Mr Justice Harbottle is a licentious and corrupt judge who is finally condemned by a dream image of himself, Chief-Justice Twofold. In 'Green Tea' the Revd Mr Jennings, a scholarly student of Swedenborg, is driven to throw himself off a cliff by the persecutions of a spectral monkey. Each of these victims has adopted a particular and distinctive attitude to Belief, but despite their philosophical divergence their fate is essentially the same.

The final story of *In a Glass Darkly*, 'Carmilla', is perhaps Le Fanu's best-known work. Though its exotic Transylvanian setting, its vampirism, and its powerfully implicit lesbianism may suggest that it is untypical of his fiction, 'Carmilla' integrates itself into the context of the novels and tales through two characteristically extreme areas—allusion and structure. The manner in which it concludes with a theory of vampirism based on the suicide of some earlier villain relates it to those novels where suicide is explicit. And the over-all structure of 'Carmilla' recalls the symmetrical form of *Uncle Silas;* first there is a straightforward narrative of a young girl introduced into a Great House as a result of her mother's need to travel; then the newcomer becomes an intimate friend of the daughter of the house while the traditional signs of vampirism—marks on the throat, listlessness, and so forth—afflict the latter girl. This narrative is then interrupted by a journey during which the victim and her father meet General Spielsdorf. The old soldier then recounts an identical story about his own daughter and the strange girl they had received as a house guest, identical except that the general's daughter had died. The two fathers proceed, with the one surviving daughter, to a place where Spielsdorf supervises the posthumous execution of the vampire who had, under the name Millarca, destroyed his daughter. She is of course identical to Carmilla who had nearly succeeded in destroying the narrator. The vampire is identified as Mircalla, the Countess Karnstein of long ago, whose portrait, after restoration, mirrored the mysterious guest and companion of the narrator. Vampirism, whatever its origins in suicide, is seen as the survival of the past at the expense of the present; just as the rediscovered portrait of 'Carmilla' recalls a similar device in 'The Haunted Baronet', so the reluctance of the narrator and her father to believe in the supernatural reality of their guest recalls the catastrophes of Schalken's demon rival. In 'Carmilla', however, the ultimate disaster is avoided by formal means, by the development of a symmetrical duality in which the narrator undergoes the ordeal and the victim of an interpolated story provides the sombre conclusion. As in *Uncle Silas*, pattern and metaphor overwhelm narrative and characterization. For it is clear that vampirism, like suicide, is exploited here for its symbolic implications. In a manner crudely parallel to the schizophrenic's attempts to escape from the insufficiently real world, the vampire tale presents a second self on which the first literally feeds; vampirism seen as a projection of this kind is suicidal in structure. 'Carmilla' emphasizes this implosive self-destruction by building up a lesbian attraction between the two girls, homosexuality providing yet another example of energies deflected and cancelled. The seductress-vampire murmurs to the narrator of 'Carmilla':

Dearest, your little heart is wounded; think me not cruel because I obey the irresistible law of my strength and weakness; if your dear heart is wounded, my wild heart bleeds with yours. In the raptures of my enormous humiliation I live in your warm life, and you shall die— die, sweetly die—into mine.[1]

Once again the pattern of *Uncle Silas* is repeated: the end of life is death; indeed death becomes a metaphor for life.

Whether in terms of the Swedenborgian 'world of spirits' where the actions of life are repeated in death, or in terms of more sensational images of suicide and vampirism, it is possible to deduce some fundamental principles of Le Fanu's perspective on reality. His view of the world is man-centred, and his depiction of nature essentially anthropomorphic. In the early *Purcell Papers* landscape is used conventionally as a mirror of human society; the sap is falling, the woods are stricken, mortal decay lies over all. By the 1860s, however, Le Fanu's treatment of landscape has become less predictable, because his view of it is no longer simple and unitary. It may appear either as a series of static scenes, presented virtually as artefacts through the framing devices of window or estate wall, or as a nervously quivering enemy to man, treacherous with revelation. This dichotomy in nature extends into every aspect of Le Fanu's work, and ultimately appears as open conflict. His characterization repeatedly

---

[1] Ibid. iii. 106–7.

suggests that we should regard separate named figures in the novels as being somehow a continuum. Austin and Silas Ruthyn are the most coherently drawn examples of this tendency, but many others might be cited. In *The Tenants of Malory*, for example, an aged housekeeper tells Tom Seddley of a dream:

I was looking toward Pendillion . . . and I saw a speck of white far away, and something told me it was his sail at last . . . and when it came very near, I saw it was Arthur himself coming upright in his shroud, his feet on the water . . . and I heard the rush of the water about his feet, and a voice—it was *your's*, not his—said 'Look at me', and I did look, and saw you, and you looked like a man that had been drowned—your face as white as his, and your clothes dripping . . .[1]

Inside the plot this passage is finally justified when we learn that Tom Seddley is the son of Mrs Mervyn (the house-keeper) and the Hon. Arthur Verney. But Arthur, in the dream, is clearly a revenant, whereas in the plot he is finally shown to be the very lively if sinister Mr Dingwell, a contradiction resolved by Dingwell's suicide. In *Willing to Die* a similar figure from the sea is presented, the survivor of a shipwreck, Richard Marston. Marston courts the narrator who also falls under the influence of Mr Carmel, a Catholic priest. Marston's spiritual allegiance in a Manichean system is underlined in a passage where he appears suddenly to Ethel Ware: 'Could it be Mr. Carmel come back again? Good Heavens! no: it was the stranger in Mr. Carmel's place, as we had grown to call it. The same window, his hands, it seemed, resting on the very same spot on the window-stone, and his knees, just as Mr. Carmel used to place his, on the stone bench.'[2] In fact, Marston is not the dark figure opposed to Carmel; he and Carmel are all but indistinguishable to the narrator. 'The Haunted Baronet' has no such unreliable narrator and presents the interrelationship of two figures more directly than the novels. When Philip Feltram returns from death by water to the house of his persecutor 'his ways and temper were changed: he was a new man with Sir Bale; and the Baronet after a time, people said, began to grow afraid of him. And certainly Feltram had acquired an extraordinary influence over the Baronet, who a little while ago had regarded and treated him with so much contempt.'[3]

---

[1] *The Tenants of Malory* (London, 1867), iii. 52.
[2] *Willing to Die* (London, 1873), loc. cit.
[3] *Chronicles of Golden Friars*, ii. 144.

Such patterns involving two or more named figures can throw light on Le Fanu's obsession with suicidal plots for, if two figures are driven towards definition as one, then the suicide of a solitary figure is a logical extension of a process inherent in his characterization. Just as decay grips the landscape and withers the trees, so his characters are reduced and refined towards absolute zero. W. J. Harvey has written of similar patterns in fiction generally and sought a philosophical explanation:

This process, wherein our sense of duality between Self and World is diminished and in which discrete identities merge into the unity of a larger spiritual continuum, we may call psychic decomposition. By this I mean that process whereby an artist's vision of the world is such that it decomposes and splits into various attributes which then form the substance of disparate characters. But the relative solidity of individual characterization does not quite conceal the fluidity of the original vision, so that characters exist not merely in the context of normal human relationships but also unite in their reference back to the single imaginative vision from which they emerged and which, so to speak, still envelopes and overflows their individual outlines.[1]

Harvey, drawing to some extent on earlier work by Dorothy van Ghent, discusses *Wuthering Heights* and *Great Expectations* as models of this process creatively utilized in literature. But in Le Fanu's fiction there is none of the positive energy and urge towards identification which marks Cathy's famous declaration in *Wuthering Heights*, 'I am Heathcliff!'; in Le Fanu's novels, though less certainly in the short stories, characters deny identities which pattern and metaphor disclose. In Dickens's great novel the continuum of Pip and Magwich or of Estella and Miss Havisham is so designed as to establish the younger figure as the centre of attention, whereas in Le Fanu's fiction it is the past which outstrips and replaces the present.

In *The Purcell Papers* heroic figures were used to explore the ramifications of the Faustian pact, and though these figures became somehow representative of social and historical processes, they remained special, distinct from the common run of men who stood around amazed and appalled. But the later fiction insists that the conditions of human existence inevitably are those of a Faustian pact; all men are bound by the same tyranny of a static

---

[1] *Character and the Novel* (London, 1965), p. 124. See pp. 247–9 below for a further discussion of this aspect of the fiction.

present and a knowing, active, and retributive past. Sweden-borgianism offers some escape from, or at least explanation of, this fallen world but the explanation disappears into solipsism and the escape is the purely formal urge towards nihilism. In advancing salvation to the seeker after truth, the Doctrines merely provide Le Fauu with a more comprehensive delineation of his anxieties.

6

THE INVISIBLE PRINCE

BETWEEN 1840 and 1860 Dublin had undergone many changes. In population it had grown in the aftermath of rural famine, and suburbs to the south of Merrion Square enclosed Le Fanu's house. Whereas in 1840 the Catholic majority had been as yet unable to capitalize on their emancipation, twenty years later social life depended to a much greater extent on their participation. Of course, the Protestant ascendency and its middle-class followers still held the 'commanding heights' in administration and the professions, but the relationship between prestige and power was now more tenuous. According to the 1861 census, members of the Established Church amounted to 12 per cent of the total population of Ireland, though half the landowners and between 70 per cent and 80 per cent of the army officers conformed to the Church of Ireland. In the professions Catholics had advanced significantly to press against the remaining restrictions which barred them from holding important legal offices.[1]

Politically, however, Dublin remained in eclipse. With the collapse of the Repeal movement the city had lapsed into provincial complacency, and such issues as arose in Irish politics in the fifteen years after the Famine were largely connected with rural society and rural problems. In this, the facts of Irish demography were at last overcoming the lingering influence of Dublin's parliamentary past. The Irish Tenant League, founded in 1850, was the first body to identify land as the issue at the heart of the Irish question, and though the League had collapsed by the end of 1852—Gavan Duffy emigrated to Australia in 1855—a new and significant note had been sounded. Following an extension of the franchise in 1850, a parliamentary pressure group emerged at Westminster, sometimes called the Irish Independent Party; among its leaders were George Henry Moore (father of the novelist, George Moore), John Sadleir (a banker and, as it turned out, swindler), and William Keogh, later a friend of

[1] See R. B. McDowell, *The Church of Ireland* (London, 1975), pp. 2–7.

Sheridan Le Fanu's. At the end of 1852 the Opposition defeated
the Conservatives, and Lord Aberdeen took office at the head of a
Whig-Peelite administration which included Sadleir and Keogh.
Their behaviour was denounced in Ireland as treachery, and the
Independent Party was soon a name only.

Nevertheless, Dublin had a function as the social capital of a
dwindling but still active ascendency, and as the centre of British
administration; Dublin Castle, the Viceregal Lodge, and the
Four Courts attracted a satellite world of some consequence. The
strongest evidence of the city's reduced status lay in the neglect
it suffered at the hands of its intellectuals. The ferment which
had stirred Trinity College in the 1830s had all but disappeared,
and no Butt or Davis enlivened student debates. Davis was dead.
Butt had departed to Westminster as MP for Harwich in 1852 and
Ireland saw little of him for the next ten years. Lever, the most
energetic of the *Dublin University Magazine* writers, had retired
to Italy; and Carleton remained preoccupied with the countryside of his youth. Only Le Fanu was actively involved in Dublin
life, connected by real but invisible threads in newspaper offices
to the city around him. If his withdrawal from national politics
after 1848 seems largely the result of internal, psychological
pressures, as an *émigré* at home he was not untypical of the
original *D.U.M.* group. This neglect of Dublin in the literature
of the mid-century in part explains the grotesque element in
George Moore's *Drama in Muslin* (1886) for in treating of contemporary city life he was breaking new ground, distracted from
conventional English settings by renewed and open violence in
Irish society:

And the darkness grows thicker, but the man still stands on the bridge.
Around him every street is deserted. On the right murder has ended
for the night; on the left, towards Merrion Square, the violins have
ceased to sing in the ballrooms; and in their white beds the girls sleep
their white sleep of celibacy. Passion and grief have ceased to trouble
the aching heart, if not for ever, at least for awhile [*sic*]: the murderer's
and the virgin's reality are sunk beneath a swift-rolling tide of dreams—
a tide deeper than the river that flows beneath the tears of the lonely
lover. All but he are at rest; and now the city sleeps; wharves, walls,
and bridges are veiled and have disappeared in the fog that has crept
up from the sea; the shameless squalor of the outlying streets is en-
wrapped in the grey mist, but over them and dark against the sky the

Castle still stretches out its arms as if for some monstrous embrace.[1]

The castle had become a centre of social life under the Victorian viceroys, and though Moore's account of high society is coloured by the rebuffs he earned in trying to gain admittance, his novel records the fragile, near-false consciousness of Merrion Square:

The weary, the woebegone, the threadbare streets—yes, threadbare conveys the moral idea of Dublin in 1882. Stephen's Green, recently embellished by a wealthy nobleman with gravel walks, mounds and ponds, looked like a school-treat set out for the entertainment of charity children. And melancholy Merrion Square! broken pavements, unpainted hall-doors, rusty area railings, meagre outside curs hidden almost out of sight in the deep gutters—how infinitely pitiful!
. . . We are in a land of echoes and shadows. Smirking, pretending, grimacing, the poor shades go by, waving a mock-English banner over a waxwork show; policemen and bailiffs in front, landlords and agents behind, time-servers, Castle hirelings, panderers and worse on the box; nodding the while their dollish cardboard heads, and distributing to an angry populace, on either side, much bran and brogue. Shadows, echoes, and nothing more. See the girls! How their London fashions sit upon them; how they strive to strut and lisp like those they saw last year in Hyde Park.[2]

Le Fanu, as the father of two daughters approaching maturity, had his responsibilities within this world. Despite his reputation as recluse—he was known at this time as the 'Invisible Prince' of Dublin society—he ensured that Emmie and Elly were introduced in the proper circles; as far as the Castle balls were concerned he delegated authority to his brother, who escorted the girls in the spring of 1864 and of 1865. At Merrion Square more intimate gatherings included Caroline Norton, Lord Dufferin (both Sheridan relatives), Percy Fitzgerald, young contributors to the *D.U.M.* such as Rhoda Broughton and Nina Cole, William and Banky Le Fanu, and some of Banky's Barrington connections. As late as 1869 Le Fanu was an irregular guest at 'Club dinners' where the company might include his brother William, Fitzgerald, Judge Keogh, M. J. Barry (who had been jailed in 1848 in Cork), the loquacious Father Healy, and a string of lawyers—John Ball, Richard Deasy, De Moleynes, and

---

[1] *A Drama in Muslin* (London, 1886), p. 220.
[2] Ibid. 158–9.

James Anthony Lawson. Charles Lever was guest of honour at one of these parties during his last visit to Ireland.

But the social world for Le Fanu remained at best a source of private amusement; to his cousin, the Countess of Gifford (Lord Dufferin's mother), he sent occasional reports:

Lady Masereene has taken a house in Dublin and came up from Oriel to take the Miss Skeffingtons [i.e. her daughters] out to balls. I paid my respects, as in duty bound, having been her guest in the country more than once and always found her very kind though very odd. I took my robust daughters with me and she received us very graciously, and kept me nearly an hour in gossip, and about a week after wrote me a kind note promising to return the girls' visit, and in about a fortnight later came from her Ladyship a large bag of mushrooms—which I acknowledged with suitable emotion, but she has never made her promised visit . . .[1]

His contacts were in fact more extensive than the merely polite and politically safe circle of soirées. Despite the crisis of 1848, in which Butt had already shown a distinctly 'national' tendency in defending Smith-O'Brien and others, Le Fanu maintained friendly if distant relations with his former ally, for in March 1864 he told Bentley that he did not think Butt had yet organized a review of *Wylder's Hand*; 'he would have sent it to me, if he had . . .'[2] As editor of the *Dublin University Magazine* from 1861 to 1869 he was in touch with every level of literate society, presiding over—if he did not always direct it—the most important organ of Irish Victorianism in literature and ideas.

According to S. M. Ellis, the *Dublin University Magazine* was 'purchased from James McGlashan's estate by Hurst and Blackett, in 1856, for £750'.[3] But a private memo of Le Fanu's makes it clear that the proprietor in 1861 was Cheyne Brady, and that Hurst and Blackett were simply the London publishers of the journal. In view of the importance of the *D.U.M.* in Le Fanu's life, his account of its acquisition is worth recording:

In the month of July 1861 I agreed to purchase the 'Dublin University Magazine' from Cheyne Brady Esq for the sum of £850—the purchase to include the July number. On the 22nd July I paid him on account

---

[1] P.R.O.N.I.: typescript copy of letter from J. T. S. Le Fanu to Lady Gifford, 11 Feb. 1866.

[2] Illinois; J. T. S. Le Fanu to R. Bentley, 31 Mar. 1864.

[3] *Wilkie Collins, Le Fanu, and Others* (London, 1951), p. 181.

by my acceptance of his draft payable 4 months after date (viz. on 25th Novr. 1861) £100. On the [day omitted] July 1861 I paid him through the hands of Mr Acton his solicitor the balance £750, by my cheque of that date on the Royal Bank, as also £2 discount on the bill already mentioned.

The transfer of the Magazine to me was registered at the Stationers Hall London by Messrs Hurst & Blackett & the date of the registered transfer is 8th August 1861.[1]

Unfortunately Le Fanu did not persist in this meticulous record of his career as proprietor and editor, and even his own contributions to the magazine have not been fully identified. In one area at least we can be reasonably certain of his output—the serial novel—for after an initial shyness Le Fanu came to sign all his longer fiction and to position it in each issue of the magazine as a major attraction. The list of his serial contributions to the *Dublin University Magazine* shows a typically Victorian prolixity:

October 1861–February 1863 *The House by the Churchyard*
June 1863–February 1864 *Wylder's Hand*
July 1864–December 1864 *Uncle Silas*
January 1865–July 1865 *Guy Deverell*
February 1866–June 1866 *All in the Dark*
February 1867–October 1867 *The Tenants of Malory*
May 1868–December 1868 *Haunted Lives*
February 1869–November 1869 *The Wyvern Mystery*

Le Fanu acknowledged authorship of these virtually from the outset, but he continued to contribute shorter fiction anonymously. *Loved and Lost*, a brief serial which appeared between September 1868 and May 1869, was never claimed as his, though it can no longer be omitted from his bibliography.[2]

Given the poor quality of much of this writing, why did Le Fanu write so prolifically? The simple answer, of course, is that he needed money, and a contributing editor was well placed to earn the maximum from his work. Not only was he able to sell book-publication rights to a London publisher such as Bentley or Chapman and Hall, but he filled much of his journal with material for which he had to make no direct payment to a contributor; every page he wrote was, in a sense, a free page. From

[1] Le Fanu papers.
[2] See Appendix 2 for a discussion of the evidence in favour of the attribution.

book publication, Le Fanu earned a modest income; for *Wylder's Hand* he had an agreement with Bentley for £200 and a further £100 contingent upon sales, for *Uncle Silas* £250 and a contingent £100, for *Guy Deverell* £300 and a contingent £100. When he negotiated the sale of *All in the Dark* (which was much shorter than the average three-decker novel) together with *A Lost Name* (this to be serialized in Bentley's *Temple Bar*) he contracted for £800. Ironically, collections of shorter tales such as *Chronicles of Golden Friars* and *In a Glass Darkly* which include his best fiction earned him significantly smaller sums; in each case he got £50 for the copyright for one year.[1]

If Le Fanu depended for his income on London publishers, the magazine's survival required a similar balancing of regional and metropolitan issues. Its editorial policy had to be broad enough to attract sales at home in Ireland and in the larger English market. When Le Fanu took over in 1861, his principal contributors were Percy Fitzgerald and L. J. Trotter. Versatility was the supreme virtue, and Fitzgerald could write fiction or biography, and Trotter felt equally competent in art-criticism and political history. The May 1862 number is not untypical; apart from verse the contents were:

> By-gone manners and customs [by Cyrus Redding]
> The latter years of William Pitt [L. J. Trotter]
> Marriage in the nineteenth century [John Morley]
> Porson [O. T. Dobbin]
> The House by the Churchyard [J. S. Le Fanu]
> Immortals by accident [D. P. Starkey]
> The terribly strange mystery in the Rue Pantalon [P. Fitzgerald]
> Irish harbours—Wexford [H. R. Hore]
> Mildrington the barrister [P. Fitzgerald]
> Mrs. Hall's last novel: Can Wrong be Right? [Author unknown]
> The freaks of fashion: a dream [L. J. Trotter][2]

Of the eight known authors, only Fitzgerald could claim to be 'native' Irish, and he was anxious to be thought a neighbour of Dickens rather than of Carleton. Morley, the only contributor of real distinction, was here making an isolated guest appearance. Trotter was a retired army officer, living in the south of England.

[1] British Library, Add. MS 36617.
[2] Attribution of these articles to the named authors is based on material in the files of *The Wellesley Index to Victorian Periodicals*, collected for publication in the fourth volume of the *Index*.

Orlando Dobbin, relative of the wretched Captain Dobbin and so a cousin of the editor, was an ordained cleric living in county Meath. By April 1867, the position has hardly changed; seven substantial articles are printed, two by Fitzgerald. There are two serial novels, one by Le Fanu himself and one by his daughter. The opening article, 'Superstitions and legends of the north of England' is by Patrick Kennedy who also contributes 'The libraries of the middle ages and their contents'. Thus, although the range of topics is wide—folklore, bibliography, the religious orders, David Garrick—the anonymous team is few in number. And for a journal with a decidedly political background, owned and edited by one who was intimately involved in the ferment of radical conservatism which surrounded the *D.U.M.* in the late 1830s and early 1840s, there is little attention to national, or even imperial, politics. And there was no reflection of the particular Protestant culture from which the magazine nominally drew its identity.

A guaranteed outlet for his fiction allowed Le Fanu to retire from Dublin with his children periodically, and in the summers of 1864, 1865, and 1866 he spent holidays at Beaumaris in Anglesey, just across the Irish Sea. In September 1865 he was staying at 10 Victoria Terrace, the last house in an austere block designed by Isambard Kingdom Brunel; the view from Beaumaris is incorporated into *The Tenants of Malory* and *Willing to Die*.[1] Dobbins, Le Fanus, Broughtons, and Bennetts had all gravitated to North Wales, Chester, or Shrewsbury, and Le Fanu was only following a pattern familiar to Irish Victorian holiday-makers and travellers. Rhoda Broughton, the daughter of his sister-in-law, Jane Bennett, began her career as a novelist in the *Dublin University Magazine* under Le Fanu's direction. In August 1865 she commenced a serial, *Not Wisely but too Well*, and her uncle wrote on her behalf to Bentley's only to receive a shocked and unfavourable reader's report. Despite this set-back, *Cometh Up like a Flower* followed between July 1866 and January 1867, and duly appeared under Bentley's imprint and with a dedication to Le Fanu.[2] By then Eleanor Frances Le Fanu, his

[1] See Enid Madoc-Jones, 'Sheridan Le Fanu and North Wales', *Anglo-Welsh Review*, vol. 17, 167–73; and 'Sheridan Le Fanu and Anglesey', *Transactions of the Anglesey Historical Society* (1961), 69–76.

[2] For an account of Rhoda Broughton see Michael Sadleir, *Things Past* (London, 1944)

elder daughter, had joined the list of contributors with another
serial novel, *Never—For Ever*. With Nina Cole and Annie
Robertson, she formed a trio of apprentice novelists whose
cause Le Fanu advanced in correspondence with his own publisher in London. Only Rhoda Broughton justified his judgement,
and the others tended through their serials to identify the *D.U.M.*
in the public mind with a distinctly feminine imagination;
during his editorship Le Fanu was the only male contributor of
fiction of ability—if we discount Mortimer Collins. Charles
Lever, to whom he dedicated *Guy Deverell* in 1865, had little or
no dealings with him between 1861 and 1872. Thus, while Le
Fanu's own fiction increasingly utilized English and Welsh
settings, and while he encouraged inexperienced ladies with a
'holiday romance' approach to literature, Lever's increasingly
trenchant analyses of Irish society and history were appearing in
The Cornhill and *Blackwood's Magazine*. Apart from the evidence
of these inclusions and exclusions, it is difficult to discover Le
Fanu's principles of selection. In a review of 1862, he had
insisted that: 'a perfect novel is as much a work of art as a perfect
play or a perfect poem. True to nature each must be. But whatever lies within the precincts of nature—no matter how wild,
how terrible, how ludicrous—provided the conditions of human
action and passion sanction it, is honestly at the disposal of the
writer.'[1] Two years later he declared editorially:

We do not deny the special merit of the Harrison Ainsworth school—
it has for many its fascination—but it is not that of truth. It is a portraiture which, in fact, no more resembles the real children of darkness
than the laced and powdered shepherds and shepherdesses, whom we
see in pink and sage-green lute-strings, and satins, and buckled shoes,
making love on old Dresden china, do the actual herds and helpers
who tend, or ever did tend, living sheep on prosaic plain or mountain.[2]

Neither as editor nor contributor did Le Fanu find the perfect
novel. His critical comments on the presence of the wild and the
terrible within nature, combined with some awareness of the
novel's requirements as art, cast a little light on the coincidence
of sensational and formal precision in *Wylder's Hand* and *Uncle
Silas*. His subsequent fiction, however, reveals greater uncertainty
as to what 'nature' may be and admits a greater dislocation

---

[1] *D.U.M.*, vol. 60 (Oct. 1862), 483.
[2] Ibid., vol. 63 (Apr. 1864), 441.

between narrative and form. Even in *Guy Deverell*, which follows immediately on *Uncle Silas*, there is evidence of a curiously effeminate sentimentalism, and by the end of the decade Rhoda Broughton's heroines were a good deal more robust than her uncle's heroes. Eleanor Frances Le Fanu did not so much imitate her father's style, as stimulate his tendency to mimic the attitudes of others, drawing him close to her own immaturity. Apart from the characteristically hyperstatic use of portrait-imagery, and the themes of revenant and suicide, *The Tenants of Malory* is all but indistinguishable from the work of the author's twenty-two year old daughter.

Quite soon after acquiring the *Dublin University Magazine* Le Fanu showed signs of impatience with it as a vehicle for his own fiction. Though there were decided short-term advantages in publishing in one's own journal, the *D.U.M.* was unlikely to launch a successful novelist or to make a meteoric career for its contributors. In May–June 1864 he was trying to place a serial—probably *Uncle Silas*—in *The Cornhill*, but without success. In 1868 he tried *Blackwood's* but with a similar result.[1] (*A Lost Name* had appeared in *Temple Bar* in 1867–8.) The sale of the *Dublin University Magazine* in 1869 to the London printer Charles F. Adams for £1,500 should therefore be seen in the light of Le Fanu's diminishing control over the full-length novel, and his growing dissatisfaction with the role of publisher/contributor. The price represents a handsome return on his 1861 investment.[2] Yet with the sale of the magazine, Le Fanu lost one of his few remaining contacts with the city of Dublin and its cultural life. The novels which he published after 1869—especially *The Rose and the Key* and *Willing to Die*, both of which appeared in *All the Year Round*—abound in the wild and ludicrous, and in their spasm-like narrative spurn the conditions of human action. Only *Checkmate* and *Morley Court* among the later novels preserve the fluency of his best work; the former is a rewritten 'sensationalized' version, and the latter virtually a reissue, of *The Cock and Anchor*.

[1] See Illinois; J. T. S. Le Fanu to R. Bentley, 5 May 1864 and 28 June 1864; National Library of Scotland (Blackwood Papers, MS 4235); J. T. S. Le Fanu to W. Blackwood, 16 Oct. 1868; see also W. J. McCormack, 'J. Sheridan Le Fanu: Letters to William Blackwood and John Forster', *Long Room*, no. 8 (1973), 29–36.
[2] Ellis, p. 181.

Wylder's Hand, serialized between June 1863 and February 1864, is ultimately a vindication of society and propriety. Though well constructed in its plot and attractive in dialogue and incidental detail, it is unhelpful to Le Fanu's biographer, for the author chose never to write again in so optimistic a style. His dissatisfaction with his success was immediately evident in the urgency with which he turned to write *Uncle Silas*, its style so different, its implications so radically pessimistic at every level, social, moral, and metaphysical. More than any other of the novels of 'an English setting and of modern times' *Uncle Silas* indirectly reveals an Anglo-Irish provenance. Geographical isolation and denominational minority reproduces in the Ruthyns an approximate model of the ascendency's position, and the novel is of course developed from two short versions of the basic plot, each with an Irish setting.[1] Austin's status in the county is compatible with this provenance:

He had been early disappointed in Parliament, where it was his ambition to succeed. Though a clever man, he failed there, where very inferior men did extremely well. Then he went abroad, and became a connoisseur and a collector; took a part, on his return, in literary and scientific institutions, and also in the foundation and direction of some charities. But he tired of this mimic government . . .[2]

This enforced withdrawal from politics is expanded in Maud's dreamings in front of Uncle Silas's portrait:

In the thin but exquisite lip I read the courage of the paladin, who would have 'fought his way', though single-handed, against all the magnates of his county, and by ordeal of battle have purged the honour of the Ruthyns. There in that delicate half-sarcastic tracery of the nostril I detected the intellectual defiance which politically isolated Silas Ruthyn and opposed him to the landed oligarchy of his county, whose retaliation had been a hideous slander.[3]

It is the stasis (and misrepresentation) of the portrait which encourages Maud's analysis. But the purist attitude to politics, or rather a purist assumption of the Ruthyns' superiority to political activity, is ironical because it depends on the ostracism of which

---

[1] 'Passage in the Secret History of an Irish Countess', *D.U.M.*, vol. 12 (Nov. 1838), 502–19; and 'The Murdered Cousin', in *Ghost Stories and Tales of Mystery* (Dublin, 1851).
[2] *Uncle Silas* i. 3.
[3] Ibid. i. 130–1.

they complain. Whether or not Silas is guilty of the crime—murder—of which he is suspected does not affect the fact that he is somehow debarred from politics; he is not apolitical but simply prevented by circumstances from speaking his political mind. Those circumstances, it is hinted, are his own excess and folly. Austin, on the other hand, lives under no suspicion and yet he too is outside the political world despite his former influence. Both the Ruthyns are politically impotent.

Other more casual allusions confirm the predominantly Anglo-Irish focus of the novelist's imagination in *Uncle Silas:* literary references to St. Kevin, Jonathan Swift, Oliver Goldsmith, and Thomas Moore. And R. B. Sheridan is introduced into the conversation of Silas himself with something of the intimacy of the family circle:

You know in that pleasant play, poor Sheridan—delightful fellow!—all our fine spirits are dead—he makes Mrs. Malaprop say there is nothing like beginning with a little aversion. Now, though in matrimony, of course, that is only a joke, yet in love, believe me, it is no such thing. His own marriage with Miss Ogle, I *know* was a case in point.[1]

These allusions in the fiction are significant because during the months when Le Fanu was writing *Uncle Silas* he was absorbed in his own family history. And the two activities were forced into alliance by the need to controvert the optimism of *Wylder's Hand* and by the delays in serialization caused by illness. From late April until the first week of June 1864, he had been the victim of influenza followed by bronchitis, and he had spent much of the six or seven week period at 11 Brennan's Terrace, Bray, a temporary retreat from Dublin. Later he revealed to his publisher:

When the short part in the July No. of the Magazine appeared I had not a line more written, & I was still not half recovered, & two days of every week are consumed in claims on my time which did not allow one moment for writing this story, the last line of which I wrote nevertheless on the 3rd of this month [November]. All then, except about 32 Magazine pages was written in 3 months only 2 thirds of which i.e. 2 months were applicable to writing the tale. I am very tired, & claim some credit for diligence.[2]

During these three months he conducted a correspondence on

[1] Ibid. iii. 63–4.
[2] Illinois; J. T. S. Le Fanu to R. Bentley, 11 Oct. 1864.

two fronts about his antecedents. His cousin, Frederick Blackwood (Lord Dufferin), was on the point of joining the Whig administration as Under-Secretary of State for India: as the son of a Sheridan (Helen, Countess of Dufferin and Gifford) he was interested in various family portraits together with details of the Le Fanu–Sheridan marriages. As he suggested, no other member of the family possessed the emotional commitment to the past which the query required: William was 'not a retrospective man'. Le Fanu's letter concluded with a ten-page summary of family history from the sixteenth century to the nineteenth, ending with an allusion to Elizabeth Le Fanu (*née* Sheridan): 'T Moore saw her & admired her eyes very much, saying (in his journal) that she had the brilliants without the carbuncles of Sheridan.'[1] His other correspondent, John Forster, recognized Le Fanu as just the kind of retrospective man to assist him in preparing a biography of Swift. Le Fanu had inherited a life interest in the Sheridan property in county Cavan, and though he had been obliged to mortgage it in 1858 to get a loan of £1,000, he now provided Forster with a nostalgic account of his last visit to Quilca:

Somewhere about 25 yards from the margin of the lake nearest the hours (I am writing from memory) there rises above its surface—but hardly above it—a rudely circular platform of loose stones. I had often wondered whether there remained any trace of the island which [Thomas] Sheridan constructed in a single night as a rejoinder to Swift's canal dug (at Quilca) in Sheridan's absence. If you have lately been looking into Sheridan's life of Swift, you no doubt remember the frollick. Well, here it was! The shrubs long departed, the verdure gone, even the clay washed away, nothing but the skeleton of the joke of 140 years ago. You can't think how odd & pathetic was the effect of meeting the bleak relic of that pleasantry so suddenly as it came upon me.[2]

It is not surprising that Le Fanu should decide, a fortnight after sending these reminiscences to Forster, to dedicate *Uncle Silas* to a latter-day Sheridan, the Countess of Gifford.[3] And if Le Fanu and Sheridan family history is traceable here and there in the novel, the duality of the narrative mirrors the past in the present.

[1] P.R.O.N.I.; J. T. S. Le Fanu to Dufferin, 18 Sept. 1864.
[2] Victoria and Albert Museum (Forster Collection); J. T. S. Le Fanu to J. Forster, 24 Oct. 1864.
[3] Illinois; J. T. S. Le Fanu to R. Bentley, 5 Nov. 1864.

But *Uncle Silas* is not a book in which one can usefully hunt for sources, because, despite a reputation for sensationalism, it is not a novel of incidents but of atmosphere. Its dominant mood is a sinister vacancy from which authority has withdrawn—'the best lack all conviction'—and with disruptive forces poised for descent. The atmosphere of *Uncle Silas* flourishes on withheld detail, and in the general context of decaying aristocracy we can see a further reflection of the Anglo-Irish world. Even the publisher's insistence on an English setting (fractured and diffused by Le Fanu's intense and static style) helped to create a symbol of Anglo-Irish decline by suggesting the remoteness and indifference of the British dimension in Ireland.

Though his published fiction does not reveal the fact in any obvious way, throughout the 1860s Sheridan Le Fanu was constantly concerned to write once again of Irish realities and of his own experience. In *Uncle Silas* he succeeded by the indirect means of suggestion and negative statement, and he was never to achieve the same degree of unity in tone, structure, and symbol in any of the later novels. His dependence on Bentley for a London imprint restricted his freedom, though in November 1865 he warned his publisher that he was 'thinking of an Irish story say in *Two* vols. to be ready in March or April'.[1] By February 1866, however, he was virtually in despair of writing: 'It seems to me so up-hill a march, so destitute of progress, so mere a treadmill, that I think if I could dispense with the little money a novel brings me in, I should never write another.'[2]

The last years of Sheridan Le Fanu's life were crowded and desolate. Between December 1861 and February 1873 he published eleven novels, two collections of tales, several new editions of earlier work, a short verse drama, and at least fifteen uncollected shorter pieces of fiction. In addition there is an unknown quantity of journalism in *The Warder* and the *Dublin Evening Mail*, with perhaps further writings awaiting identification in other papers. Against this mass of evidence there stands the brute fact that for nearly a decade it is impossible to produce any information about him relating to a consecutive period of more than two or three days; for the year 1870 virtually nothing is known, apart from his non-payment of bills and non-attendance at church. In these circumstances two question arise: if many of Le Fanu's novels are manifestly poor, is further biographical enquiry justified? And if such personal data as does emerge tends to confirm and repeat the more pedestrian aspects of his personality, is a general reassessment of his fiction possible? Taken in isolation, each of these questions would seem to demand a swift dismissal, to convict Le Fanu of complete inconsequence after *Uncle Silas*, a complex and significant novel whose ultimate nihilism appears to have exhausted its author. Yet there are overriding reasons for continuing to pursue the course of his imagination after 1864. Le Fanu's last decade, after all, was shaped by his previous experience, his reaction to Susanna's death, her religious torments, the marital difficulties which evidently fuelled her anxieties, the interaction of politics and historical romance which dominated his work between 1838 and 1848. Only mathematicians measure a writer's life in decades, and until we have understood the consequences of those earlier trials we have not fully understood their cause. In addition, an appreciation of *Uncle Silas* is in part at least dependent on (for it is suggested by) by the cruder revelations of social, religious, and sexual anxiety in the later novels. Le Fanu's art being a matter of obliquity and concealment as well as revelation and exposure, the faults of his poorer work are as helpful as the merits of his best in directing attention to fertile areas of enquiry. And if some of the later novels may be dismissed in themselves, there are still impressive short tales written as late as 1870 ('The Haunted Baronet'), 1871–2 ('Carmilla'), and 1872 ('Sir Dominic's Bargain'). As if to prove that one can never fully appreciate the early work of an evasive writer until he has dropped his pen forever, Le Fanu in his last years returned to his own first stories and novels to revise and expand them. *The Wyvern Mystery* (1869) reworks at length 'A Chapter in the History of a Tyrone Family' (1839); *Checkmate* (1871) transfers the basic plot of *The Cock and Anchor* (1845) to a modern English setting, while *Morley Court* (1873) was almost a verbatim republication of his first novel. Among the shorter pieces, 'The Haunted Baronet' and 'Sir Dominic's Bargain' were based on 'Robert Ardagh' (1838), and several new stories explicitly returned to the Limerick landscape of the author's youth. This renewed interest in Father Purcell's world draws Le Fanu once again into general agreement with the Irish view of political affairs, for by 1868 it was frequently remarked how the O'Connellite–Whig alliance had been reborn. Gladstone in November 1868 led a Liberal administration committed to the reconciliation, rather than the 'pacification', of Catholic Ireland. Agitation for the disestablishment of the Church of Ireland continued on from successes achieved in the Tithe War, and Fenian conspiracy threatened a more determined violence than Smith-O'Brien's 1848 skirmishes. In the late 1860s the opinions of the *Dublin University Magazine*'s editor were significant, especially as he had experienced so close and ambiguous a relationship with the earlier crises. And the alarms of 1867 onwards, and his reactions to them, must cast some light back into *Uncle Silas;* if sinister vacancy had been his image of Anglo-Ireland in 1864, how did the turmoil of Fenianism and Liberalism, of disestablishment and Home Rule agitation, affect his vision?

Le Fanu's politics had swung remarkably during his early years, from violent denunciations of the Liberator to a covert and short-lived endorsement of Repeal, from practical co-operation with Young Irelanders to unsuccessful canvassing for a Tory nomination. There was a consistent thread running through these widely separated corners of the fabric, which might be described variously as opposition to politicized Catholicism or attempts to redefine grounds for Protestant supremacism. Consistency of this kind did not reassure him however, perhaps because the denominational aspect—the fundamental Christian belief underlying his assumptions—had ceased to convince him. Self-questioning in religion, he inevitably came to see his political vagaries as treachery and betrayal. From 1852 onwards his life had been dominated by domestic pressures, and though these invoked similar anxieties, politics concerned him throughout the 1850s and early 1860s solely at the level of journalism. Resumed imaginative writing was soon paralleled by a new and sober interest in politics. He had become a partner with Dr Henry Maunsell in the *Dublin Evening Mail* which, as he expressed it, was 'traditionally and in point of fact, the newspaper of the Irish Tory gentry'.[1] Though he was inclined to exaggerate its influence, the paper had effectively withheld support from any of Disraeli's

[1] P.R.O.N.I.; typescript copy of letter from J. T. S. Le Fanu to Lady Gifford, 24 Feb. 1866.

Irish candidates, and this specifically at Le Fanu's insistence. Though Maunsell had supported the Irish Council negotiations in 1847, he was now cautious of such speculations and Le Fanu sought the aid of Lady Gifford in bringing him round:

Now I, of course, am an angel of goodness and wisdom. But of Doctor Maunsell, I must be permitted to say a word in diplomatic confidence. He is perhaps a little flighty and conceited and not always reasonable. He is very accessible to attention and a little complimentary recognition and likes to be listened to, and in that way is very easily manageable: and if he were in contact, ever so little, with those whom I am anxious to support, I think I should have no further trouble with him . . . Now if you think Sir R Peel would wish to make Doctor Maunsell's acquaintance I would ask my brother to furnish him with a line of introduction.[1]

Graver combinations than possible Peelite coalitions were at work in Ireland. From 1865 onwards the authorities were seriously worried by reports of gun-running, of successful Fenian infiltration of the army, and of vast number of drilled rebels awaiting the call to arms. In February 1866 Le Fanu was joking with Lady Gifford about 'Head Centre Stephens', the elusive Fenian leader, dividing the attention of the public with Lady Waldegrave, who as Chicester Fortescue's wife had just replaced Lady Emily Peel in the Chief Secretary's House. A Fenian rising finally occurred on 5 March 1867 and, though suppressed with little difficulty in a single night, it caused alarm in nervous households. Le Fanu, however, took the crisis calmly despite the nearness of danger and contamination:

It does appear very odd, that the fiddlings, dancings and flirtations of life, should enliven the throes of the Fenian conspiracy, and proceed surrounded by enemies in the field, and plotters prepared for anything, with Greek-fire and revolvers, in the streets! Our footman, hardly twenty one years old, whom we had had only a month, proved to be a sworn Fenian—was sent for on the night of 'the rising', and marched away with a small body of 150 men, to join the main body in the Wicklow Mountains. I am only thankful, his orders were not to put me to death, or burn my house before setting out, as they obey implicitly, under pain of death.[2]

This sang-froid contrasts with the religious melancholy with which

[1] Ibid.
[2] Ibid. 11 Mar. 1867.

the letter ends: 'I lay in great darkness and misery of mind—as I often do now, God help me!' suggesting that public disturbance and political disaster was now less to be feared than the uncertainties of self. The transition from the balance of gaiety and terror in *The House by the Churchyard* (1861–3) and the relative optimism of *Wylder's Hand* (1863–4) to the sustained and treacherous plotting of *Uncle Silas* might yet be explained in terms of the 'Fenian fever' steadily mounting in Ireland. Though any attempt to synchronize Le Fanu's fiction in the 1860s to political developments of the day must remain inexact, Fenianism is the background of his renewed activity as a novelist. No longer a member of any political pressure group (as he had been in the 1840s), his fiction had moved away from the overt parallelism of historical romance towards more oblique and suggestive symbols. The coincidence of these two processes—political passivity and 'sensational' fiction—is central to any understanding of his later work.

The first piece of non-fiction Le Fanu is known to have written as proprietor and editor of the *Dublin University Magazine* was a review of *The Leadbeater Papers*. Incidentally recording the doings of several earlier Le Fanus, Mary Leadbeater's memoirs record in horrifying detail the violence of the 1798 rebellion and its suppression:

As my friend and I walked out to see a sick neighbour, we looked with fearful curiosity over a wall inside of which we saw lying the youthful form of the murdered Richard Yeates. There he had been thrown after his death, his clothes undisturbed, but his bosom all bloody. For many days after I thought my food tasted of blood, and at night I was frequently awakened by my feelings of horror, and stretched forth my hand to feel if my husband was safe at my side.[1]

Such memories, stimulated by current fears of a Fenian rising, fuelled the violence of Le Fanu's fiction in the 1860s. Geraldine Jewsbury and the English critics who complained of the improbability of the later sensationalists had less militarist footmen than Sheridan Le Fanu. But the fault of his novels after *Uncle Silas* is not their improbability as life; it is their incoherence as symbolic patterns which relegates them to a position well below *Uncle Silas* or *Wylder's Hand* or even *The House by the Church-*

---

[1] *The Leadbeater Papers* (London, 1862), i. 223. For Le Fanu's review see *D.U.M.*, vol. 60 (Aug. 1862), 236–46.

yard. Dependent on English reviewers and circulation-library managers for the sales which Bentley expected, Le Fanu lived in a society where violence played a very different role. Back in the 1830s Irish violence had been localized in its organization though extensive in its effects; its targets had been individual land agents or police officers or others who had broken the taboos of a desperate peasantry. The violence which Fenianism threatened, and to a limited extent delivered, was national not only in its ideology but in its organization. Fenianism set up against Victorian society an ideal alternative, which it strove through armed rebellion and military endeavour to bring to actuality. From the point of view of Sheridan Le Fanu, the Tithe War disturbances had arisen from within a known if contorted society; Fenianism appeared to come from without, utterly alien and inexplicable. In part this stemmed from the Irish-American exile contribution to Fenian thought, which, by stressing conspiratorial methods, and a broad battle-front in Canada, England, and Ireland, impressed the Irish middle classes with the intangible and ever-present character of their enemies. While no direct link could ever be established between the two, this Fenian evasiveness has much in common with the violence of Le Fanu's late fiction, where marauders suddenly appear in the Knowl parkland, and the senseless body of a duellist is found at the narrator's feet in *Willing to Die*. When writing *The Cock and Anchor* Le Fanu had been supported by the conventions of historical romance, according to which defeat may be heroic, the enemy noble. That school of fiction, however, required an imaginative willingness to incorporate opposing ideologies into a single vision of the past, and after 1848 he did not reveal any ability or desire to reconcile opposites. In 'Richard Marston of Dunoran' (and to a significantly lesser extent in its longer and later form, *A Lost Name*) belief and doubt engage in bitter dialogue; the late fiction generally presents a solitary view of reality against which nothing creatively resists. Thus in *Uncle Silas* Swedenborgianism is unchallenged by any robust orthodoxy or concrete secularism. This development inevitably results in a diminished grasp on social and historical realities; not only are Knowl and Bartram geographically isolated, they are virtually without legend or tradition. Instead the details of social and historical commonplace—harmless spooks at Knowl, dilapidated fences at Bartram—become symbolic of a central psychological reality. In the process of interiorization Swedenborgianism is not solely an unchallenged monopoly; it is a self-challenging, contradictory, and destructive philosophy conditioning the whole fabric of the novel. During the Fenian fever Le Fanu was not uninterested in Irish politics, but his engagement was reflective. Perhaps Fenianism disturbed him less than the 1848 rebellion, because its essentially low-class basis eliminated any risk of his being personally contaminated. In retrospect, we can see that his objection to William Smith-O'Brien was not simply that he was disloyal, but that he spoke with some authority from the ascendency's heart.

Apart from observations from the *Dublin University Magazine*'s editorial chair and occasional articles in the *Evening Mail*, Sheridan Le Fanu's political initiatives in the 1860s were by and large connected with patronage. In this he had ambitions no less honourable than his peers in literature, though he worked under peculiar difficulties for, while Michael Banim and William Carleton were known to be poor, Le Fanu was assumed to be comfortably well-to-do. Lady Gifford considered that his financial problems aggravated his melancholy—as they probably did—though in the novels debt damns the central characters from the outset as if it were original sin. In March 1867 he was hopeful of official recognition through the good will of his neighbour Abraham Brewster, then Lord Justice of Appeal in Ireland; the source of this information was unfortunately Judge Keogh—hardly a reliable intermediary with the government. Lady Gifford urged Brewster to act decisively, but he (though quickly promoted to Lord Chancellor under Lord Derby) claimed that he was 'very obnoxious to certain of Lord Derby's friends' and unable to interfere in matters of patronage.[1] The following January Le Fanu reached a crisis: his debt to John Bennett, amounting to Consols worth £876. 10s. 6d., was converted into a mortgage on his lease of 18 Merrion Square.[2] And, as he explained at length to Lord Dufferin, his chances of official patronage had now disappeared:

a series of vital services were rendered to Brewster, during the most critical period of his recent life, by so insignificant a person as myself.

[1] P.R.O.N.I.; typescript copy of letter from A. Brewster to Lady Gifford, 17 May 1867.

[2] Registry of Deeds, Dublin, Memorial 1868/4/57. See p. 135 above.

Details (which are curious) I will tell you, if you permit me, at another time. These services he acknowledged, as they proceeded, again & again, with the strongest expressions of personal obligation, speaking (for instance) these words—'You have been the *making* of me, and if ever I have the power, I'll make you feel it'—and other equally strong professions. So soon as the suspense was ended, however, by his appointment to the Chancellorship, these professions were no longer conveyed to me directly, but through a very intimate common friend, one of our judges, who has always taken a strong & kind interest in me, & was intimately acquainted with all that had passed between me, & Brewster. In the communications (never initiated, or invited by me,) made by Brewster through him there gradually appeared this change, that he treated my claim as being, not upon himself personally, but politically upon the Government, and this, though accompanied with many kind expressions, amounted in effect in effect to handing me over to Lord Mayo [Chief Secretary], which for conclusive reasons, as well known to Brewster as to me, I could not but regard as simply *dropping* me. My estimate of Lord Mayo's dispositions toward me was formed on my knowledge that he had expressed himself in the severest terms of the qualified support given from time to time in the 'Evening Mail' to Lord Palmerston's Irish government, that he attributed that support to me, calling me in terms 'a whig'—opprobious epithet![1]

As far as the hostility of Mayo and Brewster was concerned, Le Fanu had little to worry about. Brewster was out of office after the November election, and the Chief Secretary had even earlier been appointed Viceroy of India. But if his letter reveals a decent man's refusal to beg before his enemies, it also demonstrates the weakness of a petitioner whose loyalty does not wholly lie with one great party or the other. In view of his earlier extremities of opinion, it is ironical that in 1868 Le Fanu's hopes of patronage were wrecked on the fact of his being too 'middle-of-the road', too much a Palmerstonian Tory.

Issac Butt returned to the Irish Bar in 1864 after several years' absence. The case which drew him home was of no importance in itself, but it had the effect of making him available for the Fenian trials of the following years, from which his Home Rule initiatives with their momentous consequences naturally followed. But Le Fanu's great ally in the councils of the Irish Metropolitan Conservative Society in 1841 was in 1864 a distant friend at best.

[1] P.R.O.N.I.; J. T. S. Le Fanu to Dufferin, 21 Jan. 1868.

His intimate associate of the period was William Keogh who, with John Sadleir, had discredited the Irish Independent Party by joining an English administration. Sadleir's career had at least one moment when it touched on Le Fanu's: in 1852 when one unsuccessfully sought a nomination for Carlow County, the other was elected for Carlow Town, and proceeded to earn in tandem with Keogh a reputation for political trimming as 'the Pope's Brass Band'. Sadleir and Keogh, apart from their considerable individual eccentricities, signalled the emergence of a new force in British public life—Irish Catholic professional men untroubled by pre-emancipation attitudes. In 1856 Sadleir committed suicide on Hampstead Heath to avoid exposure as a swindler and forger, and his partner Keogh inevitably suffered some prejudicial consequences of the scandal. But he was resilient, and by 1865 sufficiently in the government's confidence to be entrusted with trying several of the leading Fenians. For Le Fanu he was a strange confidant—a meteoric, fortune-hunting political lawyer, given to violent speeches from the Bench. Yet in 1869 he dedicated *The Wyvern Mystery* to the irascible judge. Sadleir the suicide and Keogh the lawyer seem to merge in the character of Mr Justice Harbottle in *In a Glass Darkly*. Butt and Le Fanu, on the other hand, had much in common; both were sons of the glebe-house, had worked together in the *Dublin University Magazine* and the Irish Metropolitan Conservative Society, had written their novels in mutual secrecy. Both were lawyers by training, and had invested some of their energies in politics. But when Butt returned to Ireland to resume his legal practice, Le Fanu wrote to congratulate him on abandoning 'the dreary drama of politics for a career that is *solid* as well as *brilliant*'.[1] The letter, though warmly expressed, effectively maintained a barrier of reserve between the previous allies. Like William Wilde (who lived across Merrion Square from the Le Fanus, and whose children occasionally played at No. 18), Butt was extrovert, careless with money, a little easy with women; Le Fanu shrank from all kinds of public demonstration, and his Calvinist conscience forbade him the sensations of his heroes. Such company as he chose to keep was respectably, conventionally jolly, and he was ever willing to sacrifice the

[1] National Library of Ireland (Butt Papers); J. T. S. Le Fanu to I. Butt, 1 Nov. 1865.

pleasures of society to protect his susceptibilities. In 1865 he had published an anonymous pamphlet, *The Prelude*, on the Dublin University constituency; James Whiteside was among the victims of his satire. Some time later when Charles Dickens was entertained in Dublin by Percy Fitzgerald, Le Fanu crept away unintroduced to Boz; as he arrived at the house he had noticed Whiteside among the guests. Dickens and he did correspond briefly, and the great novelist's advice confirms the fundamentally Irish focus of Le Fanu's imagination; he suggested 'such a character as this: an Irish youth who is incapable of his own happiness or anybody elses, and attributes that incapacity—not to his own faults, but to his country's real or supposed wrongs'.[1] Le Fanu does not appear to have taken up the theme; perhaps it struck him as too close to autobiography to be successful as fiction.

Reluctant to meet celebrities as sympathetic as Dickens and former colleagues as companiable as Butt, Le Fanu was always prepared to exert himself on behalf of his friend Keogh. In 1868 as a general election approached, speculation arose as to who the next Viceroy in Ireland might be, should the Liberals form an administration. Lord Dufferin's name appeared among the likely candidates, and Le Fanu put before his cousin a scheme for the further rehabilitation of Keogh in Irish politics:

You are aware that he served in the House for a long time & with how much distinction—Mr. Delane of the 'Times' who has heard him there can speak to that point. His ambition now is to return to Parliament— a change of Government might open the way for this—& I believe he would be easily arranged with. Having heard so often & through so many law-officers, how Viceroys are embarrassed & even directly thwarted by their own Secretaries, especially when they happen to be in the cabinet, & having heard that Mr. C. Fortescue has distinctly told people interested in politics, whom he knew here, that he would in the event of a change of government regard an offer of office *without a seat in the Cabinet* '*as an insult*', I was very anxious to obtain your permission to mention Judge Keogh's parliamentary ambition, because in the contingency of your being led to connect yourself as Ld Lieutenant with the Irish Government it might be very desirable that you should have in the house of Commons a brilliant & resolute debater to put your views there as occasion might require . . .[2]

[1] C. Dickens to J. T. S. Le Fanu, 7 Apr. 1870; see *The Letters of Charles Dickens* (Bloomsbury, 1938, ed. W. Dexter), iii. 770.

[2] P.R.O.N.I.; J. T. S. Le Fanu to Dufferin, 13 May 1868.

Dufferin's reaction to the proposal has not survived, though it is only fair to add in extenuation of Le Fanu's naïvety that he confessed that if his cousin were impressed with the suggestion of Keogh as Chief Secretary or Under-Secretary 'I should have to tell you some particulars—whenever you desire me'.

The new Liberal administration under Gladstone was faced with a problem in the shape of recent legislation which allowed Catholics to assume the higher legal offices. Le Fanu, 'writing as a mere spectator, & quite out of the circle of the party now on the eve of power', warned Dufferin that

with respect to the selection of an Irish [Lord] Chancellor very intense feeling begins to shew itself, & a mistake may lead to very embarrassing consequences. I ventured to send you an 'Evening Mail' of Saturday, in which I wrote an article on 'a Roman Catholic Chancellor' reflecting as nearly as I could collect it, the then state of opinion, & which at all events shews that I am not an illiberal witness. Since, then, however, I have heard from men of all shades of politics, some of them Roman Catholics, I speak of course of men of ability and influence, the un-animous expression of *increasing* uneasiness & alarm at the prospect of the selection of any Roman Catholic, for that office. The feeling grows, hour by hour stronger against selecting this stormy & critical moment for that step. Every one, of every party assumes that return to Brady & the old *regeme* [sic] is impossible. Lawson remains. *Personally* there would be no protestant sympathy with Lawson, should he be superceded [sic]. He has forfeited his seat by his connection with the anti-church policy of Mr. Gladstone. But that sacrifice & his protracted official & parliamentary service, give point to the question on what ground other than that of accomplishing an exciting religious triumph, does his political patron meditate passing him over in favour of a Roman Catholic? And coming simultaneously with this great & agitat-ing change, all parties would read in it a menace & a triumph very unfavourable to the success of the government.

I am not in this matter a prejudiced witness. My sympathies are all in favour of a liberal Roman Catholic as Chancellor. But considering the Herculian [sic] labours before the government, & the fact that even with most cautious & tender handling, the process, it is now too plain, will stir Irish society to its depths, I thought you might not approve, my withholding this information.[1]

As far as Keogh and Lawson are concerned, Le Fanu's motives are probably quite conventional; both men were regular guests

[1] Ibid. 7 Dec. 1868.

at the club dinner-parties which he less frequently joined. But, in reversing an anonymous opinion published as *Evening Mail* policy, his conduct is less clear. What is certain, however, is the increasing liberalism—in non-party terms—of his political attitudes. Though bitterly antagonistic to Cardinal Cullen, Le Fanu favours a Catholic Lord Chancellor, in principle at least. His private reservations are similarly broad-minded: 'The reality is only beinning to open upon the protestant people here. When it arrives with its tremendous excitement, the government, will see the humanity of having spared them every aggravation that could be even *mis*-interpreted as an insult.'[1] The crisis came with Gladstone's decision to disestablish the Church of Ireland, and the November election had been fought to a great extent on that single issue. From 1865 onwards English liberals had actively sought to remove the anomaly of Ireland's minority state church, and in Ireland Sir John Gray (MP for Kilkenny and proprietor of the *Freeman's Journal*) had been preparing the ground for Gladstone's initiative. The Fenian rebellion, apparently unconnected with issues of denominational subsidy, had in fact persuaded many English liberals that some decisive reform was needed in Ireland to ensure Irish votes for the party, and to counteract the appeal of agitation and unrest. As in 1834 and 1838, the Church of Ireland provided a convenient focus for issues which went deeper into the heart of the Irish question: the ownership of land and the aspiration towards self-government in some form. Le Fanu, a consistent Tory in terms of social policy, was able to countenance disestablishment in 1869 because he had abandoned that nervous devotion to the Protestant religion which had characterized his earlier politics. 'Countenancing', however, is the attitude of a spectator of politics, and his more profound reaction to the 1868 election and the victory of Gladstone may be traced (imprecisely) under the fabric of the last four year's fiction. As for the Chancellorship, Gladstone appointed a Catholic (Thomas O'Hagan) and chose the Earl Spencer as Viceroy and Fortescue as Chief Secretary. In his journal Lord Kimberly commented drily on Dufferin's chances of leading a Dublin administration: 'it would have been a mistake to place the Irish government entirely in the hands of two Irishmen, neither of

[1] Ibid.

them possessing much backbone'.[1] Sheridan Le Fanu wrote more
sympathetically to his cousin:

your friends will congratulate you on a very happy escape. With
O'Hagan, who is completely in the hands of Cardinal Cullen & Arch-
bishop Manning, the latter of whom is in communication with Gladstone, for Chancellor, & with a Chief Secretary in the Cabinet, every
one says that the Lord Lieut*t* will be *absolutely without power* & so will
be a mere effigy sharing in the unpopularity of acts in which he has no
part. With the protestant as well as the Roman Catholic population in
a most unpleasant & difficult temper, and without even a chance of one
of those mock-rebellions which gave Lords Abercorn & Kimberly each
a step in the peerage, it would seem to lead to nothing, for a statesman
of your energies and genius, but pain & danger. I am told, *parva si
licet componere magnis*, that it was this state of things which made
Lawson, who liking power, would otherwise have much preferred the
Atty. Generalship, elect to take the puisné Judgeship . . . My daughters
are of course, in despair at your not coming as Viceroy with Lady
Dufferin. But they see only the flowers at top, & don't know that just
now, all rests upon a quaking bog.[2]

Perhaps Le Fanu's concern for his cousin's viceregal prospects
was no more altruistic than his daughters'; perhaps he too longed
for the place in Phoenix Park society which had been his birth-
right fifty years earlier. He may have hoped that Dufferin might
provide for him what Mayo and Brewster had refused, yet he
cannot have hoped, as a barrister who had scarcely handled a
brief, for any official appointment or sinecure. If he sought
patronage from his cousin, it must have been as an acknowledgement of his merit as a writer. There are other explanations of his
conduct: Dufferin he saw as a link with the Sheridan past, whose
radicalism (now tempered by Victorian rectitude) no longer
threatened his own position in society. In class terms, one could
say that he had reconciled himself to the middle-class role which
only ascendency illusions had previously obscured; he was now a
tenant and not a landlord, a working newspaperman, and not the
oracle of hierarchic wisdom. In more personal terms, he himself
tried to relate political progress to his own cast of mind: 'I suppose
everything is tending ultimately to improvement, but the process
is disgusting & I am so sea-sick, that I almost wish at times that

[1] Quoted by Leon O Broin, *Fenian Fever* (London, 1971), p. 244.
[2] P.R.O.N.I.; J. T. S. Le Fanu to Dufferin, 14 Dec. 1868.

the ship & all hands wd go down to those caverns so deep that
no undulation disturbs . . .'[1] If the realistic political assessments
of these letters suggest a new clarity of vision for the novelist, the
gain was quickly cancelled, for melancholy and private obsession
coloured his last novels and robbed them of the formal elegance
of *Wylder's Hand* and *Uncle Silas*. The spectator of politics when
he returned to fiction perceived in the manner of a Maud Ruthyn,
subjectively, intermittently, and with an imagination caught up
in abstract emotions. Though all was not loss and decline, it was
in shorter forms (the novella 'Squire Toby's Will' for example)
that Le Fanu maintained his balance as an artist. The full-length
novel had virtually passed beyond his control.

In theory it should be possible to correlate Le Fanu's private
expression of political interest with the editorial policy of his
Dublin University Magazine. Le Fanu was at first content to
allow others to write his political columns, and only gradually
replaced Trotter and J. B. Heard with his own man, J. A. Scott,
a rising Dublin journalist. Scott, who was also associated with
The Warder, acted as a kind of secretary to the new proprietor of
the *D.U.M.*, kept the accounts for a while, and contributed an
occasional political commentary. In 1862 and again in 1864 a
temporary excitement about the status of the Irish Church
brought in Christopher Robinson and Daniel Foley as visiting
pundits, but the bulk of the month-by-month political writing
fell to Scott, who wrote almost as much on the American Civil
War as on British affairs. Then, with the death of Palmerston in
October 1865, Le Fanu undertook to write the political column
himself. In the last paragraph of his obituary for the Prime
Minister, he called for the formation of Palmerston Clubs. In
February 1866 he continued his campaign by proposing a 'middle
party' the aim of which would be the outwitting of Gladstonian
radicals; while supporting moderate reform it would defend the
Church's inviolability. In May he defined his ideal as 'constitutional repose', while still advocating a Palmerstonian compromise
party in Parliament. By September the factions at Westminster
had become more clearly defined, and he praised Lord Derby's
policy of 'showing the Roman Catholic gentry [of Ireland] that
he will administer the Act of '29 [i.e. the Emancipation Act]
generously, in the true spirit of liberality, by refusing to rule the

[1] Ibid. 13 May 1867.

country through the priesthood . . .'[1] Running through these
attitudes, isolated as they are in the list of Le Fanu's publications,
are two related themes: a distinction between the Catholic laity
and the Ultramontane priesthood led by Paul Cullen, and a
deliberate use of the term 'liberal' to describe the political and
social philosophy appropriate to this strategy.

Le Fanu's renewed interest in politics, though sustained in his
correspondence with Dufferin, did not survive in the *Dublin
University Magazine*, whose commitment to political commentary
—by whomever—continued to waver and then to disappear. Of
the thirty issues published between July 1867 and December 1869,
only seven carried political articles, and these were:

1867	July	'Lord Dufferin on Irish Tenure' (a book review)
	August	'The Scotch Reform Bill'
1868	January	'England and her Fenian Enemy'
	June	'Irish land "pacification"'
	July	*Ireland in 1868* (a book review)
	October	'Parties and the Irish Church'
1869	February	'The Railway Problem in Ireland and Belgium'

Thus, 1868, a year of two general elections and the final victory
of the Gladstonians, produces just four articles on politics—none
of them known to be by Le Fanu—and the year of disestablishment is marked by a piece on railway fares. To underline the
political indifference, or apathy, of this policy, the opening paragraph of the October 1868 article on the Royal Commission on
the Irish Church declared that

No purpose sufficient to justify the effort would be served by entering,
in these pages, into the rude conflict of argument going forward in
every part of the country, on the question of the Irish Church. The
contest is one of party politics, and discussion of principles amid the
roar and bustle of the combat would be as much out of place as a
wrangle on a battle-field over the right and wrong of the *casus belli* . . .[2]

Two explanations of this eclipse of the Magazine's political commitment to Protestantism spring to mind: first of all, the proprietor was already attempting to sell his property to a London agent, and so was anxious to de-Hibernicize its image; secondly, and as a further analysis of the urge to sell, Le Fanu had come to despair of the political future, had no interest in writing or publishing political commentary. The most striking instance of his apathy is the magazine's abandonment of the church during the disestablishment debates; though it sounded the trumpet in 1862 and 1864, the battle itself is virtually unrecorded. In its place, however—and this is a characteristic mannerism of Le Fanu's already evidenced in his suggestion that his brother should take holy orders—he provides a surrogate. Beginning in October 1868, the same issue which included 'Parties and the Irish Church', the magazine published a series of articles on the New Testament and related religious questions: 'St. Matthew's Gospel in a new light' (October 1868), 'Christ, mythical and real' (November 1868), 'The Gospel of St. Luke in its relation to St. Paul' (January 1869), etc. Of the twelve issues published in 1869, eight contained an article of this kind, and while religious subjects had been occasionally discussed from 1865 onwards, this concentration in 1868–9 is quite exceptional. The author remains unidentified—he certainly was not Le Fanu, for the articles are clearly the work of a professional churchman, scholarly in method, orthodox in tone. If Le Fanu felt unable to provide a political leadership for the Protestants of Ireland, he ensured that their biblical knowledge was fostered, side by side with his own sensational fiction.

The advent of Gladstone with his revolutionary Irish policies (as Le Fanu saw them) had immediate repercussions in Protestant circles. The year before disestablishment, a general church congress met in Dublin to debate the church's place in society and its attitudes to a changing world. As the proprietor of the leading journal of the Irish Protestants, and sometime publisher of biblical criticism, Le Fanu might have been expected to participate. But he had too long absented himself from the life of the orthodox community to join in any public soul-searching. Two of the five vice-presidents of the congress were old enemies— Frederick Shaw (Tory opponent of the Metropolitan Conservatives in 1841) and James Whiteside, whom Le Fanu had lampooned anonymously in *The Prelude*. The general committee, on the other hand, included his brother William and a Dobbin relative. A paper on 'The Church and the Periodical Literature of the Day', read by Archdeacon William Lee, made not a single allusion to Le Fanu's magazine, but in the ensuing debate Stopford Brooke (sometime fiction critic for the *D.U.M.*) declared: 'We cannot understand [Christ], we cannot enter into the profound truth of His teaching if we have habituated our mind to morbid excitement, our conscience to a continual violation of its sensitiveness, in French and English novels, and our emotions to a mood of hysteria . . . sensational literature is denatural.'[1] Sheridan Le Fanu's reaction is of course unrecorded, though it is worth noting that his subsequent fiction displays a curious juxtaposition of sensational incident and religious exclamation. The unreliable narrator of *Willing to Die* prefaces her story: 'I begin to discover through the mist who was the one friend who never forsook me through all those stupendous wanderings, and I long for the time when I shall close my tired eyes, all being over, and lie at the feet of my Saviour.'[2] With his gift for (or affliction by) mimicry, some of this religious zeal may be attributed to Lady Gifford, with whom he corresponded in the months before her death, swapping texts and exchanging consolation. But religion did not come in a single undisputed form, to be rejected or accepted in one decision. Behind the disestablishment debate lay several anxieties, some political, some denominational: that the Catholic Church better deserved state subsidy was a proposition stemming from democratic head-counting, a notion Le Fanu shrank from as an instinctive Tory. Yet Catholicism, with its universal claim to exclusive salvation, exerted a powerful attraction on wavering Victorians. In Ireland, William Maziere Brady, one of the few Irish churchmen to support disestablishment, went so far over to Rome as to become a private secretary in the Vatican; the fourth Earl of Dunraven (a distant relative of the Le Fanus) became a Catholic, while Isaac Butt, once both a bitter Orangeman and a close associate of Sheridan Le Fanu's, passed his last years in a half-hearted adherence to Catholic rites—Mr Terence de Vere White indexes

---

[1] *Authorised Report of the Church Congress* (Dublin, 1868), p. 357. That Le Fanu was on familiar terms with Lee may be deduced from his asking Lord Dufferin to support Lee's membership in the Athenaeum (P.R.O.N.I., 7 Feb. 1871). See also p. 49 above and p. 269 below.

[2] *Willing to Die*, i. 54.

these as 'curious religious practices'.[1] Le Fanu, in the days of his closest intimacy with Butt, had written stories in which Catholic Jacobitism stood symbolically for modern Protestant insecurity; and now, in the wake of disestablishment his mind was once again assimilating Catholic imagery.

Politically, he was unwilling to follow Butt. In The Metropolitan Conservative Society they had stood side by side, though in the years following they had written their historical romances without confiding in each other. When a declaration of loyalty was published in the Dublin newspapers in 1848, Le Fanu's name appeared, but his friend's did not. If the responsibilities of a barrister's brief retrospectively excuse Butt's absense from the lists, they do not explain his subsequently consistent advocacy of 'national' principles and nationalist prisoners. Le Fanu and Butt shared a respect for what Dr Thorley has recently described as old-fashioned protectionist and Palmerstonian values. The *laissez-faire* economics of the 1840s had driven these instinctive Tories into a radical posture, and now in a Gladstonian world their contrasting personalities pulled in opposite directions. Or rather, Butt characteristically took up a decided stance, whereas Le Fanu presented a Janus-like ambiguity. In the aftermath of disestablishment, the Protestant middle classes felt betrayed rather than defeated, and betrayal by their English masters and guarantors prompted a sense of rebellion in them. Not since the days of The Metropolitan Conservative Society and Young Ireland—bodies so similar and dissimilar—had conservative separatism (or Repeal) seemed attractive to the Irish gentry and their urban followers. Many of Le Fanu's associates in the newspaper world, figures on the margin of politics, were prepared at least briefly to look to Butt and George Henry Moore for leadership, and if a different element in Irish society ultimately adopted Butt as their spokesman it was the Protestant professional classes who steadied his course back into national politics.[2] The Home Rule movement of which he was the first leader—Parnell was the second and last—was a combination of constitutional politicians, ex-Fenian republicans, and land-tenure activists. But in 1870 when the Home Government Association was founded Protestant conservatives also had a voice in the new coalition. The inaugural

---

[1] *The Road of Excess* (Dublin, n.d.), p. 387.
[2] See D. Thornley, *Isaac Butt and Home Rule* (London, 1964), pp. 83–97.

meeting of the association in May 1870 included Fenians and Whigs; less predictably, Sir William Wilde, Professor Samuel Haughton, E. H. Kinahan (an ex-high sheriff), Major Laurence Knox of the *Irish Times*, and Dr Henry Maunsell of the *Dublin Evening Mail* also participated, together with two Fellows of Trinity College and several landowners. Wilde and Haughton had been contributors to the *Dublin University Magazine*; Kinahan had been a close friend of George Bennett; Knox and Maunsell were newspaper proprietors, Knox a rival of Le Fanu's, Maunsell a partner. Though these recruits did not stay long with Butt's organization, their presence underlines Le Fanu's absence, draws attention to his lack of initiative in the crisis. It was not that he lacked the ability to respond to altered circumstances—his private correspondence and the articles of early 1866 refute any accusation of political rigidity. It was not that the Home Government Association proposed dangerously new solutions; Butt emphasized continuity between pre-Famine Repeal agitation and his own latest proposals. Rather, Le Fanu's response to 1870 was specifically to *do* nothing, revealing a deep-seated resistance to action, a fundamental inertia of spirit. He had come to embody in his own attitude to public life the essential feature of his own fictional characters, a stolid and yet vulnerable opposition to movement, a hyperstatic reaction to the flux of experience.

The association founded in 1870 was a temporary phenomenon, which gave birth to a greater and different organization. David Thorley has written of it: 'from the very outset the Home Government Association was divorced from the main sources of Irish political energy . . . [by] its orange reputation, which discouraged the liberals and the catholic clergy from joining it . . .'[1] But within eighteen months the movement's character had changed; symptomatic was the defection in October 1871 of the *Irish Times*, whose proprietor had been one of the founding members of the association.

Checkmate, Le Fanu's revision of *The Cock and Anchor*, itself a near-programmatic Young Ireland plot, was serialized between September 1870 and March 1871 in, significantly, an English journal. The villain is no longer single-minded Whig or Tory, as Blarden, Ashbrooke, and O'Connor had been in the first version. Depoliticized, the new villain Walter Longcluse had disfigured

[1] Ibid. 96.

himself by plastic surgery, obliterating his original identity as Yelland Mace. But Mace, so altered, finds that his thorough wickedness has been altered too; he is finally destroyed through the incompleteness of his evil intentions. Any tincture of virtue is fatal to his intended role. So Longcluse/Mace dies a suicide, whereas his prototypes in *The Cock and Anchor* died with an historical aptness on gallows and battlefield. A real continuity of assumption links Le Fanu's early and late novels, though the logic is extreme. If Scott-ish romance assumes that the triumphant are morally suspect, Le Fanu's hero/villains demonstrate that guilt (which he presents again and again as social pre-eminence or respectability *is* punishment. Taking *The Cock and Anchor* as the epitome of his Young Ireland tendencies, we must surely find *Checkmate* a revelation of his later politics. Introspection replaces action, and the condemnation of authority proceeds from within rather than through 'Jacobite' rhetoric. Thus *Checkmate* parallels the altering role of the old conservative radicals in the Home Rule movement; in depoliticizing *The Cock and Anchor*, and in merging his Tory and Whig heroes and villains in the self-negating figure of Mr Longcluse, Le Fanu perhaps speaks a political truth; he recognized and anticipated the pointlessness of conservative investment in Home Rule. This, of course, was a creed of despair, the fundamental tenet of which was that if at first (1845?) one doesn't succeed there is nothing to be gained by trying again. The years 1845 and 1870 were perhaps less similar in their political circumstances than Butt pretended, and experience is rarely if ever merely a flux; nevertheless Le Fanu's withholding himself from the new movement seems grounded in such assumptions. As a symbol of this paradoxical involvement and indifference, *Checkmate* lacks the neatness of its prototype, the multi-dimensional quality of *Uncle Silas*. Leaning on Wilkie Collins and on *Edwin Drood*, its detective aspect vitiates any profound reading of its plot. It marks the low point of despair among Le Fanu's fellow Tories—the ebullience of Standish O'Grady's *Toryism and the Tory Democracy* lay fifteen years ahead, in 1886, the year of *A Drama in Muslin*. If there were not biographical or psychological explanations of Le Fanu's disintegration as a novelist, one might advance the stylelessness of *Checkmate* as a deliberate and fitting reflection of Anglo-Irish realities.

Willing to Die, Le Fanu's last novel, was serialized in *All the*

Year Round in 1872 and appeared posthumously in three-decker
form early in 1873. The principal difficulty confronting the critic
anxious to assess the merits of the novel lies in determining
whether the numerous echoes of earlier work reflect a jaded
imagination engaged in mechanical repetition or a deliberate or
obsessive attention to crucial themes. The Jesuit Mr Carmel
echoes the name of Carmel Sherlock in *A Lost Name*, and does
more than this for both men are religious speculators, lovers of
Italian literature, pale-featured dreamers. Opposed to him is
Richard Marston, a name reaching back to the 1848 tale which
bears his name; Marston is still associated with scepticism and
sexual treachery. Between these two the narrator is spancelled, a
vacillating, passive female voice almost drained of personality.
The central plot revolves round the interception by the Jesuits
of an inheritance expected by the Ware family, a catastrophe which
leads to Francis Ware's suicide and Ethel's destitution. What is
unclear is Le Fanu's attitude to the Jesuits; he leaves the reader
trapped—as Ethel Ware, the narrator, is trapped—between conflicting views of the order. On the one hand they are scheming
and avaricious; on the other, they are attractive ascetics. Ethel
sees her own life divided by these alternatives:

So it seemed to me my life was divided between frivolous realities and
a gigantic trance. Into this I receded every now and then, alone and
unwatched. The immense perspective of a towering cathedral aisle
seemed to rise before me, shafts and ribbed stone lost in smoke of
incense floating high in air; mitres and gorgeous robes, and golden
furniture of the altar, and chains of censers and jewelled shrines,
glimmering far off in the taper's starlight, and the inspired painting
of the stupendous sacrifice reared above the altar in dim reality.[1]

The attractions of Catholicism are described by Ethel in a near-
hypnotic manner, and she seems unaware of the implications of
her observation that the painting of the stupendous sacrifice of
Christ is remote in its 'dim reality'. There are indications of a
rushed ending to the story which strains plausibility on a realistic
level, without making sense on any formal or symbolic level. Yet
the discussion of Catholicism is a radically new element in Le
Fanu's fiction; only in 'Wicked Captain Walshawe, of Wauling'
(1864) had he attempted to discuss contemporary Catholicism,

[1] *Willing to Die*, i. 144.

and that in hostile and satirical terms. Between 1864 and 1872 he had corresponded with Lord Dufferin, and in doing so commented frequently on the status of Catholics in public life. He was happy to see a liberal policy towards the laity, but remained intransigent in the letters on the question of the priesthood; intending to send Cardinal Cullen's pastoral letters to his cousin, he was amused to encounter difficulties:

You would have thought that potatoes & pastorals were abundant in Ireland. But of Doctor Cullen's documents there is no collective copy . . . Duffy who publishes them had no copy. His printer had sent his away as waste paper—a priest whom we 'approached' declared that he never dreamed of keeping them. In fact not withstanding their violence, they are treated with a curious contempt by the Cardinal's own party.[1]

The fatal flaw in *Willing to Die* may well be that Le Fanu, in opting to place his narrator between two conflicting views of Catholicism, placed himself at the centre of an argument he could neither resolve nor abandon. The Swedenborgianism of *Uncle Silas* collaborated with the author by providing an ideology in which such contradictions were accepted and rationalized. In addition, the Swedenborgianism of the Ruthyns presented no political problems; indeed their denominational isolation mirrored the Protestant presence in Irish society.

From the moment when he bought the *Dublin University Magazine*, Le Fanu's public role was curious. He had returned as proprietor to the scene of his past success as an author, had returned to the past as the nostalgia of *The House by the Church-yard* loudly declared. Yet the past was instinct with accusation, unpredictable in its revelation, potent with menace for the future. Had he not been obliged financially to accept Bentley's insistence on English settings and modern times, he might have developed a form of novel capable of holding together those important imaginative forces—past, place, and the revenants who link the one to the other. But apart from *Wylder's Hand* and *Uncle Silas* his novels of the 1860s are loose and shapeless. Far from being a hack-writer's easy escape from reality, however, the subjectivism of Le Fanu's lesser novels is recognizably close to his own marital experience and his growing melancholia: it was his ironic mis-

---

[1] P.R.O.N.I.; J. T. S. Le Fanu to Dufferin, 13 May. 1868.

fortune to achieve a harmony of inner and outer worlds. Around him, the city of Dublin was changing, acknowledging the recent emergence of the Catholic majority, assimilating new ideas about the link with Britain. And Le Fanu was prepared to change also, to moderate his political tone, almost to obliterate it. It is impossible to pin-point the moment when this chameleon tendency became dominant in his personality, but two instances may be noted. First of all, Le Fanu's political initiatives of 1866 in calling for a 'middle party' lead into his calm response to Fenian outrage in March 1867; and secondly, his political neglect of the Irish Church in 1869, coupled with his sponsorship of biblical criticism, prefaces the contradictory Catholicism of *Willing to Die*. There is, however, a vital difference between the chameleon's ability to *appear* indistinguishable from its surroundings, and the urge to achieve an actual homogeneity with one's imaginative context. The latter, ultimately, threatens the distinctive existence of the subject, is another form of the nihilism already noted in other aspects of Le Fanu's work. His public role, then, was to have no role, to merge invisibly with the contradictions and warring factions of Irish culture. Of course, such urges are unconscious and may seem to be repressed in individual, isolated conscious acts, but the over-all pattern of Le Fanu's imagination—the ventriloquism of *The Purcell Papers* and *The Cock and Anchor*, the suicidal heroes of 'Richard Marston', *Uncle Silas*, *The Tenants of Malory*, *A Lost Name*, *Checkmate*, and *Willing to Die*, the lesbianism and vampirism of 'Carmilla'—is self-consuming. Such a fiction can unwittingly encourage a vulgarly existentialist criticism, as when Michael Begnal announces that the Le Fanuesque hero

can make no sense out of the absurd universe which is revolving around him. It is an impossible world which Le Fanu is presenting, in which there is neither order nor harmony, where characters move blindly and aimlessly like the ignorant armies on Matthew Arnold's darkling plain. One might wonder if the struggles in the novels here somehow foreshadow the futile striving of some of Irishman Samuel Beckett's characters, as poor Watt seeks to solve the mystery of the establishment of Mr. Knott.[1]

[1] M. Begnal, *Joseph Sheridan Le Fanu* (Lewisburg, 1971), p. 69. Begnal's interpretation of Le Fanu's late stories is based on the ingenious translation of *Imago Mortis* (the drug used in 'The Room in the *Dragon Volant*') as 'the death of illusion'.

Le Fanu's characters in fact see things all too clearly, see things with an intensity which imposes their truth with a distorting emphasis. V. S. Pritchett surely is right when he stresses the extreme logicality of these heroes, supernatural and natural:

Le Fanu's ghosts are what I take to be the most disquieting of all: the ghosts that can be justified, blobs of the unconscious that have floated up to the surface of the mind, and which are not irresponsible and perambnlatory figments of family history, mooning and clanking about in fancy dress. The evil of the justified ghost is not sportive, wilful, involuntary or extravagant. In Le Fanu the fright is that effect follows cause.[1]

It might be feasible therefore to correlate the guilty past of Le Fanu's fiction with the politics of his time, and particularly of his caste, to argue as it were from the specific instance of *Checkmate* that his novels mirror the dilemma of Messrs Knox, Maunsell, and Kiriahan. Leaving aside the theoretical problems involved in such an undertaking, one is left with the perplexing contrast between Le Fanu's novels and his short stories, a contrast central to the theoretical issue, for any simple view of literature as a reflected of social reality must come to terms with or founder on the diversity of literary forms: as proprietor of the *Dublin University Magazine* Le Fanu contributed not only his novels and short stories, but also reviews, poems, and a verse drama. Inevitably, any account of his published work and his public life leads into a further examination of his inner life; the two form a continuum, inform each other with autobiographical allusion in the fiction and conscious self-dramatization in the psychic life.

[1] *The Living Novel* (London, 1946), p. 96.

7

TOWARDS NIGHTFALL

MUCH OF Le Fanu's later fiction deserves the silence it has provoked; of *The Wyvern Mystery* (1869) or *The Rose and the Key* (1871) little may be usefully said. And as such information as we possess relating to his last years is scant and typical of thousands of Victorian lives, it will be possible to press on rapidly to a broader consideration of his significance. If one were to pause to examine *Guy Deverell* (1865) for example, three aspects of the novel might detain the patient reader's attention. First of all, the nominal hero is presented as a sickly, pallid, effeminate boy whose fate is entirely decided by others—this is the obverse of the sensitive heroine of *Uncle Silas*. Secondly, at the heart of this long chronicle of murder and delayed retribution, there is a short story (read by one character to another) in which the same themes are treated in explicitly supernatural terms. And, finally, there are two instances of Le Fanu's momentary recognition of a formalism which might have redeemed his sensational fiction. The hero is on the point of obeying an irksome request:

Perhaps it was a bore. But habitual courtesy is something more than 'mouth honour, breath.' Language and thought react upon one another marvellously. To restrain its expression is in part to restrain the feeling; and thus a well-bred man is not only in words and demeanour, but inwardly and sincerely, more gracious and noble than others.[1]

This recognition of the potency of language is, however, used solely to cloak the characters in a shoddy ambiguity rather than to deepen the implications of formal control evident in *Uncle Silas*. In *Guy Deverell* the intending agent of retribution reassures Lady Alice: 'Certainly madam, I mean what I say; and if I did *not* mean it, still I would say I do.'[2] Such evasion may be special to the speaker, but in the light of the hero's theory of

---

[1] *Guy Deverell* (London, 1865), ii. 186.
[2] Ibid. iii. 55.

language it may warn of the novelist's tendency to elevate manner and surface at the expense of character and action. Were this attitude intensified the result might be the dissolution of individual free will in the characters, a central element in the novelist's view of character and one implicitly under pressure in the repetitive symmetry of *Uncle Silas*. Le Fanu's novels give the appearance of accepting the need to conform to the rules of verisimilitude and plausibility, but after *Uncle Silas* they recurringly insinuate disclaimers, denials, and counterpointing interpolated tales. The corollary of that hyperstasis which dominated his best fiction was a restlessness and lack of control which marks virtually all the novels after 1864.

All in the Dark, which he published in 1866 in two volumes, represents an attempt to modify the surface sensation of *Guy Deverell* but without any return to the historical dimension (explicit or implied) which had previously proved so fruitful. The story was English and contemporary in setting, and universally disappointing. After the tension of *Uncle Silas* and the violence of *Guy Deverell*, here he had composed 'a little story without conspiracy or villain in it'. Instead of sensation he produced sentiment in a colourless tale of village wooings, ridiculous seances, and hesitant heroes. Yet *All in the Dark* is the fulcrum of a transition in Le Fanu's fiction, a reorientation which he never completed. The Great House is disregarded in favour of a more recognizably Victorian household; semi-aristocrats and landowners are replaced by struggling law-students and spinsterish aunts. A relaxed, humorous narrative style suggests that he was aiming at a bourgeois realism in which some of his own personal inner experience might be analysed. If *Uncle Silas*'s metaphysics had been a macrocosm of Anglo-Irish society, then *All in the Dark* aimed to present in a domestic scene psychological explorations rather than political symbols. The flippant account of Aunt Dinah Perfect's seance recalls Le Fanu's letters to Bessie Bennett, and William Maubray's somnambulism resembles Susanna Le Fanu's visions and trances. But the plot lacks any coherence apart from these purely private echoes: William Maubray is urged to go into holy orders when all he wants to be is a decent barrister (does this mirror Le Fanu's ambitions for himself and his brother William in 1842?); Violet Darkwell, Maubray's fiancée, has an absentee father, also a barrister but powerful and dreaded where Maubray is feeble and insipid. *All in the Dark* is not fiction, but 'decomposed' autobiography. Nevertheless, it casts light on an important area of Le Fanu's better fiction, for the hero's sickly expressions of love demonstrate by contrast the contribution of the female narrator to the success of *Uncle Silas*. Though Maud Ruthyn may not accommodate herself very clearly to the novel's Swedenborgianism, Le Fanu's preference for a female narrator explains in part the attractiveness for him of that negating, solipsistic symbolism. His male heroes in *Guy Deverell* and *Haunted Lives* are emotionally paralysed figures before whom feminine strength displays itself; and the aggressive vampire of 'Carmilla', far from being an exotic in Le Fanu's range of characters, is typical in one crucial aspect, for she demonstrates in the most palpable way an underlying feature of his characterization. Feminine nature is powerful, destructively powerful, and its objects become hypnotized (or hyperstatically controlled) in its power.

The 1866 two-decker had not been a success with the public, and by 1 August Le Fanu found himself forced to defend his departure from the overt sensationalism of *Guy Deverell*:

I am half sorry I wrote 'All in the Dark' with my own name to it. I am now convinced it is a great disadvantage to give the public something quite different from what your antecedents had led them to expect from you, although it may be better. Lady Gifford thinks it the very best thing I have written. If I go hereafter on that tack I must do so experimentally & anonymously—& build up a circulation if I can upon that basis.[1]

That he did resort to anonymity in seeking a new style is certain. Yet the conscious search for a style was perhaps a way forward for which Sheridan Le Fanu was ill-suited; his most controlled and resonant fiction had been the result of methods of composition other than deliberate planning and design. While it is legitimate to analyse *Wylder's Hand* or *Uncle Silas* or *Willing to Die* in terms of its implied view of social, political, and spiritual reality, it is less certain that Le Fanu was aware of all that he was doing. If his fiction reveals a symbolic use of death as an account of wider dimensions, he was also quite capable of straightforward Victorian morbidity in his private conversation and correspondence. A great deal of Sheridan Le Fanu was 'the bundle of

[1] Illinois; J. T. S. Le Fanu to G. Bentley, 1 Aug. 1866.

accidents' that sits down to breakfast, with this additional compli-
cation which did not fit into the Yeatsian view of the artist: he
did not generally regard himself as a conscious artist. Lacking
the professionalism of Trollope and the philosophical self-
awareness of George Eliot, he succeeded in *Uncle Silas* and in a
reasonable proportion of the shorter tales through the synchronization of his own temperament with the inner logic of the
material he chose. Walter Allen has remarked how novelists of the
generation born around 1810–14 did not possess any concept of
the novel as a particular art-form, and Le Fanu was at least
typical of his generation in this regard.[1] The criticism to which
his fiction was subjected never assisted any development of
artistic conscience, either because sensational conventions had
become unfashionable by the time he resumed novel-writing,
or because personal considerations were elevated above literary
judgement. Caroline Norton reviewed *Uncle Silas* for *The Times*,
and while her observations on the coexistence of angels and
human beings suggests that she appreciated the underlying
Swedenborgian pattern of the novel, her criticism can hardly be
taken as independent and disinterested.[2] In Dublin, Le Fanu had
from the moment he acquired the *Dublin University Magazine*
contrived to have each monthly issue favourably reviewed in *The
Warder*, the weekly paper in which he retained a financial interest.
As the anonymous reviewer was Patrick Kennedy, concurrently a
contributor to the *D.U.M.* and a friend of the proprietor's, his
criticism is no more a measure of public response than Mrs
Norton's.

The move towards sentiment in *All in the Dark* was clearly
linked to the altering roles of hero and heroine, though the
innovation had not yet justified itself for 'Carmilla' lay some five
years in the future. Lady Gifford's admiration of the 1866 novel—
if Le Fanu had not been simply bluffing to impress Bentley—was
very likely motivated more by motherly concern than critical

---

[1] *The English Novel* (Harmondsworth, 1958), p. 211.

[2] Mrs Norton reviewed three of Le Fanu's novels for *The Times: Uncle Silas*
(14 Apr. 1865, p. 4); *Guy Deverell* (18 Jan. 1866, p. 7); *A Lost Name* (21 Sept.
1868, p. 4). It was in the last of these that she revealed an understanding of
Uncle Silas more complex than the merely sensational: 'His characters stand
out distinct and definite, with a breadth of colouring and mastery of outline
such as prove him a skilled anatomist of the human heart. Its inmost variations
are known to him, whether in the depths of malicious perversit yor the high
religious soaring that brings us into neighbourhood with angels.'

insight. With the death of his mother in 1861, she had become the head of the family in Le Fanu's eyes. Such a relationship obscured his own position as *pater familias*, a role for which his personality and financial insecurity made him increasingly unsuited. At the end of Stepember 1866 he took his daughters (Elly was now twenty-one and Emmie twenty) to Clandeboye, near Belfast, where Lady Gifford was staying with her son. After a fortnight Le Fanu returned to Dublin, leaving the girls behind him. A light-hearted note to his elderly cousin acknowledged the welcome break from routine:

I wrote some little verses as I flew along the rails, addressed to you, but today they seem too unworthy of the subject, and so are condemned to darkness. No adventure have I to tell, except that the wheels of the carriage in which I was penned, smoked furiously at every station at which we stopped, and axle-boxes, &c had all, to be drenched with water, at each successive halt. We were an hour and a half late in Dublin. Was it my verses, the fire, or the ponderosity?[1]

But five days later his mood had changed: 'I left Clandeboye in low spirits, thinking that I was at last near a break down or up, and had looked my last on your beloved face . . . I doubt whether people ought to try to write when they are moved more than sentimentally. Language is drowned in the roar of their emotions . . .'[2] On 22 October he wrote to Emmie and to her hosts, at last delivering the verses to Lady Gifford: 'They are very bad, but the feeling is true. I have omitted only a little bit, which I have destroyed. I have grown hippish again, and "the fear of death is fallen upon me", and this is another excuse for sending you my limping verses.'[3] The poem ends:

> Broken by the iron rod,
>   Upon the voiceless stones I lay,
> Forgotten clean by man and God,
>   I thought for many a day.
>
> Thy sweet voice made my spirit start,
>   As songs of birds in prisoners' ears
> With a strange rapture pierce the heart,
>   And drown the eye with tears.

[1] P.R.O.N.I.; typescript copy of letter from J. T. S. Le Fanu to Lady Gifford, 14 Oct. 1866.
[2] Ibid. 19 Oct. 1866.
[3] Ibid. 22 Oct. 1866.

> When I lie sightless in the dust,
>   A happier hour and hope be thine,
>   A steadier light and surer trust
>   Than ever yet was mine![1]

Three letters written within eight days demonstrate Le Fanu's tendency to cultivate his morbidity. Perhaps external causes prompted him for, when he reached Merrion Square after his fortnight in Ulster, his elder son 'little Philie' (he was nineteen) had gone off without warning or explanation, the first evidence of the boy's latent irresponsibility. But the accelerating despair of the letters is clearly integral to Le Fanu's mind, and matched by an increasing willingness to release the poor verses.

He had confessed that any progress on the lines of *All in the Dark* must be anonymous, and complained that language may be drowned by emotion. The evidence in favour of his authorship of *Loved and Lost* (serialized anonymously in the *D.U.M.* in 1868–9) is set out in Appendix 2. If the case is proven, then this short serial may help to confirm the increasing subjectivity and privacy of Le Fanu's fiction. The tale is narrated by a mature woman who recounts the follies and disappointments of her youth. In her love for both a male admirer and for that admirer's mother, the narrator's emotions are febrile, uneasy, and self-accusing, features also present in the heroes of *Guy Deverell*, *All in the Dark*, and *Haunted Lives*. But *Loved and Lost* is basically an example of *folie de grandeur*, in which snobbery and class pride are retrospectively condemned in a narrative which depends substantially on them for interest. Differences of class, and financial tribulation, have fractured the Aubrey family whose 'fallen state' and 'fallen human nature' are repeatedly stressed. They are 'not, as a rule, a church-going family'. But it is in the accounts of domestic life that one may see both a reflection of the Le Fanu household, and an explanation for the anonymity which Le Fanu maintained for his brief novel:

Sunday was a day of rest to [my mother], and her devotions were generally said at home. My father was at this time with us for a flying visit. Things had evidently gone cross with him, for even with me he was testy, and the scenes between him and my mother were of daily recurrence . . . How vividly the whole scene comes before me. My

[1] Ibid.

father with clouded brow and a sneer on his lip is handling with much
disgust an unfortunate joint from which a gory stream is issuing,
certainly an unattractive bill of fare . . . The cook was sent for—a sturdy
Welshwoman—whose wages being long in arrear gave as good as she
got. A general row ensued; my father scolding; my mother retorting
with injudicious reproaches, ending at last by her sudden exit in tears,
and sullen dejection, accompanied by immense contrition on the
part of my father.[1]

As the finances of this unhappy household depend on the narrator's
uncle—despised because he is in trade—there is a general resemblance to the sibling relationship of Joseph and William Le Fanu.
The novelist's reluctance to sign this unremarkable record of
marital distress may be merely Victorian rectitude, contributing
indirectly to the legend of his unusually contented marriage. It
may, on the other hand, indicate a broader need to explore such
conflict covertly. For *Loved and Lost* is dominated at every level
by emotional paralysis and sporadic, uncontrolled energy: the
narrator is a passive observer, a powerless girl bewildered in a
world of anger and frustration; her few allies are a deformed
cousin, a stammering admirer, and a lost lover who is ultimately
drowned as a consequence of her impulsive misunderstanding of
their relationship. The characters, virtually without exception,
are emotionally crippled, limping from pride to self-abasement,
faith to cynicism, energy to apathy. Le Fanu has too readily
accepted the late romantic view that literature *expresses* the
spiritual life of the artist, and *Loved and Lost* is the unhappy
revelation of insecurities, marital, social, and religious, previously
noted in the 1858 diary. Though the choice of a female narrator
may appear to reveal a disturbed identification between novelist
and narrator, or even a psychological abdication from sexuality,
a more positive interpretation is available. In Edith Aubrey's
demi-monde, the young unmarried woman is both impotent and
prized, powerless to determine events and yet the centre of
attraction; the female narrator occupies a vantage point from
which the triviality and treachery of her world is inescapable. Le
Fanu fails to exploit Edith's position as a fictional character
being content to make her the vehicle of private compensation
and (for the reading public) conventional sentimental expressions.
The novel of entertainment, to use a phrase of Georg Lukacs,

[1] *D.U.M.*, vol. 72 (Sept. 1868), 264.

offered no mediating form between experience and expression, no transforming style through which order and meaning might be engendered.

It is perhaps too easy to accuse Le Fanu of these private and public offences against artistic conscience. Given that he possessed no great measure of creative originality, what models had he to emulate? With only Carleton and Lever on hand as witnesses, it is not possible to speak of an Anglo-Irish tradition in fiction. And, as Le Fanu's initial contract with Bentley revealed, the absence of a native publishing industry in Ireland placed the writer at the mercy of the English market. His cousin, Lord Dufferin, speaking at a Walter Scott centenary banquet in Belfast in 1871, deplored the lack of an Irish school of historical romance,[1] though forty years earlier there had been several claimants to the title of the Irish Scott—Le Fanu with *The Cock and Anchor* made a belated entry into the lists. Not only did his society lack any outstanding literary mentor, it had never experienced the impact of any major critical intelligence—no Carlyle or Newman or Arnold had ever analysed the state of civilization in Ireland. Even at the political level, Ireland's role in the United Kingdom found no coherent expression during Le Fanu's lifetime.

The novel, however, was not Le Fanu's only form of literary expression, and his short stories reveal the extent to which he sought to escape from the inertia of his social surroundings and the conventions of the entertainment novel. That he had gradually liberated himself from the loyalties of his inheritance is evident from his choice of friends in his last years. At the time when he earned the nickname 'Invisible Prince', when all but a few relatives were virtually banned from the house on Merrion Square, he struck up a lasting friendship with Patrick Kennedy, a book-dealer in Anglesea Street. Kennedy was as unlikely a companion as Judge Keogh; he was a Catholic of humble origins with whom Le Fanu worked in complete harmony until death claimed them both in the early months of 1873. By October 1861, the *D.U.M.* editor was already writing in comparatively frank and personal terms to his recruit, offering Lady Mary Montagu's memoirs for review: 'There is in her correspondence some

---

[1] 'Speech as Chairman of the Scott Centenary Banquet; Belfast, August 15, 1871', *Speech and Addresses of the . . . Earl of Dufferin* (London, 1882), pp. 133–8.

colour undoubtedly for Pope's atrocious & cowardly innuendos
[*sic*] (referring to Sappho) which are worthy of nothing in modern
times but the London "Satirist" & the Dublin "World" in their
youth of malignity, cowardice & corruption.'[1] Six years later he
described Kennedy as 'my quaint, kind, and clever little book-
seller', and in the interim he had come to rely much on him.
Between November 1861 and January 1869 the *D.U.M.* carried
over one hundred articles of Kennedy's. Often two pieces
appeared in the same issue, as in January 1867 when Kennedy
published 'Parisian Booklore in the Fourteenth Century' and
'Modern Writers of Spain'. He was not an original critic nor a
scholarly researcher, but his wide-ranging interests met a particular need in Le Fanu's journal—the need for articles which
would appeal to a readership outside Ireland. In addition,
Kennedy's regular non-fiction contributions left the editor free
to concentrate on the succession of serial novels which dominated
the magazine for eight years.

Patrick Kennedy's influence on his editor's writing is more
pervasive than merely convenient. As a collector of folklore (much
of it published in the *D.U.M.*) he surely directed Le Fanu's
remarkable return to Irish traditional material in his later short
stories and tales. Though nothing explicit survives of Tithe War
alarms and of Catherine Le Fanu's anxieties and her family's
genteel poverty, four stories recreate the landscape of Father
Purcell's county Limerick. In those first stories which Le Fanu
had published in the *D.U.M.* thirty years earlier elements of
folklore intruded only to provide a comic or pseudo-Gothic
effect; fears of Purgatory and graveside battles were transformed
into the cosy humour of 'The Ghost and the Bonesetter'. But in
the later stories, 'The White Cat of Drumgunniol', 'Sir Dominic's
Bargain', 'The Child that Went with the Fairies', and the 'Stories
of Lough Guir', legend now becomes the material of conscious
fiction, at once relaxed in style and intense with implication.

'The Child that Went with the Fairies', as the title makes
manifest, is based on the common belief that supernatural agents
seduce the young. But whereas W. B. Yeats's 'Stolen Child'
dwells on the hostility between the natural and supernatural
worlds, Le Fanu's story concentrates on human acceptance of
death. Beginning with an account of the various protections

[1] University College, Dublin; J. T. S. Le Fanu to P. Kennedy, 3 Oct. 1861.

against evil which the poor employ (horseshoes and holy water), it advances to relate the seizing of a child by two ladies in a glass coach: one is sweet-voiced and gentle, and the other (a negress) is speechless with suppressed and angry laughter. This ambiguous balance, which is never disturbed, leads on to the gradual reconciliation of the child's family to the fact of his disappearance. To the biographer, certain names in the final paragraph are significant:

'Fairy doctors' . . . did all that in them lay—but in vain. Father Tom came down, and tried what holier rites could do, but equally without result. So little Billy was dead to mother, brother, and sisters; but no grave received him. Others whom affection cherished, lay in holy ground, in the old church-yard of Abington . . .[1]

The death of a child and Abington cemetery may recall Catherine Le Fanu's early death, and the use of William as the 'stolen child's' name is striking for, in the Revd William Wylder of *Wylder's Hand* and William Maubray of *All in the Dark*, Le Fanu uses it as a surrogate assocated with a priestly vocation. But to the critic this late story is quite without the disruptive personal element which had marred earlier accounts of death and bereavement and which persisted in novels written as late as 'The Child' itself. The narrator neither seeks consolation nor requires it; in his remoteness he is at peace, and being at peace he can approach once again the reality of death.

The five 'Stories of Lough Guir' repeat this calm and benign treatment of supernatural attraction and death; each story tells of an unsuccessful attempt by the past to lure a human being into complicity with evil or death. The implication is that evil *is* death and the fear of death. But the remaining two stories are less reassuring on the question of diabolical power: in 'The White Cat of Drumgunniol' the appearance of a spectral animal has always announced death to some member of the Donovan family, and 'Sir Dominic's Bargain' retells the Faustian career of Robert Ardagh. Despite the division into accounts of resisted temptation and of diabolic destruction, these stories are united as a group by the stylistic precision and relaxed distance of the narrator's stance. Not only Father Tom (O'Brien Costello?) and Abington in 'The Child', but other names—Killaloe, Nenagh, Murroa,

---

[1] *All the Year Round* (new series), no. 62, 5 Feb. 1870, 233.

and Ballyvoreen—indicate without being obtrusive that the
focus of the stories is Le Fanu's experience in county Limerick.
By renaming Robert Ardagh as Dominic Sarsfield, Le Fanu also
makes explicit the Jacobite loyalties of his early heroes. And this
too confirms the Limerick provenance of these stories as a group,
for the historical Sarsfield's most renowned exploit was a rapid
night march through the district immediately to the north and
west of Abington to destroy a Williamite munitions convoy. This
precision of reference would be pointless, however, were it not
for the narrative style which employs detail to effect; the opening
of 'Sir Dominic's Bargain' adopts a useful nonchalance:

In the early autumn of the year 1838, business called me to the south
of Ireland. The weather was delightful, the scenery and people were
new to me, and sending my luggage on by the mail-coach route in
charge of a servant, I hired a serviceable nag at a posting-house, and,
full of the curiosity of an explorer, I commenced a leisurely journey
of five-and-twenty miles on horseback, by sequestered cross-roads
to my place of destination.[1]

The Faustian legend of Sir Robert Ardagh is adjusted to avoid
the neat divisions of the early version into melodrama and
stoicism with the one adding full credence to the supernaturalism
of the other. 'Sir Dominic's Bargain' creates a tension between
narrators, the first to whom Dunoran (Richard Marston's seat
in 1848) and Murroa are new and incidentally pleasing, and the
second for whom the Sarsfields are an intimate and ancient
ritual, an historical *credo*. The thematic emphasis, channelled
through these figures rather than through Sarsfield, now lies on
the acceptance of death's inevitability. Whereas Father Purcell
had remained a distant and a distancing figure, the narrator of
these tales leans towards the reader in confidence of his integrity.
A relaxed style brings the revelation of explicit Jacobitism; or,
to invert the phrase, the admission of Jacobite loyalty in the
characters results in a transformation of style. This is not to say
that the mature Le Fanu could admit political parallels which, as
a youth, he had suppressed or disguised. Instead he uses his
material symbolically, without fear of a superficial interpretation.
As 'The Haunted Baronet' makes explicit, every man contains
within himself the psychological polarities of noble defeat and

[1] Ibid., no. 118, 6 July 1872, 186.

guilty success, of impotence and power. Woe to him in whom the *conquistador* characteristics preponderate, for the pressure of the past must inevitably reduce him to the condition of his previous victims. In this sense, Le Fanu expands his Scott-ish analysis of Irish history into a theory of human personality. In a more limited sphere, the late folklore stories may be read as an oblique and indirect critique of current developments within the Protestant ascendency in Ireland: the expropriators are subtly transformed (in their own imagination at least) into the helpless dupes of a political system which now disowns them; the fierce loyalist and anti-Papist of 1842 (Isaac Butt, for example) becomes the centre of separatist discontent.

Both the fact of Le Fanu's friendship with Patrick Kennedy, a countryman Catholic of meek orthodoxy, and the evidence of the folklore of 1868–72 might suggest that he had learn to control his combative obsession with Calvinist fears and the attendant social attitudes. And the Swedenborgianism of *Uncle Silas* and the mockery of spiritualism in *All in the Dark* support this gradual rationalization of religious unease. But what Le Fanu gives with one hand he simultaneously refuses with the other; while 'The Child that Went with the Faries' calmly accepts death, *Willing to Die* (despite its title) is frantically disrupted by religious anxieties and aspirations and by lapses of narrative consciousness. The merit of his fiction does not so much lie in method or theme as in its explorations of form and pattern; where traditional themes and devices are available—as in the 'damsel in distress' aspect of *Uncle Silas*—he is able to exploit a highly patterned idea to create a synthesis on which private or neurotic details, together with stock-in-trade genre effects, are held together in a larger order. Both Swedenborgianism and folklore attempt to place the events, particularly the disturbing events of life, in the context of a higher rationality. Their 'rage for order' appealed to Le Fanu who was, almost by cultivated instinct, incapable of accepting any final view of the world. In their gods and heavens he may have temporarily believed, but his consuming passion was for their comprehensive methodology. Swedenborg's metaphysics and the Irish folk world's infinite power of absorption and transformation offered symbols and not creeds. Le Fanu never had any institutional commitment to the New Jerusalem Church and never corresponded with its functionaries. As for folklore, he lacked any scholarly appreciation of Gaelic myth or bardic tradition; to Kennedy he denounced 'the Ossianic fables' as insupportable curiosities, and preferred a story of the 'wicked old fellow in the coffin who pursued the girl looking for work'.[1] Against his blindness to the heroic dimension in folklore and mythology, a dimension soon to be so very influential, one might weigh Le Fanu's delicate treatment of 'the stolen child' theme in which style and pattern take command of crude materials, with a touching effect.

This concurrent decay of Le Fanu's abilities as a novelist and the late flowering of his talent as a short-story writer could be demonstrated in many instances. Such tales as 'Squire Toby's Will' or 'Borrhomeo the Astrologer' compare oddly with the awkwardness of *Haunted Lives* or *The Rose and the Key*. His last novel, *Willing to Die*, attempts to rationalize his declining powers by advancing as narrator a hysterical and untrustworthy woman whose efforts of memory obscure rather than reveal the past. Ethel Ware is the culmination of a series of female narrators, beinning with the inexperienced and (in Elizabeth Bowen's opinion) sexless Maud Ruthyn and including Edith Aubrey of *Loved and Lost* and the naïve victim of lesbianism and vampirism in 'Carmilla'. *Willing to Die* marks a further climax in relation to the role of the Great House in Le Fanu's fiction: in *Wylder's Hand* Brandon Hall is preserved for the rightful heirs in plenitude and integrity; in *Uncle Silas* Maud marries and redeems her father's faith and property; in *The Tenants of Malory*, however, the house is threatened and remote, while in the last novel the Wares suffer ejection, poverty, and humiliation. This gradual separation of house and heroine may be read as a symbolic dimension in the author's exploration of authority and esteem, or it might be related directly to his own financial difficulties resulting in the mortgage on his life-interest in Merrion Square. The year 1866 had seen a major collapse in the fortunes of many small investors, and Le Fanu may have suffered the consequences for the remainder of his years.

While *All in the Dark* and *Haunted Lives* do not stress the importance of the Great House, an underlying logic links the new concern with sexual psychology with the theme of political

[1] University College, Dublin; J. T. S. Le Fanu to P. Kennedy, dated 'Tuesday':

decay. Both the elimination of the hero and the more violent exposures of a criminal inheritance at Bartram-Haugh and Brandon Hall symbolize an assault on authority as understood in Le Fanu's generation. A society which was patriarchal, hierarchical, and, ultimately, justified by God the Father, depended at every level on the supremacy and potency of the male. Le Fanu's fiction speaks against that supremacy, even in his least controlled work. It is not merely that the 'social élite' is corrupt; Silas Ruthyn is powerless to resist a general pattern which condemns him actively to repeat accusations of guilt which were previously mere passive rumour; Sir Bale Mardyke must become the victim of victimized Philip Feltram. These transformations are not isolated and individual, but typical and systematic. Not surprisingly this anti-authoritarianism is frequently resisted in Le Fanu's fiction; it engenders a further level of guilt in those who recognize spiritual entropy at work. Significantly, those who resist and recognize are women, gifted with sexual strength but burdened with the knowledge that they are the beneficiaries of chaos. Perception is resisted by loss of consciousness: Maud Ruthyn perceives her father's violent nature through the unconsciousness of dream, and lapses once again into unconsciousness when Silas's murderous plans become evident; in *Willing to Die* the same swooning is related to violence. During a period of poverty and despair, Ethel Ware contemplates suicide but is distracted on her journey to Waterloo Bridge by the sight of her enemy, Droqville, in a jeweller's shop:

I drew nearer. What occurred next appeared to me like an incident in a dream, in which our motives are often so obscure that our own acts take us by surprise.

An icy chill seemed to stream from my brain through to my feet, my finger tips; as a shadow moves, I had leaned over, and the hand that holds this pen had struck the dagger into Droqville's breast . . . Was it real? For a second I stared, freezing with horror; and then, with a gasp, darted through the shop door.[1]

Subsequently Droqville looms up through the mist, standing at the prow of a boat on a northern lake. Given the dreamy uncertainty of the stabbing, these reappearances are less than fully authenticated by the narrator. All we can be sure of is her

---

[1] *Willing to Die*, ii. 280.

sense of guilt, her own imperfect, interior recollection of the
violent scene. And when Richard Marston reveals that he had
witnessed Ethel's attempt on Droqville, she swoons again, her
own act surprising her once more. This loss of consciousness,
either in the form of actual swooning or a merely vague apprehension of her surroundings, defines Ethel's guilt. *Willing to Die*
is coherent only as a thorough dislocation of the plot of 'Richard
Marston of Dunoran', dispersing elements of the central theme
among several characters. Francis Ware commits suicide beside
an open Bible; Ethel bears the guilt of unsuccessful murder;
Marston's name reappears and with it the old bigamous sub-plot
of the 1848 tale. But the essence of the novel is that its narrator
is totally unreliable; her narrative is repeatedly an attempt to
create a hyperstatic constancy which resists certain perceptions—
even her attack on Droqville is a *pause en route* to suicide. Thus,
the hyperstasis of Le Fanu's fiction is not so much a barrier
against dynamic action, but a last ditch defence against implosion,
self-destruction, entropy. Within the conventions of sensationalism, his art is literally a circumscription of death.

As *Willing to Die* reveals the novelist's imagination was nearly
exhausted, and exhaustion remained a theme on which he wrote
convincingly; even the successful short stories look forward to
eternal rest. The Christmas 1872 number of *London Society*
included advertisements for two forthcoming works by Le Fanu
to appear the following year, a novel called *The House of Bondage*
and a shorter piece, 'Premature Sepulture'.[1] Behind the banal
titles one can perceive an element of continuity, a stress on
forms of constriction and hyperstasis or paralysed consciousness,
emotional bondage, emotional burial. Nothing is known of these
projects; probably they were never completed, but a notebook
preserved in the National Library of Ireland includes a number of
fragments and notes towards fiction:

Hints for the story
A person supposed to be most harmless taken in from charity, turns
out to be the dreaded enemy of the House, & becomes its cruel tyrant.
    Old Mr Beaufort is rich & severely virtuous. Has been in commerce—
is a member of Pt not a speaking but a voting one. He married early
had one son, who has been his disgrace—a proud man having sustained

[1] See advertisements preserved in the set in The National Library of Ireland.

a repulse he had married in pique very early a woman whom he did not love.

The first paragraph recalls 'The Mysterious Lodger', the second aspects of *Loved and Lost;* but the attempt to relate the Great House and marital distress is near unique in Le Fanu's work. And the physical position of the last two words of this fragment—they appear overleaf from the main body of the note, though there is ample space on the same page—testifies to his extreme reluctance to pursue loveless marriage as a fictional theme. A further note scarcely aspires to the status of fiction:

It is easy enough for stupid people to renounce that which it requires some intellect to enjoy. They call that, or a few similar renunciations, going out of the world. They carry some tastes with them. But they like eating & they love money; they prosecute their spites, & kill character with a sanctimonious relentlessness. The man shirks half his duties as a country gentleman; the woman, if she is indolent, dresses like a slut, & with her fingers through her gloves & her eyes turned up, pauses upon points of faith she does not understand. They love adulation better even than defamation, & surround themselves with flatterers whom they call the Lords people, & in the luxury of this [word illegible] & impious routine spend their useless lives.

The tone here is infinitely more bitter than the parallel account of religious differences between man and wife in 'The Mysterious Lodger' and the 1858 diary, and the male figure has been assimilated into complicity in a useless life. The National Library notebook also contains a draft for the stabbing of Droqville in *Willing to Die*, and a deletion and revision reveal further subjective considerations in the composition of fiction; the female narrator has asked for change of a pound note: ' "Sorry I cant oblige you—you must try elsewhere" he said in a rather sharp parenthesis (to judge by his face was taken with my looks . . .)' The parenthetical comment on physical attraction has been altered to read 'looking hard at me, but apparently satisfied at a glance that I was no thief'.[1] All of these fragments, with their hesitation over a topic of loveless marriage, their condemnation of hypocritical and sluttish women, and their avoidance of what would in a fictive world be a natural comment by a male character on a female character's appearance, indicate the morbid sensitivity of Le Fanu's approach to the

[1] National Library of Ireland; Joly MS 22.

materials of his fiction. It is as if he were fearful of unwittingly composing a *roman-à-clef*.

It may seem that Le Fanu's imagination had become a rag-bag filled with random and unrelated obsessions—Swedenborgianism, suppressed sexuality, radical Toryism. But R. L. Wolff has suggested a means of reconciling such diverse interests through the fantasy of a bisexual God 'whose feminine characteristics often almost overwhelm the traditional masculine ones of God the father'.[1] This paradoxical theology, traceable to Swedenborg, had a particular subversive value for distressed Victorians who were only in part conscious of the direction of their sexuality. That Le Fanu may have been a latent homosexual has a certain clinical interest; more important in the life of a writer is the consistency and unity of feeling achieved through literary forms of little or no complexity and buoyancy. The Swedenborgian world, and indeed other symbolic systems in his fiction (the Great House, relations between the sexes, crime, and innocence), strive towards the reconciliation of opposites by a process of osmosis. The innocent are compromised by association with the guilty, and guilt may emerge from a past which is virtually impersonal and abstract. Indeed guilt is a necessary condition by which characters find their identities. Yet so guilty a figure as Yelland Mace in *Checkmate* is destroyed by a residual virtue. Given this urge towards homogeneity, there is also a tendency towards division, diffusion, and repetition. Every man casts a shadow or possesses a dual portrait-image, and those images develop a separate life of their own. In this pattern there is no sense of a Hegelian dialectic in which reality perpetuates itself through contradiction and destruction; rather, it is the *praecox* phenomenon of schizophrenia which offers a comparison to Le Fanu's logic. There is little evidence in the fiction or elsewhere that he was conscious of these features of his imagination.

He employs a form of dualism in the presentation of character; in the novels, this is usually implicit, that is, the reader may come to see Austin and Silas Ruthyn as in some way related (beyond the conventions of individual identity) as he gradually adopts a particular reading of the novel. The same, more crudely achieved, is true of Marston and Carmel in *Willing to Die*. In the short

[1] *Strange Stories and Other Explorations in Victorian Fiction* (Boston, 1971), p. 126. For Wolff's discussion of Le Fanu see pp. 31-7.

stories and tales, however, the process is frequently explicit as when Philip Feltram expounds his concept of man and shadow in 'The Haunted Baronet' or when Mr Justice Harbottle recognizes Twofold as 'a dilated effigy of himself'.[1] The short story encourages an ideological framework, whether supernatural or otherwise, in which these concepts find articulation: the prefatory note to *In a Glass Darkly* outlines a theory of identity which is then studied in the several case histories of Dr Hesselius. This approach to character is not unique by any means to Le Fanu; at a more sophisticated level, Charles Dickens adopts a similar technique. Dorothy van Ghent has summarized it:

> Dickens uses a kind of montage in *Great Expectations*, a superimposing of one image upon another, with an immediate effect of hallucination, that is but one more way of representing his vision of a purely nervous and moral organisation . . . This device, of doubling one image over another, is paralleled in the handling of character. In the sense that one implies the other, the glittering frosty girl Estella, and the decayed and false old woman, Miss Havisham, are not two characters but a single one, or a single essence with dual aspects, as if composed by montage—a spiritual continuum, so to speak. The boy Pip and the criminal Magwich form another such continuum. The relationship between Joe Gargery, saintly simpleton of the folk, and Orlick, dark beast of the Teutonic marshes . . . has a somewhat different dynamics, though they too form a spiritual continuum. Joe and Orlick are related not as two aspects of a single moral identity, but as the opposite extremes of spiritual possibility—the one unqualified love, the other unqualified hate—and they form a frame within which the actions of the others have their ultimate meaning. A commonplace of criticism is that, as Edmund Wilson puts it, Dickens was usually unable to 'get the good and bad together in one character'. The criticism might be valid of Dickens' were a naturalistic world, but it is not very relevant to Dickens' daemonically organised world.[2]

Much of this could be translated into an analysis of *Uncle Silas* or 'Richard Marston of Dunoran', with the important difference that Dickens's montage is rationally justified by his wish to relate the inner life of his characters to the hidden complexity of social existence. For it is explicitly society and corrupted social values which make Magwich who he is and Pip what he is. By contrast, Le Fanu establishes his dualistic montage as if it were a her-

[1] *In a Glass Darkly*, i. 275.
[2] *The English Novel; Form and Function* (New York, 1953), pp. 132–4.

metically sealed and self-regulating world. Of course, this urge towards homogeneity in division leads to implosion and suicide in form and character. W. J. Harvey relates Mrs van Ghent's notion of montage to the question of identity, by this meaning 'that process whereby an artist's vision of the world is such that it decomposes and splits into attributes which then form the substance of disparate characters'.[1]

To speak of psychic decomposition is to move outside the fictional world of effects and to presume to causes in the author's life. The cause may be 'some emotional nexus outside the book which is too painful to be brought into the novel in a pure state'.[2] In Le Fanu's case there is abundant evidence that these painful causes existed—the treacherous reversals in politics between 1842 and 1848, and the marital and domestic crises between 1850 and 1858. The playful mimicry of his letters to Bessie Bennett and the brief confessional diary of 1858 indicate that he felt deeply ill at ease in the role of the dominant male, the *pater familias*. It is not only the insipid heroes who reflect this desire to sap energy and responsibility from the male; the preference for female narrators allows the novelist to speak through a role of apparent passivity and weakness which is also subversively a source of strength and integrity. This, at least, is the impression given by Maud Ruthyn in *Uncle Silas*. But Le Fanu's heroines display the same urge towards homogeneity as other aspects of the fiction, and progressively they crave for identification with the fallen male. Maud has yearned to serve Silas; Edith Aubrey speaks collectively of her family, warring father and mother, as a unit whose characteristics she epitomizes; Ethel Ware precipitately gives herself to the daemonic Marston of *Willing to Die*.

With the growing subjectivity of Le Fanu's fiction adequately documented—doubtless further echoes of his private life could be detected in both novel and short story—it would seem relatively simple to place him and his work in the context of his contemporaries. If Victorian middle-class Dublin has remained in obscurity, declining to provide a convenient yard-stick by which to measure the (ab)normality of his social behaviour, then the nature of Anglo-Irish literature, especially of the nineteenth-century novel, may

[1] *Character and the Novel* (London, 1965), p. 124.
[2] Ibid. 127.

provide a surer guide in judging his writing. The Anglo-Irish novel, starting with *Castle Rackrent* (1800), is accepted as being above all else a social form, actively concerned with and influential upon the life of the community from which it arose. (Ruskin believed that *The Absentee* revealed more of Irish conditions than a thousand Blue books, and prefaces by John Banim and William Carleton belabour the immediate relevance of their themes.) Yet the apparent solidity of the novel tradition in Ireland is largely an illusion generated in the minds of recent historians. If we leave aside the ephemera of the day, it is difficult to point to a period when more than two or three novelists of any ability were at work simultaneously. Banim becomes ill and Maria Edgeworth abandons Irish fiction at about the moment when Carleton takes up the pen. Griffin takes holy orders as Le Fanu begins to publish. Lever departs for Italy as Young Ireland springs to life. Kickham and Moore effectively open their careers when Lever and Le Fanu die. Far from constituting a unified school of writing, the Anglo-Irish novelists are better regarded as, in Thomas Kinsella's phrase for his own generation, 'a scattering of incoherent lives'. As for the ephemera of the day, the productions of George Brittaine, Eyre Evans Crowe, William Hamilton Maxwell, and so forth, we know in fact so little of their publishing history and of the reading habits, critical standards, and preconceptions of their public that it is premature and impertinent to declare any of them irredeemably ephemeral and worthless. The groundwork for even the crudest sociology of the Anglo-Irish novel has hardly been mapped out, let alone tackled. Any enquiry into a possible homology between the structure of Irish fictional forms and the structure of Irish society must await a great deal of research into the types of fiction actually produced and consumed in Ireland; for the moment we have to be content with the term 'novel' as covering a variety of types of fiction, and the terms 'tale' and 'short story' have here been used almost interchangeably. From a purely aesthetic point of view, Charles Lever and Sheridan Le Fanu may scarcely merit such ponderous attention, but the minor crises of 1845 and 1870 in which they played a part prefigure the infinitely greater crisis of the Parnellite period, a period which produced a vigorous and modern literature—Yeats, Wilde, Shaw, Synge, and after a pregnant delay, James Joyce.

Such a decidely Irish bias in discussing an author, beloved of
M. R. James and Montagu Summers and remembered primarily
for stories ostensively set in Derbyshire and the Lake District, is
not perverse. Not only have we seen that landscape and setting
in Le Fanu's fiction are consciously symbolic, but that landscape
was originally presented as the extension of figures emblematic
of Irish historical realities. The tawdry metaphysic of Swedenborgianism and the impositions of the English publishing market
indeed restricted and contorted his material, but these influences
were in a sense an appropriate product of Le Fanu's relationship
with the Irish past and present. The eighteenth century (beginning albeit in 1688!) had been an era of power and privelege for
Le Fanu's Irish ancestors, had seen the consolidation of their
well-being and the nurture of their deliberate identification with
the ascendency. But according to a different reading of history,
one gaining in articulation and accuracy in the years of Le
Fanu's adolescence, that era had been characterized by corruption, expropriation, conquest, and extermination waged by those
whom he acknowledged as the founding fathers of his historical
existence. A chasm necessarily separates such a figure from the
landscape of his immediate surroundings, for he sees in them
the active survival and transformation of a previous landscape,
once the land promised by the Glorious Revolution and now the
treacherous haunt of his enemies. A similar dual reading of the
nineteenth century was already in circulation in Le Fanu's
youth: to the Irish Catholics it spoke of hope and an end to legal
restrictions; to the ascendancy it meant an end to hegemony and
the harmony of Church and State. The past survives; conquest
and expropriation have failed; or, to state the same proposition
conversely, the present is pure revenant, a mere extension of
something more real. Given such a cultural diagnosis, it is almost
inevitable that Le Fanu should cleave to the language both of
schizophrenia and of crude Calvinism. Estrangement from the
present may be motivated by a recognition of the accusations it
conveys, but by driving the solitary back towards the past it
simply confronts him with the origins of these accusations, for
the Battle of the Boyne (retrospectively considered) cannot alter
the outcome of the Tithe War. Indeed, if there is any historical
determinism it must argue that success at the Boyne leads to
humiliation in a thousand glebe gardens. So too, the sinner who

acknowledges that his offences have separated him from God finally confronts that Original Sin which has predisposed him to fall. *The Purcell Papers* place the hero between two conditions, neither of which is accessible to the reader: a life before the story opens, before the hero has returned to Ireland, and a destiny in or beyond death. The intervening space—for even in the Faustian 'Sir Robert Ardagh' Le Fanu is concerned with space rather than time—is a near vacuum, attenuated society or withered vegetation. To move abruptly from *The Purcell Papers* to the novels of the 1860s may seem outrageous, and yet both bodies of work share one important feature: neglect of the intricate, limited world we call human society in favour of realities which are at once larger (the metaphysical dimension) and smaller (the solitary individual). In the sensational novels this neglect is entirely paradoxical, for the Wilkie Collins—Charles Reade school emphasized social didacticism and the investigation of 'problems' —asylums, legal anomalies, etc.—as the justification of their fiction. Le Fanu's sensationalism is therefore categorically different from theirs. Though all the surface elements of his late fiction are part of the stock-in-trade of romanticism in decline, it is precisely those elements he does *not* assimilate from his English models which identify the distinctive provenance of his work. The continuation from *The Purcell Papers* to *Willing to Die* outweighs the disruptive place-names which replace any solider evidence of society in the novels of 1864 and after. Yet if the place-names are spurious, the disruption is both authentic and necessary, for it acknowledges once again the separation from his immediate context which had always characterized Le Fanu's fiction. Bartram-Haugh is not England writ small, nor is its desolation a reflection of English society. Bartram-Haugh, it is fairer to say, is an image produced by the diminished reality of the British dimension in Ireland, the declining potency of an ascendency in recession. And, as in 'Sir Robert Ardagh', *Uncle Silas* exploits space and distance as symbols of history and time: if Bartram is the self-accusing image of Victorian Protestant Ireland, Knowl in its ignorance of self is a miniature of eighteenth-century exclusivism. This is not to say that the novel is a *roman-à-clef* of the ages, in which site and character codify specific periods. On the contrary, *Uncle Silas* possesses a pattern, *is* a pattern and structure which reveal an openness to interpretation, in the sense that it embodies that awareness of history's multiple levels which preoccupied the Protestant élite in its more attentive moments. And to judge by Le Fanu's fiction, attentive moments occurred when the relationship between Britain and Ireland came under active political reconsideration. The periods 1838–45 and 1868–70 constituted such minor crucial moments; in both Le Fanu's friend Isaac Butt played a central role, and it was Butt who paved the way for Parnell's more trenchant and paradoxical expression of the same question.

The Purcell Papers at the end of the Tithe War; *The Cock and Anchor* among Young Ireland's reassessments of the Jacobite past; *Uncle Silas* composed in 'Fenian fever', and the folk tales of 1868–70 with their Home Government Association background— if these go some way towards substantiating such a correlation of fiction and politics, what may be said of Le Fanu's remaining fiction, written during lulls in the political debate? Neither sensationalism nor the discrete 'tradition' of Anglo-Irish fiction can throw any positive light on *Guy Deverell* or *Haunted Lives*. Too much of the plotting conforms to the demands of the circulating libraries, with the result that style placates the reader without invigorating the characters. In a word, much of Le Fanu is commercialized romanticism, and even his characteristic devices— the recurrent portrait image and the presentation of character in duplicate—reach back through Emerson and Poe, Arnold and Keats, to Horace Walpole and the Gothic novel. Influence is perhaps the most overrated notion in the literary critic's bag of tricks. English romanticism made only a late and limited impact on Anglo-Irish literature; no Irish literary figure of Wordsworth's generation (and only George Darley of Byron's) had responded more than fitfully to the new mode of feeling. Or, rather, the conditions which permitted and encouraged the flowering of romanticism in England did not pertain to Ireland. As far as the novel is concerned, Walter Scott (coming from a culture more readily compared to the Irish) was the impetus to whom Anglo-Irish writers responded, and Scott as interpreted in Ireland was more realist than romantic. Though the present state of scholarship gives scant recognition to the fact, Irish culture between the close of the eighteenth century and the opening of the Victorian age was responsive to influences from beyond Britain. Dr Patrick O'Neill has recently drawn attention to the exceptional sensitivity of the *Dublin University Magazine* during Le Fanu's lifetime to German romanticism.[1] Between 1833 and 1850 more than one hundred and forty articles of a German literary interest appeared in the magazine, and in excess of half of these were published in the first seven years of its existence, that is, during the Tithe War emergency. Though this emphasis on German culture may in part be explained by John Anster's influence—he was a founder of the *D.U.M.* and the first translator of Goethe's completed *Faust*—there was a general affinity between certain central concepts of the German romantics and the needs of emerging Anglo-Irish writers, especially those of a Tory hue. Goethe had long argued that social conditions in Germany did not favour the development of some literary forms: Frank O'Connor's argument that the short story is a peculiarly Irish (and Russian) phenomenon, being the art-form of submerged populations, is a late variation on the Goethean theme. Yet the novel in nineteenth-century Ireland appealed to both middle-class Protestant supporters of the Union with Britain and to figures such as Carleton or Michael Banim whose origins were Catholic and humble. To the latter, the novel opened up the possibility of dignifying the Irish peasantry's historical experience with the solidity and stability which the form readily expressed at the hands of a Jane Austen, a Thackeray, or a George Eliot. To others, like Le Fanu, the novel was an important area in which the continuity and homogeneity of the United Kingdom was maintained across the Irish Sea. For both social groups, the choice of the novel form was in part determined by their dependence on the economics of the British publishing industry—it is significant that Le Fanu's 1840s novels (in which a *radical* adjustment of history and of Anglo-Irish relations is posited) were issued from a Dublin publishing house, whereas the fiction after *The House*

---

[1] 'German Literature and the *Dublin University Magazine* 1833–1850: a Checklist and Commentary', *Long Room*, no. 14/15 (1977), 20–31. Morgan and Hohlfeld analyse the contents of 164 British and Irish magazines with reference to the popularity of German literature in the period 1750–1860. Though the comparison is very rough indeed the following figures suggest that the appeal of German romanticism did not extend to the Catholic and (in origin, at least) the Irish *Dublin Review:*

References to German literature 1836–60
    Dublin Review 9
    D.U.M. 135
(See *German Literature in British Magazines* (Madison, 1949), pp. 115–18.)

by the Churchyard (which was 'privately' published in that the author saw it through the press locally) utilizes English settings and displays London imprints. But the novel also revealed the contradictory view of Irish social reality implict in both the ascendency novelists and those who came from the ranks of the Catholic population. A solid and stable Catholic bourgeoisie had not established itself during the lifetime of Carleton or Banim or Kickham, and the difficulties these writers experienced in integrating the linguistic, structural, and formal elements of the novel form are related to this undefined social order. On the ascendancy side, it is equally true that the Union had not achieved any actual unity or homogeneity of social behaviour in Ireland and Britain, and economically the two islands evolved in differing directions during the nineteenth century. Irish society, then, was undergoing a particularly complex transition: no new dispensation had come to power, and the *ancien régime* (though shaken) resembled the Bartram paling in being both decayed and strong. These divisions of course were in part generated by the need of less clearly defined factions to perceive and determine such divisions— it is notable that Trollope in his early novels sees a more recognizably bourgeois Ireland than his Irish contemporaries in the 1840s, Lever and Le Fanu. Novelists whose needs, as adherents to a particular view of history, drew them to neglect this coexistence of non-congruent worlds found that the novel form in their hands was lifelessely remote from society or myopically and sentimentally focused on parochial oracles. No nineteenth-century Anglo-Irish novel speaks of Irish society as a totality for they either defined that society as explicitly a dual system (the legacy of Scott as seen in Banim, Carleton, and early Le Fanu) or as an integral if threatened part of a larger British society (the provincialism of early Lever and the exile provenance of later Le Fanu at his erratic best). An issue which future sociologists of Anglo-Irish literature must surely face is the extent to which the novel was an imposed form in the Victorian age.

To appreciate that transitional states of sensibility were far from unique to Ireland one has only to recall Matthew Arnold's 'Stanzas from the Grande Chartreuse' where the speaker is 'wandering between two worlds, one dead, The other powerless to be born'. Such a poem as this, or 'Dover Beach' with its

darkling plain from which the sea of faith has withdraw
reminds us that the Victorian religious crisis formed part of
wider disjunction of feeling and belief. In Arnold the religio
imagery is also symbolic of anxieties which are not religious
psychological, social, political. But in Anglo-Irish experien
religious imagery was at all times explicitly political: despite t
ironies and inexactitudes of nomenclature, the new Whigs a
liberals were overwhelmingly Catholic, the defenders of abs
lutism and ascendency Protestant. It is therefore inevitable r
only that Anglo-Irish literature should differ from English in tl
social conditions on the two islands continued to diverge (or,
least, signally did not converge), but also that Anglo-Iri
literature should exploit religious imagery with an explicit a
literal intensity unparalleled in Britain. The Gothicism of *T
Purcell Papers*, the Swedenborgianism of *Uncle Silas* and *In
Glass Darkly*, the missionary Catholicism of *Willing to Die* ¡
instances in Le Fanu's fiction of a pervasive symbolism fro
which it is impossible to amputate political implications.

In *Dichtung und Wahrheit*, in his conversations with Eckerma
and on a score of other occasions, Goethe spoke of his experien
of the 'daemonic' as a force intensifying certain crucial qualit
in a man at times of stress. In the English language 'daemoni
like 'genius' with which it has affinities, has taken on a prec
and limited meaning, positive in the case of 'genius' but negati
in the case of 'daemon'. To Goethe, however, the daemonic

was not divine for it seemed irrational: it was not human, for it had ¡
reason; not devilish, for it was beneficent; not angelic, for it oft
allowed room for malice. It resembled the accidental, for it was witho
consequence; it looked like providence, for it hinted at hidden co
nections. Everything that restricts us seemed permeable by it; it seem
to arrange at will the necessary elements of our existence; it contract
time, it expanded space. It seemed at ease only in the impossible, a
it thrust the possible from itself with contempt.[1]

Though in Goethe's humanist *weltanschauung* the daemonic
ethically neutral and allied to no extra-human dimension

[1] For the original see J. W. von Goethe, *Dichtung und Wahrheit* (Zuric
1948), pp. 839–40. I quote the passage as translated by Anna Bostock in Geo
Lukacs, *The Theory of the Novel* (London, 1971), p. 87. I am very grateful
Dr Dennis Tate for discussing with me the implications of Goethe's theory
the daemonic and Lukacs's use of it.

reality, it is clear that the daemon could serve a different function in a different philosophical system. In the framework of Christianity, he became virtually synonymous with devil, and was presented as perennially hostile to man's ultimate spiritual welfare. Le Fanu's heroes in *The Purcell Papers* are the victims of daemonic temptation, and if their descent from the Byronic *âme damnée* is evident, so too is the ambiguity of the daemon's identity. For Robert Ardagh and the last heir of Castle Connor were not simply returned Jacobites and Catholics destroyed by Satan; they were destroyed by the agency of their adherence to these values and beliefs—recourse to Europe. Seen in this light, the diffused but unmistakable element of suicide in these stories is necessary and inevitable; adhering to an ideology which, in the historical moment of *The Purcell Papers*' setting, is redundant and decaying, Ardagh and O'Connor die through loyalty to their outmoded beliefs. But *The Purcell Papers* possess also a historical moment of *composition*, in which the author and his caste (or a significant portion of it) considered a major political initiative, a breach of the Union, an adoption of their traditional foes' tactics and terminology, Repeal. By this reading, France was Jacobin as well as Jacobite; the heroes of the stories not only adhered to their own redundant ideology but also conspired with everything most hostile to their self-interest. In this latter context, they aligned themselves with a world 'powerless to be born', a world of sterile contradiction or romantic fantasy. This dual nature of the hero reveals that it is young O'Connor as much as Fighting Fitzgerald, Robert Ardadh as much as his melodramatically evil servant, who is 'daemonic'. George Lukacs, writing of Goethe's concept, translates the psychology of creativity seen in *Dichtung und Wahrheit* into an account of the transformation of literary forms in *The Theory of the Novel*:

Fallen gods, and gods whose kingdom' is not yet, become demons; their power is effective and alive, but it no longer penetrates the world, or does not yet do so: the world has a coherence of meaning, a causality, which is incomprehensible to the vital, effective force of a god-become-demon; from the demon's viewpoint, the affairs of such a world appear purely senseless.[1]

The novel, for Lukacs, expresses 'transcendental homelessness',

---

[1] Lukacs, pp. 86-7.

and though *The Theory of the Novel* concerns itself solely with a few novels of the highest rank, much of its theoretical commentary is illuminating when focused on Le Fanu's hesitant and inconclusive exercises in fiction. In contrast to the restlessness and estrangement of the novel,

the short story is the most purely artistic form; it expresses the ultimate meaning of all artistic creation as *mood*, as the very sense and content of the creative process, but it is rendered abstract for that very reason. It sees absurdity in all its undisguised and unadorned nakedness, and the exorcising power of this view, without fear or hope, gives it the consecration of form; meaninglessness as *meaninglessness* becomes form: it becomes eternal because it is affirmed, transcended and redeemed by form.[1]

The relation between Le Fanu's novels and short stories could hardly have been more finely expressed. *The Purcell Papers* offer static, self-contained studies of daemonic temptation: predicament rather than action determines their movement, and the double telling of the story in 'Sir Robert Ardagh' enacts this preference for mood over melodrama. *The Cock and Anchor*, in contrast, strives both in fear and hope to rationalize the past and to bring a world to birth, a world reconciling history and self-interest, Protestant and Catholic, male and female. From a later period of Le Fanu's life we have taken as exemplary the tension between novels such as *Willing to Die* and the 'Stories of Lough Guir'. In the latter, mood predominates because the narrative is not of an action but of reactions to an action; as with the framed landscape of *Uncle Silas* distance achieves a stilling and chilling effect.

The unexpected aptness of Lukacs's analysis may in part be explained by his debt to Goethe and Hegel and by the special appeal of German romanticism for the *Dublin University Magazine* and its radical Tory authors. And while the groundwork for an intensive investigation of mid-century literary relations in Ireland—relations between reader and publisher, publisher and author, to take but two elementary examples—has not been prepared, there is still much to be gained by advancing along the path indicated (in a very different context) by Lukacs's *Theory of the Novel*. For the late emergence of the novel not only signals

[1] Ibid. 51–2.

the retarded condition of Irish society, but allows some limited applications of theories of the European novel's origins generally to the problem of nineteenth-century Anglo-Irish fiction. Indeed, if one does not recognize that the Anglo-Irish novel exists, as it were, within two timetables—one, of its own delayed evolution; and another, of the English novel's more advanced condition— then many of its peculiar features will remained unnoticed and unexplained. (The uncertain relationship between irony and inhumanity in *Castle Rackrent* is a good example of this dual timetable, for readers who react excessively to one of these poles generally fail to observe the other. The political implications are clear.) Lukacs describes the novel as revolving round a problematic character whose degraded search for authentic values is conducted in a world of conformity and convention.[1] The daemonic hero journeys to find goals which are altered and distanced by his journeying; he has moved out from one world and has not yet found any other of comparable density and intensity. He carries with him values which remain effective for him but not for those he encounters, and the degree to which they remain effective for him measures the extent to which his journey is purely interior. Le Fanu's fiction presents several instances of the problematic character *en voyage*, and the literalness with which he abides by this convention is a further index of the primitive condition of Anglo-Irish fiction. None of these figures is more starkly daemonic (in both the German and English senses of the word) than Richard Marston. In 'Some Account of the Latter Days of the Hon. Richard Marston of Dunoran' we saw how Le Fanu produced an anomalous hero who throws 'a guilty and furious glance' at those whose guilt he discovers, only to advance into complicity against convention and 'the ceremony of innocence'. Twenty years later in 1868 the story is rewritten in three-decker form as *A Lost Name;* the fair seducer is now only French-educated and no longer French born; the hero's name has become Mark Shadwell (enigmatically the novel's title hints at Marston as a name which might have appeared instead). Le Fanu's obsession with this figure remains, and it is not surprising to find that the figure opposed to pious Mr Carmel in *Willing to Die*, the figure who survives shipwreck and who lures the narrator

---

[1] This summary of Lukacs's view of the novel is based on Lucien Goldmann's *Towards a Sociology of the Novel* (London, 1975), pp. 1–17.

towards a bigamous marriage, is once again named Richa
Marston. It may be that the concept of the daemonic, as defin
by Goethe and extended by Lukacs into the study of litera
forms, offers a new perspective on Le Fanu's later fiction, ev
if our criticism of *Willing to Die* should continue to stand.

Le Fanu's fiction is dominated by transitional stasis, a sta
of consciousness in which the inevitability of change is bo
acknowledged and resisted. The hero or narrator moves throu
a landscape in which the stimuli requiring change reveal ther
selves; the search for authentic values—purgation of the pa
recovery of belief, the establishment of identity, the stabilizati
of sexual energy—is conducted among figures who reciproca
in a purely negative manner. Silas thwarts Maud's commitme
to the Trust by confirming past rumour as present crime. Marst
and Carmel adhere to ideologies which present themselves
oscillations between remote and sumptuous reality on the o
hand, and cynical, Machiavellian deception on the other; bo
priest and daemon fluctuate in Ethel's consciousness betwe
attraction and repulsion; only a willingness to die can offer
pretext for the most attenuated religious statement. Experien
whether sexual or social, criminal or blandly sentimental, tak
the characters towards a point of potential transformation. B
transformation into a new self involves annihilation of the ol
and so suicide becomes the pervasive metaphor of change. In l
Fanu's fiction the future either does not exist or it portends pu
nihilism in requiring an alteration from the past. In politi
terms, it recognizes the outer necessity of change, but stresses t
inner impossibility of adjustment: 'transitional stasis' describ
the contradictions implicit in the dilemma of the Anglo-Iri
ascendancy in the 1850s and 1860s. For the parallel between l
Fanu's fiction and the world of the Anglo-Irish is not diffic
to draw, and Standish O'Grady was to define with a characteris
extremity the political consequences of an emotional conditi
within ten years of Le Fanu's death. *The Crisis in Ireland* (188
exposed a deep vein of gloomy fatalism among the ascendenc
especially the landowners, and *Toryism and the Tory Democra*
(1886) accused the Anglo-Irish upper classes of moral cowardi
and class treachery. But by then land war had made explic
contradictions which were merely latent in Le Fanu's life time. I
Fanu's fiction, however, is a relevant precursor to O'Grady's *sae*

indignatio, for it symbolizes in alienated setting and dislocated character the emotional consequences of a political condition.

Just as the narrator moves between a dead but yet contaminating past and a future powerless to be born, so the author must be seen as a transitional figure in the evolution of literature in Ireland. When Joseph Thomas Sheridan Le Fanu was born in 1814 Maria Edgeworth was at the height of her career; her fiction presented a rationality which looked back to the eighteenth century and the Enlightenment; her knowledge of the Irish social cobweb was balanced by her training in English 'utilitarian' analysis. Malthus and Ricardo were her mentors; for Swedenborg she would have entertained nothing more than impatient incomprehension. But, abandoning Irish fiction in the 1830s, she despairingly acknowledged that her father's contractual notion of society no longer could effectively relate their people to 'the people'. The history of Sheridan Le Fanu's family in the nineteenth century traces the contortions and convulsions resulting from that realization. The great crises of Le Fanu's early life—Catholic emancipation, the Reform Act, the Tithe War, Protestant Repeal, Famine, 1848—all centred round the tensions generated by the appearance that the United Kingdom of Great Britain and Ireland was a homogeneous social entity; each crisis defined an area in which that appearance was punctured. Added to these outer climaxes, there was the writer's difficulty of constructing a literary form which accommodated itself to both actual and apparent forms of society.

That Irish Victorian life laboured under these general difficulties—the rule of conventions dicated from differing conditions in England—did not prevent the hidden growth of very particular and peculiar difficulties also. If Le Fanu's domestic life in the 1850s and 1860s seems eccentric, one has only to turn to George Bernard Shaw's *Sixteen Self Sketches* to appreciate that it was not unique. The Shaws, like characters from Le Fanu's *Loved and Lost*, had slipped down the social ladder of Irish Protestantism to become suburban bohemians. Though their status was comparatively low, they still existed by virtue of the sectarian system within the Anglo-Irish pale, within an ill-defined élite which W. B. Yeats was soon to condemn as

a class which, through a misunderstanding of the necessities of Irish

Unionism, hated all Irish things, or felt for them at best a contemp
tuous and patonising affection, and which through its disgust at th
smoky and windy fires of popular movements had extinguished thos
spiritual flames of enthusiasm that are the substance of a distinguishe
social and personal life, a class at whose dinner-tables conversation ha
long perished in the stupor of anecdote and argument, and on whos
ears the great names of modern letters fall to awaken no flutter o
understanding, or even of recognition, and into whose churches n
joyous and mystical fervour has ever come.[1]

Provincialism in culture, philistinism in art, mindless evan
gelicalism in religion—these are the features of the culture i
which Le Fanu lived, and in which Yeats many years later was t
rediscover

> A law indifferent to blame or praise,
> To bribe or threat; habits that made old wrong
> Melt down, as it were wax in the sun's rays;
> Public opinion ripening for so long
> We thought it would outlive all future days.[2]

That, however, was the past seen from the vantage point of 191{
another moment of crisis in Irish history from which the pas
might be reassessed and recreated. Edward Stephens, writing
biography of his uncle J. M. Synge, stayed closer to the day-to
day experience of Dublin's Victorian middle classes:

These people, who had lost much of their money and most of the
libraries and learning, increased their class consciousness in sel
defence. They clung together like members of a secret society, an
refused to mix with the prosperous townspeople whose neighbou
they had become. Their emotions had suffered violence; their belie
had become restrictive; if anyone among them chanced to inherit th
genius of their race, he found himself unhonoured by his kin. I
suburban life there was no outlet for the energy of their children, wh
cut off from their traditions, tended to seek abroad scope for the
enterprise.[3]

All of Le Fanu's children who survived into the 1890s con
formed to this pattern of permanent exile; indeed emigratio

[1] W. B. Yeats, *Uncollected Prose* (London, 1970), i. 405. The article, fror
which the passage is quoted, is a review of Lady Ferguson's *Sir Samuel Fergusc
in the Ireland of his Day*, published in the *Bookman* in May 1896.
[2] *Collected Poems* (London, 1963), p. 233, 'Nineteen Hundred and Nineteen
[3] Edward Stephens, *My Uncle John* (London, 1974), p. 16.

better describes their choice of voluntary separation from Ireland. The Huguenot immigrants of the seventeenth and eighteenth centuries simply departed—in so far as Sheridan Le Fanu's direct descendants are concerned—in the nineteenth and twentieth centuries. His life was an interlude between journeys.

The occasion of Yeats's outburst against his own class was the publication of Lady Ferguson's memoir of her late husband, Sir Samuel Ferguson. And in the 1880s and 1890s Yeats was actively engaged in establishing contacts with the generation of which Le Fanu had been a part—commemorating Ferguson in a series of explicitly nationalist articles, investigating Mangan's unhappy life, and co-operating with Sir Charles Gavan Duffy in a projected library of Irish literature. Gavan Duffy, who had introduced Mangan to the press association in 1838, advised Le Fanu in writing *Torlogh O'Brien*, and brought together O'Connell and Isaac Butt, Charles Lever and William Carleton, William Smith-O'Brien and Ferguson and Le Fanu, in a John Banim Commemoration Committee, had emigrated to Australia after the failure of 1848 and subsequently had become Prime Minister of Victoria. In drawing up their lists of Irish books deserving republication, Yeats and Gavan Duffy in their different ways acknowledged the centrality of the period from 1838 to 1848—the period of *The Purcell Papers* and *The Cock and Anchor* and, of course, 'Richard Marston'. Yeats praised Carleton's *Fardorougha the Miser* and *The Black Prophet* 'written when a true Irish public had gathered for a brief while round the [*Dublin*] *University Magazine*'.[1] In compiling a list of the best Anglo-Irish fiction, Yeats had little difficulty in choosing titles from the pre-Famine period, and if his sense of proportion seems eccentric—one novel by Maria Edgeworth to three by John Banim and three by Carleton—it must be remembered that his purpose was frankly propagandist. In choosing novels from the second half of the nineteenth century, however, Yeats encountered more serious problems. Apart from three titles by Standish O'Grady, he recommended *Flitters, Tatters and the Councillor* (May Laffan), *Maelcho* (Emily Lawless), *Irish Idylls* (Jane Barlow), and *Ballads in Prose* (Norah Hopper). Though Oscar Wilde, George Moore, and Bernard Shaw had all published fiction by this date, Yeats's choice is determined by his insistence on a combination of Irish

[1] *Uncollected Prose*, i. 143–4, written in 1889.

settings and non-naturalist techniques. *A Drama in Muslin* fai
to meet the technical requirement; Wilde's fairy stories offer
the local and propagandist one. His choice of late nineteentl
century Anglo-Irish fiction, while of little critical importance i
itself (being part of a passing and purely journalistic debate), m;
serve to draw attention to the lack of interest in fiction general
evinced by the giants of the Literary Revival. Irish authors wl
sought to develop the novel were obliged to seek models abroa
passing over contemporary English examples in favour of Frenc
naturalism: Moore's *Drama in Muslin* and Somerville's ar
Ross's *The Real Charlotte* are both indebted to France. Whi
it is often acknowledged that Moore's influence on the your
James Joyce was considerable, it is worth recording that tl
opening chapters of *The Real Charlotte* are perhaps the neare
prior parallel to Joyce's treatment of his native city in *Dubliner*
One hundred years after *Castle Rackrent* there was still *i*
coherent critical definition of Anglo-Irish fiction. Indeed tl
same superficial criteria—geographical setting, for the most part-
dominate the discussion today.

Le Fanu's relationship to the early revival is of course tenuous
Several of his novels were republished, but the impetus cam
from *émigrés* in London (Edmund Downey and his own sc
George Brinsley Le Fanu) rather than from enthusiasts i
Dublin.[2] That Yeats was acquainted with his work is certain;
is equally certain that the poet saw no relevance in *Uncle Silas*
even *The Purcell Papers* for his own historic mission to reviv
Anglo-Irish literature. It is—perhaps strangely—among tl
dramatists that one finds a fruitful area for comparison. Le Fanu
occasional dialect tales may be counted among the exampl
available to J. M. Synge when he began to experiment with tl
artistic adaptation of dialect for dramatic purposes. Edwar

---

[1] For a comment on his influence on Somerville and Ross see John Croni
Somerville and Ross (Lewisburg, 1972), p. 27. Apart from Joyce's incorporatic
of *The House by the Churchyard* into the referential structure of *Finnegans Wak*
Le Fanu's twentieth-century influence is most evident in the work of Elizabei
Bowen.

[2] Downey established himself as a publisher in London in the 1890s, ar
issued several new editions of Le Fanu's novels with illustrations by G. B. L
Fanu, e.g. *The Cock and Anchor* (1895), *The Evil Guest* (1895), *A Chronicle
Golden Friars and Other Stories* (1896), *The Fortunes of Colonel Torlog
O'Brien* (1896), *The Poems of Joseph Sheridan Le Fanu* (ed. A. P. Graves, 1896
Checkmate (1898), *Wylder's Hand* (1898), etc.

Stephens has outlined a reading of Synge's plays as reflections of
the playwright's experience, and though he confines himself to a
strictly biographical level, a more profound enquiry into Synge's
plays as symbolic products of the Anglo-Irish ascendancy at the
crux of its historical development is clearly possible and indeed
urgently needed. Like Le Fanu's novels, Synge's plays from *In
the Shadow of the Glen* to the unfinished *Deirdre* conclude with
images of death, of death necessitated and desired as the culmination of life. (It is my belief that *The Playboy* does not stand
outside this pattern, but rather is central to it.) If Le Fanu
was forced to choose Derbyshire and the Lakes as his fictional
settings, Synge (having had *When the Moon has Set* summarily
dismissed by Yeats and Lady Gregory) forsook a setting which
resembled his own professional-cum-landowning background in
favour of a 'peasant community'. His contemporary reputation
as a peasant playwright is of course part of the concern for a
fiction which emphasizes the local and national.[1] Synge, unlike
Le Fanu, had a clear conception of the nature of literature and of
dramatic form; he studied the work of Wilde, Shaw, and Ibsen
and appreciated the essentially symbolic role of language in
literature. Le Fanu, caught in the restrictive notions of his period
and prevented by his morbid sensitivity from developing his art
fully, constantly took the word for the deed, the deed for the word.
Symbolic his landscapes may well have been, but they resisted
any opportunity to transform themselves. Considered as event,
the past was something fixed and accusing, the present being
determined by this past and therefore unalterable. In Synge, and
more especially in Wilde, the transformation of the past is
central to the symbolic action of the drama. *An Ideal Husband*
and *A Woman of No Importance* abound in evidences of Puritan
thinking—moral absolutism in characterization, echoes of Haw-
thorne, etc.—but the movement of the plays suggests that art
transforms the past, releases man from what the theologian calls
Original Sin. The parallel with Le Fanu is necessarily a faint one,
and the case requires a fuller enquiry into Wilde's concept of
comedy and his view of the Parnellite crisis which all but over-
shadows his own tragic fate. Nevertheless, one point is starkly

[1] For a useful discussion of this point see Thomas Kilroy, 'Synge and
Modernism', in *J. M. Synge: Centenary Papers 1971* (Dublin, 1972, ed. M.
Harmon), pp. 167–79.

clear; for Le Fanu landscape and setting are not susceptible to the artist's control. They speak of sin, not of symbol. If Wilde's comedies may be related to the Anglo-Irish crisis of the 1890s by being seen as achieving that reformation of society and elimination of the *tyrannos* which is the object of classical comedy, Le Fanu's fiction (at its humbler level) advances a more pessimistic view of the adjustments possible in Irish society. Writing at a time when the political base of the crisis was still unrecognized or misunderstood, he produced a body of work which willynilly appears ill-defined, divided in its objectives.

The study of Anglo-Irish literature is still at what may be aptly called an infantile stage, obsessively concerned with certain prominent and important figures—Yeats, Joyce, Synge—but neglectful of the larger body of writing amongst which the masters must ultimately be placed. This uneven application of scholarship has particularly affected the Victorians, for their achievement (flawed and awkward though it was) was rejected as irrelevant by the exponents of cultural nationalism. To an extent which is too infrequently recognized, critics of Anglo-Irish literature have derived their techniques from Yeats, and so have entered into a conspiracy with that formidable reviser of history. Others, following the directions of the New Criticism, have illuminated the inner structure of some major texts. By both factions, however, the element of continuity and mutual clarification which can exist between texts of varying quality has often been neglected. The need to apply techniques of the new school of literary historians to the study of Anglo-Irish literature is overwhelming, and in no way conflicts with the equally urgent need for biographical and sociological inquiries into the careers of Sir Samuel Ferguson, Sir Charles Gavan Duffy, Thomas Davis, James Clarence Mangan, James McGlashan, Mortimer and Samuel O'Sullivan (to name but a few), and into the inner organization and public influence of the *Dublin University Magazine*, *The Nation*, and *The Warder*. Beyond this one could outline a programme involving the relationship between Anglo-Irish literature and Gaelic culture on the one hand, and metropolitan English literature on the other.

Hovering above all these comparatively concrete objectives there is the infinitely more difficult theoretical question of seeking a definition of 'Anglo-Irish literature', identifying its boundaries and analysing its distinctive choice of literary forms. Protracted speculations on these issues would be out of place here, but it may be useful to suggest that the first shibboleth deserving challenge is the anthropomorphic metaphor which pervades our criticism. When we speak of the founding fathers of a literature, we employ a dangerous image. A literature, an individual work of literature, has no limited 'parentage', no descendants, no familial boundaries of exclusion or inclusion. But when claims are made that a particular novel 'belongs' to Anglo-Irish literature or French literature or whatever, it is frequently assumed that these claims are exclusive, just as a human individual can only have one father, two grandfathers, and so forth. If we say that Edmund Burke is the father of Anglo-Irish literature we must be prepared to admit that Jonathan Swift and Walter Scott may have equally legitimate claims to that paternity. The problem may be only a special instance of a wider tendency to spatialize literature as we speak of it, to refer to 'areas', 'boundaries', 'levels' without reflecting on the purely metaphorical role of these terms. But in a literature where the exclusivism of Nation, Race, and Creed is constantly at hand, it is imperative to avoid taking these metaphors literally. If conditions in Goethe's Germany bore some resemblance to those experienced by sections of the Irish population in the 1820s and 1830s, there are also sinister parallels between the growth of 'volkish' thought in nineteenth-century Germany and the origins of Irish Catholic nationalism.[1]

Le Fanu's life and work provides an effective focus for these larger considerations. As a transitional figure standing between the ge. ierations of Maria Edgeworth and J. M. Synge, his career touches on many aspects of Irish culture—the Established Church, the urge towards radical politics among the Tories, the influence of English journalism and literature, the attractions of native folk traditions, the pressure of Victorian rectitude—which have not been analysed in the context of one individual's experience. Marked by his eighteenth-century social inheritance, and anticipating certain twentieth-century assumptions about sexuality, Le Fanu offers the biographer a broad spectrum of attitudes on

[1] For an account of the relationship between racism and the cult of the peasant in German literature see G. L. Mosse, *The Crisis of German Ideology* (London, 1970). Dr Mosse does not of course draw any parallel between German experience and Irish, but his analysis suggests a further area in which a compa rative study is desirable.

which he may base a still wider investigation into cultural con
tions. If we were to seek a single image of those conditions
Le Fanu's work, we would inevitably turn to *Uncle Silas*. In
earliest tales he had created specific crucial encounters which t
place in an implied society which is actually based on n
social assumptions. In *Uncle Silas* this paradox is translated i
Swedenborgian terms; seeking to warn Maud of the danger
Bartram, Dr Bryerly points to a passage in *Heaven and Hell*.
Maud recalls:

> It was in that awful portion of the book which assumes to describe
> condition of the condemned and it said, that independently of
> physical causes in that state operating to enforce community of habi
> tion, and an isolation from superior spirits, there exist sympathi
> aptitudes, and necessities which would, of themselves, induce t
> depraved gregariousness, and isolation too.[1]

Irish Victorian society was doubtless a more complex interacti
of class than the traditional terminology suggests; nevertheli
to speak of an 'ascendency' is to reflect an important sense
common purpose felt by various elements in the population
landowners, the established clergy, the genteel professions, t
Protestant commercial classes. Given the discrepancy betwe
terminology and reality, given the desperate urgency with wh
this pseudo-hegemony was maintained, Le Fanu's summary
hell is most apt—'depraved gregariousness, and isolation too'.

Le Fanu's last five years were passed largely in isolation. Havi
sold the *Dublin University Magazine* in 1869 his principal cont
with the world beyond Merrion Square disappeared. In Septeml
of the previous year some medical alarm had prompted him
make a will; it was a simple document hastily drawn up 'les
should be the will of God to call [him] hence' before making
more formal disposition of such property of mine as may rem
disposable after all my just debts are paid.'[2] The family portraits
of Colmans, Sheridans, and Le Fanus—were bequeathed
Philip, his eldest child. For George Brinsley, the youngest,
made provision to provide £600 for educational expenses. Th
was no reference in the will to land or real estate of any kind.

---

[1] *Uncle Silas*. London, 1864. ii. 196–7.
[2] P.R.O., Dublin; 'The Will of Joseph Thomas Sheridan Le Fanu made
the 18th September 1868' (T. 9958).

1870 George Brinsley (variously known as Brin or Bush) was at
school at Rugby. Though the boy was sixteen his father's
correspondence blended baby talk with incongruous allusions
to the deaths of the great:

I enclose 4 three pences as a little tip. I have been very low in consequence of my great friend Mr Dickens's death. I enclose six stamps.
You must tell me whenever you lay out any money of your own on
stamps. Tell me if you have spent any on them (stamps), & how much,
that I may send it to you.

Womsie is very well & sends kind love. Sir Zosimus shall be placed
in your drawer for the future instead of being sent to Rugby, & you
will find the Numbers when, please God, you come home.

Ever your affectionate & fond
Wob[1]

The habitual mimic finally forgets that his subject is constantly
changing and developing, is not frozen linguistically at the level
of a child's speech. With Ellie marrying Patrick Robertson of
the 92nd (Gordon Highlanders) in 1871, Le Fanu's domain was
further reduced. Only Philie and Emmie remained at home, and
the elder boy was displaying signs of irresponsibility and dissolution. In December 1872 Emmie became engaged to marry
her cousin George Bennett, and sought Lord Dufferin's assistance
in finding her future husband 'a mastership at one of the public
schools or an inspectorship of either National or Grammar
schools'.[2] But before she could leave the parental nest, her father
had died and the speedy break-up of the Le Fanu family was
under way.

As late as April 1871, however, he could be persuaded to dine
at Hewitt Poole Jellett's (Jellett was married to a sister of
Mrs W. R. Le Fanu's) and go on later to a musical evening at the
home of Archdeacon Lee. In May when Charles Lever made a
final appearance at the Club dinners in the Shelbourne Hotel,
his old comrade from the *Dublin University Magazine* made no
appearance. His brother William continued to prosper, finding
it possible to adjust to the new constitution of the Church of
Ireland, just as he had taken 1848 and the arrival of Morgan John
O'Connell in polite society, in his stride. Within sight of Joseph's
house, St. Stephen's Church had in the aftermath of disestablish-

---

[1] J. T. S. Le Fanu to G. B. Le Fanu, 11 June 1870.
[2] P.R.O.N.I.; E. L. Le Fanu to Dufferin 9 Dec. 1872.

ment become an independent parish, though it saw little or nothing of Sheridan Le Fanu. In 1872 it had still been a chapel of ease attached to St. Peter's—where in 1843 Joseph and Susanna had been married—but in 1873 William was appointed as one of the first churchwardens of the new parish. As he had done in Susanna's lifetime, William called to 18 Merrion Square after Sunday service, to see his stay-at-home brother.

On 29 January 1873 William called to find his brother very weak. He spent all the morning of the next day at Merrion Square, and by Friday January 31 the patient was a little better. Emmie was preoccupied with her correspondence with Dufferin over her cousin's prospects. She duly reported her father's attack of bronchitis which 'made us all very uneasy for some time'.[1] The day following this report of his recovery, Sheridan Le Fanu died at half past six in the morning. His brother spent most of the day at Merrion Square, and coincidence would sardonically have it his diary records that 'Joe's bill £83' fell due for renewal on the day of his death. The funeral took place to Mount Jerome cemetery on Tuesday 11 February, and Sheridan Le Fanu was placed in the Bennett tomb beside his wife and five other members of the Bennett family. The sandstone Victorian Gothic Monument which now marks the grave is so defaced by time that no trace remains of Le Fanu's name.

Reactions to his death were, at least as recorded, strictly conventional. Emmie wrote to Lord Dufferin to reassure him of her father's peaceful end:

He had almost got over a bad attack of Bronchitis but his strength gave way & he sank very quickly & died in his sleep . . . . His face looks so happy with a beautiful smile on it. We were quite unprepared for the end. My brother Philip & I never left him during his illness & we were so hopeful and happy about him even the day before he seemed to be so much better. But it comforts me to think he is in Heaven, for no one could have been better than he was. He lived only for us, and his life was a most troubled one.[2]

Though Philie had been appointed his father's executor it fell to William to arrange the children's affairs. Under the terms of Joseph's mortgage of 1868, now that he was dead his heirs had no tenancy at Merrion Square and the great terrace house quickly

[1] Ibid. 6 Feb. 1873.
[2] Ibid. 9 Feb. 1873.

passed into other hands. Financially, Le Fanu's children had little to rely on: he had raised £4,300 by way of of mortgage on lands at Ballywilliam (originally mortgaged in Dean Le Fanu's will), and this sum had been divided equally between his four children some time before his death. £1,250 had been repaid, and the balance fell due in April 1873. To add to William's problems, various bills in Philie's name had to be met immediately. The Le Fanu inheritance had between 1845 and 1873 profited nothing by the growth of Victorian prosperity and stability; apart from William's success in assimilating himself into the new bourgeois society and the new disestablished church, all that survived were paintings of the past, engraved silver, relics.

Even these were soon at risk. Philie Le Fanu, already showing signs of dissipation and now deprived of his home on Merrion Square, became a persistent trial to his patient uncle. Some time after February 1873, Sheridan Le Fanu's papers were put on the market: the Dublin antiquarian William Frazer bought eight manuscript letters, two of which Le Fanu had published in the *Dublin University Magazine* in 1839. None of Le Fanu's literary papers sold at this time have been traced.[1] Paintings and other heirlooms were preserved only by the intervention of William Le Fanu himself, who bought back his brother's property for the family.[2]

Philie Le Fanu was fated to survive his father by less than seven years. Though the over-all impression he has left is of 'depraved gregariousness' the record scarcely does justice to the difficulties under which he grew up or to the pressures of Protestant conformism in the Dublin of the 1870s. A letter to his uncle William revolves touchingly round a familiar phrase:

I cannot tell you how sorry I am for what is past, or what agony of mind to me to think of my foolishness and the pain I have given you. I know you would not believe me if I were to say it so I would rather write to you. I *really* intend to make quite a change for the future. I have written to that woman to say that I don't intend to see her any more.[3]

[1] See Frazer's note in *Notes and Queries* (6th series), vol. 5 (1882), 321. All attempts to trace Frazer's papers have failed.
[2] Personal information supplied to the present writer by W. R. Le Fanu, Esq., of Chelmsford.
[3] T. P. Le Fanu to W. R. Le Fanu (undated).

By October 1879, William did not even know his nephew's address, and considering an edition of his brother's poems, was forced to use a solicitor as intermediary: 'I could hold no communication with Philip himself.'[1] And A. P. Graves, relaying this information to the publisher Bentley, held out only a slight hope of better success with Philip who was now 'a disgrace to family, a confirmed scamp. I have lost sight of him, though without a rupture, & as we were friends as lads he will I think give his content to the publication of the stories if needful.'[2] Philie, in fact, was living at 3 Gloucester Place, on the north side of Dublin, not far from where his father had taken his first digs as a hopeful law student. But William was soon to resume contact with Philie, though briefly. On 19 December 1879 he was summoned to the young man's bedside, and shortly after he left Philie died. 'It is so sad—he was such a dear . . . little fellow long ago.'[3]

With Brinsley set on a career as illustrator and painter in England, Ellie married to her soldier, and Emmie to her schoolmaster at Sutton Valence, and with Philie now dead, Sheridan Le Fanu's descendants severed their connections with Ireland. As with the development of his fictional settings, distance and migration removed them from the scene of their father's success and failure.

[1] W. R. Le Fanu to A. P. Graves, 31 Oct. 1879; copy in Graves to G. Bentley, 1 Nov. 1879 (Illinois).
[2] Illinois; A. P. Graves to G. Bentley, 1 Nov. 1879.
[3] Diary 19–20 Dec. 1879.

APPENDIX 1

A checklist of Joseph Sheridan Le Fanu's Writings

SEVERAL ATTEMPTS to compile a comprehensive bibliography of Sheridan Le Fanu's writings have come to naught, and the checklist which follows is intended only to fulfil a limited role—that of directing the reader to the full canon of Le Fanu's work. Details of the first edition of each book are provided but prior publication (serialization of the novels, printings of short stories and poems individually in magazines) is not indicated. Piracies, adaptations, translations, reissues, and further editions are similarly excluded. The list of first editions is augmented by a list of uncollected writings—fictional, journalistic, and political—so that the two-part checklist gives access to all of Le Fanu's known publications.

Inevitably, there are anomalies. Though I exclude collections of Le Fanu's stories, gathered eclectically by later editors, I have included *The Purcell Papers* (1880) on the grounds that, despite its posthumous appearance, the stories in it were originally written as an organic unity: their being collected was, as it were, authorized by Le Fanu himself. (As a result, the 1838–40 magazine publication of the *Papers* is not detailed below.) Three other posthumous publications are listed: *Willing to Die*, which appeared very shortly after Le Fanu's death, and which had been serialized in his lifetime; the fragmentary 'Hyacinth O'Toole', which was sent to *Temple Bar* by the author's son; and the *Poems* of 1896 which neatly disposes of an otherwise untidy and unimportant area of Le Fanu's work.

Further difficulties arise in relation to variant texts and revisions. For example, *The Cock and Anchor* (1845) was republished with alterations as *Morley Court* in the year of Le Fanu's death, and some subsequent editions reverted to the original title while retaining the later text. A number of short stories appeared in several forms and this, together with Le Fanu's habit of using his early work as a source for later fiction, poses a problem in distinguishing between original compositions and amended versions.

Doubtless, the solutions I have adopted will not please everyone. I have, however, deliberately listed the original magazine appearances of 'Richard Marston' despite the subsequent inclusion of a variant under the title 'The Evil Guest' in *Ghost Stories and Tales of Mystery;* my reason for this is simply that a change of location— Chester instead of Dunoran—though textually slight, constitutes a significant rewriting of the tale's meaning. (See pp. 117–18 above.)

Readers who require bibliographical descriptions of Le Fanu's books should turn to Michael Sadleir's *XIX Century Fiction.* It will be noted that all the new attributions in part two of this list are to be found in the *Dublin University Magazine.* My work in this area was facilitated by my appointment in 1973 as Assistant Editor of *The Wellesley Index to Victorian Periodicals*: I am happy to record my debt of thanks to the *Index*'s general editor, Walter E. Houghton, for permission to include in this checklist some material destined to appear in his fourth volume.

BOOKS

[Anon.], *The Cock and Anchor being A Chronicle of Old Dublin City,* Dublin, William Curry; London, Longmans; Edinburgh, Fraser, 1845, 3 vols.

[Anon.], *The Fortunes of Colonel Torlogh O'Brien; A Tale of the Wars of King James,* Dublin, James McGlashan; London, William S. Orr, 1847

[Anon.], *Ghost Stories and Tales of Mystery,* Dublin, James McGlashan; London, William S. Orr, 1851

The House by the Churchyard, London, Tinsley Brothers, 1863, 3 vols.

Wylder's Hand: A Novel, London, Richard Bentley, 1864, 3 vols.

Uncle Silas: A Tale of Bartram-Haugh, London, Richard Bentley, 1864, 3 vols.

[Pseud.], *The Prelude, Being a Contribution towards a History of the Election for the University, by John Figwood Esq., Barrister at Law,* Dublin, G. Herbert, 1865

Guy Deverell, London, Richard Bentley, 1865, 3 vols.

All in the Dark, London, Richard Bentley, 1866, 2 vols.

The Tenants of Malory; a Novel, London, Tinsley Brothers, 1867, 3 vols.

A Lost Name, London, Richard Bentley, 1868, 3 vols.

Haunted Lives; a Novel, London, Tinsley Brothers, 1868, 3 vols.
The Wyvern Mystery; a Novel, London, Tinsley Brothers, 1869, 3 vols.
Checkmate, London, Hurst and Blackett, 1871, 3 vols.
The Rose and the Key, London, Chapman and Hall, 1871, 3 vols.
Chronicles of Golden Friars, London, Richard Bentley, 1871, 3 vols.
In a Glass Darkly, London, Richard Bentley, 1872, 3 vols.
Willing to Die, London, Hurst and Blackett, 1873, 3 vols.
The Purcell Papers, London, Richard Bentley, 1880, 3 vols.
The Poems of Joseph Sheridan Le Fanu, London, Downey, 1896

UNCOLLECTED WRITINGS

'Original Letters (No. 1): Swift', *D.U.M.*, September 1838
'Original Letters (No. 11): Political', *D.U.M.*, April 1839
'Pawn-broking in Ireland: Mr. Barrington's Suggestions—Charitable Institutions of Limerick', *D.U.M.*, December 1839
'Spalatro, from the Notes of Fra Giacomo', *D.U.M.*, March and April 1843
'The Fatal Bride', *D.U.M.*, January 1848
'Some Account of the Latter Days of the Hon. Richard Marston of Dunoran', *D.U.M.*, April, May, and June 1848
'The State Prosecutions', *D.U.M.*, June 1848
'The Irish League', *D.U.M.*, July 1848
'The Mysterious Lodger', *D.U.M.*, January and February 1850
'Ghost Stories of Chapelizod', *D.U.M.*, January 1851
'Some Gossip about Chapelizod', *D.U.M.*, April 1851
'An Account of Some Strange Disturbances in Aungier Street', *D.U.M.*, December 1853
'Ultor de Lacy: a Legend of Cappercullen', *D.U.M.*, December 1861
'Borrhomeo the Astrologer: a Monkish Tale', *D.U.M.*, January 1862
'The Leadbetter Papers [a review]', *D.U.M.*, August 1862
'Two Gossiping-Books of Travel [a review]', *D.U.M.*, September 1862
'An Authentic Narrative of a Haunted House', *D.U.M.*, October 1862
'Cyrus Redding's New Novel [a review]', *D.U.M.*, October 1862

'*Mildrington the Barrister* [a review]', *D.U.M.*, June 1863
'*Lispings from Low Latitudes* [a review]', *D.U.M.*, July 1863
'*Their Majesty's Servants* [a review]', *D.U.M.*, February 1864
'My Aunt Margaret's Adventure', *D.U.M.*, March 1864
'Fitzgerald's *Life of Sterne* [a review]', *D.U.M.*, March 1864
'Felon Biography [a review]', *D.U.M.*, April 1864
'Wicked Captain Walshawe, of Wauling', *D.U.M.*, April 1864
'Lord Palmerston', *D.U.M.*, November 1865
'Beatrice: A Verse Drama in Two Acts', *D.U.M.*, November
    and December 1865
'The Opening Session', *D.U.M.*, February 1866
'The Reform Bill of 1866', *D.U.M.*, May 1866
'Lord Dufferin on Ireland', *D.U.M.*, July 1866
'The Session of 1866', *D.U.M.*, September 1866
'Squire Toby's Will', *Temple Bar*, January 1868
'Loved and Lost', *D.U.M.*, September 1868–May 1869
'The Child that Went with the Fairies', *All the Year Round*,
    5 February 1870
'The White Cat of Drumgunniol', *All the Year Round*, 2 April
    1870
'Stories of Lough Guir', *All the Year Round*, 23 April 1870
'The Vision of Tom Chuff', *All the Year Round*, 8 October 1870
'The Dead Sexton', *Once a Week*, Christmas Number 1871
'Sir Dominic's Bargain', *All the Year Round*, 6 July 1872
'Laura Silver Bell', *Belgravia*, Annual 1872
'Dickon the Devil', *London Society*, Christmas Number 1872
'Hyacinth O'Toole', *Temple Bar*, August 1884

APPENDIX 2

Some problems in the attribution of anonymous fiction

IT IS widely recognized among specialists that existing checklists of Sheridan Le Fanu's publications are incomplete.[1] As he was a contributor to the *D.U.M.* from 1838 to 1869, and its proprietor and editor from 1861 to 1869, it is likely that some further identifications of his work may be attempted in this area. However, both the archives of the magazine and of Le Fanu's literary papers survive only in part, a factor which has discouraged research.

The preservation, then, of Charles Lever's monthly accounts for the *D.U.M.* for the best part of his editorship (1842–5) uncovers a period of Le Fanu's apparent silence. From these records it is clear that he published a two-part story 'Spalatro: from the Notes of Fra Giacomo' in March and April 1843. Lever's entry in the March accounts reads: 'Spalatro. Lefanu 13 pages'. And the April entry reads: 'Spalatro. 2 part Lefanu 13 pages 18: 18: o'. The evidence is incontrovertible. The first instalment of the story appeared on pp. 338–51 of vol. 21, and the second on pp. 446–58. The fee of eighteen guineas is a little above average to judge by other entries in Lever's accounts.[2]

'Spalatro' may seem to be something of an erratic in Le Fanu's canon, with its continental setting, though *The Papers* (published

[1] See M. R. James (ed.), *Madam Crowl's Ghost and Other Tales of Mystery*, by Joseph Sheridan Le Fanu (London, 1923), pp. 265–77; T. P. Le Fanu, *Memoir of the Le Fanu Family*, pp. 77–9; S. M. Ellis, *Wilkie Collins, Le Fanu, and Others*, pp. 179–91; Michael Sadleir, *XIX Century Fiction; a Bibliographical Record*, i. 179–204; George Watson (ed.), *The New Cambridge Bibliography of English Literature* (Cambridge, 1969, vol. 3, 1800–1900), cols. 942–3.

Sadleir writes (i. 198): 'A full-dress bibliography of Le Fanu by Dudley Massey and M. J. MacManus is in preparation and will, in due course, be published by the Bibliographical Society.' Twenty-five years later the Society is unable to provide any information on the project. The *New Cambridge Bibliography* entry is unreliable on biographical detail.

[2] Lever's accounts are preserved in the Pierpont Morgan Library, and these details are cited by kind permission of the Library Trustees.

in the *D.U.M.* between 1838 and 1840) include 'Schalken the Painter' which is set in the Low Countries. The discovery of 'Spalatro', however, is useful as a link in a chain of evidence leading to another identification. 'Borrhomeo the Astrologer: a Monkish Tale' appeared in the *D.U.M.* in January 1862, while Le Fanu's famous (but pseudonymous) novel *The House by the Churchyard* was being serialized. A reviewer in the Dublin newspaper, *The Warder*, attributed the tale to the author of 'Ultor de Lacy' which had been printed in the *D.U.M.* in the previous December.[1] The last mentioned story was identified as Le Fanu's by M. R. James, and included in *Madam Crowl's Ghost and Other Tales of Mystery*; none of James's attributions has been challenged. The authorship of 'Ultor de Lacy' is unassailable, fragments of it being preserved in a manuscript notebook of Le Fanu's in the National Library of Ireland.[2] Two additional factors reinforce the case for Le Fanu's authorship of 'Borrhomeo'. Firstly, he had owned for years a substantial interest in *The Warder*, and was influential in its editorial direction; the review would not have passed unnoticed or uncorrected had it been inaccurate. Secondly, the tale is listed without attribution or fee in a *D.U.M.* account book compiled by J. A. Scott, an associate of Le Fanu's in the newspaper business. Other contributions known to be by Le Fanu are similarly recorded—without fee or attribution—in Scott's accounts.

This evidence, being less exact than that of Lever's accounts in the case of 'Spalatro', can be augmented with some stylistic observations. Both tales are set in Italy, are transmitted through priestly confessors, and relate the terrible fate of a hypocritical

---

[1] See *The Warder*, 4 Jan. 1862, p. 5; and also a review of the *Dublin University Magazine* in 1 March 1862 issue of *The Warder*: 'The tales of Ultor de Lacy and Borrhomeo . . . from their style and spirit we are induced to believe that they may claim brotherhood with the story under notice [i.e. the serialization of *The House by the Churchyard*.]' These anonymous notices may have been written by Patrick Kennedy, a friend of Le Fanu's and a contributor to the *D.U.M.* For Kennedy's association with *The Warder*, see Michael Banim to Kennedy, 23 Feb. 1865, in a disbound volume of letters to Kennedy in the library of the Department of Irish Folklore, University College, Dublin. Kennedy, in a review in an unknown paper, assumed 'Ultor de Lacy' and 'Borrhomeo' to be by the same author—see cutting on unnumbered p. between pp. 113–14 in vol. A of Kennedy Cuttings in UCD—and elsewhere identifies this writer with the author of *The Purcell papers* i.e. Le Fanu (see vol. A, p. 96).

[2] National Library of Ireland; Joly MS 22.

(or daemonic) figure. Both 'Spalatro' and 'Borrhomeo' associate female beauty with moral or metaphysical revulsion—a theme powerfully present in 'Schalken the Painter' (1839) and 'Carmilla' (1871–2). All four stories (which span Le Fanu's career) utilize a beautiful woman's portrait as a prominent symbol. These collocations, together with the unchallenged and significant circumstantial evidence of *The Warder*'s review, seem conclusive in establishing 'Borrhomeo' as Sheridan Le Fanu's work. It may be added that, as editor and proprietor of the *D.U.M.* in 1862, he had an unrivalled opportunity to publish anonymously.

Apart from the short stories and tales for which he is best remembered, Le Fanu also published extensively as a novelist. Historical romance, sensationalism, and sentiment attracted him; often a Le Fanu novel combined two or more of these fashions. Undoubtedly, he wrote too many novels, but in the least flawed one finds a recurring interest in two areas of experience— domestic unhappiness and religious anxiety. In *Uncle Silas*, and to a lesser extent *A Lost Name* and *Willing to Die*, he created a unified image of an individual's struggle against despair. The full-length novels admit a broad depiction of society, albeit an impoverished and guilt-ridden society, while the short tales emphasize interior fears and supernatural possibilities. Consequently, a knowledge of the short tales may not provide much assistance in identifying any anonymous serial novel which Le Fanu may have published.

After *Uncle Silas* (1864) and *Guy Deverell* (1865), in which sensationalism was the dominant narrative fashion, he experimented in *All in the Dark* (1866) with a new interest in sentimental psychology. The novel was a failure, being generally regarded as an insipid story of village wooing. Le Fanu's publisher, George Bentley, had found the text too short for convenient conversion into three-decker form. Nevertheless, the novelist replied to these complaints with some confidence:

I am half sorry I wrote 'All in the Dark' with my own name to it. I am now convinced it is a great disadvantage to give the public something quite different from what your antecedents [*sic*] had led them to expect from you, although it may be better.

Lady Gifford thinks it the very best thing I have written. If I go

hereafter on that tack I must do so experimentally & anonymously—&
build up a circulation if I can upon that basis.[1]

In *The Tenants of Malory* (1867) and *Haunted Lives* (1868) Le
Fanu maintains his sentimental treatment of character, but
balances it with sensational narrative also. Furthermore, both
these modest experiments were published by Tinsley in three-
decker form, Le Fanu having fallen out of favour with George
Bentley.

A sentimental serial novel appeared in the *D.U.M.* in nine
instalments between September 1868 and May 1869. The first
instalment appeared under the title *Loved and Lost*, but from the
second onwards the title was *My Own Story; or Loved and Lost*.
The story is narrated by Edith Aubrey, eldest child of the
Aubreys of Vere, an aristocratic but impoverished family.
Quarrels between her mother, a self-righteous and querulous
woman, and her father, an impetuous (perhaps rascally) fellow
are exacerbated by the Aubreys' dependence on relatives who
have married into the lower classes. Edith's narrative is principally
concerned with her relations with various suitors: Sir Benjamin
Hopper, a vulgar millionaire to whom her father is in debt;
Sir Richard Airey, who has a kind heart and a stammer; and
Richard's friend Philip Warrender whom Edith truly loves.
Despite her pride in class, she has come to sympathize with
Scarsdale, a deformed, wealthy, but low-born, cousin. Her
inexperience and quick temper lead to confusions at the height of
which she tells Philip that she loves Richard. Philip is almost
immediately drowned, and his death virtually coincides with
Scarsdale's; subsequently Edith experiences a reverie in which
their faces merge. In reaction to Philip's death she despairs and
prays for death; then she hears two voices, one offering death and
annihilation, the other life, atonement for her sins, and ultimate
happiness with Philip in heaven. She chooses life and gradual
readjustment to her surroundings.

Loved and Lost, as we shall refer to it, is sentimental rather than
sensational; in this it would align itself with *All in the Dark* and
The Tenants of Malory rather than the more violent *Uncle Silas*.
But there is no external evidence—editorial notebook or con-

---

[1] Le Fanu to George Bentley, 1 Aug. 1866; text printed in Walter C. Edens,
'A minor Victorian novelist and his publisher' (University of Illinois Ph.D.
thesis 1963).

temporary review—on which to begin to base an attribution to
Sheridan Le Fanu. It is true that he admitted to Bentley that
further work in the style of *All in the Dark* might have to be
anonymous, and as editor and proprietor of the *D.U.M.* he was
free to experiment secretly if he so wished. And, having discovered 'Spalatro' and 'Borrhomeo', we are entitled to regard
the question of further identifications as open. In place of solid
documentary evidence, *Loved and Lost* reveals a network of
stylistic clues which in combination amount to a substantial case
for Le Fanu's authorship:

1. The plot as outlined above bears a general resemblance to
Le Fanu's fictions of the 1860s. A girl, visiting a house she does
not previously know and confronted with a number of suitors,
appears prominently in *Uncle Silas* and *Willing to Die*, and less
prominently in *All in the Dark* and *Wylder's Hand*. The social
world of *Loved and Lost* is the same sub-aristocratic or upper-
middle-class setting of most of his novels; the immediate settings
are country houses, and the general context the English countryside. In length, *Loved and Lost* is shorter than most of Le Fanu's
novels, but longer than *All in the Dark*.

2. *Loved and Lost* is narrated by its heroine, and the plot is
occasionally lost in her reveries and moments of unconsciousness.
Both *Uncle Silas*, written five years earlier, and *Willing to Die*
of four years later, are narrated by heroines who are subject to
momentary loss of consciousness, ominous dreams, and reveries.
In *Loved and Lost* and *Uncle Silas* a house soliloquizes, and in
each case the house is the home of an attractive woman of the
world who stands in some contrast to the other characters. In
Uncle Silas, the house is Elverston; in *Loved and Lost* a place
called Ulverston is mentioned.

3. The family of *Loved and Lost* are the Aubreys of Vere; on
one occasion, the author refers to them as 'Aubrey de Vere'.[1]
Aubrey de Vere, of course, was the name of a contemporary Irish
poet, and Sheridan Le Fanu uses literary names in several of his
novels, e.g. Marlowe (in *Guy Deverell*), Berkeley (*The Evil Guest*),
Wycherly (*A Lost Name*), and Marston (*Willing to Die*). In *Loved
and Lost* family names are twice given at length: 'Marmaduke
Henry Vere Aubrey de Vere' (the narrator's father) and
'Rosamond Vincent Vere Aubrey de Vere' (her mother). These

[1] *D.U.M.*, vol. 73 (Jan. 1869), 26–7.

repetitious signatures, though not unusual in high society, may recall similar ones in *Uncle Silas*. Thus *Loved and Lost* in its use of names resembles half-a-dozen Le Fanu novels, and does so in two distinct ways—in the choice of literary names and the use of repetitious forms as letter-signatures.

4. There are further name echoes. In *Loved and Lost* the female narrator's cousin is Scarsdale; in *Uncle Silas* her counterpart meets her cousin at Church Scarsdale. Cousin Scarsdale belongs to a low-born branch of the family; in *Uncle Silas*, the narrator's cousin has secretly married a barmaid. The transference of a name from a person to a place (or vice versa) is not unheard of in Le Fanu's fiction; in *Uncle Silas* a village, Feltram, is mentioned; in 'The Haunted Baronet' the hero's name is Philip Feltram.

5. The disaster of *Loved and Lost* is the death by drowning of Philip Warrender, which follows Edith's false rejection of him. She experiences a waking dream of his return: 'I could have sworn I saw Philip standing at the end of the old hall. He was all dripping, and drenched with water, and his eyes looked reproachfully at me.'[1] In 'The Haunted Baronet' Le Fanu's hero (another Philip) is drowned; when his corpse is brought back to the Great House, his tormentor, Sir Bale Mardyke, has a nightmare which coincides with the 'resurrection' of Philip Feltram. In *Loved and Lost*, Edith's waking dream occurs between her rejection of Philip Warrender and the discovery of his death, and so may be said to coincide with his death.

6. *Loved and Lost* does not explicitly announce Philip's death as suicide; references to a storm hint at a natural explanation, while family legends are cited to implicate fatalistic elements. In *A Lost Name*, Mark Shadwell dies by drowning also; both he and Warrender have just learned that their lovers are fickle and have fled from the scene. *Loved and Lost* elsewhere raises the issue of suicide, when Edith's father threatens to kill himself on learning of her rejection of the millionaire, Sir Benjamin Hopper; in *Willing to Die* another female narrator's father actually commits suicide on hearing disastrous financial news.

7. In the third chapter of *Loved and Lost*, the narrator goes to church and sees on the gallery a face which closely resembles a portrait familiar to her since childhood, a portrait by Velasquez

---

[1] Ibid. (Apr. 1869), 395.

of Philip of Spain. Subsequently she meets Philip Warrender and identifies him as the figure on the gallery. Three points are of interest: first, there is the apparent emergence of a figure whose portrait would lead one to assume him or her to be long dead (cf. 'Spalatro' and 'Carmilla'); second, a living person is frequently described in terms of a painter's style (Velasquez in *Loved and Lost*, Rembrandt in *Uncle Silas*, Guido in *The Tenants of Malory*); finally, and less importantly, there is the encounter of future lovers in church. Not only can each of these be paralleled in several of Le Fanu's novels, but at the opening of *The Tenants of Malory*, there is a church scene which incorporates references to a Guido portrait, while at the opening of *Guy Deverell* there is a church scene in which a man thought to be long dead appears as a young man on the gallery. Although the church as a location of a lovers' first meeting may be trite enough *Loved and Lost* incorporates other more distinctive Le Fanuesque features.

8. If we compare *Loved and Lost* with two Le Fanu novels narrated by girls, we find that each contains an opening scene of a similar kind. In *Loved and Lost* and *Willing to Die*, the girls (now matured and older, of course) begin their recollections by placing themselves by a window; in *Loved and Lost*, the window is 'abbey-shaped'; in *Willing to Die* it overlooks a churchyard; very early in *Uncle Silas*, the narrator gazes through a window towards a family tomb. Here we have a perfect example of three quite minor points of resemblance combining to become something of a trade-mark.

No one of these points of similarity constitutes evidence of Le Fanu's authorship of *Loved and Lost*. However, the probability of his writing the serial is established in proportion to the number and variety of similar details. Collocations of a female narrator, of setting and plot in general, of portrait imagery in particular, of character—and place-names, may be regarded by some as evidence establishing authorship 'beyond all reasonable doubt'. When we recall Le Fanu's suggestion (admittedly made two years prior to the appearance of *Loved and Lost*) that he might resume anonymity to experiment in the style of *All in the Dark*, stylistic similarity to his work in the anonymous serial must be granted a large measure of credibility. There is, however, another perspective from which the case can be considered: if Sheridan Le Fanu did not write *Loved and Lost*, then some other unknown

author did write it. As Le Fanu was proprietor and editor of the
D.U.M. in 1868, this would involve him in accepting for publication a serial so demonstrably similar to his own work that, of the
two propositions, it seems more likely that he wrote *Loved and
Lost* than encouraged a plagiarist. Finally, though Le Fanu's
personal and business correspondence contains no reference to an
anonymous serial at this date, it must be remembered that he had
broken off communications with George Bentley (whose file is the
only surviving extensive record of Le Fanu's dealings with
publishers) while his surviving personal letters are notoriously
few.

The preceding stylistic argument was based exclusively on a
comparison of an anonymous serial with published fiction by
Sheridan Le Fanu. Though examples cited from his work of the
years prior to 1868 might conceivably have been available as a
model for an imitator, references to *Willing to Die* (1873) are not
open to this objection. If an unknown author wrote *Loved and
Lost* he chose to reproduce features of Le Fanu's fiction which
Le Fanu himself then subsequently developed—a remote possibility. Furthermore, during the period of Le Fanu's editorship
of the *D.U.M.*, there are no other serial novels which cannot be
reliably attributed to known authors. If Le Fanu's authorship is
rejected we are forced to conclude that the only unattributed
serial which he published as editor was *Loved and Lost*, which
bore a very striking resemblance to his own signed work.[1] The
existence of a fragment of an unfinished and unpublished story
by Sheridan Le Fanu provides a point of comparison to which an
unknown author can have had no access. As William Le Fanu has
noted, the story is a version of 'A Chapter in the Histroy of a
Tyrone Family' which Sheridan Le Fanu published in the
D.U.M. in 1839; significantly, the incomplete manuscript recasts
the story in an English setting, retaining the female narrator of
the 1839 story.[2] Between 1839 and 1864 (when *Uncle Silas* was
serialized in the *D.U.M.*) Le Fanu had not experimented with a
female narrator, and it is likely that the incomplete story in
manuscript dates from the latter period of Le Fanu's career as a

[1] See the forthcoming fourth volume of *The Wellesley Index to Victorian
Periodicals*. I am grateful to Professor Walter E. Houghton for discussing
aspects of this attribution with me in an exchange of letters.

[2] See W. R. Le Fanu, 'Notebooks of Sheridan Le Fanu', *Long Room*,
nos. 14/15 (1977) 37–40.

writer. The contents of the notebook in which it is preserved would indicate 1848 as the earliest date for the story. Though the manuscript was never completed—the narrative breaks off in mid-sentence and mid-page—it is clear that Le Fanu was writing a rough draft of a tale in which the narrator tells of her wicked infatuation with a powerful public figure, whom she meets through his brother, a sympathetic and sensitive cripple. Passages from this manuscript and *Loved and Lost* may be compared, thus:

(*Manuscript*)

He was a young man & in person by no means attractive. He was pale, thin & with a certain sickly & habitual expression of pain which is sometimes fixed upon the countenance by early & protracted ill health. So it had been in his case, for when a mere child he had encountered an accident which had for years made him a prisoner to his room & often to his bed & the consequences of which were permanently entailed upon him in a very perceptible lameness. He was gentle, rather shy but at the same time a pleasant & even a lively companion.[1]

(*Loved and Lost*)

A little boy who had been clinging to my uncle's hand now came towards me—a small attenuated child, with a perceptible hump, and that wizened, pitiable, old man's expression that deformed children acquire. His eyes, even then, had a most wonderful power in them—large, lustrous, and dark, they seemed to fill up all his face, and attracted and rivetted your attention. Although I was disgusted by his appearance, I could not resist their influence, and I allowed myself to be drawn into a corner, where we indulged in mutual confidences, and cemented a friendship.[2]

The verbal description of the two deformed confidants of female narrators provides no clinching identity of phrasing, but the parallel roles which the two figures play in the unpublished Le Fanu manuscript and the anonymous serial surely confirm *Loved and Lost* as Le Fanu's.

Loved and Lost is an undistinguished piece of writing, and the value of identifying its author may be challenged. Apart from the importance of the discovery to a biographer of Sheridan Le Fanu—interested in his psychological constitution or in his financial difficulties, for the recourse to anonymity has a bearing

[1] The fragment is preserved in the notebook listed as no. 4 in W. R. Le Fanu's article (see previous note).
[2] *D.U.M.*, vol. 72 (Sept. 1868), 260.

on both of these issues—there is the continuing task of establishing the *modus operandi* of *D.U.M.* editors and contributors, and
of completing a list of the writers who maintained the *D.U.M.*
as the premier organ of Irish Protestant conservatism in the
Victorian age.

The issue of Le Fanu's previously unidentified fiction might
properly be regarded as settled with the evidence for three new
attributions given above. Yet with an author whose bibliography
is notoriously obscure and whose use of pseudonyms is so
extensive, it would be unwise to declare the lists closed. Two
further, admittedly marginal, considerations also encourage
continued enquiry: (a) Le Fanu's journalistic writings (in the
Dublin Evening Mail, the *Protestant Guardian*, *The Warder*, and
elsewhere) have certainly not been fully identified; (b) the literary
activities of his family (notably his daughter 'Russell Gray')
remain to be investigated, and these might well shed light on Le
Fanu's own career. For these reasons *My Own Story* by Marian
Leigh (New York, 1865) enters the discussion.

My Own Story is a one-volume novel, the distinctly confused
plot of which defies summary. The setting is English—Wrexham
and Richmond are mentioned—and the characters are drawn
from the middle classes. Three factors encourage us to challenge
the veracity of the title-page: first, nothing is known of an author
called Marian Leigh, publishers' records, library catalogues, and
biographical dictionaries making no reference to any writer, either
British or American, of this name; second, the female narrator
of the novel is called Marian Leigh, and the running-title throughout is 'Friends of My Youth'. These details suggest that the novel
is best regarded as an anonymous work, entitled *My Own Story
by Marian Leigh*. Thus, the question of attributing it to some
other author is at least open.

In comparing *My Own Story* and Le Fanu's known fiction,
there are two significant areas of similarity and one crucial area
of dissimilarity. Parallels of incident or scene could be constructed on the basis of a female narrator whose loss of consciousness blends with an inability at times to distinguish between
dreaming and waking. To this might be added a crippled young
man and a portrait suggesting the identity of an ancestor and a
living character—all features of Le Fanu's fiction. These and other

passing details—references to homeopathy and the sensuous embrace of the narrator and other female characters (cf. *Loved and Lost*, 'Carmilla', and *Willing to Die*)—might provide a prima-facie case for Le Fanu's authorship. At this point, therefore, evidence against that conclusion may be timely.

By comparison with even the weakest of Le Fanu's novels—*All in the Dark* or *Haunted Lives*—*My Own Story* is crudely written, not simply in the confused sequence of events or the proliferation of indistinguishable characters, but in the texture of its phrasing. A few examples will dismiss the case for Le Fanu's authorship:

During our walk, I had cast imploring looks towards Rachel, which silent demur had availed me naught; and I had ventured to remonstrate otherwise against the unparrelled [*sic*] verlocity of our transit (p. 288).

And a few pages later:

While I dubitated as to the safest course of procedure the cry was reiterated (p. 293).

Or conclusively:

'Have your provided yourself with a sufficiency of hair-pins?' asked Mabel, when I returned, having obeyed her directions.
'I do not possess such a commodity,' said I.
'Luckily, I have a superfluity,' said Mabel (pp. 313–14).

If such a random sample effectively dismisses Le Fanu as an author, what of the second area of similarity between *My Own Story* and the Le Fanu canon? This second area of resemblance being a pattern of name echoes, an extended examination of the 1865 novel may yet be justified, for such a pattern has figured in earlier attributions. These interlocking name echoes in *My Own Story* may be tabulated thus:

My Own Story (1865)	Le Fanu's known fiction
Barton (place), Montague (character), p. 63, etc.	Barton and Montague (characters in 'The Watcher' 1847)
Grace Willoughby (character), p. 142	Grace Willoughby (character in *Torlogh O'Brien* 1847)

Beatrice Percy, p. 170, alias the Italian singer Signorina Foresti, p. 359	Percy Neville (character in *Torlogh O'Brien*) 'Beatrice' (title-character of the Italian-set verse drama, Nov.–Dec. 1865)

The interlocking of these echoes is particularly compact. Two names can be traced back to one short story; that a character-name should become a place-name is not unexpected in the context of Le Fanu's fiction. Furthermore, the repeated combination 'Grace Willoughby' seems to confirm a debt to *Torlogh O'Brien*. Both 'The Watcher' and *Torlogh O'Brien* date from 1847, so the close echo of names is concentrated in a period of one year. To see a three-stage link (Percy Neville–Beatrice Percy/ Foresti–Beatrice) may seem strained, yet in this too there is a concentration in time, both *My Own Story* and 'Beatrice' date from 1865. (For good measure the verse drama has a double-dealing monk called Spalatro, thus recalling the 1843 story of that name!) But we do not pause here, because *My Own Story* offers no less than three literary names of the kind which Le Fanu gave to his prominent characters: Aytoun, Allingham, and Marston. The first and second are the names of nineteenth-century minor poets; Marston we already know from Le Fanu's 1848 story, another echo in the time-compact of 1847–8 as a source for *My Own Story*.

If the style of *My Own Story* rules out Le Fanu's authorship, how are we to account for the pattern of name-echoes? The solution sketched here is entirely speculative but it goes some way towards reconciling the conflicting analyses. I suggest that *My Own Story* was written by someone close to Le Fanu (possibly his wife) who was familiar only with his early work. Susanna Le Fanu, it will be remembered, died in 1858, and in the years between 1848 and 1858 Le Fanu had not produced much fiction. I suggest that Mrs Le Fanu (the most likely candidate) wrote her novel during the period of her recurring illness, taking names from her husband's fiction. The jerky uncertainties of *My Own Story* are not incompatible with what we know of Susanna Le Fanu's state of mind. The novel then remained unpublished for fifteen years or so, until (I suggest) Sheridan Le Fanu arranged for its pseudonymous publication in America perhaps as an expiation of the guilt he evidently felt in relation to his dead wife.

But *My Own Story* does not impinge solely upon Le Fanu's *previous* fiction. In particular, three details connect the American novel to *Loved and Lost*, the anonymous serial of 1868–9 which treats quite explicitly domestic and marital unhappiness, frustrated and misconstrued emotion, in the life of the female narrator:

1. The anonymous serial appropriates, after its first instalment, the title of 'Marian Leigh's' novel as its own, and becomes *My Own Story*; *or Loved and Lost*. (For the sake of clarity, I refer consistently to the serial as *Loved and Lost*.)

2. The literary names in the two works—Allingham in *My Own Story* and Aubrey de Vere in *Loved and Lost*—belong to Irish poets of Le Fanu's own generation. William Allingham first came to prominence in the early 1850s, and his name adds weight to the case for dating *My Own Story* to that period. Aubrey de Vere was born in the same year as Le Fanu, and like him raised in county Limerick.

3. The motto at the head of *Loved and Lost* is taken from the ballad 'Robin Gray', while in *My Own Story* Robin Gray is debated as a possible name for a pet. (Further trivial name echoes, for example 'Mabel' in each work, could be tabulated.)

Let us finally distinguish between speculations and reasonable deductions. It is probably that *My Own Story* was written within Le Fanu's circle at a date considerably earlier than 1865. From this we may deduce that he was involved in its publication and possibly in its revision for publication. That Susanna Le Fanu was the author remains unproven: however psychologically suggestive we may find the evidence it is purely circumstantial. Nevertheless, if *My Own Story* prompted Le Fanu to write 'Beatrice' and *Loved and Lost* (and to include Spalatro in the former), then the nexus of anxieties which concerned him in the 1840s still obsessed him as late as 1865 or 1869. And given the chameleon quality which we noted in his personality, it is tempting to see the longing for death and the preference for female narration as the product of his imitation of his dead wife's feeble literary exercise. By this line of argument, the fiction of Le Fanu's last years is to some significant extent determined by the experience of his early manhood—the end of the Tithe War, the death of Catherine Le Fanu, the dream of Protestant Repeal, and courtship in the Bennett household. Such a causality is of course repeatedly endorsed in his fiction where the past frequently re-presents itself.

BIBLIOGRAPHY

A. MANUSCRIPT SOURCES

The vast majority of manuscript papers quoted in this study are preserved in four collections:

1. *Le Fanu Papers*

    A large collection of family papers, including material relating to Jonathan Swift, the Sheridans, and other eighteenth- and nineteenth-century notables. No calendar of these papers has been compiled though microfilm copies are available—with the permission of the owner—through the National Library of Ireland (N. 2973–88; P. 2594–609). During the period when this present study was in preparation, the Le Fanu Papers included the diaries (1846–94) of William Richard Le Fanu, the novelist's brother: these have now been deposited in the library of Trinity College, Dublin.

2. *Bennett Papers*

    A collection of letters written to and by various members of the family of George Bennett, the novelist's father-in-law. During the preparation of this study, these papers were in the possession of Mrs Susan Digby-Firth who very kindly made them available. They are now preserved in the Brotherton Library, University of Leeds.

3. *Dufferin and Ava Papers*

    A very large collection relating to the family of the first Marquis of Dufferin and Ava, and including copies of letters from Sheridan Le Fanu to Helen, Lady Dufferin; the papers are now in the Public Record Office of Northern Ireland whose staff very kindly gave me access to this yet uncalendared material.

4. *Bentley Papers*

    The reconstructed correspondence of the publishing firm of Bentley, now preserved in the library of the University of Illinois. The Le Fanu–Bentley letters have been transcribed by Walter C. Edens (see Section B below).

Where references have been made to manuscript material outside these four major sources, details are provided in the relevant annotations.

B. SELECT PRINTED SOURCES

ALLEN, WALTER, *The English Novel: a Short Critical History*, Harmondsworth, 1958.

[ANON.], 'Joseph Sheridan Le Fanu', *Dublin University Magazine*, vol. 81 (Mar. 1873), 319–20.

[ANON.], 'The late J. Sheridan Le Fanu', *Irish Builder*, vol. 15 (15 Feb. 1873), 50.

[ANON.], *Memoirs of Father Healey of Little Bray*, London, 1895.

BECKETT, J. C., *The Anglo-Irish Tradition*, London, 1976.

BLEILER, E. F., 'Introduction' to *Best Ghost Stories of J. S. Le Fanu*, New York, 1964, pp. v–xi.

——, 'Introduction' to *J. S. Le Fanu: Ghost Stories and Mysteries*, New York, 1975, pp. v–ix.

BOWEN, ELIZABETH, *Collected Impressions*, London, 1950.

——, 'Introduction' to *The House by the Churchyard*, London, 1968, pp. vii–xi.

BRIGGS, JULIA, *Night Visitors: the Rise and Fall of the English Ghost Story*, London, 1977.

BROEKER, GALEN, *Rural Disorder and Police Reform in Ireland 1812–36*, London, 1970.

BROOKE, RICHARD SINCLAIR, *Recollections of the Irish Church*, London, 1877 (also 2nd series 1878).

BROWN, MALCOLM, *The Politics of Irish Literature from Thomas Davis to W. B. Yeats*, London, 1972.

BROWNE, NELSON, *Sheridan Le Fanu*, London, 1951.

BUTLER, MARILYN, *Maria Edgeworth: a Literary Biography*, Oxford, 1972.

BYRNE, PATRICK F., 'Joseph Sheridan Le Fanu: a Centenary Memoir, *Dublin Historical Record*, vol. 26, no. 3 (June 1973), 80–92.

CARLETON, WILLIAM, *The Autobiography of William Carleton*, London, 1968 (revised ed.).

'CATALOGUE of the Library of the Very Rev. Thomas P. Le. Fanu LL.D. . . . to be sold by Auction by Charles Sharpe . . . 22nd November 1845' (no imprint).

CHASE, RICHARD, *The American Novel and its Tradition*, London, 1958.

COBBETT, WILLIAM, *Rural Rides* (ed. G. D. H. and Margaret Cole), London, 1930, 3 vols.

COMBE, J. C., 'Huguenots in the Ministry of the Churches in Ireland', unpublished Ph.D. thesis, Queen's University of Belfast, 1970.

CORKERY, DANIEL, *Synge and Anglo-Irish Literature*, Cork, 1966 (first published 1931).

DAGG, T. S. C., *College Historical Society: a History 1770–1920* (privately printed for the Society, 1970).

DAVIE, DONALD, *The Heyday of Sir Walter Scott*, London, 1961.

DELANEY, JAMES, 'Patrick Kennedy', *The Past*, vol. 7 (1964), 9–87.

DICKENS, CHARLES, *The Letters* (ed. Walter Dexter), Bloomsbury, 1938, 3 vols.

DISKIN, PATRICK, 'Poe, Le Fanu and the Sealed Room Mystery', *Notes and Queries* (new series), vol. 13 (Sept. 1966), 337–9.

EDENS, WALTER C., 'A Minor Victorian Novelist and his Publisher, unpublished Ph.D. thesis, University of Illinois, 1963.

ELLIS, S. M. 'Bibliography of Joseph Sheridan Le Fanu', *Irish Book Lover*, vol. 8 (Oct.–Nov. 1916), 30–3.

——, *Mainly Victorian*, London, [1925].

——, *Wilkie Collins, Le Fanu, and Others*, London, 1951 (first published 1931).

FALKINER, C. LITTON, 'The Phoenix Park—its Origin and Early History with some Notices of its Royal and Viceroyal Residences', *Proceedings of the Royal Irish Academy* (3rd Series), vol. 6, no. 3 (1901), 465–88.

FERGUSON, LADY MARY, *Sir Samuel Ferguson in the Ireland of His Day*, Edinburgh, London, 1896, 2 vols.

FFOLLIOT, ROSEMARY, *The Pooles of Mayfield and other Irish Families*, Dublin, 1958.

FITZPATRICK, W. J., *The Life of Charles Lever*, London, 1901 (revised ed.).

FLANAGAN, THOMAS, *The Irish Novelists 1800–1850*, New York, 1959.

FRAZER, WILLIAM (ed.), 'A Series of Eight Anonymous and Confidential Letters to James II about the State of Ireland', *Notes and Queries* (6th series), vol. 5 (1882), 321–3, 361–3, 401–2, 484–5; vol. 6 (1882), 2–4, 21–3, 61–3.

GAVAN DUFFY, CHARLES, *Four Years of Irish History 1845–1849*, London, 1883.

——, *My Life in Two Hemispheres*, London, 1898, 2 vols.

——, *Thomas Davis: the Memoirs of an Irish Patriot 1840–1846*, London, 1890.

——, *Young Ireland: a Fragment of Irish History 1840–1845*, London, 1880, 2 vols.

GETTMANN, ROYAL A., *A Victorian Publisher: a Study of the Bentley Papers*, Cambridge, 1960.

GOLDMANN, LUCIEN, *Towards a Sociology of the Novel* (trans. by Alan Sheridan), London, 1975.

GRAHAM, KENNETH, *English Criticism of the Novel 1865–1900*, Oxford, 1965.

HARE, A. J. C. (ed.), *The Life and Letters of Maria Edgeworth*, London, 1894, 2 vols.

HARVEY, W. J., *Character and the Novel*, London, 1965.

HAWTHORN, JEREMY, *Identity and Relationship: a Contribution to Marxist Theory of Literary Criticism*, London, 1973.

HOUGHTON, WALTER E., *The Victorian Frame of Mind 1830–1870*, New Haven, London, 1957.

——, *The Wellesley Index to Victorian Periodicals 1824–1900*, Toronto, London, 1966—(in progress).

KENTON, EDNA, 'A Forgotten Creator of Ghosts: Joseph Sheridan Le Fanu. Possible Inspirer of the Brontes', *Bookman* (July 1929), 528–34.

LE FANU, THOMAS PHILIP, *Memoir of the Le Fanu Family*, Manchester, [1924].

LE FANU, WILLIAM RICHARD, *Seventy Years of Irish Life*, London, 1893.

LONGFORD, CHRISTINE, 'Introduction' to *Uncle Silas*, by J. Sheridan Le Fanu, West Drayton, 1940, pp. 7–10 (an abridged edition).

——, 'Joseph Sheridan Le Fanu', *The Bell*, vol. 4, no. 6 (Sept. 1942), 434–8.

LOUGHEED, W. E., 'An addition to the Le Fanu Bibliography, *Notes and Queries* (new series), vol. 11 (June 1964), 224.

LOZES, JEAN (ed.), 'Fragment d'un journal intime de J. S. Le Fanu . . . 18 Mai 1858', *Caliban* (Annales de l'Université de Toulouse— Le Mivail), new series, vol. 10, no. 1 (1974), 153–64.

LUKACS, GEORG, *The Historical Novel*, (trans. from German by Hannah and Stanley Mitchell), London, 1962.

——, *The Theory of the Novel: a Historical-Philosophical Essay on the Forms of Great Epic Literature* (trans. from German by Anna Bostock), London, 1971.

LYONS, F. S. L., *Ireland since the Famine*, London, 1971.

MCCORMACK, W. J., 'Joseph Sheridan Le Fanu and the Fiction of the Anglo-Irish Ascendancy in the Nineteenth Century, unpublished D.Phil., thesis, New University of Ulster, 1974.

——, 'J. Sheridan Le Fanu; Letters to William Blackwood and John Forster', *Long Room*, no. 8 (Autumn 1973), 29–36.

——, 'J. Sheridan Le Fanu's Richard Marston (1848): the History of an Anglo-Irish Text, in *1848: the Sociology of Literature* (ed. Francis Barker and Others), [Colchester], University of Essex, 1978, pp. 107–25.

——, 'Sheridan Le Fanu's *Uncle Silas:* an Anglo-Irish Provenance', *Long Room*, no. 4 (Autumn/Winter 1971), 19–24.

——, 'Swedenborgianism as Structure in Le Fanu's *Uncle Silas*', *Long Room*, no. 6 (Autumn 1972), 23–9.

MAC DONAGH, OLIVER, *The Nineteenth Century Novel and Irish Social History: Some Aspects*, Dublin, [1971].

McDOWELL, R. B., *Public Opinion and Government Policy in Ireland 1801–1846*, London, 1953.

McDOWELL, R. B., and D. A. WEBB, 'Trinity College in 1830', *Hermathena*, no. 75 (May 1950), 1–23; no. 76 (Nov. 1950), 1–24.

MACMANUS, M. J., 'Some points in the Bibliography of Joseph Sheridan Le Fanu', *Dublin Magazine* (2nd series), vol. 9, no. 3 (July/Sept. 1934), 55–7.

MADOC-JONES, ENID, 'Sheridan Le Fanu and North Wales' *Anglo-Welsh Review*, vol. 17, no. 40, 167–73.

MAXWELL, J. C., 'J. S. Le Fanu's *The Cock and Anchor;* notes for O.E.D.', *Notes and Queries* (new series), vol. 6 (July/Aug. 1959), 284–5.

MILLER, NORBERT, 'Ein Dunkler Spiegel der Wirklichkeit: Sheridan Le Fanu und der viktoriansche Kriminalroman', [postscript to] *Onkel Silas, oder Das verhängnisvolle Erbe*, Munich, 1972, pp. 543–64).

MORROW, H. L., 'Sheridan Le Fanu's Ghosts', *The Word* (Roscommon) (Oct. 1973), 16–19.

MURCH, A. E., *The Development of the Detective Novel*, London, 1968.

NETHERCOT, ARTHUR H., 'Coleridge's "Christabel" and Le Fanu's "Carmilla"', *Modern Philology*, vol. 147 (Aug. 1949), 32–8.

NOWLAN, K. B., *The Politics of Repeal*, London: 1965.

O'BRIEN, R. B., *Thomas Drummond, Under-Secretary in Ireland 1835–40: Life and Letters*, London, 1889.

O BROIN, LEON, *Fenian Fever*, London, 1971.

O'CONNOR, FRANK, *The Lonely Voice: a Study of the Short Story*, London, 1963.

O'DONOGHUE, DAVID JAMES, *The Poets of Ireland; a Biographical and Bibliographical Dictionary of Irish Writers of English Verse*, New York, London, 1970.

O'NEILL, PATRICK J., 'German Literature and the *Dublin University Magazine* 1833–1850: a Checklist and Commentary', *Long Room*, nos. 14/15 (1977), 20–31.

PENZOLDT, PETER, *The Supernatural in Fiction*, New York, 1965.

PHILLIPS, WALTER, C., *Dickens, Reade and Collins: Sensation Novelists; a Study in the Conditions and Theories of Novel Writing in Victorian England*, New York, 1919.

PRITCHETT, V. S., *The Living Novel*, London, 1946.

RASHID, SALIM, 'Political Economy in the *Dublin University Magazine* 1833–1840', *Long Room* nos. 14/15 (1977) 16–19.

RAY, GORDON N., 'The Bentley Papers', *The Library* (5th series), vol. 7 (Sept. 1952), 178–200.

RUER, J. M. L., 'Sensation in English Fiction in the 1860s', unpublished M.A. thesis, Manchester University, 1957.

SADLEIR, MICHAEL, *Dublin University Magazine; its History, Contents and Bibliography*, Dublin, 1938.

——, *XIX Century Fiction; a Bibliographical Record Based on his own Collection*, London, 1951, 2 vols.

SCOTT, KEN, 'Le Fanu's "The Room in the Dragon Volant"', *Lock Haven Review*, no. 10 (1968), 25–32.

SHAW, JACK, 'Dickens in Ireland', *Dickensian*, vol. 5 (1909), 33–41.

SMITH, WILBUR J., 'Le Fanu's *Ghost Stories* Dublin 1851', *Book Collector*, vol. 17 (1968), 78.

STANG, RICHARD, *The Theory of the Novel in England 1850–1870*, London, 1959.

STEELE, E. D., *Irish Land and British Politics: Tenant-Right and Nationality 1865–1870*, Cambridge, 1974.

STEPHENS, EDWARD, *My Uncle John: Edward Stephens's Life of J. M. Synge* (ed. Andrew Carpenter), London, 1974.

STEVENSON, LIONEL, *Dr. Quicksilver: the Life of Charles Lever*, London, 1939.

STONE, L., 'Joseph Sheridan Le Fanu: a Critical Study', unpublished Ph.D. thesis, National University of Ireland, 1953).

SULLIVAN, KEVIN, 'The House by the Churchyard: James Joyce and Sheridan Le Fanu', *Modern Irish Literature: Essays in Honour of William York Tindall* (ed. R. J. Porter and J. D. Brophy), New York, 1972, pp. 315–34.

——, 'Sheridan Le Fanu: The Purcell Papers 1838–40', *Irish University Review*, vol. 2, no. 1 (Spring 1972), 5–19.

SUMMERS, MONTAGUE, 'Joseph Sheridan Le Fanu and his Houses', *Architectural Design and Construction*, vol. 2, no. 7 (May 1932), 296–9.

SWIFT, THEOPHILUS, *The Touchstone of Truth: Uniting Mr. Swift's Late Correspondence with the Rev. Doctor Dobbin, and his Family; and the Detailed Account of their Subsequent Challenge and Imposture*. Dublin, n.p., 1811.

SYMONS, JULIAN, *Bloody Murder: from the Detective Story to the Crime Novel: a History*, London, 1972.

THORNLEY, DAVID, *Isaac Butt and Home Rule*, London, 1964.

TIERNEY, DOM MARK, *Murroe and Boher: the History of an Irish Country Parish*, Dublin, 1966.

TOKSVIG, SIGNE, *Emanuel Swedenborg: Scientist and Mystic*, London, 1949.

TRENCH, W. S., *Realities of Irish Life*, London, 1869.

TROWBRIDGE, GEORGE, *Swedenborg and Modern Thought*, London, 1899.

WHITE, TERENCE DE VERE, *The Parents of Oscar Wilde: Sir William and Lady Wilde*, London, 1967.

WHITE, TERENCE DE VERE, *The Road of Excess*, Dublin, [1945].

WOLFF, ROBERT LEE, *Strange Stories and Explorations in Victorian Fiction*, Boston, 1971.

WRIGHT, A. B., 'The Life and Novels of Joseph Sheridan Le Fanu', unpublished B.A. thesis, Trinity College, Dublin, 1952.

ZETLER, ROBERT L., 'Life and Works of J. S. Le Fanu', unpublished Ph.D. thesis, University of Pittsburg, 1944.

INDEX

The following index does not include references to the lists in Appendix I and the Bibliography. Footnotes are indexed selectively and without reference to book-titles. Holders of titles appear under their family names (e.g. the Marquis of Dufferin and Ava under Blackwood). Married women appear under the form used in the text (e.g. Le Fanu, Eleanor Frances; and Le Fanu, Mrs Henrietta Victorine, *née* Barrington); these forms are generally those by which the persons concerned were known during the period covered by the book. The many variants of Irish place-names accepted in the nineteenth century are not separately indexed. I am grateful to W.E. Mackey, research librarian at Trinity College, Dublin, for his assistance in tracing some of the more obscure *dramatis personae*.

1. William Richard Le Fanu, brother.

2a. Catherine Le Fanu, sister. No other picture
of the novelist's sister is known to survive.

2b. The Glebe-House, Abington, County Limerick. The
house is now in private possession.

3. Part of the manuscript draft of *Torlugh O'Brien*.
Note the doodle-drawings representing the—as yet—nameless factions of the novel's central conflict.

4. Susanna Le Fanu (*née* Bennett), the novelist's wife. The Victorian photographer has superbly caught the subject's nervous forward-inclination of the body and her anxiously folded hands.

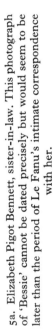

5b. No. 18 Merrion Square South, Dublin, now No. 70 Merrion Square, Dublin 2, the headquarters of An Comhairle Ealaíon, The Irish Arts Council; note the plaque commemorating Le Fanu's residence here for the two decades prior to his death in 1873.

5a. Elizabeth Pigot Bennett, sister-in-law. This photograph of 'Bessie' cannot be dated precisely but would seem to be later than the period of Le Fanu's intimate correspondence with her.

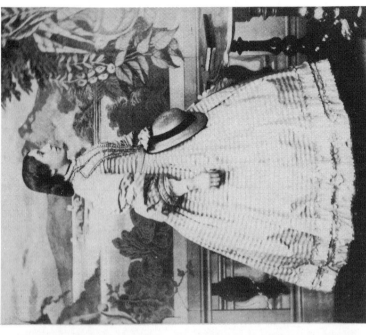

6a. Philip Le Fanu, elder son, regarded by some of his contemporaries as the classical 'wastrel son'. This curious studio study seems to provide some phreno-

6b. Emma Le Fanu, younger daughter. The studio backcloth suggests the unreal, or fragile, status of the Irish Victorian 'ascendancy' family.

7. Pages from a notebook in Le Fanu's hand. Note the uncalled-for gap before the words 'not love'.

8. The Bennett/Le Fanu tomb, Mount Jerome Cemetery, Dublin.